THE NEW FOXE'S BOOK OF MARTYRS

THE NEW FOXE'S BOOK OF MARTYRS

JOHN FOXE

REWRITTEN AND UPDATED BY
HAROLD J. CHADWICK

Bridge-Logos *Publishers*

Gainesville, Florida 32614 USA

The Scripture quotations in this publication are from the King James Version of the Bible.

We are grateful to the following for their contributions to this volume:

The Voice of the Martyrs, Inc.
P.O. Box 443
Bartlesville, OK 74005-0443
Tel: 918-337-8015
Fax: 918/337-9287

Christian Solidarity International
Mission to the Persecuted
P.O. Box 70563
Washington, DC 20024
Tel: 301-989-0298 Fax: 301-989-0398
800-323-CARE (2273)

Reproductions of Copper engravings from **The Martyr's Mirror,** taken from the 1685 edition, courtesy of: **Mennonite Historical Society**
2215 Millstream Road
Lancaster, PA 17602
Tel: 717-393-9745

Open Doors
with Brother Andrew
P.O. Box 27001,
Santa Ana, CA 92799
Tel: 714-752-6600
e-mail: usa@opendoors.org
Web site: http://www.opendoors.org

The New Foxe's Book of Martyrs 2001
by John Foxe
Rewritten and updated by Harold J. Chadwick
ISBN: 0-88270-875-9
Library of Congress Catalog Card Number: Pending
Copyright© 2001 by Bridge-Logos Publishers

Published by:
Bridge-Logos *Publishers*
Gainesville, FL 32614

Contents

Section II - The Next Three Centuries

Section III - Modern Martyrs

Foxe's Book of Martyrs

I cannot remember a time when *Foxe's Book of Martyrs* was not on a shelf in my father's home. I was taught to read it very early in my Christian life, and it made a lasting impression on me. I am thrilled that Bridge-Logos is making it available in a modern English version. I highly recommend that all believers read this important work.

Dr. Judson Cornwall

This book challenges the individual to radical commitment to Jesus, by providing examples from history of people who gave much, including their lives for their faith in God. May we all be inspired by their testimonies. May we give our lives to extending the kingdom of Almighty God. Let this book ignite your passion!

Dr. Mark Virkler, President
Christian Leadership University

For centuries we have enjoyed the benefits of Christianity, often forgetting the countless courageous believers who laid down their lives for the cause. It has been the blood of these precious saints of Christ that has watered the fields of harvest, accelerating the growth of Christianity around the world. But, amazingly, as a new century dawns, the persecution of believers globally is greater today than ever before.

That's why I commend *The New Foxe's Book of Martyrs,* the updated and revised edition of an ageless classic. With numerous stories of recent martyrs, photos, expanded historical information ... I believe this work, more than ever, *remains one of history's greatest reminders that Christ's body ultimately will triumph.*

Dick Eastman
President of Every Home for Christ

Introduction
to John Foxe and His Book

John Foxe (Figure 1) was born at Boston in Lincolnshire county, England, in 1516. He died on April 18, 1587. This work, for which he is famous, was first published in English in 1563 under the title, *Acts and Monuments of These Latter and Perillous Dayes*, but it became known almost immediately as the *Book of Martyrs*. Over the years it has gone through many editions, and also many versions as others added to Foxe's work. Although the book's popularity decreased somewhat in the 19th century, it has rebounded in recent years as even non-Christians have come to realize that it contains much information about 16th-century England that is not available elsewhere. So much information, in fact, that when William Shakespeare wrote his play, *The Life of King Henry VIII*, in about the year 1613, he relied upon Raphael Holinshed's *Chronicles* (1577) for his material, and John Foxe's *Book of Martyrs*.

John Foxe did not write his book for historians, however, he wrote it to document the persecution against Christ's Church by pagans and by those who called themselves Christians but were not. It's a book about God's grace and Christian faithfulness. It's a spiritual book of the highest order, and its historical information is only there to set the times, the people and places, and the circumstances. For over four-hundred years Foxe's book has endured as a memorial to the martyrs, and a legacy of inspiration and courage to the true Church of Christ.

Without question the book began in Foxe's mind when he was at Magdalen College at Oxford University, where he held a fellowship for seven years. He had first been sent by his parents to Brasenose College at the University when he was sixteen. During that time Reformation doctrines were strong throughout Oxford and Cambridge Universities, and Foxe was highly influenced by them. He began intensive study of the Scriptures and began to question the doctrines and practices of the Roman church. Before long he was an affirmed Protestant and nothing ever turned him from that path. This so changed his conduct that before long suspicions began to arise about his allegiance to the Church of Rome. Then it was reported that Foxe was taking solitary walks in the evening and could be heard sobbing and pouring out prayers to God. When questioned about this practice, he openly stated his new religious opinions, and was almost immediately expelled from the college as a confirmed heretic.

Foxe's friends found him employment as tutor to the children of Sir Thomas Lucy of Warwickshire, whose house was just a short distance from Stratford-on-Avon where Shakespeare was born in 1564. While there Foxe met and married Agnes Randall of Coventry, who shared his beliefs in Jesus Christ and His completed work. About that time the pope's inquisitors began to delve into the religious affairs of private families. So Foxe and his wife left the Lucy household to stay at her father's house in Coventry, even though Mr. Randall, in reply to a letter Foxe sent him, had written, "it seems to me a difficult thing to take a person into my house who I know is guilty and condemned for a capital offense. And I am not ignorant of the hazard I will undergo by so doing. I will, however, show myself a kinsman, and neglect my own danger. If you should change your mind about your beliefs, you may come and stay as long as you like. If you cannot be persuaded to do that, however, you will have to be content with a shorter stay, and not bring me and my wife into danger." Foxe accepted the conditions, especially after his mother-in-law wrote him not to fear her husband's severity, that he wrote that way because he felt that he needed to, but his actions would more than make up for it. In fact, Foxe was better received by both of them than he hoped to be.

By this means and others, Foxe kept himself concealed for some time from the papist inquisitors. This continued from the reign of King Henry VIII, through the open and peaceful days of Edward VI, and into the reign of Queen Mary I, who brought back into England all of the Roman Catholic doctrines and the pope's power. Knowing then what was to happen, Foxe and his family left England and traveled first to Strasbourg, France, then to Frankfurt, Germany, and then to Basel, Switzerland. There he found a number of English refugees who had fled England to avoid the cruelty of the persecutors, and there began work on his now famous book. When it was noised abroad that he was working on such a book, many who had been persecuted, or witnessed persecutions, in various countries, including England, sent him their stories.

Queen Elizabeth I ascended to England's throne in 1558, and in 1559 Foxe and his family left Basel and returned to England. He there expanded his book through to Archbishop Cranmer's death in 1556 and published his English edition in 1563. Because his book was highly criticized as having many inaccuracies, Foxe continued to revise his material for the next seven years, checking closely the details and accounts of persecutions that had been reported to him from England. In 1570 he published a corrected and greatly improved second edition titled, *Ecclesiastical History, Contayning the Actes and Monuments of Things Passed in Every Kynges Tyme.*

That same year, the Anglican Convocation ordered this edition to be placed in every collegiate church in England.

Although Foxe was ordained an Anglican priest in 1560, soon after he returned from Switzerland, he refused all church offices because he was now a staunch Puritan. He did, however, continue to preach and publish his sermons so that many could benefit by them.

Even though the recent recollection of the persecutions under "Bloody Mary" put more bitterness into his writing than he may have realized, Foxe himself was the most conciliatory of men, and while he heartily disowned the Roman Church into which he had been born and raised, he was one of the first to attempt to bring harmony among the Protestants in England. He was truly a messenger of toleration and reconciliation.

When the plague broke out in England in 1563, and many ministers left their duties to go where they were safe from it, Fox remained at his post to help the sick and friendless and distribute the money the wealthy gave to him for their aid. He was tolerant and open-hearted and could not refuse help to anyone who asked for it in the name of Christ. While he was able, he did all he could to influence Queen Elizabeth to confirm her intention to no longer continue the cruel practice of executing those of opposing religious views. She respected Foxe highly and often referred to him as "Our Father Foxe," and yet he wasn't able to stop her from driving the Puritans underground for their continual pressure on her to make extensive changes in the Church of England.

Before he died in 1587, John Foxe had the joy of seeing the fruits of his labor come to pass. His book went through four large editions, and the Council of Bishops ordered it placed in every cathedral church in England. Like the Bible, it was often chained to the pulpit so that over-zealous readers would not take it as their own.

Eventually there came a time, not only in England but all over the English-speaking world, when a home wasn't considered to be Christian unless it openly displayed a Bible and Foxe's *Book of Martyrs*.

Foreword to
The New Foxe's Book of Martyrs

Original sentence in *Foxe's Book of Martyrs*: "But because there were put to no fewer green faggots than two horses could carry upon their backs, it kindled not by and by, and was a pretty while also before it took the reeds upon the faggots."

New sentence in *The New Foxe's Book of Martyr*s: "But too many green *faggots had been used, almost as many as two horses could carry, and it took some time for the reeds to ignite the faggots."

When John Foxe wrote his *Book of Martyrs* during the mid-1500s, persecution of Christians was in full fury throughout Europe. Most of the stories in his book were not from times past, but from events swirling around him everywhere. Many of the events he undoubtedly witnessed himself, like a newspaper reporter today. Other stories were sent to him by Christians who had been persecuted themselves or who had witnessed the persecution and martyrdom of others. They were living in some of the most turbulent times in history and in Christendom. During those times, religion was the force that determined the destiny of their countries and controlled their lives. Few were unaffected by its benefits when it was benevolent and of God, and few escaped its wrath when it was malevolent and of the devil.

Because Foxe wrote about current events, as did those who followed him and added to his book, he did not explain or define those things that were common knowledge to all, or go into details about the persons and places he wrote about, especially in England, because most of the people of his day were familiar with them. He did not, for example, explain what a *Halberd* was, or a *pike*, or *faggots*, or procedure for burning a person, or where *Smithfield* was and what it was notorious for, or about *Fleet Prison*, or about the many wives of *King Henry VIII*, or about *Archbishop Thomas Cranmer's* participation in Henry's marriages and divorces. Nor did he explain the intrigues of the social and religious politics of his day that so affected Christianity—perhaps because he did not know what they were, or because he did not consider them important, or more likely, because only history can look back and see the effects in their proper perspective. In many cases we know more about those things today than Foxe could have in his day, simply because we have the accumulated historical data that enables us to look back over many dates and events, people and places, and see their relationships and interaction.

Foxe wrote his book in Middle-English, the language of his day. It's putting it mildly to say that Middle-English is a difficult language for us to understand. We no longer use words like *abscond, assoil, belike, bethinking, bruit, ambassage*, and *eftsoons*. Also, many of the words that we still use today don't mean what they did in Foxe's day, such as *discover*, which meant "to reveal or expose." And to *exorcise* someone meant to give them a demon, not deliver them from one. There is also the problem of sentence construction and length. Semicolons and commas were in popular use in Foxe's time, and a creative writer could maintain a sentence for well over a hundred words, and go off in several directions before blessing the reader with a period. Since we normally don't think about what a sentence means until we reach the period long, complex, sentences are difficult for us to understand—and virtually impossible to understand when combined with Middle-English language.

In *The New Foxe's Book of Martyrs*, we have removed unknown Middle-English words, untwisted the sentences, and rewritten everything in modern American English. Most of the Middle-English words that were taken out are in Appendix A along with the modern words or expressions that best fit Foxe's context. In some cases, no definition for a word could be found in current dictionaries, and so the context alone guided the translation. Where the Middle-English word seemed the most suitable for the context, and there was a clear definition available, the original word was left but preceded by an asterisk and the definition included in Appendix A. This was also done with words that are still in use but not commonly known, such as certain ecclesiastical words. An asterisk also precedes questionable dates and spelling of names. Plus names of persons, places, organizations, and other items, for which additional information is provided are preceded with an asterisk. Occasionally, remarks or words are inserted in the text to clarify a statment—when done, the remark or word was enclosed in brackets [like these] to show it's an editorial comment.

Because certain people and places were often mentioned by Foxe, and people and their positions often changed, appendixes are included that list the popes, the kings and queens of England, and the colleges at Cambridge and Oxford universities during the times covered by Foxe's book. There is also an appendix containing Martin Luther's *Ninety-Five Theses*, which he nailed to the Castle Church in Wittenberg, and there is an "Index of Persons and Places" for your convenience and research.

Rewriting and updating Foxe's book has not been an easy task, mentally, emotionally, or physically, and it has been highly personal—I worked as much with my heart as with my head. To translate the language and the times properly, I tried to sit in Foxe's chair and imagine him as he was when he wrote. I tried to live in the times, places, and culture where the events took place, and I tried to suffer the persecution, torture, and burning of the martyrs. I was their scribe in freedom and in prison, in life and in death. A scribe who could only watch and listen and record the events as they unfolded, but who could not intervene.

I wish I could have told John Huss that Holy Roman Emperor Sigismund was not going to uphold his guarantee of safe conduct. I wish I could have warned William Tyndale that the man he had so quickly befriended was a Judas sent to betray him. And I still wonder what King Henry of Navarre did to escape being killed during the St. Bartholomew Day massacre when almost every Huguenot in Paris was slaughtered.

When they burned John Lambert and held him up out of the fire with their halberds so that he would burn more slowly I sat at my computer and wept. And when John Hauker raised his flaming hands over his head and clapped them together three times I rejoiced at the amazing grace of God. Just as I did when that same grace returned a repentant Archbishop Thomas Cranmer to the truth of Christ, and when it gave Mary Dyer the strength to return to Boston to give her life fighting an unjust Puritan law against the Quakers.

Most of all, I marveled at the steadfast faithfulness of so many men, women, and children who rejoiced that they were counted worthy to suffer for their Lord, and whose sufferings and deaths gave witness and strength to the true Church of Christ. Their stories continue to haunt me, as I ask this question: *Could we, with our soft and self-serving modern Christianity, follow their examples of such courage and love for Christ that we would suffer being tortured, mutilated, and burned alive rather than recant our faith in Him?*

There are thousands of Christians around the world today that answer with a resounding "Yes!"

But what is *your* answer to that question?

Harold J. Chadwick,

July 4, 1997

Addendum

On the afternoon of the last day of preparing the *New Foxe's Book of Martyrs* for printing, July 22, 1997, it was announced that the U.S. State Department had just released an 86-page *Religious Freedom Report* that assessed our countries policies in support of religious freedom around the world, with a special emphasis on the persecution of Christians. The report examines specifically the treatment of Christian believers in 78 countries.

In the report, China was accused of violating constitutional pledges of religious freedom by putting all religious activity under government control. It said that the Chinese constitution stated that citizens "enjoy freedom of religious belief," but that "the Government of China has sought to restrict all actual religious practice to government-authorized religious organizations and registered places of worship."

Foreword To New Updated Edition

In a recent issue of *Newsweek*, this brief statement appeared in an extensive article on Christianity around the world:

What many U.S. Christians fail to realize is that when Asians convert to Christ it requires enormous courage. Converts typically are ostracized by family and neighbors—and often targeted for persecution. Over the last six months, Chinese communists have demolished some 1,500 houses of worship—most of them Christian—whose members refused to accept direction from the state. In officially secular India, scores of Christians have been murdered and their churches trashed since the rise of militant Hindu groups. On Christmas Eve, churches in nine Indonesian cities were bombed, killing at least 18 believers and wounding 100 more. An additional 90 Christians were murdered for refusing to convert to Islam, and some 600 more are still being forcibly detained on the island of Kasiui.

In India, where Graham Staines and his two young sons, Philip and Timothy, were burned to death in their jeep by a raging mob of Hindus, on January 23, 1999, the Indian Home Minister stated soon after that attacks on Christians were on the increase. In a report to the upper house of the Parliament, he said: "A total of 116 incidents of attacks on Christians including five killings were reported across the country since January 1998."

On June 20, 2000, Muslim warriors attacked the village of Duma in the Maluku islands, Indonesia, and slaughtered more than 100 Christians. Since 1995, more than 500 Christian churches in Indonesia have been burned.

In January of this year, 2001, Mullah Mohammed Omar, spiritual leader of the Taliban militia in Afghanistan, issued an edict stating a penalty of death for any Muslim who converts to Christianity. There are currently no known Christians in Afghanistan.

Even as I am writing this, additional news is being received of new violence against Christians in Indonesia and other countries. It is difficult to stay up to date with the persecution.

VOM News - May 17, 2001 - Muslims Again Attacking Churches in Indonesia - Following a lull of several months, radical Muslim mobs are once again attacking Christians and their churches in Indonesia. Poso, a Central Sulawesi Island, has been a hotbed of anti-Christian activity. During the four days of April 9 to 12, three church buildings and more than a dozen Christian homes were burned. In retaliation, Christians burned an abandoned Muslim school. The following day, Muslims set fire to an additional 13 Christian homes.

On April 22, a mob of several hundred Muslims burst into the Oikumene Christian Church during services. Three policemen arrived and prevented the mob from burning the church. At the Elim church, an angry Muslim mob arrived early in the morning and began throwing stones at the building—nothing was done to prevent the attack. Later that day, they returned and burned the church to the ground.

On April 23, Muslims destroyed at least five Christian homes. Another church in Central Jakarta under renovation from a previous burning was destroyed in April. Meanwhile, more than 21,000 radical Muslim troops are reportedly poised to wage jihad (holy war) in the Muluku and North Muluku Islands.

Obviously, this updated edition of the *New Foxe's Book of Martyrs* is not intended to be a comprehensive report on the thousands of incidences of persecution and hundreds of deaths of Christians since the publication of the first edition in 1997. No single book could contain a record of the multitude of persecutions and atrocities of every imaginable kind that are committed against Christians throughout the world in any given year. Indeed, many of those that are committed are never reported because of threats and fears of greater persecution and violence.

The intent of this updated edition is to bring to the attention and hearts of its readers the inescapable fact that many of their brothers and sisters in Christ around the world are being persecuted even this day. Since all Christians are part of the mystical body of Christ, to persecute them is to persecute us— and to persecute Christ Himself. When they suffer, we suffer. When they cry, we cry. Thus our prayers and our help, in whatever form we can give it, should constantly go out to them.

This updated edition contains stories of persecution up to 2001—so it now covers a period of 1966 years, starting from the time of the death of Stephen, the first martyr, in A.D. 35. The Index has been updated to include these new stories

There are 13 new photographs in this new edition. Some of them so horrifying in their brutality that you want to turn away from them. But they are pictures of our brothers and sisters in Christ who are suffering for their faith in our Lord, and should be viewed with open hearts that cry for their pains and that send prayers rising to the throne of God for them.

After spending fourteen years in Romanian prisons, Richard Wurmbrand and his wife, Sabina founded *The Voice of the Martyrs* to minister to the persecuted Church. At Pastor Wurmbrand's 90th birthday party, Sabina Wurmbrand shared a most marvelous truth that all Christians should think deeply upon.

"Leprosy is a disease without pain. No remedy is found because the nerves don't work. Lepers lose their fingers and toes in accidents because they cannot feel any pain . . . When the Church does not feel pain with those that are part of them, the Church's nerves also become dead. Then the Church loses parts of its body. It loses power to touch souls. The Church loses its credibility before the world. On the other side, the suffering Church gives the whole Church strength to fight for Christ. Suffering makes the soul to cry out and look for help, to draw strength from the source of help—Jesus Christ."

I want to give special thanks to *The Voice of the Martyrs* for their great help in gathering these new stories and for giving us permission to use the photographs of Kamerino, Mila Wenno, Dominggus Kenjam, Abuk, Rose, Marina , and Emiliana — and for the updated Prayer Map. VOM is a blessing to persecuted Christians all over the world. No finer Christians can be found anywhere. If you wish to contact them, their telephone number is 800-747-0085, and their e-mail address thevoice@vom-usa.org. They also have a Web site at http://www.persecution.com.

I also want to express our thanks to Gospel Literature Service Publishing for their permission to print the photographs of Graham Staines and his family, their burned out jeep, and the burned church in India, from their book, *Burnt Alive.* Also for the information about the Staines that was obtained from the book. Their Web site is at http://www.glsindia.com. You may purchase the book from their site.

I pray that as this updated edition of the *New Foxe's Book of Martyrs* goes forth, it will encourage and motivate you to stand fast with your persecuted brothers and sisters in Christ all over the world, and to lift them up daily in your prayers to their Lord and yours.

Harold J. Chadwick
June 4, 2001

Section I

The First Sixteen Centuries

1

The First Christian Martyrs

In Matthew 16:18, it is recorded that Jesus told His disciples, "I will build My church, and the gates of hell [Hades] shall not prevail against it."

Three major points can be noted in Jesus' words:

1. Christ will have a Church in this world;

2. His Church will be mightily attacked;

3. None of the devil's attacks will destroy it.

Looking back through the history of the Church, we can see that Jesus' words have been fulfilled in every century—its glorious history verifies His words. First, that there is a true Church of Christ in this world is without question. Second, every level of secular and religious leaders and their subjects have publicly and forcefully, with every cunning and deceitful means at their disposal, *denounced and persecuted that true Church. Third, that Church has endured and held its testimony of Christ through every attack brought against it. Its passage through the storms caused by violent anger and hate has been glorious to see, and much of its history is written in this book so that the wonderful works of God might be to Christ's glory and that the knowledge of the experiences of the Church's martyrs might have a beneficial effect upon its readers and strengthen their Christian faith.

Jesus (see Figure 2)

The first to suffer for the Church was Jesus Himself— not a martyr, of course, but the inspiration and source of all martyrdom. The story of His suffering and crucifixion is so well told in the Holy Scriptures that we have no need to document it here. It's enough to say that His subsequent resurrection defeated the intent of the Jews and gave fresh courage and new direction to the hearts of His disciples. And after they received the power of the Holy Spirit on the Day of Pentecost, they were further filled with the confidence and boldness they needed to proclaim His name. This new confidence and boldness completely confused the Jewish rulers and astonished all who heard them.

Stephen

The second person to suffer and die for the Church was Stephen, whose name means "crown" (Acts 6-8). He was martyred because of the faithful way in which he proclaimed the Gospel to those who had killed Jesus. They became so enraged at what he said to them that they drove him out of the city and stoned him to death. Stephen's martyrdom came about eight years after His Lord's crucifixion, which would place his death in the year A.D. 35, since it is supposed that Jesus was actually born in 6 B.C., about two years before Herod the Great died in 4 B.C. (see Matthew 2:16).

The same hate generated against Stephen apparently brought great persecution to all who professed faith in Christ as the Messiah. Luke writes, "At that time a great persecution arose against the church which was at Jerusalem; and they were all scattered throughout the regions of Judea and Samaria, except the apostles." (Acts 8:1). During that time, about **two thousand Christians** were martyred, including **Nicanor**, who was one of the seven deacons appointed by the Church (Acts 6:5).

James (see Figure 3)

James the son of Zebedee and Salome was the elder brother of the Apostle John. He was the first of the twelve apostles to be martyred (Acts 12:2). He was executed about A.D. 44 by order of King Herod Agrippa I of Judea. His martyrdom may have been a fulfillment of what Jesus foretold about him and his brother John (Mark 10:39).

The eminent writer, Clemens Alexandrinus, wrote that when James was being led to his execution, his extraordinary courage impressed one of his captors to such a degree that he fell on his knees before the apostle, asked his forgiveness, and confessed that he was a Christian too. He said that James should not die alone, whereupon they were both beheaded.

5

About the same time, **Timon** and **Parmenas**, two of the seven deacons, were executed—one in Philippi and the other in Macedonia.

Exactly ten years later, in A.D. 54, the Apostle **Philip** is said to have been scourged, thrown into prison, and then crucified at Hierapolis in Phrygia.

Matthew (see Figure 4)

Little is known about the Apostle Matthew's later life and the time and manner of his death, but legendary accounts say that he traveled to Ethiopia where he became associated with Candace (see Acts 8:27). Some writings say he was pinned to the ground and beheaded with a *halberd in the city of Nadabah (or Naddayar), Ethiopia, in circa A.D. 60.

James (the Less)

This James was the brother of Jesus and the writer of the epistle. He seems to have been leader of the Church at Jerusalem (see Acts 12:17; 15:13-29;21:18-24). The exact time and manner of his death is not certain, although it's believed to be about A.D. 66. According to Flavius Josephus, the Jewish historian, the high priest Ananus ordered James killed by stoning. But Hegesippus, an early Christian writer, quoted by the third-century Christian historian Eusebius, says James was cast down from the Temple tower. This version of his death further states that he was not killed by the fall, and so his head was smashed in with a fuller's club, which may have been a club used to beat clothing, or a hammer used by blacksmiths.

Matthias

Elected to fill the vacant place of Judas, almost nothing is known about him. It is said he was stoned at Jerusalem and then beheaded.

Andrew (see Figure 5)

Andrew was the brother of Peter (Matthew 4:18). Tradition says he preached the Gospel to many Asiatic nations and was martyred in Edessa by being crucified on an X-shaped cross, which came to be know as St. Andrew's Cross.

Mark

Little is known about Mark except what is written in the New Testament about him. After Paul's mention of him in 2 Timothy 4:11, he disappears from view. Tradition says he was dragged to pieces by the people of Alexandria when he spoke out against a solemn ceremony for their idol Serapis.

Peter

The only account that we have of the martyrdom of the Apostle Peter is from the early Christian writer Hegesippus. His account includes a miraculous appearance by Christ. When Peter was old (John 21:18), Nero planned to put him to death. When the disciples heard of this, they begged Peter to flee the city [said to be Rome], which he did. But when he got to the city gate, he saw Christ walking toward him. Peter fell to his knees and said, "Lord, where are you going?" Christ answered, "I've come to be crucified again." By this, Peter understood that it was his time to suffer the death of Jesus which would glorify God (John 21:19). So he went back to the city. After being captured and taken to his place of martyrdom, he requested that he be crucified in an upside down position because he did not consider himself worthy to be crucified in the same position as his Lord.

Paul

The Apostle Paul was imprisoned in Rome in A.D. 61, and there wrote his prison Epistles: Ephesians, Philippians, and Colossians. His imprisonment ended approximately three years later during the year that Rome burned, which was in May, A.D. 64 (see Acts 28:30). During his brief freedom, Paul may have visited western and eastern Europe and Asia Minor—he also wrote his first Epistle to Timothy and his Epistle to Titus.

At first, Nero was blamed for setting fire to Rome, so to direct the blame away from himself he blamed the Christians. As a result, a fierce persecution broke out against them. During it, Paul was arrested and put back into prison in Rome. While in prison this second time he wrote his second letter to Timothy. It was his last.

Not long after, he was judged guilty of crimes against the Emperor and condemned to death. He was taken to the execution block and beheaded. It was A.D. 66, just four years before Jerusalem fell.

Jude

The brother of James, he was crucified at Edessa, an ancient city of Mesopotamia, about A.D. 72.

Bartholomew

Tradition says he preached in several countries, then translated the Gospel of Matthew into the language of East-Indian and taught it in that country. His pagan enemies cruelly beat and crucified him.

Thomas (see Figure 6)

Thomas preached the Gospel in Persia, Parthia, and India. In Calamina, India, he was tortured by angry pagans, run through with spears, and thrown into the flames of an oven.

Luke (see Figure 7)

Luke was a Gentile, possibly Greek. It's not known as to when or how he was converted. He was a physician in Troas and probably converted there by Paul, especially since it was at Troas that he attached himself to Paul's party and started traveling with them. Notice in Acts 16:8-10, that it is at Troas that Luke switches from "they" to "we" in his text—"And they passing by Mysia came down to Troas. And a vision appeared to Paul in the night; There stood a man of Macedonia, and prayed him, saying, Come over into Macedonia, and help us. And after he had seen the vision, immediately we endeavoured to go into Macedonia, assuredly gathering that the Lord had called us to preach the gospel unto them."

Luke went with Paul to Philippi, but was not imprisoned with him and did not travel with him after his release. He apparently made Philippi his home and stayed for some time. It's not until Paul's visit to Philippi (Acts 20:5-6) about seven years later, that we again meet with Luke. From this time he again traveled with Paul and stayed with him during his journey to Jerusalem (Acts 20:6-21:18). But he disappears once more during Paul's imprisonment at Jerusalem and Caesarea, and only shows up again when Paul starts for Rome (Acts 27:1). He then stayed with Paul through his first imprisonment (Philemon 1:24; Colossians 4:14). Many Bible scholars believe that Luke wrote his Gospel and Acts while in Rome with Paul during this time. During Paul's second imprisonment, Luke apparently stayed nearby or with Paul, because just before his martyrdom, Paul wrote to Timothy and said, "only Luke is with me" (2 Timothy 4:11).

After Paul's death, Luke apparently continued to evangelize as he had learned to do with Paul. Exactly when and how he died is unknown. One ancient source states, "He served the Lord without distraction, having neither wife nor children, and at the age of eighty-four he fell asleep in Boeatia (place unknown), full of the Holy Spirit." Another early source says that he went to Greece to evangelize, and was there martyred by being hung from an olive tree in Athens in A.D. 93.

John

The Apostle John, brother of James, is credited with founding the seven churches of Revelation: Smyrna, Pergamos, Sardis, Philadelphia, Laodicea, Thyatira, and Ephesus. It was from Ephesus, it is said, that he was arrested and sent to Rome where he was cast into a large vessel filled with boiling oil that did not harm him. As a result, he was released and banished by the Emperor Domitian to the Isle of Patmos, where he wrote the Book of Revelation. After being released from Patmos he returned to Ephesus where he died about A.D. 98. He was the only apostle to escape a violent death.

Even with all the continual persecutions and violent deaths, the Lord added to the Church daily. The Church was now deeply rooted in the doctrine of the apostles and watered abundantly with the blood of saints. She was prepared for the cruel persecutions that were to come.

2

The Beginning of General Persecutions Against the Church

(A.D. 54-304)

The first persecution, under Emperor Nero (A.D. 54-68)

Nero was the sixth emperor of Rome and reigned for fifteen years. He was a paradox—a man of great creativity combined with a vicious temper and extreme cruelty. It is said by many that it was Nero who ordered Rome to be burned and then blamed it on the Christians to turn the wrath of Rome's citizens away from himself. Others say he was not in Rome when it burned. Whichever way it was, Christians were blamed for the fire that lasted nine days, and during which the hunt for Christians increased and became a dreadful persecution that lasted for the rest of Nero's reign.

The barbarous acts against the Christians were worse than any they had previously endured, especially those committed by Nero. Only a Satan-inspired imagination could have conceived them. Some Christians were sewn inside skins of wild animals and torn at by fierce dogs. Shirts stiff with wax were put on others, and they were then tied to poles in Nero's garden and set on fire to provide light for his parties.

This cruel persecution spread throughout the Roman Empire, but it only succeeded in strengthening the spirit of Christianity rather than killing it. Along with **Paul** and **Peter**, several of the seventy appointed by Jesus (Luke 10:1) were martyred, also. Among them were **Erastus**, treasurer of Corinth (Romans 16:23); **Aristarchus** the Macedonian (Acts 19:29); **Trophimus** the Ephesian (Acts 21:29); **Barsabas**, who was surnamed Justus (Acts 1:23); and **Ananias**, bishop of Damascus, whom the Lord sent to Saul (Acts 9:10).

The second persecution, under Emperor Domitian (A.D. 81-96)

Domitian was a cruel person who killed his own brother and brought the second persecution against Christians. In his hatred, Domitian issued an order "That no Christian, once brought before the tribunal, should be exempted from punishment without renouncing his religion."

Numerous lies were made up during this time to harm the Christians, some so outrageous that only unthinking hate could believe them—such as the Christians were responsible for every famine, epidemic, or earthquake that afflicted any part of the Roman empire. Money was offered to those who would testify against the Christians, and many innocent people were slaughtered for financial gain. When Christians were brought before Domitian's council, they were told that if they swore an oath of allegiance to him they would be set free. Those who refused to take the oath were killed.

The martyr during this time with whom we are most familiar was **Timothy**, who was the celebrated disciple of the Apostle Paul and overseer of the Church in Ephesus until A.D. 97. In that year, the Ephesian pagans were celebrating a feast called "Catagogion." When Timothy saw their pagan procession, he blocked their way and severely rebuked them for their idolatry. His holy boldness angered the pagans and they attacked him with clubs and beat him so badly that he died of his injuries two days later.

The third persecution, under Emperor Trajan (A.D. 98-117)

In the third persecution, Pliny, known as "the Younger," a Roman consul and writer, took pity on the persecuted Christians and wrote to Trajan, assuring him that there were many thousands of them put to death daily who had not done anything contrary to Roman laws. In his letter, he said:

> The whole account they gave of their crime or error (whichever it is to be called) amounted only to this: namely, that they were accustomed on a stated day to meet before daylight, and to repeat together a set form of prayer to Christ as a God, and to bind themselves by an obligation, not indeed to commit wickedness; but, on the contrary, never to commit theft, robbery, or adultery, never to falsify their word,

13

never to defraud any man: after which it was their custom to separate, and reassemble to partake in common of a harmless meal.

The degree to which Pliny's letter lessened the persecution, if at all, is not recorded.

During this persecution, in the year A.D. 110, **Ignatius** (see figure 8), who was the overseer of the Church in Antioch, the capital of Syria, where the disciples were first called Christians (Acts 11:26), was sent to Rome because he professed and taught Christ. It's said that when he passed through Asia, even though guarded by soldiers, he preached the Word of God in every city they traveled through and encouraged and strengthened the churches. While in Smyrna, he wrote to the Church at Rome and appealed to them not to try to deliver him from martyrdom, because they would deprive him of that which he most longed and hoped for. He wrote:

> Now I begin to be a disciple. I care for nothing of visible or invisible things so that I may but win Christ. Let fire and the cross, let the companies of wild beasts, let breaking of bones and tearing of limbs, let the grinding of the whole body, and all the malice of the devil, come upon me; be it so, only may I win Christ Jesus.

Even when he was sentenced to be fed to lions and could hear their roaring, he was filled with such desire to suffer for Christ (see Acts 5:41) that he said, "I am the wheat of Christ: I am going to be ground with the teeth of wild beasts that I may be found pure bread."

Emperor Adrian

Trajan was succeeded by Adrian, who continued this third persecution with as much cruelty as his predecessor.

About **ten thousand Christians** were martyred during his reign. Many were crowned with thorns, crucified, and had spears thrust into their sides in cruel imitation of Jesus' death.

Eustachius, a successful and brave Roman commander, was ordered to join in an idolatrous sacrifice to celebrate his victories, but his heart-faith in Christ was so much greater than his vanity that he refused. Enraged at this, Adrian forgot Eustachius's noble service to Rome and had him and **his entire family** martyred.

Two brothers, **Fausines** and **Jovita**, bore their tortures with such patience that a pagan named Calocerius was so struck with admiration that he cried out in a kind of ecstasy, "Great is the God of the Christians!" For this, he was immediately arrested and put to the same tortures.

The relentless persecutions against the Christians continued until Quadratus, who was overseer of Athens, made a scholarly defense in their favor before the emperor, who was in Athens for a visit. At the same time, Aristides, a philosopher in the city, wrote an elegant epistle to the emperor, also in their favor. These combined to cause Adrian to become more lenient and relax his persecution.

Adrian died in A.D. 138, and was succeeded by Antoninus Pius. Emperor Pius was one of the most amiable monarchs that ever reigned, and stopped all persecutions against the Christians.

The fourth persecution, under Emperor Marcus Aurelius Antoninus (A.D. 162-180)

Marcus Aurelius was a philosopher, and wrote *Meditations*, a classic work of stoicism, which is an indifference to pleasure or pain. He was also fierce and merciless toward Christians and responsible for the fourth general persecution against them.

The cruelties against Christians in this persecution were so inhuman that many of those who watched them shuddered with horror, and were astonished at the courage of the sufferers. Some of the martyrs had their feet crushed in presses, and were then forced to walk over thorns, nails, sharp shells, and other pointed objects. Others were whipped until their sinews and veins were exposed. Then after suffering the most excruciating tortures that could be devised, they were killed in terrible ways. Yet few turned from Christ or begged their torturers to lessen their pains.

When **Germanicus**, a young man and true Christian, was delivered to the wild lions on account of his faith, he behaved with such astonishing courage that several pagans were converted to the faith that inspired such bravery.

Polycarp, who was a student of the Apostle John and the overseer of the church in Smyrna, heard that soldiers were looking for him and tried to escape but was discovered by a child. After feeding the guards who captured him, he asked for an hour in prayer, which they gave him. He prayed with such fervency, that his guards said they were sorry that they were the ones who captured him. Nevertheless, he was taken before the governor and condemned to be burned in the market place.

After his sentence was given, the governor said to him, "Reproach Christ and I will release you."

Polycarp answered, "Eighty-six years I have served him, and he never once wronged me. How then shall I blaspheme my King who has saved me?"

In the market place, he was tied to the stake rather than nailed, as was the usual custom, because he assured them he would stand immovable in the flames and not fight them. As the dry sticks placed around him were lit, the flames rose up and circled his body without touching him. The executioner was then ordered to pierce him with a sword. When he did, a great quantity of blood gushed out and put out the fire. Although his Christian friends asked to be given his body as it was so they could bury him, the enemies of the Gospel insisted that it be burned in the fire, which was done.

Felicitatis, a well-known lady of a wealthy Roman family was a devout and pious Christian. She had seven sons who were also devout Christians. All were martyred.

Januarius, the eldest, was scourged, and pressed to death with weights. **Felix** and **Philip**, the two next, had their brains dashed out with a club. **Silvanus,** the fourth, was thrown from a precipice. The three younger sons, **Alexander**, **Vitalis**, and **Martial**, were beheaded with a sword. Felicitatis was then beheaded with the same sword.

Justin, the Greek theologian who founded a school of Christian philosophy at Rome and wrote the *Apology* and the *Dialogue,* was also martyred during this time of persecution. He was a native of Neapolis in Samaria, and was a great lover of truth, and a universal scholar. After his conversion to Christianity when he was thirty years old, he wrote an elegant epistle to the Gentiles, and employed his talents in convincing the Jews of the truth of the Christian faith.

When the pagans began to treat the Christians with great severity, Justin wrote a defense in their favor that prompted the emperor to publish a decree in favor of the Christians.

Soon after, he entered into frequent debates with Crescens, a celebrated cynic philosopher. Justin's arguments overpowered Crescens and so disturbed him that he resolved to destroy Justin. The second defense that Justin wrote on behalf of the Christians gave Cresens the opportunity he needed, and he convinced the emperor that Justin was dangerous to him, whereupon he and **six followers** were arrested and ordered to sacrifice to pagan idols. When they refused, they were scourged and then beheaded.

Soon after, the persecutions ceased for a while because of a miraculous deliverance of the emperor's army from certain defeat in a battle in the northern providence through the prayers of a legion of his soldiers who were all Christians. But it began again in France where the tortures almost exceed the powers of description.

Sanctus, a deacon of Vienna, had red hot plates of brass placed upon the tenderest parts of his body and left there until they burned through to his bones.

Blandina, a Christian lady of a weak constitution who was not thought to be able to resist torture, but whose fortitude was so great that her tormentors became exhausted with their devilish work, was afterward taken into an amphitheater with three others, suspended on a piece of wood stuck in the ground, and exposed as food for wild lions. While awaiting her suffering, she prayed earnestly for her companions and encouraged them. But none of the lions would touch her, so she was put back into prison—this happened twice. The last time she was brought out, she was accompanied by 15-year-old **Ponticus**. The steadfastness of their faith so enraged the multitude that neither her sex nor his youth were respected, and they were subjected to the severest punishments and tortures. Blandina was torn by the lions, scourged, put into a net and tossed about by a wild bull, and placed naked into a red-hot metal chair. When she could speak, she exhorted all near her to hold fast to their faith. Ponticus persevered unto death. When Blandina's torturers were unable to make her recant her faith, they killed her with a sword.

The fifth persecution, starting with Emperor Lucius Septimus Severus (A.D. 193-211)

For a short period, Severus was favorable toward Christians because it was said he had recovered from a severe fit of sickness after being ministered to by a

Christian, but it wasn't long before the prejudice and fury of Rome's citizens prevailed and obsolete laws were revived and used against the Christians. And, once again, they were blamed and punished for every natural misfortune that occurred.

Regardless of the renewed persecution, the Church and Gospel stood firm and bright through it, and the Lord increasingly added to His Body throughout the Roman empire. Tertullian, the Carthaginian theologian who converted to Christianity about A.D. 193, said that if the Christians all left the Roman provinces, the empire would be nearly empty.

During this persecution, **Victor**, bishop of Rome, was martyred in A.D. 201. **Leonidus**, the father of Origen, the Greek Christian philosopher known for his interpretations of the Old Testament, was beheaded. Many of Origen's hearers also suffered martyrdom: **Plutarchus**, **Serenus**, **Heron**, and **Heraclides** were beheaded. A woman named **Rhais** had boiling tar poured upon her head and was then burned, as was her mother, **Marcella**. Her sister **Potainiena**, met the same fate that she did, but during her torments, **Basilides**, an army officer ordered to attend her execution, was converted to Christ. Later, when he was required to swear an oath on Roman idols, he refused on the basis that he was a Christian. At first those with him could not believe what they heard, but when he repeated it, he was dragged before a judge, condemned, and beheaded.

Irenaeus, (AD 130-202), Greek church father and bishop of Lyons, was born in Greece, and received both a secular and a Christian education. It is believed that he wrote the account of the persecutions at Lyons. He was beheaded in A.D. 202.

The persecutions now extended into northern Africa, which was a Roman province. Many were martyred in that area. Here are but a few.

Perpetua, a young married woman who was still nursing a child; **Felicitas**, who was then pregnant, and **Revocatus** of Carthage, a slave who was being taught the principles of Christianity. Other prisoners who suffered at the same time were **Saturninus**, **Secundulus**, and **Satur**. These latter three were made to run between two rows of men who severely lashed them as they passed.

After an appearance before the proconsul Minutius in which she was offered freedom if she sacrificed to the idols, Perpetua had her still-nursing baby taken from her and was thrown into prison. Describing her faith and life in prison, she told her father, "The dungeon is to me a palace." Later she and the other prisoners appeared before Hilarianus, the judge. He, also, offered to set her free if she would sacrifice. Her father was there with her baby and begged her to do so. She replied, "I will not sacrifice."

"Are you a Christian?" asked Hilarianus.

"I am a Christian," Perpetua replied.

All of the Christians with her stood fast for Christ, and they were ordered to be killed by wild beasts for the enjoyment of the crowd on the next pagan holiday. The men were to be torn by lions and leopards and the women set upon by bulls.

On the day of their execution, Perpetua and Felicitas were first stripped naked and hung in nets, but were removed and clothed when the crowd objected. Upon returning to the arena, Perpetua was tossed about by a mad bull and was stunned but not seriously hurt; Felicitas, however, was badly gored. Perpetua hurried to her side and held her while they waited for the bull to charge them again, but he refused to do so, and they were dragged from the arena, much to the crowds disappointment.

After a short time, they were brought back to be killed by gladiators. Felicitas was killed quickly, but the young, inexperienced gladiator assigned to kill Perpetua trembled violently and could only stab her weakly several times. Seeing how he trembled, Perpetua held his sword blade and guided it to a vital area in her body.

The fate of the men were similar. Satur and Revocatus were killed by the wild beasts, Saturninus was beheaded, and Secundulus died of his wounds in prison.

The sixth persecution, under Emperor Marcus Clodius Pupienus Maximus (A.D. 164-238)

Maximus was a despot who ordered all Christians hunted down and killed. So many were killed that at times they buried them fifty and sixty together in large pits.

Among those killed were **Pontianus**, bishop of Rome, who was exiled to Sardinia for preaching against idolatry and was there killed. His successor, **Anteros**, was also martyred after only forty days in office for offending the government by compiling a history of the martyrs. A Roman senator, **Pammachius and his family** and **forty-two other Christians** were beheaded the same day and their heads displayed on the city gates. A Christian minister, **Calepodius**, was dragged through the streets of Rome and then thrown into the Tiber River with a millstone tied around his neck. A refined and beautiful young virgin named **Martina** was beheaded, and **Hippolitus**, a Christian minister, was tied to wild horses and dragged along the ground until he died.

Maximus died in A.D. 238 and was succeeded by Gordian, who was then succeeded by Philip. During the latter two reigns, the Church was free from persecution for a period of 6-10 years. In A.D. 249, however, a violent persecution in Alexandria was instigated by a pagan priest without the emperor's knowledge. During that persecution, an elderly Christian, **Metrus**, was beaten with clubs, pricked with needles, and stoned to death for refusing to worship idols. A Christian woman, **Quinta**, was scourged, then dragged over flint stones by her feet, and stoned to death. A seventy-year-old woman, **Appolonia**, who confessed that she was a Christian, was fastened to a stake to be burned. After the fire was set, she begged to be set free, which the mob did thinking that she was going to recant Christ. To their amazement, however, she hurled herself back into the flames and died.

The seventh persecution, under Emperor Decius (A.D. 249-251)

This persecution was initiated by Decius because of his hatred for his predecessor Philip, who was believed to be a Christian, and by his anger that Christianity was rapidly increasing and the pagan gods were being forsaken. He decided, therefore, to eliminate the Christian religion and all its followers. The heathen citizens of Rome were eager to enforce Decius's decree, and considered the killing of Christians to be beneficial to the empire. During this persecution, the martyrs were too numerous for anyone to record. Here are a few of them.

St. Chrysostom, the patriarch of Constantinople in A.D. 398, wrote that **Julian**, a Cilician, was arrested for being a Christian, put into a leather bag with several snakes and scorpions, and then thrown into the sea.

A young man, **Peter**, who was known for the superior qualities of his mind and body refused to sacrifice to the goddess Venus when told to do so. In his defense, he said, "I'm amazed that you sacrifice to an infamous woman whose debaucheries your own writings record, and whose life consisted of such perverted actions as your laws would punish. No, I shall offer the true God the acceptable sacrifice of praises and prayers." When the governor of Asia, Optimus, heard this, he ordered that Peter be stretched upon a wheel until all his bones were broken and then beheaded.

A weak Christian, **Nichomachus**, was brought before Optimus and ordered to sacrifice to the pagan idols. Nichomachus replied, "I cannot pay the respect to devils that is due only to the Almighty." He was immediately placed on the rack, and after enduring his torments for only a short time, recanted his faith in Christ. As soon as he was freed from the rack, he was seized with a great agony and fell to the ground and died.

Seeing what seemed to be a terrible judgment, **Denisa**, a sixteen-year-old girl who was among the observers, exclaimed, "O unhappy wretch, why would you buy a moment's ease at the expense of a miserable eternity!" When Optimus heard this he called her to himself, and when Denisa confessed that she was a Christian, he had her beheaded.

Andrew and **Paul**, two Christian companions of Nichomachus, held fast to Christ and were stoned to death as they called on their blessed Redeemer.

In Alexandria, **Alexander** and **Epimachus** were arrested for being Christians. When they confessed that they were, they were beat with thick sticks, torn with hooks, and then burned to death. On the same day, **four female martyrs** were beheaded; their names are unknown.

In Nice, **Trypho** and **Respicius**, prominent men and Christians, were arrested and given over to the torturers. Nails were driven through their feet, they were scourged, dragged through the streets, torn with iron hooks, scorched with torches, and then beheaded.

Quintain, governor of Sicily, lusted after a Sicilian lady, **Agatha**, who was as much known for her piety as her remarkable beauty. When she resisted all of Quintain's advances, he had her placed in the hands of a notorious woman, Aphrodica, who ran a brothel. But that she-devil was unable to turn Agatha to prostitution so that Quintain could satisfy his lust with her. Upon hearing this, Quintain's lust turned to rage and he called her before him and questioned her. When she confessed that she was a Christian, Quintain had her scourged, torn with sharp hooks, and laid naked upon live coals mixed with broken glass. Agatha bore these tortures with great courage, and was carried back to prison where she died from her wounds on February 5, 251.

Lucius, the governor of Crete, ordered **Cyril**, the 84-year-old overseer of the church at Gortyna, to be arrested for refusing to obey the imperial edict to perform sacrifices to the idols. When Cyril appeared before him, Lucius exhorted him to perform the sacrifices and thereby save himself from a horrible death. The godly man replied that he had long taught others the way to eternal life in Christ, and now he must stand firm for the sake of his own soul. He displayed no fear when Lucius condemned him to be burned at the stake, and suffered the flames joyously and with great courage.

In A.D. 251, Emperor Decius erected a pagan temple in Ephesus and commanded all those in the city to sacrifice to its idols. Seven of his soldiers who were Christians refused to do so and were placed in prison. They were: **Constantinus, Dionysius, Joannes, Malchus, Martianus, Maximianus,** and **Seraion**. Decius tried to turn them from their faith by a show of leniency, and gave them until he returned from an expedition to change their minds. During his absence the seven escaped and hid themselves in a cave in nearby hills. When Decius returned, however, their hiding place was discovered, and he ordered the cave to be sealed so they would die from thirst and starvation.

It was during this persecution under Decius that sixty-four-year-old **Origen**, the renowned Christian philosopher whose father, **Leonidus**, was martyred during the fifth persecution, was arrested and thrown into a foul prison in Alexandria. His feet were bound with chains and put into the *stocks, and his legs were spread as far apart as possible. He was continually threatened with burning, and tormented with every means that would keep him barely alive for some time before dying.

Fortunately, during this time Decius died, and his successor Gallus was immediately involved in repelling an invasion by the Goths, a Germanic peoples from the north. This temporarily stopped the persecution on the Christians, and Origen obtained his release and went to Tyre, where he stayed until his death five years later in about A.D. 254

The eighth persecution, under Emperor Valerian (A.D. 253-260)

This persecution began in the fourth month of A.D. 257, and lasted for three and a half years. The number of martyrs and the degree of their tortures were as great as under any previous persecution. We cannot tell all of their stories, so we have chosen a few that represent the many

Rufina and **Secunda**, the beautiful and educated daughters of a prominent man in Rome, were engaged to two young men of some wealth, Armentarius and Verinus. All four were professed Christians. When the persecutions began, however, and the young men realized they were in danger of losing their money, they renounced their faith, and tried to persuade the young ladies to do the same. When they would not, the gentlemen informed against them and they were arrested for being Christians and taken before the governor of Rome, Junius Donatus, and condemned and beheaded. The overseer of the church in Rome, **Stephen**, was also beheaded.

About the same time, in Toulouse, which was part of Roman Gaul, **Saturninus**, the godly overseer of the church, refused to sacrifice to idols in their temple when ordered to do so, and was taken to the top of the temple steps and tied by his feet to the tail of a wild bull. The beast was then driven down the steps, dragging Saturninus behind him.

By the time the bottom step was reached, the pious man's head was split open and he was dead.

In Rome, **Sixtus** succeeded Stephen as overseer of the church, but his time in office was short. In A.D. 258, the year after Stephen's martyrdom, Marcianus, governor of Rome, obtained an edict from emperor Valerian authorizing him to kill all the clergy in Rome. Sixtus and **six of his deacons** were immediately put to death.

Also in the church in Rome was a godly man named **Lawrence**, who was a minister of the Gospel and in charge of distributing the church's goods (see Acts 6:3). Marcianus greedily demanded that Lawrence tell him where the church's riches were hid, thinking he could take them for himself. Lawrence requested three days in which to gather the riches together and present them to the governor.

When the third day came, Marcianus demanded that Lawrence keep his promise. Whereupon Lawrence stretched out his arms over some poor Christians that he had gathered in the place with him and said, "These are the precious riches of the Church. They are the treasure in which faith in Christ reigns, in whom Christ has His dwelling place. What more precious jewel can the Church have than those in whom Christ promised to dwell?"

Upon hearing this, Marcianus raged in the fury and madness of devils, and screamed out his anger: "Light the fire, do not spare the wood! This villain has tried to deceive the emperor. Away with him, away with him! Whip him with scourges, jerk him with hooks, buffet him with fists, brain him with clubs. Does the traitor joke with the emperor? Pinch him with fiery tongs, wrap him in burning plates, bring out the strongest chains, and the fire-forks, and the grated bed of iron. Put the bed on the fire and when it's red-hot, bind the traitor on it hand and foot and roast him, broil him, toss him, turn him. Torment him every way you can or you will be tormented yourselves."

No sooner had he finished ranting than the tortures began. After many cruel torments, this meek slave of Christ was laid on his fiery bed. But in God's providence, it was as a bed of soft feathers, and the godly Lawrence laid there and perished as if taking a nourishing rest.

In Africa, the full fury of the persecutions raged. **Thousands** were martyred for Christ. Again, we can only tell the stories of a few of them.

In Utica, just northwest of Carthage, the provincial governor ordered **three hundred Christians** to be placed around the rim of a burning lime kiln pit. A pan of coals and incense for worshipping idols were prepared, and the Christians were told that they would either sacrifice to the god Jupiter or be thrown into the pit. All refused, and then together jumped into the pit to suffocate and burn in the terrible fumes and flames.

Not far from there, three Christian virgins, **Maxima, Donatilla**, and **Secunda**, were condemned for refusing to give up Christ, given gall and vinegar to drink to perhaps lessen their pains, or in imitation of Jesus (see Matthew 27:34). They were then horribly scourged and their wounds rubbed with lime. After that they were hung and tortured on a gallows, scorched on a *gridiron, torn by wild animals, and finally decapitated.

In Spain, **Fructuosus**, the overseer of the church in Tarragona, and his two deacons, **Augurius** and **Eulogius**, were martyred in the flames.

In Palestine, **Alexander, Malchus, Priscus**, and an **unnamed woman** were sentenced to be eaten by lions after publicly stating that they were Christians. Their sentence was carried out immediately.

In A.D. 260, Valerian's son, Gallienus, succeeded him. During Gallienus's reign the Church was free from general persecution for several years.

The ninth persecution under Aurelian (Lucius Domitius Aurelianus) (A.D. 270-275)

Historians know Aurelian as the Roman Emperor who held the barbarians in check beyond the Rhine River and regained Britain, Gaul, Spain, Syria, and Egypt for the empire. Christians know him as just another barbarian and persecutor of the Church of Jesus Christ.

The overseer of the church in Rome, **Felix**, was the first martyr during Aurelian's reign. Felix was beheaded in A.D. 274.

In Praeneste, a city about thirty miles from Rome, a wealthy young man named **Agapetus** sold all that he had and gave the money to the poor. As a result, he was arrested as a Christian, tortured, and beheaded.

Aurelian was assassinated by his own officials and succeeded by Tacitus. Several other emperors followed: Propus, Carus, and his sons Carnious and Numerian. During these reigns the Church was at peace.

The tenth persecution, under Diocletian (A.D. 284-305)

The previous persecutions were only preliminaries for the persecution under Diocletian—it was the worst of all. His desire to revive the old pagan religion of Rome led to what was to be not only a massive persecution of Christians, but the last major persecution in the Roman empire.

In the beginning of his reign, Diocletian was favorable toward the Christians. Several were, however, martyred before any major persecution broke out. Here are some of them.

In Rome, the twins **Marcus** and **Marcellianus** had been brought up as Christians by their tutors, even though their parents were heathens. Their faithfulness to Christ laid at rest the arguments of those who wanted to make them pagans, and eventually resulted in the conversion of their entire family. For their faith, their arms were tied over their heads to posts and their feet nailed to the posts. They remained that way for a day and night and then were thrust through with lances.

Because of the steadfastness of their faith, **Zoe**, their jailer's wife, was also converted to Christ. Not long after, she was martyred by being hung upon a tree with a straw fire burning under her. After she perished from the flames, a large stone was tied around her body and it was thrown into a nearby river.

Faith, a Christian female, in Aquitaine [or Aquitania], a region in South France, was laid upon a gridiron and broiled, and then beheaded.

In Rome in A.D. 287, **Quintin** and **Lucian** were determined to preach the Gospel in parts of Gaul. For a while they preached together in Amiens in northern France. Then Lucian went to another city where he was martyred. Quintin went to Picardy, and was fervent in his evangelism. Not long after going there, however, he was arrested and condemned to die for being a Christian. For his death agonies, ropes were tied to his arms and legs and he was stretched with pulleys until his joints dislocated, then he was scourged with a wire whip, had boiling oil and pitch poured on his naked body, and had fire applied to his sides and armpits. After these tortures, he was put back into prison where he soon died from his wounds. A heavy stone was tied to his body and it was thrown into the Somme river.

On June 22, 287, a Christian named **Alban** became the first British martyr. The city of St. Alban's in the county of Hertfordshire is named after him. Alban was originally a pagan, but a Christian minister named Amphibalus convinced him of the truth of Christ. When Amphibalus was sought by the authorities because of his religion, Alban hid him in his house. When soldiers came there seeking him, Alban said he was Amphibalus in order to give him time to escape. The deception was discovered and the governor ordered Alban to be scourged and then beheaded.

The Venerable Bede, the Anglo-Saxon theologian and historian who wrote the *Ecclesiastical History of the English Nation* in A.D. 731, states that **Alban's executioner** suddenly became a convert to Christianity and begged Alban that he be allowed to die for him or with him. He was given permission for the latter, and they were both beheaded by a soldier who volunteered to act as executioner.

It was during Diocletian's reign that Galerius, his adopted son and successor, agitated by his mother who was a bigoted pagan, convinced the emperor to eliminate Christianity from the Roman empire.

The day scheduled to begin the bloody work was February 23, 303. It began in Nicomedia, the capital of Diocletian's Eastern Roman Empire. Early that morning, the chief of police and a large number of officers and assistants made their way to the main Christian church and forced open its doors and ransacked the building and burned all its sacred books.

Diocletian and Galerius had accompanied them to witness the beginning of the end of the Christian religion—not satisfied with the burning of the books, they had the building leveled to the ground. Following this, Diocletian issued an edict that all Christian churches and books were to be destroyed, and all Christians were to be arrested as traitors to the empire.

When the edict was posted in a public place, **a bold Christian** immediately tore it down and denounced the name of the emperor for his injustice. For his public display of contempt for the emperor, he was arrested, tortured, and burned to death.

Every Christian in Nicomedia was arrested and put into prison. To ensure the certainty and severity of their punishment, Galerius secretly ordered the imperial palace set on fire and Christians blamed as the arsonists. From this a general persecution started throughout the empire and lasted ten years, during which **thousands of Christians** were martyred. It mattered not their age or sex, none were spared. In A.D. 286, Diocletian had divided the empire into East and West in an attempt to rule the territory more effectively, and the persecution was especially fierce in the East, which was under his rule. In A.D. 293, he made Aurelius Valerius Constantius, the father of Constantine, caesar of the West areas of Gaul and Britain.

"Christian" became a hated name among the pagans, and any who bore that name received no mercy from them. Once again they were blamed for every disaster and misfortune that befell the pagans. The worst lies and most unreasonable stories could be told about them and they were believed. The forms of torture that were devised exhausted imagination.

Many Christian houses were set on fire, with entire families perishing in the flames. Heavy stones were hung about the necks of many and they were tied together and driven into the Sea of Marmara. Racks, scourges, fire, swords, daggers, crosses, poison, and starvation, were all used individually and collectively. In the region of Phrygia, a city in which **all the citizens** were Christians was burned and all the inhabitants forced into the flames to perish.

Finally weary with the slaughter, the governors of several provinces appealed to the emperor on the basis that such conduct on the part of Romans was improper. Thus many Christians were saved from death, but were mutilated in such ways as to make their lives miserable. Many had their ears cut off, their noses slit, one or both eyes put out, bones torn out of their sockets, and their flesh burned in conspicuous places so they were ever marked as Christians.

As with all general persecutions, only a few stories can be told, but they represent the thousands who were tortured unmercifully and died horrible deaths.

Sebastian was an officer in the emperor's guard at Rome. During the persecution, when he refused to recant his faith in Christ and worship idols, Diocletian ordered him shot through with arrows, which was done until he was supposedly dead. When some Christians came to take his body and bury it, however, they saw signs of life in him and immediately took him to a secure place where he recovered from his wounds. His respite from death was nevertheless short, for soon as he was able he accosted Diocletian in the streets and rebuked him for his cruel and prejudice treatment of Christians. Though surprised at seeing Sebastian alive, the emperor immediately ordered him arrested and taken to a place of execution and beaten to death. To prevent the Christians from finding his body this time, he ordered it thrown into Rome's sewers. But Lucinda, a pious woman, found a way to remove it from the sewers and had it buried in the catacombs among the bodies of other martyrs.

Vitus was taught the principles of Christianity by a nurse who raised him. When his pagan father, Hylas, discovered this, he tried to convert him to paganism but failed. To appease his gods for his son's insults to their deity, he sacrificed Vitus to them on June 14, 303.

The good Christian **Victor** spent much time visiting the sick and weak, and gave considerable money to the poor. Being so well known as a charitable Christian, he soon came to the attention of the emperor and was arrested and ordered to be bound and dragged through the streets, all the while being beaten and stoned by pagans along the way. His steadfastness was condemned as stubbornness and he was ordered to be stretched on the rack and tortured while it was being done. Victor endured the ordeal with great courage, and when his tormentors grew tired of their work, they put him into a cell. There, he preached Christ to his jailers and three of them, **Alexander, Longinus**, and Felician received Christ.

When news of this reached the emperor, he ordered the three jailers to the executioner's block where they were beheaded. Victor was remanded to the rack and beaten with clubs and then returned to prison.

The third time he was examined, a pagan altar with an idol on it was brought in and he was given incense and ordered to offer it to the idol. Incensed at this, Victor drove his foot against the altar and overturned it. This so enraged the emperor, who was there, that he ordered Victor's foot to be cut off. He was then thrown into a grain mill and crushed beneath the millstones.

Once when Maximus, the provincial governor of Cilicia, was in Tarsus, three Christians, **Tarchus, Probus** and **Andronicus** were brought before him and repeatedly tortured and exhorted to recant their faith in Christ. When they would not, they were sent to the amphitheater for execution. There several hungry animals were released to attack the Christians, but none of them would do so. The animal keeper then brought out a ferocious lioness and a large bear that had killed three men that same day, but both refused to attack the men. Being frustrated in his attempts to torture them to death with the teeth and claws of wild beasts, Maximus had them killed with a sword.

Romanus was deacon of the church in caesarea. There arrested, he was taken to antioch where he was condemned for his faith, scourged, racked, torn with hooks, cut with knives in his body and face, his teeth beaten out, his hair plucked from his head, and then strangled to death.

Pious **Susanna**, who was the niece of Caius, the overseer of the church in Rome, was ordered by Diocletian to marry a noble pagan relative of his. When she refused, he had her beheaded.

Peter, a eunuch and slave to the emperor, became a Christian of great modesty and humility. When the emperor heard of this, he had him tied to a gridiron and broiled over a low fire until he died. It took several hours.

Eulalia was a remarkably sweet young lady of a Spanish Christian family. When she was arrested for being a Christian, the civil officer tried to convert her to paganism, but she so ridiculed the pagan gods that he was enraged and ordered her to be tortured with the greatest severity. During her torture, hooks were inserted into her sides and then pulled through the flesh, and her breasts were burned until they were charred. Her pain was so great from this that she died. This was in December 303.

In A.D. 304, the governor of Tarragona in Spain, ordered **Valerius** the overseer, and his deacon, **Vincent**, arrested, weighted with chains, and imprisoned. Both held fast in their faith, but for unknown reasons the overseer was only banished from Tarragona while his deacon suffered horrible tortures. He was tied upon a rack and stretched until his joints dislocated, hooks were inserted into loose parts of his flesh and then pulled through, then he was tied to a gridiron that had spikes on the top that pressed into his flesh while a fire burned beneath it. When none of these tortures either killed him or changed his steadfastness, he was put into a filthy prison cell that had bits of sharp flint and broken glass covering its floor. In that torment he died on January 22, 304.

The persecution of Christians reached the peak of its magnitude and cruelty in A.D. 304, the year before Diocletian resigned as Roman Emperor. It was almost as if the pagans sensed that a change was coming and were determined to afflict the Christians as horrendously as they could before the time of persecution was over. Again, we can tell the stories of only a few who were martyred that year.

In Africa, a Christian minister named **Saturninus** was tortured, put into prison, and starved to death. His **four children** suffered the same fate.

At Thessalonica, in what was then the Roman province of Masedon, the sisters **Agrape, Chionia**, and **Irene**, were arrested and burned to death on March 25, 304. Irene was given special treatment by the governor who was attracted to her beauty. When she rebuked his advances, he ordered her to be driven naked through the streets of the city, and in that condition be hung from the city wall and burned.

Four brothers, **Victorius, Carpophorus, Severus,** and **Severianus**, were employed in high offices by the city of Rome. But when it was heard that they were Christians and spoke against the worship of idols, they were arrested and scourged with whips like the cat-o'-nine-tails that had lead balls fastened to the ends. The scourgings were so severe that all four brothers died at the whipping posts.

Timothy, a deacon in a church in the Roman province of Mauritania, and **Maura** had been married only a few weeks when the persecution struck them and they were arrested for being Christians. Soon after their arrest, they were taken before the provincial governor, Arrianus, who was aware that Timothy was in charge of maintaining the Holy Scriptures in his church, and so ordered Timothy to turn the Scriptures over to him to be burned. To which order Timothy replied, "If I had children, I would sooner turn them over to you to be sacrificed than I would the Word of God."

Incensed at this answer, Arrianus ordered Timothy's eyes to be burned out with a red-hot iron, saying, "The books will at least be useless to you, for you will have no eyes with which to read them."

Timothy's courage through the horrible pain so infuriated Arrianus that he commanded him to be hung by his feet with a weight tied around his neck and a gag in his mouth, thinking that thereby he could overcome his steadfastness.

Timothy's wife, Maura, who had been forced to watch all this, begged him to recant for her sake that she not have to face such tortures. But when the gag was taken out of his mouth so he could reply to her entreaties, instead of agreeing with her, he charged her with mistaken love and declared his determination to die for his faith in Christ. The result was that Maura resolved to follow her husband's courage and to either accompany or follow him to glory. Failing to break her new resolution, Arrienus ordered her to be given the severest tortures. When their torments were finished, Timothy and Maura were crucified next to each other.

Sabinus, bishop of Assisium in the province of Tuscany, refused to sacrifice to Jupiter, the supreme god of Rome, and shoved the idol away from him. Whereupon, the governor had his offending hand cut off. While in prison, however, Sabinus converted **the governor and his family** to Christianity. Upon their confession of their newfound faith in the true God, they were all executed. Soon after, Sabinus was scourged until he died. This was in December 304.

In Phoenicia, where he was born, **Pamphilus** was noted for being so intelligent and well educated that he was called a second Origen. He became a member of the clergy in Caesarea, the capital of Roman Judea, established a public library, and devoted himself to every manner of Christian charity and work. As part of his work, he copied by his own hand the greatest part of Origen's writings, and assisted by another minister, Eusebius, produced a correct copy of the Old Testament, which had suffered greatly because of the ignorance or negligence of former transcribers. For doing such work, he was arrested, tortured, and put to death.

In A.D. 305, Diocletian resigned as supreme emperor of Rome and turned the empire over to Aurelius Valerius Constantius, whom he had made caesar of the West in A.D. 293, and Gaius Galerius Valerius Maximianus, who was his son-in-law and who had reigned as co-emperor with him in the East. Constantius was a mild mannered man of good temper and character. Under his rule, the Christians in the West had the first respite from persecution that they had had in many years. In the East, however, the cruel persecutions continued under the rule of Galerius, for it had been he who had incited Diocletian to the great persecution that was going to wipe the Christian Church from the face of the earth. It failed to do so, however, as have all persecutions, for Christ will have His Church upon the earth until He returns.

The failure of the pagan's to destroy Christ's Church was the beginning of the end of persecution in the Roman Empire, for God had a champion whom He would soon place as emperor over all of Rome.

3

Constantine the Great

(Emperor of Rome: A.D. 306-337)

In A.D. 293 when the emperor Diocletian made Constantius Caesar of Gaul and Britain, Constantius's son, Constantine, was kept at the court of Galerius, the Eastern emperor, as a hostage. In A.D. 305, he escaped and joined his father in the West.

When Diocletian resigned as emperor of Rome that same year, Galerius, who succeeded him, chose Maximian and Severus as Caesars under him. Constantius chose his son, Constantine, as Caesar under him. Although Italy and Africa were part of the empire in the West, Constantius refused to rule there because of the difficulty of governing them. He chose to rule only in France, Spain, and Britain. So Italy and Africa came under the rule of Maximian in the East. Although persecutions continued in the East for some time, they virtually stopped in the West under the rule of Constantius and Constantine, both of them being eager to maintain good relations with their citizens and support and treat all equally.

Constantius was a civil, caring, meek, gentle, and liberal man who desired to do good to all who were under his authority. Cyrus "the Younger"(424?-401 B.C.) once said that he got treasure for himself when he made friends rich, and Constantius often said that it was better that his subjects had the public wealth rather than have it hoarded in his own treasure house. He was by nature a man content with a simple life, and ate and drank from earthenware vessels rather than those elaborate in style. As a result of his splendid virtues, there was great peace and tranquillity in the provinces he governed.

In addition to his virtues, it is said that he had love and affection for the Word of God, and guided his life and rule by its principles. Because of this, he did not engage in wars that were contrary to piety and Christian doctrine, and he refused to assist other leaders who were engaged in unjust wars, he stopped the destruction of churches, and commanded that Christians be preserved, defended, and kept safe from all injuries caused by persecution. In the other regions of the empire, however, the persecution continued unabated—only Constantius permitted Christians to practice their faith unharmed.

On one occasion Constantius decided to test which members of his court were good and sincere Christians. He called together all his officers and servants and told them that only those who were willing to make sacrifices to devils would stay with him and keep their offices, and that those who refused to do so would be thrust out and banished from his court. Upon hearing this, the attendants of his court divided themselves into groups, from which the emperor separated those he knew to be strong in faith and godly.

The emperor sharply rebuked those who would sacrifice; he called them traitors to God and unworthy to be members of his court and commanded that they be banished. He commended those who refused to sacrifice to devils and confessed God, declaring that they alone were worthy to be in his presence. He commanded that they be placed as his trusted counselors and defenders of his person and kingdom. He said that not only were they worthy to be in office, but he regarded them as his true friends, esteeming them more than the wealth in his treasury.

Constantius died in A.D. 306 and the army hailed Constantine as Caesar. Many Christians believed Constantine was a second Moses whom God had sent to deliver His people out of captivity into joyful liberty.

Flavius Valerius Constantinus (Constantine), was born about A.D. 280 in the city of Naissus in the Roman province of Moesia, an ancient region of southeast Europe that later was Serbia. His father, Constantius, was a member of an important Roman family. His mother, Helena, was the daughter of an innkeeper.

Before A.D. 312, Constantine appears to have been a tolerant pagan who was willing to accumulate heavenly protectors to help him but was not committed to any one god. During the period of A.D. 312 to 324, however, he began to adopt the true God and several times granted favors to individual churches and overseers [bishops]. After his defeat of his political rival, Emperor Licinius, at Chrysopolis on September 18, 324, Constantine openly confessed Christianity.

Though a benevolent ruler like his father before him, Constantine ruled with absolute power, oppressive and tyrannical. And though he admitted bishops to his council, and his laws concerning the treatment of slaves and prisoners show the influence of Christian teachings, he had his oldest son, Crispus, and his second wife, Fausta, put to death. Like many during his time, Constantine's life and conduct were a mixture of Christianity and paganism.

Three important events marked Constantine's reign. He was the first Christian emperor of Rome, he made Christianity a lawful religion, and he founded the city of Constantinople. Constantinople became the capital of the Eastern Roman Empire and a symbol of Christian triumph. Constantine died on May 22, 327. Prior to his death, he divided the Roman empire among his three remaining sons.

When Constantine first became emperor of the West, he faced many problems with other claimants of the throne. Maximian had resigned as emperor, and his son, Maxentius, was elected emperor of Rome by the army. Since Italy was part of the West empire, he also considered himself to be superior emperor of the entire Roman empire. His military rule in Rome continued during the rule of Constantine. The Roman senate greatly feared Maxentius, and they hesitated to resist him. Upon their urging, his father, Maximian, who was once emperor, began to plot a means by which he might take control of the region away from his son. He attempted to get Diocletian to join him in his effort to overthrow Maxentius, but Diocletian refused to help. The soldiers that had elected Maxentius emperor learned about his father's plans to depose him, and made it clear to Maximian that they would not tolerate such a move.

When he could not move against Maxentius, Maximian turned his attentions toward France where Constantine ruled. He went to Constantine under the pretense of complaining to the emperor about his son, but his actual intent was to kill Constantine and take over the West empire. Constantine, however, had married Maximian's daughter, Fausta, and when she discovered her father's plot, she carried the news to Constantine. Maximian was arrested as he tried to flee France and executed.

All the while, Maxentius reigned at Rome with intolerable wickedness. He was so that many considered him to be another Pharaoh or Nero because he put most of the nobility to death and took their goods. Often he would fly into violent rages and command his soldiers to kill large numbers of Roman citizens. He left no lustful or monstrous act untried. He was also addicted to the magical arts. Often he called upon devils for help in his wickedness, and sought wisdom from them by which he might repel the wars that he believed Constantine was preparing against him.

Maxentius also pretended to be favorable toward Christians. Hoping to make the people of Rome his friends, he commanded them to no longer persecute the Christians, and he himself stopped his arrogant accusations against them. But this lasted only a short time and he once again became their open persecutor.

Weary of the bloodshed and Maxentius's tyrannical rule, the citizens of Rome complained to Constantine. They implored him to intervene and to release their city and country from Maxentius. Constantine listened to their appeals and sympathized with them over their plight. He wrote to Maxentius and appealed to him to stop his corrupt actions and cruelty. But when his letters did no good, he gathered his armies in Britain and France and prepared to march on Rome in A.D. 313.

Maxentius was alerted to the coming of Constantine's army, and not wanting to meet him in open battle, set up hidden garrisons along the way to the city to ambush Constantine's forces. Although there were many skirmishes but, Constantine won each of them.

Constantine, being still influenced by pagan superstitions, was concerned about Maxentius's supposed powers of sorcery, and tried to think of some way to overcome his magic. The story is told that as they drew near Rome, Constantine looked up many times toward heaven hoping for some sign of help. At about twilight one evening, he looked up toward the southern sky and saw a great brightness in the form of a cross, and on the cross this inscription: *In hoc vince,* which means, "In this overcome." Eusebius Pamphilus, an officer in Constantine's army, said that he often heard Constantine tell about his vision of the cross, and swore that he also saw it and the inscription. Many of the soldiers confirmed Constantine's vision as well.

Constantine did not know what the vision meant and consulted with many of his men about it, but no one had an answer. That night Christ appeared to him in a dream holding the same cross and told him that if he would make such a cross and carry into his battles with him he would always win.

> The cross was not given to Constantine as a superstitious symbol that had power in itself to win battles, but rather as a continual reminder to him and his men to seek knowledge and faith in the One in Whose name they would fight, for His glory, and for the spread of His kingdom.

The next day, Constantine had a cross made of gold and precious stones that they carried in place of his standard. With the cross before them, and renewed hope and confidence within them, Constantine and his men hurried toward Rome.

Maxentius now knew that he must meet Constantine's forces in open battle, so he moved his forces to a field beyond the Tiber River. He then destroyed the bridge they crossed over, and had another one made of various sized rowboats covered with boards and planks so that the construction looked like a bridge. His plan was to trick

Constantine's forces into trying to cross the imitation bridge, and then attacking as it collapsed beneath them.

But as the Psalmist wrote:

> *He made a pit and dug it out, And has fallen into the ditch which he made.*
>
> *His trouble shall return upon his own head, And his violent dealing shall come down on his own crown.*
> (Psalm 7:15-16)

When the two forces engaged in battle, Maxentius's men were not able to withstand the newfound strength of those fighting under the banner of the cross, and he and his men were hurled back toward the city. In their haste to escape the fury of Constantine's attack, they sought to cross the bridge they had made to trap Constantine's army, and were trapped themselves. The makeshift bridge collapsed and overturned, tossing many soldiers and Maxentius and his horse into the river, where his heavy armor pulled him to the bottom and he drowned. It was as if Pharaoh's army drowning in the Red Sea were a prophetic symbol of Maxentius and his army.

As the children of Israel had suffered in Egyptian captivity for 400 years, so had the Christians suffered persecution under the heels of the Roman empire for 300 years. The blood of the lamb had saved the Israelite's when the death angel passed over Egypt to deliver them from Pharaoh's iron grip, and now the Cross of the Lamb of God had led an army of deliverance into the last stronghold of Roman tyranny and set God's people free. Nearly 1600 years had passed, and the same LORD was watching over His people.

Constantine became emperor over all of the Roman empire, and in A.D. 324 moved his seat of government from

Rome to the East. For his capital he chose the ancient Greek city of Byzantium in the Bosporus, which is a strait that lies between the Black Sea, to the north, and the Sea of Marmara. It has been an important trade route since ancient times. Constantine enlarged and enriched the city at great expense. In A.D. 330, he dedicated it as "New Rome," but it was commonly called Constantinople, "the city of Constantine."

Constantine was the first Christian emperor of the Roman Empire, and Constantinople became the capital of Christianity in the West, but Rome dominated Christianity in the East. The Western Roman Empire that Constantine established survived for more than a thousand years, and during those years Christians lived in relative peace.

Although there was no longer a general, systematic persecution of Christians, such as there had been under the Roman emperors, Christians still suffered persecution in isolated areas of the world, as they always would. As the much afflicted Apostle Paul wrote to his disciple Timothy from prison in Rome just before he was beheaded, "all who desire to live godly in Christ Jesus will suffer persecution" (1 Timothy 3:12).

4

Persecutions During the Thousand Years of General Peace

(About A.D. 320-A.D. 1079)

Because the persecutions during these thousand years were isolated and widespread, we have only a few records of those who were martyred for Christ. Yet each tell the same story of suffering and pain and eventual death for love of their Lord and faith in Him. Surely He was with them no matter where they suffered, giving them His strength and patience to endure unto eternal glory, just as He endured and is now waiting with open arms for all who die in His name. Here are a few of their stories and the places where they died.

Persia: About A.D. 320

Many in Persia were sun worshippers, and when the Gospel began to spread into that country, their pagan priests became concerned that they would lose the influence they had over the lives of the people. So they complained to their king, Sapores, that Christians were enemies of the state and were in communication with the Romans, who were the hated enemies of the Persians. Almost every war with Rome had ended disastrously for the Persians. Sapores immediately commanded that Christians be persecuted throughout his empire. Thus many godly and prominent people in the Church and in the government of Persia were immediately seized and martyred.

When Emperor Constantine was told of the persecutions in Persia, he wrote to Sapores and told him of the tragedies that always seemed to befall those who persecuted Christians, and how great success always seemed to befall those who treated them well. He sighted his own victories over rival Roman emperors, and said, in effect, "I defeated them by faith in Christ alone, and because of this faith, God helped me in every battle and made me victorious. He has also extended my empire from the Western Ocean to the farthest parts of the East. To obtain all of this, I never offered sacrifices to any ancient gods nor made use of any of the magical arts. I prayed only to God Almighty and followed the cross of Christ that was given to me as my banner. Consider all this, for I would rejoice if you also abounded in glory because you treated the Christians well, and that you and I, and you and them, may enjoy enduring peace."

As a result of Constantine's appeal, the persecution in Persia ended for a while, but was renewed years later when a ruler unsympathetic to Christians became king of Persia.

Egypt: About A.D. 325-340

About A.D. 318, Arius, a Christian priest in Alexandria, Egypt, published a doctrine that declared that Jesus Christ was only a created being who did not exist from eternity and was therefore not coequal with God. To deal with this doctrine, Constantine called an *ecumenical council to convene in Nicaea. The council condemned Arius and his teachings, now called *Arianism*, and declared the complete equality of God the Father and the Son, and that the Father and Son were composed "of one substance."

In spite of the council's decisions, the problem of Arianism was not solved. The emperor Constantius II, Constantine's son, supported Arianism after the death of his father, as did Valens, one of his successors, who shared rule of the empire with his brother, Valentinian I, who made him emperor of the East. With Constantius II on the throne, the Arians rose in power and began to persecute orthodox Christians; that is, those Christians who held to faith in the divinity of Christ. Athanasius, the Greek patriarch of Alexandria, who was a leading defender of Christian orthodoxy against Arianism, and many of his bishops were banished from Alexandria and their positions filled with Arians.

The commander of the Roman forces in Egypt, **Artemius**, who admitted to being a Christian, had his commission taken from him, then his property, then his head.

Rome: A.D. 361

In A.D. 361, Constantius II died and was succeeded by Julian, who ruled as Roman emperor for two years. Although raised in the Christian faith, Emperor Julian renounced Christianity and declared that he was a pagan and was going to revive the old Roman religion. He made no public edicts against Christianity, but restored idol worship and recalled all banished pagans. Although he allowed free practice of religion to everyone, he banned Christians from holding a government or military office and revoked all privileges given to the clergy by Constantine.

The bishop of Arezzo in Italy, **Donatus**, the hermit, **Hilarinus**, and the Roman magistrate, **Gordian** were tortured and executed

Ancyra or Ankara, Turkey: A.D. 362

In the eastern city of Ancyra, **Bishop Basil** was put into prison for his fervent opposition to paganism. While he was in prison, the emperor Julian came to Ancyra and had Basil brought before him, determined that he would examine Basil himself. During the examination, Julian did everything he could to convince the bishop to stop his activities against the pagans, but Basil would not relent, and then prophesied the death of the emperor and said that he would be tormented in eternity. Julian was enraged when he heard this and commanded that Basil's flesh be torn every day in seven different places until his skin and flesh had no parts unmangled. Before this condition could be brought to pass, however, Basil died under the severity of his wounds. The date was June 28, 362.

Palestine: About A.D. 363

There are no records left of the individuals martyred in Palestine. We know only in general the ways in which they gave their lives for Christ. Many were burned alive, some were dragged by their feet through the streets naked until they died from loss of blood or pain, others were scalded to death or stoned, and many had their brains beaten out with clubs.

Alexandria: About A.D. 363

In Alexandria the Christians who were martyred were almost too many to count. They were killed by the sword, burned, crucified, and stoned. Several had their stomach cut open and grain put inside. Pigs were then let loose upon them to feed upon the grain and their intestines. How long the martyrs lived during this torture depended, of course, upon the hunger of the pigs.

Thrace: About A.D. 363

A Christian named **Emilianus** was burned at a stake, and one named **Domitius**, was slain by swords in a cave where he had tried to hide from his persecutors.

Emperor Julian died in A.D. 363 from wounds in a battle with Persia, and was succeeded by Jovian, who made peace with the Persians by giving up all Roman territories beyond the Tigris River. Jovian reigned for only one year and restored temporary peace to the Church. In A.D. 364, Valentian I become Emperor of Rome in the West and ruled jointly with his brother Valens in the East. Valens was an Arian, and once more the true Church was subjected to persecution. Valentian I ruled in the West from 364 to 375, and Valens ruled in the East from 364 to 378. He was killed in A.D. 378 in a battle fought with the Visigoths (West Goths) near the city of Adrianople.

It is noted that many Goths were Christians; Christianity having been spread among them by a converted Goth, a saintly scholar named **Ulfilas**. For more than forty years he labored, first making a Gothic alphabet so that he could translate the Bible, and then teaching his people faith in Christ.

Alexandria: A.D. 386

The emperor gave George, the Arian bishop of Alexandria, the authority to persecute the true Christians in that city, which the bishop proceeded to do with extreme malice. Assisting him were several leaders of the government, the general of the Egyptian forces, and a high-ranking Roman officer.

During the persecution, orthodox clergy were driven out of Alexandria and their churches closed. The harshness of the punishments inflicted on the Christians were as great as any of those inflicted by the pagans. If a Christian escaped from the persecution, his entire family was executed and his property seized.

Spain: A.D. 586

Hermenigildus was the oldest son of Leovigildus, a king of the Goths. Originally an Arian, was converted to orthodox faith by his godly wife, Ingonda. When his father heard of his conversion, he removed him as governor of Seville in southwest Spain, and threatened to execute him unless he recanted his faith in Christ.

To prevent his execution, Hermenigildus gathered around him an army of orthodox believers who would fight for him. Because of Hermenigildus rebellion, the king began a persecution against the true believers and led a powerful army toward Seville. Hermenigildus first took refuge in Seville itself, and then when the battle went badly, fled to Asieta [city unknown], where he was captured after a short besiegement.

Encased in chains, Hermenigildus was taken back to Seville, where at the feast of Easter he refused to receive the communion host from an Arian bishop, and on order of his father was immediately cut to pieces by his guards. This was on April 13, 586.

Lombardy (Italy): A.D. 683

The bishop of the city of Bergamo in the region of Lombardy, whose name was **John**, joined forces with the bishop of Milan to erase the errors of Arianism from the Church. Together they were increasingly successful in combating the heresies until John was assassinated on July 11, 683.

Germany: A.D. 689

Kiffien was a pious Roman bishop who preached to the pagans in Franconia, Germany. At Wurzburg he converted the governor, **Gozbert**, whose testimony was so godly that over a period of two years it inspired most of the citizens of that town to convert. In A.D. 689, Gozbert convinced the governor that his marriage to his brother's widow was sinful, whereupon the widow had him beheaded.

Spain: A.D. 850

Born in Corduba, Spain, and raised in the Christian faith, **Perfectus** was highly intelligent and read all the books that he could. He was also known for his extreme piety. While still a young man, he was ordained a priest and performed his duties in a most admirable fashion. In A.D. 850, he publicly declared that *Mohamet was an imposter, for which he was soon after beheaded, for most of Spain had been dominated by the Muslims since A.D. 711, after they defeated the Visigoths.

Persia: A.D. 997

The bishop of Prague, **Adalbert** became increasingly burdened for the conversion of infidels, so he traveled to a city in Persia and then converted and baptized many. This so infuriated the pagan priests so they attacked him and killed him with long darts.

Poland: 1079

Bolislaus, who was the second king of Poland, apperd an amiable man, but had a cruel heart. He soon became known for his sadistic actions. **Stanislus**, bishop of Cracow on the Vistula River, couragously took it upon himself to tell the king his faults in a private conversation in the hopes that he would cease his cruelties against his people. Although freely admitting the enormity of his crimes, Bolislaus was enraged at the repeated opportunites the bishop took to chastise him. Bolislaus had no intentions of changing, he sought an opportunity to rid himself of the bishop who was faithful to his Christian duties.

One day Bolislaus heard that the bishop was alone in a nearby church, sent soldiers kill him. They found the bishop alone, but they were awed by his godly presence and afraid to kill him. When they reported back to the king, he flew into a violent rage and snatched a knife from one of them and raced to the chapel and there stabbed Stanislus several times as the good man knelt at the altar. Stanislus died immediately.

The persecution of Christians was spasmodic for nearly a thousand years, but then Satan again fastened himself on Rome and sent his workers forth in another systematic attempt to destroy the Church. Only this time the persecutions would not come from pagans, but from those who called themselves Christians, and whose fury and sadistic actions against those who held in faith to Christ would far exceed the cruelest imaginations of the pagans.

5

Papal Persecutions and the Inquisition
(1208-1834)

Papal Persecutions

Up to about the 12th century, most of the persecutions against true believers in Christ came from the pagan world, but now the church in Rome discarded the truths of the Scriptures and the commandments of love and took up the sword against all who opposed the false doctrines and traditions that had increasingly become part of it since the time of Constantine. During that time the Roman church drifted away from the orthodox beliefs for which so many had been martyred. It began to lay aside holiness, piety, humility, charity, and compassion, and take upon itself pagan superstitions and doctrines that were materially, physically, and socially beneficial to its clergy and gave them total domination in all Church matters. Any who disagreed with them or their doctrines were branded as heretics who must be brought into agreement with the papal church by whatever force necessary, and if the heretics did not repent and swear allegiance to the pope and his *prelates, they must be executed. They justified the horrors they committed by wresting Old Testament Scriptures, and by appeal to Augustine, who had interpreted Luke 14:23 as endorsing the use of force against heretics: "Then the master said to the servant, 'Go out into the highways and hedges, and compel them to come in, that my house may be filled.'"

For several centuries the papal church raged throughout the world like a hungry beast, slaughtering thousands of true believers in Christ and torturing and mutilating thousands more. It was the "Dark Age" of the Church. The **Waldenses** in France were the first victims of the fury of the papal persecution.

About A.D. 1000, when the light of the true Gospel had almost been put out by darkness and superstition, a few who plainly saw the great harm that was being done to the Church became determined to show the light of the Gospel in its real purity, and to drive off the clouds that scheming priests had raised over it to blind the people and hide its true brightness. The effort began with a man named Berengarius, who boldly preached the holy Gospel as plainly seen in the Scriptures. Down through the years others took up the torch of truth and brought light to thousands, until by the year A.D. 1140 there were so many reformed believers that the pope became alarmed and wrote many princes that they should drive them out of their principalities. He also had many of his most educated officials write letters against them.

Persecution of the Waldenses

About 1173, Peter Waldo, or Valdes, a wealthy Lyon merchant, well-known for his piety and learning, gave his goods to the poor and became a traveling preacher and strenuous opposer to papal prosperity and oppression. Before long a large number of the reformed in France joined with him—they became know as the Waldenses. At first, Waldo sought papal recognition, thinking that he could influence the church in Rome, but, instead, he was excommunicated for heresy in 1184.

Waldo and his followers then developed a separate church with its own ministers. They preached religious discipline and moral purity, spoke out against unworthy clergy and the abuses of the church, and rejected the taking of human life under any circumstances. The papal church, however, would not allow such heresy to be taught, and separation from Rome could not be tolerated, so in A.D. 1208 the pope authorized a crusade against the Waldenses and other reformed groups, especially the Albigenses.

In A.D. 1211, eighty of Waldo's followers were captured in the city of Strasbourg, tried by inquisitors appointed by the pope, and burned at the stake. Shortly thereafter, most of the Waldenses withdrew into the Alpine valleys in northern Italy to live. Waldo died in 1218, still preaching the true Gospel of Christ.

Persecution of the Albigenses

The Albigenses were reformed-religion people who lived in southern France during the 12th and 13th centuries. They obtained their name from the French town of Albi, where they were centered. They lived by a rigorous ethical code, and counted many prominent people among their members, such as the Count of Toulouse, the Count of Foix, the Count of Beziers, and others of similar education and ranking. To suppress them, Rome first sent Cistercian and Dominican friars to their region to reaffirm papal teachings, but it was of no use for the Albigenses remained true to reformed doctrine.

Not even the threats of the second, third, and fourth Lateran councils (1139, 1179, 1215), each of which prescribed imprisonment and confiscation of property as punishment for heresy and threatened to excommunicate princes who failed to punish heretics, brought any of the Albigenses back into the Roman fold. At the second Lateran Council in 1179, they were condemned as heretics by order of Pope Alexander III. This was the same pope who had excommunicated Frederick I, Holy Roman Emperor and King of Germany and Italy, in 1165. The emperor subsequently failed to subdue papal authority in Italy, and so conceded supremacy to the pope in 1177.

In 1209, Pope Innocent III used the assassination of a friar in the dominion of Count Raymond of Toulouse as justification to begin a crusade of persecution against the count and the Albigenses. To accomplish this, he sent agents throughout Europe to raises forces to act together against the Albigenses, and promised paradise to all who would come and fight for forty days in what he called a Holy War.

During this most unholy war, which lasted from 1209 to 1229, Count Raymond defended the city of Toulouse and other places in his dominion with great bravery and some measure of success against the army of Simon de Montfort, Count of Monfort, and a bigoted Roman Catholic nobleman. When the pope's army was unable to defeat Count Raymond openly, the king and queen of France and three archbishops raised an even greater army, and on the basis of their military strength persuaded the count to come to a peace conference and promised him safe conduct. But when he arrived, he was treacherously seized and imprisoned, forced to appear bareheaded and barefooted before his enemies to humiliate him, and by various tortures was made to recant his oppositions to papal doctrine.

In the beginning of the persecution in 1209, Simon de Montfort massacred the citizens of Beziers in what is but a small example of the cruelties that were brought against the Albigenses by the pope's army for twenty years. During the massacre, a soldier asked how he could separate Christians from heretics. His leader is said to have replied, "Slay them all. God knows His own."

After the capture of Count Raymond, the pope decreed that the laity should not be allowed to read the sacred Scriptures, and for the rest of the thirteenth century, the Albigenses, along with the Waldenses and other reformed groups, were the main targets of the inquisition throughout Europe.

The Inquisition

The Inquisition was a medieval church court appointed to prosecute heretics, those so named who opposed the errors and superstitions of the papal church. The infamous name is used to mean the institution itself, which was episcopal (governed by a bishop or bishops) or papal, regional or local; the members of the court; and the operation of the court.

In the crusade against the Albigenses, Pope Innocent III appointed special inquisitors like the friar Dominic, who during the crusade founded the Dominicans in 1215. There was not yet, however, a specific office of Inquisition. In 1231, Pope Gregory IX formally instituted the papal Inquisition. Copying a law that Holy Roman Emperor Frederick II enacted for Lombardy, Italy, in 1224, and extended to his entire empire in 1232, Gregory ordered convicted heretics to be seized by the secular authorities and burned. He also commanded that heretics be sought out and tried before a church court.

Pope Gregory IX entrusted this heinous task to the Dominican and Franciscan order of friars, and gave them the exclusive rights to preside over the various courts of Inquisition, unlimited powers as judges in his place, and power to excommunicate, torture, or execute any whom were accused of the slightest heresy or opposition to the papal government. He further gave them authority to declare crusades against any who were judged to be heretics, and to enter into agreements with sovereign princes and combine their crusades with their forces. They were also given the authority to function independent of any local church officials, and to include them in their inquisition examination if they interfered with their work in any way. Naturally, this independent authority of the Inquisition was a frequent cause of friction with the local clergy and bishops.

It is said that this zeal to persecute the enemies of the Roman church was inspired by rumors circulating throughout Europe that Gregory intended to renounce Christianity and become a Muslim. To counteract the rumors, Gregory began a crusade of cruelty against the enemies of Rome, which included Protestants, Jews, and Muslims.

Each Inquisition was comprised of about twenty officials: a grand inquisitor; three principal inquisitors or judges; a finance supervisor; a civil officer; an official to receive and account for money fines; a similar one for confiscated property; several assessors to evaluate property; a jailer; counselors to interview and advise the accused; executioners to conduct tortures, stranglings, and burnings; physicians to oversee the torture; surgeons to repair body damage caused by torture; clerks to record the proceedings and confessions in Latin; doorkeepers; and familiars who wormed their way into the confidences of those suspected of heresy and then testified against them. Each trial also had witnesses or informers against the accused, and favored visitors, who were sworn to keep secret any procedures and proceedings that they witnessed.

At first the Inquisition was only concerned with charges of heresy, but it soon expanded it's authority to include charges of such things as sorcery, alchemy, blasphemy, sexual aberration, infanticide, reading the Bible in the common language, or reading the Talmud of the Jews or the Koran of the Muslims. [As heresy charges became less popular in the late 15th century, an increasing number of witches and sorcerers were burned, thereby justifying and prolonging the existence of the Inquisition.]

Regardless of the charges, the inquisitors performed their examinations with the utmost severity, having little or no mercy on anyone no matter what their age, sex, race, high birth, distinguished rank or social standing, or physical or mental condition. And they were especially cruel to those who opposed papal doctrine or authority, most particularly those who once were Roman Catholics and now were Protestants.

A defense before the Inquisition was of little use, for having been charged was sufficient evidence of guilt, and the greater the wealth of the person charged, the greater his danger. Often a person was executed not for heresy, but for his property. Many times great lands and homes and even provinces and principalities were acquired by the papal church or by the sovereignty cooperating with the Inquisition in their work.

Those charged by the Inquisition were never allowed to know the names of their accusers, and two informants were usually sufficient for a charge. Every method of persuasion was used by the inquisitors to make the accused persons confess to the charges, and thereby prove the evidence against them and convict themselves. To do this, every method of physical torture known or that can be imagined was used—such as stretching limbs on the rack; burning with live coals or heated metals; breaking fingers and toes; crushing feet and hands; pulling out teeth; squeezing flesh with pincers; inserting hooks into fleshy parts and pulling the hooks out through the flesh; cutting off small pieces of flesh; sticking pins into the flesh; inserting pins under fingernails or toenails; tightening ropes around flesh until they cut through to the bone; scourging with rods or various kinds of whips; beating with fists, rods, and clubs; twisting limbs and dislocating joints. The methods used by the sadistic inquisitors are too numerous and horrendous to list.

At the beginning of the questioning, which was recorded in papal Latin by a clerk, suspects and witnesses had to swear under oath that they would reveal everything. If they would not take the oath, then it was interpreted as a sign of agreement with the charges. If they denied the charges without proof that they were not guilty, or if they stubbornly refused to confess, or persisted in the heresy, then they were given the most severe punishment, their properties were confiscated, and almost without exception they were sentenced to death by burning. In its great hypocrisy, the papal church said it was not allowed to shed blood, and so the condemned heretic was turned over to the cooperating secular authorities for punishment and execution.

After the Inquisition completed its judgments, a solemn ceremony was held at the place of execution; it was known as the *sermo generalis* ("general address") or, in Spain, as the *auto-de-fé* ("act of faith). It was attended by local officials, the papal clergy, and all, whether enemies or friends of the heretics, who wished to view the penalties and executions. If the condemned heretics confessed their heresies and recanted, then they were given their penalties, which might range from being severely whipped to being sent to the *galleys. In any case, all their properties and goods were confiscated for use by the papal church or the local authorities.

If the accused obstinately clung to their heresies, they were solemnly cursed and turned over to the executioner to be burned immediately for all to see. By this public display, the Roman clergy hoped that fear of the Inquisition would be burned into the minds and hearts of those watching the flames consume heretics who opposed the papal church. But those who had true faith in Christ were actually strengthened in their faith as they saw the courage of the martyrs and the grace of God that sustained them through their tortures and in the flames.

Of all the offices of the Inquisition throughout the world, the Inquisition in Spain was the most active and sadistic, and is an example of the terrible danger of giving unlimited power over the bodies and lives of people to unholy men who claim to be holy.

Spain

Although there are almost no records of the number of people killed or tortured throughout the world by the Inquisition, a few records concerning the Spanish Inquisition have come down to us.

There were seventeen tribunals in Spain, and each burned an average of 10 heretics a year, and tortured and mutilated thousands of others who were never able to fully recover from their wounds. Over the years of the Spanish Inquisition it is estimated that about 32,000 people, who were guilty of nothing more than disagreeing with papal doctrine, or who had been accused of superstitious crimes, were tortured beyond belief and then burned alive.

In addition, the number of people who were burned in effigy or condemned to penance, which usually meant exile, confiscation of all property, physical punishment to the shedding of blood, and total ruination of everything in their life, amounted to 339,000. But there are no records of the multitudes who died in dungeons from torture; from being confined in filthy, diseased, rat and vermin infested holes; from broken bodies or broken hearts; or the millions of lives who were dependent upon them for their survival, or who were hurried to the grave by the death of the victims. That is a record that is known only in heaven for the Day of Judgment.

In 1483, at the insistence of the Roman Catholic rulers of Spain, Ferdinand II of Aragon and Isabella I of Castile, Pope Sixtus IV created an independent Spanish Inquisition to be presided over by a high council and grand inquisitor. In 1487 Pope Innocent VIII appointed Spanish Dominican monk, Tomas de Torquemada, as grand inquisitor. Under his authority, thousands of Christians, Jews, Muslims, suspected witches, and others were killed or tortured. Those in the greatest danger from the Inquisition were the Protestants and the *Alumbrados* (Spanish mystics).

Torquemada's name became synonymous with cruelty, bigotry, intolerance, and hate. He was the most feared man in Spain, and during his reign of terror from 1487 to 1498 he *personally* ordered more than 2000 people to be burned at the stake. This amounted to 181 people a year, when the average Spanish tribunal was burning only 10 a year.

With the support of the Roman Catholic rulers, the early Spanish inquisitors were so savage in their methods of torture and terror that even Pope Sixtus IV cringed at the reports, but was unable to lessen the horrors that he had unleashed on Spain. When Torquemada was made grand inquisitor, it was even worse, and he conducted the Inquisition as if he were the god of Spain. Anything that he could classify as a spiritual offense was given to the attention of his inquisitors. The cruel Inquisition in Spain had not known what pure cruelty was until Torquemada became its leader.

In 1492 the Inquisition was used to expel all Jews and Moors from Spain or to force their conversion to Roman Catholicism. At Torquemada's urging, Ferdinand and Isabella expelled from Spain more than 160,000 Jews who had not converted to the papal religion.

For political purposes, the inquisitors also held their cruel investigations among the colonists and converted Indians in the Spanish colonies in America.

Despite an eventual decline in its cruelties, the Inquisition remained in effect in one form or another until the early 19th century—1834 in Spain, and 1821 in Portugal—when it was simply renamed but not abolished. In 1908, the Inquisition was reorganized under the title *Congregation of the Holy Office*, and redefined during Vatican Council II in 1965 by Pope Paul VI as the *Congregation for the Doctrine of the Faith*. It has today, it is said, the more positive task of furthering right doctrine rather than "censuring" heresy.

6

Work and Persecution
of John Wycliffe
(About 1377-1384)

John Wycliffe was a native of Yorkshire, England. He studied at Oxford University where he majored in scholastic philosophy and theology, and later taught there, and became known as a brilliant scholastic theologian and the most respected debater of his time. In 1374 he entered royal service and was sent to Bruges, a city in northwest Belgium, to negotiate with the pope's representatives on the issue of tribute payments to Rome, which all Roman Catholic monarchs were required to pay.

For some time he was associated with John of Gaunt, Duke of Lancaster, in his opposition to the influence of the church or the clergy in political affairs. During that time, Wycliffe attacked the rights claimed by the church, and called for a reformation of its wealth, corruption, and abuses. He considered the king to be the legitimate authority for purifying the church in England. His views were in radical opposition to the practices and teachings of the Roman Catholic Church. For this reason prelates, friars, and priests rose against him and his followers, who were now called *Lollards.

Wycliffe was an eminent Oxford scholar and philosopher. Even those who were enemies of his doctrines recognized this and were impressed by his strong and logical arguments. Years after Wycliffe's death, one of them, a man named Walden, wrote to Pope Martin V and said, "I am wonderfully amazed by his most strong arguments, with the sources of authority that he gathers, and with the emotional intensity and force of his reasons."

Wycliffe's influence came at a time when organized religion was depraved and corrupted. People gave lip-service to the things of the Lord, but they denied His converting power by the way they lived. The traditions and ceremonies of men were important to many, and few had a saving relationship with Jesus Christ. It was a time of spiritual blindness. Because they had no way of obtaining direct knowledge of the Scriptures, most people were led into realms of darkness and doubt, and taught by the clerics that the ceremonies and practices of the church would save them.

The early Christians were persecuted and often martyred by the people of the world, but John Wycliffe had to face persecution from those who named the sacred name of Christ. The Catholic clergy were enraged by his teachings. They opposed him with every means possible. At first, only the friars and monks rose in opposition to

Wycliffe. Then they were joined by the priests, bishops, and archbishops. One archbishop, Simon Sudbury, removed Wycliffe from his post at Oxford. Ultimately, the pope took measures against Wycliffe as well.

For a period of time, Wycliffe had been able to avoid the power of the Catholic Church because of the intervention and favor he enjoyed from John of Gaunt, Duke of Lancaster, and Lord Henry Percy, first earl of Northumberland, who was killed on February 20, 1408, in a rebellion against Henry IV at Bramham Moor. Eventually, however, even the support of these two noblemen proved fruitless, and in 1377 the bishops succeeded in inciting the archbishop, Simon Sudbury, to take action against Wycliffe.

Sudbury had previously deprived Wycliffe of any means of teaching his "erroneous doctrines," and now he summoned him to appear before a council of bishops. The secular leaders who supported Wycliffe found four friars who were willing to stand with Wycliffe in front of the bishops. The council was conducted at St. Paul's Cathedral in London.

The dukes and barons sat together with the archbishops and bishops in Our Lady's Chapel. Wycliffe was required to stand before them. Lord Percy told Wycliffe to take a seat because he had "many things to answer to," and he would need to sit down. This angered the bishop of London who said Wycliffe should remain standing. An intense argument followed that lasted so long, the crowd became restless and began to voice their impatience, especially when the argument deteriorated into each side threatening the other—the secular side threatening with secular action against the clergy, and the religious side threatening with spiritual action against the noblemen. The argument ended when the Duke of Lancaster whispered an insult against the bishop of London to a person next to him loudly enough so all could hear it. This raised such an outcry from many of the crowd, who said they would not allow their bishop to be treated that way, that the meeting broke down entirely in scolding and brawling and the council was dissolved before nine o'clock that morning. It was not reconvened.

Not long after Richard II succeeded his grandfather, Edward III, as king of England in 1377, the Roman bishops moved against Wycliffe again on the basis of several articles they extracted from his sermons.

> 1. The Holy Eucharist, after the consecration by a priest, is not the actual body of Christ.
>
> 2. The Church of Rome is not the head of all churches; nor did Peter have any more power given to him by Christ than to the other apostles.
>
> 3. The pope has no more the keys of the Church than does any other in the priesthood.
>
> 4. The Gospel by itself is a rul sufficient to rule the life of every Christian person on the earth, without any other rule.
>
> 5. All rules that are made to govern religious people add no more perfection to the Gospel of Jesus Christ than does white color to a wall.
>
> 6. Neither the pope, or any other *prelate, should have prisons in which to punish transgressors.

Wycliffe was commanded by the bishops and prelates to keep silent and not teach his doctrines, but he simply became stronger and bolder in his determination to teach the truth of the Scriptures. He continued to enjoy the support of many noblemen, and attempted again to stir up his doctrine among the common people.

In the first year of King Richard II's reign, the pope reacted by issuing a *bull directly to Oxford University, rebuking them sharply for not "excising the Wycliffe doctrine," and for allowing it to be expressed so long as to take root. The proctors and masters of the University counseled among themselves as to whether they should honor the bull by receiving it, or refuse and reject it as something shameful. The bull stated:

It has been made know to us by many trustworthy persons that one John Wycliffe, rector of Lutterworth, in the diocese of London, professor of divinity, has gone to such a level of detestable foolishness, that he does not fear to teach, and publicly preach, or rather to vomit out of the filthy dungeon of his breast, certain erroneous and false propositions and conclusions, savoring even of heretical moral corruption, that tend to weaken and overthrow the status of the whole Church, and even the secular government.

These opinions he is circulating in the realm of England, which is so glorious in power and abundance of wealth, but still more so for the shining purity of its faith, accustomed to producing men illustrious for their clear and sound knowledge of the Scriptures, mature in seriousness of manners, conspicuous for devotion, and bold defenders of the catholic faith. Some of Christ's flock he is defiling with his doctrines, and misleading from the straight path of the sincere faith into the pit of perdition.

Wherefore, being unwilling to ignore and thereby encourage so deadly a pest, we strictly charge that by our authority you seize or cause to be seized the said John, and send him under trusty keeping to our venerable brethren, the archbishop of Canterbury and the bishop of London, or either of them.

Two other letters from the pope indicated his strong feeling against John Wycliffe. One of these letters indicated that the pope wanted Wycliffe to appear before him if the bishops were not able to resolve the case within three months. The second was to the English bishops, exhorting them to admonish the secular authorities, including the king, not to give any credit to the doctrine of Wycliffe. These letters served to solidify the case against Wycliffe among the bishops, and they were determined to bring Wycliffe before them to receive the justice they perceived was due him for his heresies.

But when the day for Wycliffe's examination came, a person from the prince's (King Richard II) court, named Lewis Clifford, entered in where the bishops were and commanded them not to proceed any further with a definite sentence against John Wycliffe. His words so stunned the bishops that many of them were speechless. And so, by the wonderful works of God's providence, John Wycliffe escaped the bishops' wrath a second time.

Wycliffe was thrilled to have more time to teach and to preach. The more he did so, however, the more wrathful the bishops and other ecclesiastical authorities became. Then in March 1378, Pope Gregory XI, the leader who had stirred up much trouble for Wycliffe, died unexpectedly. This began the "Great Papal Schism" in the western church at Rome. It was a period of papal strife and confusion that continued until the Council of Constance elected Martin V as pope in 1417.

Around the same time, for about three years, a violent division took place in England between the common people and the nobility. During the trouble, Simon of Sudbury, the archbishop of Canterbury, was taken by some of the more violent ones and beheaded. He was succeeded as prelate by William Courtney, a Catholic leader who was no less diligent in rooting out heretics.

Nevertheless, Wycliffe's sect of Lollards continued to grow to a greater force and influence in England until William Berton, the Chancellor of Oxford University, called together eight monastical doctors [monks] and four others, and issued an edict declaring severe penalties would be imposed upon anyone who associated with Wycliffe and his followers. Berton threatened Wycliffe himself with excommunication from the church and imprisonment. The edict gave Wycliffe and his followers three days to repent of their "misdeeds and false teachings."

In response, Wycliffe thought to bypass the pope and the clergy and make an appeal directly to the king. The Duke of Lancaster, however, forbade him to do so and said he should submit himself to the censure and judgment of the bishop of the dioceses. Thus Wycliffe, surrounded by problems and adversaries, had to once again publicly state his doctrines before the Roman clergy.

On St. Dunstan's Day in 1382, around 2:00 in the afternoon, the archbishop of Canterbury and his assistants, certain doctors of divinity, lawyers, professors, and other clergy assembled at Blackfriars in London to consult with one another about Wycliffe's books and teachings. At about that time, a devastating earthquake occurred throughout England. Many of those present at Wycliffe's examination thought it was an omen, and some even suggested that they should abandon their purpose. The archbishop, however, said they were misinterpreting the meaning of the earthquake, and succeeded in encouraging them to continue their mission. He then read some of Wycliffe's writings to the group, boldly declaring that his doctrine was clearly heretical inasmuch as it did not coincide with the traditions and teachings of the church. Not only were the teachings erroneous, the archbishop declared, but they were irreligious as well.

Having been somewhat disarmed by the earthquake, the leaders were not totally convinced by the archbishop. One member reported that a similar natural phenomenon had happened at a particular church when a previous *disputation against Wycliffe had taken place. He said that the door of that church had been broken open with a bolt of lightning. The people who were there barely escaped the fires from heaven. The discussion of Wycliffe and his teachings went on for several hours.

As a result of the meeting at Blackfriars, the archbishop of Canterbury sent a mandate to the bishop of London against John Wycliffe and his supporters:

It is come to our hearing, that although, by church laws, no man, being forbidden or not sent, ought to take upon himself the office of preaching, publicly or privately, without the authority of the apostolic *see or of the bishop of the place; yet notwithstanding this, certain persons, who are sons of perdition hiding under the veil of great holiness, are brought into such a state of mind, that they take upon themselves authority to preach, and are not afraid to affirm, and teach, and generally, commonly, and publicly to preach, as well in the churches as in the streets, and also in many other common places of our said province, certain propositions and conclusions, heretical, erroneous, and false, condemned by the Church of God, and repugnant to the determinations of holy church; who also infect therewith very many good Christians; causing them lamentably to err from the catholic faith, without which there is no salvation.

We therefore admonish and warn that no man henceforth, of whatever estate or condition, do hold, teach, preach, or defend the aforesaid heresies and errors, or any of them; nor that he hear or pay attention to any one preaching the said heresies or errors, or any of them; nor that he favor or support him, either publicly or privately; but that immediately he shun and avoid him, as he would avoid a serpent putting forth infectious poison; under pain of the greater curse.

And furthermore, we command our fellow brethren, that of such presumptions they carefully and diligently inquire, and do proceed effectually against the same.

At that same time, the new Chancellor of Oxford University was Master Robert Rygge, who apparently favored John Wycliffe and the preaching of the Gospel of Jesus Christ. Often he blocked certain moves against Wycliffe and thus helped move forward the Gospel, which was then in great danger from church authorities. Also, when sermons were needed to be given to the people, he sent ministers who he knew greatly favored John Wycliffe. Two of them were John Huntman and Walter Dish, who openly approved Wycliffe as much as they dared.

Later that same year (1382), Philip Reppyngdon and Nicholas Hereford were appointed to preach to the people at the feast of the Ascension and at the Feast of Corpus Christi. They delivered pro-Wycliffe addresses in the cloister of St. Frideswide [now called Christ's Church] before the people.

Hereford said that Wycliffe was a faithful, good, and innocent man. The friars who were present were stunned by his presentation, and stood up in strong and vocal protest. The Carmelite Order of the church, led by a Peter Stokes, was particularly noisy against him.

As the feast of Corpus Christi drew near, some of the friars wondered if Reppyngdon would give a presentation similar to the one delivered by Hereford. They began to appeal to the archbishop of Canterbury to block Reppyngdon's sermon. Peter Stokes, the Carmelite, was appointed to defame the minister and the teachings of Wycliffe publicly, and the archbishop of Canterbury wrote to the Chancellor of Oxford, urging him to reconsider the appointment of Reppyngdon as the preacher at the feast of Corpus Christi.

The chancellor grew bold in the face of this opposition, and he reprimanded the archbishop and Peter Stokes for undermining the authority of the university and troubling its peaceful state. He declared that the archbishop had no authority over the university and that the university would make its own decisions regarding these matters. He publicly stated that he would not assist the Carmelites in any way.

Reppyngdon, therefore, went ahead with his sermon on the feast day. He said, "In all moral matters I will defend Master Wycliffe as a true catholic doctor." He also praised the support that the Duke of Lancaster gave to the Gospel movement. He concluded his sermon by praising the work and ministry of John Wycliffe.

When the sermon was over, Reppyngdon went into St Frideswide's Church accompanied by many of his friends, who, as their enemies thought, had weapons concealed under their garments in case there was an attack against Reppyngdon. Friar Stokes, the Carmelite, hid himself in the church's sanctuary, thinking that they were going to attack him, and did not dare to leave until Reppyngdon and his party did. Throughout the university there was great rejoicing over their chancellor's boldness, and they were encouraged by Reppyngdon's clear sermon.

After a short time of banishment, Wycliffe was able to return to the parish of Lutterworth where he became parson [parish priest]. He died in his sleep on December 31, 1384, at the age of fifty-six. It was said of him: "the same thing pleased him in his old age that pleased him when he was young."

Wycliffe's worst enemies were members of the clergy. But he also enjoyed the support of many of the common people and the nobility, among them John Clenbon, Lewis Clifford, Richard Stury, Thomas Latimer, William Nevil, and John Montague. After Wycliffe's death, these men removed the statues and icons from his church in honor of his doctrines and teachings.

The opposition to Wycliffe and his teachings continued for many years after his death. On May 4, 1415, the Council of Constance decreed:

> This holy council declares, determines, and gives sentence, that John Wycliffe was a notorious heretic, and that he died obstinate in his heresy; cursing alike him and condemning his memory. This council also decrees and ordains that his body and bones, if they might be discerned from the bodies of other faithful people, should be taken out of the ground, and thrown away, far from the burial of any church, according as the canons and laws direct.

Thirty-one years after Wycliffe's death, the Council of Constance removed his remains from their burial place, burned them, and threw the ashes into the river. His persecutors thought they would kill his continuing influence by such an act, but it was not to be so. In the same way that the Pharisees thought they had killed Christ, and put His body in a dark grave, thinking He was gone forever, the council who opposed John Wycliffe thought their symbolic act of disinterring the "heretic" and throwing away his ashes would kill his memory among his followers. But as the Pharsisees learned to their dismay, nothing could stop Jesus Christ, and nothing can stop the truth.

Though they burned Wycliffe's body and threw its ashes into the river, the Word of God and the truth of Wycliffe's doctrines could not be destroyed, and others would soon continue the work he started.

7

Persecution and Martyrdom of John Huss (1415)

John Huss was born at Hussenitz, Bohemia, in 1372. He studied theology at the University of Prague, and was ordained a priest and appointed preacher at the Bethlehem chapel in Prague in 1402. In 1409, Huss was made *rector of the University.

Huss was greatly influenced by the writings of Wycliffe, especially his rejection of any biblical basis for the Roman Catholic pope having authority over the Church; his insistence that the Scriptures were the foremost authority in all Church matters; his insistence on extensive reforms in the wealth, corruption, and abuses of the Roman church; his denial of the church's doctrine of transubstantiation, which is the doctrine that says that the communion bread and wine become the actual body and blood of the Lord Jesus Christ when the priest prays over them, although their appearances remain the same; and his argument that Christians should have a Bible in their own language that they could read for themselves. At that time, all Bibles were in Latin and for use only by the clergy; some Bibles used for saying mass were chained to the pulpit so they could not be taken out of the building by a layperson.

Huss not only believed the doctrines of Wycliffe but began to teach them from his church pulpit and at the University. By so doing, there was no way he could long escape the attention of the pope and his supporters, against whom Huss protested loudly and strongly.

The Roman Catholic archbishop of Prague, finding the reformists, as they were now called, daily increasing, issued a decree to suppress the further spreading of Wycliffe's writings. But this had an effect different than what he expected, for it stimulated Wycliffe's and Huss's supporters to greater effort until almost everyone in the University was united to spread the teachings as far as they could.

Because he so strongly agreed with the doctrines of Wycliffe, Huss opposed the archbishop's decree personally and from the pulpit. The archbishop then obtained an official document from the pope, giving him the authority to stop anyone from publishing Wycliffe's doctrines in his province. Upon receiving the *papal bull, the archbishop immediately condemned Wycliffe's writings, and commanded any who had such writings to turn them over to him. When four doctors of divinity did not, he issued a decree that they were forbidden to preach to any congregation. Huss and four members of the university protested the decree and appealed the sentence to the archbishop.

When the pope heard of this, he commissioned a Cardinal Colonna to summon John Huss to Rome and answer the accusations that he was preaching errors and heresies. Upon Huss's request, King Winceslaus and his wife, certain noble people, and the university leaders, requested that the pope dispense with Huss's personal appearance in Rome, and that the pope not permit any in Bohemia to be accused of heresy, and permit all priests in Bohemia to freely preach the Gospel in their churches

Three representatives appeared for Dr. Huss before Cardinal Colonna to explain why he could not appear, and said they could answer any questions on his behalf. But the cardinal declared that Huss was stubbornly disobedient, and immediately deprived him of any further rights of church membership by excommunicating him. Huss's representatives appealed to the pope, who commissioned four cardinals to review the process. The cardinals not only confirmed the sentence but enlarged the excommunication to include all of Huss's friends and followers, which included his four representatives.

Huss appealed the sentence but it was no use, and since he could no longer preach in the Bethlehem Chapel in Prague, he retired to his home town of Hussenitz, where he continued to teach his new doctrine from the pulpit and in writing. During this time he wrote numerous letters and a long discourse in which he insisted that no one had the authority to forbid anyone from reading books by reformers like Wycliffe. He also wrote books against the corrupt vices of the Roman Catholic pope, cardinals, and clergy. Huss's arguments were biblically sound and forceful and convinced many that he was right.

In November 1414, a council was called in Constance, Germany, for the purpose of bringing to an end the schism in the Roman Catholic church that had resulted in three competing popes. It was called together by the *antipope John XXIII at the insistence of the Holy Roman Emperor Sigismund. During the proceedings, the council declared itself to be superior to the papacy, and removed two of the popes, John XXIII and Benedict XIII, and requested that the third, Gregory XII, relinquish his office. They then elected a new pope, Martin V. Before they adjourned in 1418, the council also degreed that general councils, which had powers superior to popes, would meet regularly to determine church policies and doctrines. But when the Council of Basel met in 1431-37, the pope declared the council heretical and reaffirmed the papacy's superiority over any such council. Ultimately, little came of the council's effort to reform the Roman Catholic church, and it's vices and corruption continued.

John Huss had been invited to attend the Council of Constance, and was guaranteed safe conduct by Emperor Sigismund. Nevertheless, charges of heresy were drawn up against him and presented to the pope and the members of the council. Soon after Huss arrived in Constance, about January 1415, he was arrested and confined to a room in the palace. When some of Huss' friends pointed out to the council that this was a violation of the law and of the emperor's vow of safe conduct, the pope replied that he himself had never granted any safe conduct, and he was not bound by anything the emperor had said. When an appeal was made to Emperor Sigismund based on his vow of safe conduct, he refused to intervene and protect Huss. This later caused the emperor much grief after he became the Bohemian king in 1419 and was drawn into the devastating Hussite Wars.

Since there were no papal inquisitors to try Huss, the council itself assumed that role. In their foolishness, they first condemned John Wycliffe, who had died in 1384, and ordered his body to be dug up and burned to ashes, and the ashes thrown into the Rhine River.

When Huss was brought before them, they read forty articles against him, most of them taken from his writings, and most of them perverted to prove their accusations. To the accusations, Huss replied: "I appealed to the pope, who died before my appeal was determined, so I then appealed to his successor, John XXIII. But since I was not allowed to defend my cause for over two years, I appealed to the high judge Jesus Christ."

When John Huss finished speaking, his inquisitors demanded to know whether he had received *absolution from the pope or not. He answered, "No."

The council then asked if it was lawful to appeal to Christ or not. To which he answered, "Truethfully I say before you all that there is no more just or effective appeal than an appeal that is made to Christ. For the law says to appeal is to ask a higher judge to right the wrong done to you by a lesser judge. I ask you, who is a higher judge than Christ? Who can judge them at term or justly, or be more impartial and fair? There is no deciet in Christ, and He cannot be decieved, so who can help the miserable and oppressed better than He can? While Huss was speaking he was laughed at and mocked by all the council members, who then became enraged at his words and condemed him to be burned.

Seven came forward and comanded Huss to put on the garments of a priest, which he did. They then began to degrade and mock him as they removed the priest's garments from him one at a time. At one point they debated how they should remove the *shaven crown of his head. Huss commented, "I am amazed that scince you are all odf one cruel mind, you cannot agree on the manner of performing this cruelty."

The bishop's decided that they should cut off the crown of his head with a pair of shears, which they proceeded to do. Then on his bloodied head they put a paper bishop's hat that had demons painted on it and the words, "A ringleader of heretics." When Huss saw it, he said, "For my sake, my Lord Jesus Christ worn a crown of thorns, so for His sake why should I not wear this light crown, even though it is a shameful thing."

When the bishop put the paper *miter on Huss's head, he said, "Now we commit your soul to hell."

Huss lifted his eyes toward heaven and said, "But I commend into Your hands, O Lord Jesus Christ, my spirit that you have redeemed."

Huss was then led past a fire where they were burning his books and was bound to a stake with a chain. As the executioner wrapped the chain around him, Huss smiled and said, "My Lord Jesus Christ was bound with a harder chain than this one for my sake, so why should I be ashamed of this rusty chain?"

The bundles of sticks were piled up to his neck, and then the duke of Bavaria tried to get him to recant his teachings. Huss replied, "No, I never preached any doctrine that was evil, and what I taught with my lips I will now seal with my blood." When the faggots were lit and the flames engulfed him, Huss sang a hymn so loud and cheerful that he could be heard above the crackling of the burning sticks and the noise of the crowd watching him burn. Soon, however, his voice stopped as the flames reached his throat and face, and he slumped forward against his chains.

With continued foolishness the bishops carefully gathered Huss's ashes and cast them into the Rhine River so that no remnant of Huss would remain on the earth. They could not, however, by torment, fire, or water, erase his memory or his teachings out of the minds of his supporters. Through them, his memory and teachings would continue to be honored and spread far and wide. In death, Huss was more of a threat to the papacy then in life.

Out of his death were born the Hussites, who were Czech religious reformers that followed his teachings. They formed the nucleus of a national movement in Bohemia and Moravia after his death on July 6, 1415. Huss's condemnation for heresy at the Council of Constance and his execution, despite the guarantee of safe conduct given by Holy Roman Emperor Sigismund, were regarded by the Czech people as a national affront. It was an affront that many never forgot and that led to the   Hussite Wars.

8

Persecution and Martyrdom of Jerome of Prague (1416)

Jerome of Prague was born in 1370. He was a Bohemian church reformer and wandering scholar. He attended several universities and seminaries in various cities: Prague, Paris, Heidelberg, Cologne, and Oxford, during which he learned to speak excellent English. At Oxford, he became acquainted with the writings of John Wycliffe, and while there translated many of them from English into the Czech language. His books were circulated throughout Bohemia, and it was from these that John Huss learned of the doctrines of Wycliffe.

When Jerome returned to Bohemia, he found that his books were widely read in the city and the university, and that John Huss had become the chief promoter of them and Wycliffe's teachings. So he immediately associated himself with Huss and they worked together in the endeavor from that time on.

After Huss was betrayed and arrested at the Council of Constance, Jerome went to Constance, arriving there on April 4, 1415, about three months before Huss was burned. He entered the city secretly for fear of being arrested, and consulted with some of the leaders of those who also believed in Wycliffe's doctrines. They easily convinced him that he could be of no service to Huss because of the Council's unchangeable determination to condemn and burn Huss as a heretic. Jerome then went to Iberling, an imperial town that was under the protection of the emperor, and sent a letter to Emperor Sigismund stating that he was willing to appear before the Council on Huss's behalf if the emperor would give him safe-conduct—this was refused. He then wrote to the Council of Constance concerning the same matter, and was refused both an appearance on Huss's behalf and safe-conduct.

Jerome then started back to Bohemia, taking with him several certificates signed by nobles in Constance and Iberling, which stated that he had done all he could to obtain a hearing on Huss's behalf. He never made it back to Bohemia, however. In the city of Hirshaw, Germany, he was illegally seized by an officer on the orders of the duke of Sultsbach, who was certain he would receive thanks from the Council of Constance for such an acceptable service to them. The Council was notified that Jerome was in custody, and they requested he be brought to them immediately. A German prince on horseback assigned to guard Jerome met them on the way with numerous attendants. He had Jerome's feet shackled and a long chain attached around his neck. He then triumphantly and with great fanfare led Jerome back to Constance, where Jerome was put into a foul dungeon to await the pleasure of his inquisitors.

Jerome's treatment was much like that given to Huss, except that he was confined considerably longer and was often moved to a different prison. It was nearly a year after his capture before he was brought before the council. There he asked to plead his own cause and was refused, whereupon he shouted forth these words:

What cruelty is this? For three-hundred-and-forty days I've been confined in various prisons. There is not a misery or a want that I have not experienced. You have allowed all my enemies to accuse me as much as they wish, and you have denied me the smallest opportunity to defend myself. Not one hour will you give me to prepare for my trial.

You have swallowed the most malicious statements against me. You have represented me as a heretic without knowing my doctrine; as an enemy of the faith without knowing what faith I professed; as a persecutor of the priest before you have had an opportunity to know my view on that matter.

You are a general council, and in you is contained all that this world can impart of wisdom, solemnity, and holiness; but you are still men, and men are often fooled by words and appearances. The higher your character is for wisdom, the more you should be careful not to fall into foolishness.

The cause I wish to plead is my own cause, the cause of men, the cause of Christians. It is a cause that will affect the rights of future generations, no matter in what way the testing process is applied to me.

Jerome's outburst did not affect the council, and when he finished they read the charges against him, which can be summed up under five headings:

1. That he ridiculed the papal dignity.

2. That he opposed the pope.

3. That he was an enemy of the cardinals.

4. That he was a persecutor of the bishops.

6. That he was a hater of the Christian religion.

Jerome denied all the charges and was returned to prison. There he was hung repeatedly by his heels over a period of eleven days. Brought back to the council and threatened with worse torture, Jerome agreed that the writings of John Wycliffe were false and that John Huss had been fairly condemned and burned as a heretic. He was returned to prison but was no longer tortured and received better treatment. Before long, however, it became obvious that Jerome had not truly agreed with the council. He retracted his denunciation of Wycliffe and Huss, and 107 new articles of heresy were drawn up against him.

Although there were many bigoted people who did not want Jerome given an opportunity to speak because they were afraid his persuasive way of speaking might change the minds of even the most prejudiced, the council allowed him to defend himself. In his defense, Jerome made an excellent distinction between evidence that is based on facts, and evidence that is supported only by malice and lies. He detailed for the council the course and conduct of his life, and said that even the greatest and most holy men had been known to differ in their opinions, and openly discuss them so they could find the truth, not conceal it. He spoke contemptuously of those who would try to make him retract his beliefs and teachings, defended the doctrines of Wycliffe, spoke highly of Huss, and said that he was willing to follow that holy martyr to his death. As before, however, the council paid no attention to his words.

He, like Huss, was condemned and sentenced to be burned at the stake as a heretic. Since he was not a priest, however, he did not have to experience the degradation that Huss did. The council gave him two days in which to recant, and during which the cardinal of Florence did his utmost to win him over. But his words had no more effect on Jerome than Jerome's words had on the council.

On the way to the stake, Jerome sang several hymns, and when he was taken to the exact spot where Huss was burned, he knelt down and prayed fervently. Then he embraced the stake before being chained, and when the executioner went behind him to light the faggots, he said to him, "Come here in front of me and light the fire where I can see it. If I were afraid of it, I would not have come to this place."

The fire was lit, and because the faggots were extremely dry they flared into flames that quickly enveloped him. Jerome sang a hymn for a short time, but was soon silenced by the searing fire. His last words that could be heard by the witnesses were, "This soul in flames I offer Christ to Thee." The day of his martyrdom was May 30, 1416.

Though the papal inquisitors hoped otherwise, the flames of martyrdom spread the fire of the true Gospel throughout the civilized world. Jerome had translated Wycliffe's writings from English into Czech, and thereby planted seeds of truth that would never stop growing. Soon God would raise up another man who would translate the New Testament from the papist Latin, which kept knowledge of the Scriptures hidden from the common people, into English. In Revelation 2:12, the risen Christ wrote to the church at Pergamos, "Repent; or else I will come unto thee quickly, and will fight against them with the sword of my mouth." Now the Word of God, which is the sword of the Spirit (Ephesians 6:17), was about to come against an unrepentant church.

9

Persecutions in England

(1401-1541)

During King Edward III's reign (1327-1377), the Church of England was corrupted with errors and superstition. The light of the true Gospel of Christ had been virtually extinguished by the darkness of man's doctrines, burdensome ceremonies, and gross idolatry. At the same time, Wycliffe's followers, reformers called Lollards, had become so many that the clergy was annoyed, and though the clergy molested them in underhanded ways, they had no authority to put them to death.

After the usurpation of the English throne by Henry IV in 1399, the Lollards were subject to increasing persecution. Soon after, the papist clergy prevailed upon the king to introduce a bill into parliament to condemn the Lollards who remained obstinate in their reform beliefs, and turn them over to the secular authorities for burning as heretics. Despite strong Lollard resistance in the House of Commons, the statute *De haeretico comburendo* (On the Burning of the Heretic) was passed by Parliament in 1401, and was immediately put into effect. It was the first time in Britain that a law was passed to burn people for their religious beliefs.

The first martyr to die under the new law was a priest named **William Santree** [or Santee]—he was burned in *Smithfield.

Soon after, the archbishop of Canterbury, Thomas Arundel, and his bishops began to move against **Sir John Oldcastle** (Lord Cobham), a popular Wycliffe follower and personal friend of Henry IV, whom they accused of commissioning others to preach who were not licensed by the bishops, and of encouraging false teachings against the sacraments of the church, images, pilgrimages, and the pope. Before they could charge him, however, they knew they had to enlist the aid of the king. The king listened to them politely, and then told them to deal with Sir John with respect, and restore him to the church through gentleness. He also offered to reason with Sir John on their behalf. Soon after, he sent for Sir John and admonished him to return to his mother the Holy Church, and, like an obedient child, acknowledge that he deserved punishment because he had been wrong.

Sir John replied:

> Most worthy king, you know I am always prompt and willing to obey, because I know that you are a

Christian king and the appointed minister of God, and that you bear the sword with which to punish the evildoers and protect the virtuous. Next to my eternal God, I owe you my obedience, and I am ready, as I have always been, to submit all that I have of money or properties to fulfill whatever you command me in the Lord. But, concerning the pope and his clergy, I owe them neither attendance nor service, since I know by the Scriptures that he is the antichrist, the son of perdition, the open adversary of God, and the abomination of Daniel standing in the holy place.

When the king heard this, he made no answer and left the room.

The archbishop again approached the king about Sir John, and was given authority to charge him, examine him, and punish him in accordance with their devilish decrees: *The Laws of Holy Church.* But when Sir John did not appear before them as he was told to, the archbishop condemned him for contemptuous resistance to authority. Then when he was told that Sir John mocked him; disdained everything he did; maintained his same opinions; viewed with contempt the church's powers, a bishop's dignity, and the order of the priesthood; he raged openly and excommunicated him.

In response, Sir John Oldcastle wrote out his personal confession of faith and took it to his friend, Henry IV, whom he expected would gladly receive it. Instead, the king refused it and commanded it to be delivered to the archbishop and his council of bishops who would judge him. When Sir John appeared before the council, and in the king's presence, he asked that a hundred knights be assembled to hear his case and judge him, for he knew they would clear him of all heresies. To clear himself, he even offered to the fight to the death any man who disagreed with his faith, according to the Law of Arms. Finally, he gently stated that he would not refuse any manner of correction that was according to the Word of God, but would obey it meekly. When he finished, the king took him into his private chambers, where Sir John first told him that he had appealed to the pope, and then showed him what he had written. At this, the king angrily told him to wait for the decision of the pope, and if it was that he should submit to the archbishop, then Sir John should do it, and he should not appeal again. All of this Sir John refused, and the king commanded him to be arrested and imprisoned in the Tower of London.

Because of Sir John Oldcastle's great popularity and esteem, the archbishop proceeded slowly with his trial over a period of several weeks from September until December, but the judgment had already been predetermined, and Sir John's condemnation for heresy and sentence of death by hanging and burning surprised no one.

In his defense, Sir John had written this:

As for images, I understand that they are not a matter of faith, but were intended, since faith in Christ was tolerated by the Church, to represent and bring to mind the passion of our Lord Jesus Christ and the martyrdom and good living of other saints. But whoever gives to dead images the worship that belongs to God, or puts hope and trust in getting help from them as he should to God alone, or has greater affection toward them than toward God, he is committing the great sin of idol worship.

Also, I know this fully, that every person in this earth is a pilgrim toward bliss or toward pain, and he who does not know the holy commandments of God and keep them in his life here, even though he may go on pilgrimages to all the world and die doing so, he shall be damned; but he who knows the holy commandments

of God and keeps them, he shall be saved, even though
he never in his life went on a pilgrimage, as people do
now, to Canterbury, or to Rome, or to any other place.

On the day appointed for his execution, Sir John
Oldcastle was brought out of the Tower of London with
his hands tied behind him. He smiled cheerfully at those
around him. Then he was laid upon a frame as if he were a
heinous traitor to the crown, and dragged to St. Gile's field.
When they reached his place of execution and he was taken
off the frame, Sir John knelt down and asked God to forgive
his enemies. Then he stood up and exhorted the people who
had come there to follow the laws of God written in the
Scriptures, and to beware of teachers whose conversation
and living are contrary to Christ. Then chains were tied
around his stomach, and he was lifted into the air, and a
fire was started under him. As the fire consumed him, he
praised God until he could praise Him no more. Throughout
the crowd who watched him there was great weeping and
grief, for a godly and good man had died. The year was
1417.

In August, 1473, **Thomas Granter** was arrested in
London and accused of openly declaring that he believed
the teachings of Wycliffe, for which he was condemned as
a stubborn heretic. On the day of his execution, Thomas
was taken to the sheriff's house where he was given a meal.
While eating, he said to the people there, "I am now eating
a good meal, for I have a strange conflict to engage in before
I eat again." When he finished eating, he gave thanks to
God for the abundance of His gracious providence, and then
asked that he be taken instantly to the place of execution
so that he could bear testimony to the truth of those
principles that he had declared. Accordingly he was taken
to Tower-hill and chained to a stake. There he was burned
alive, still declaring the truth until his last breath.

In 1499 in Norwich, which is northeast of London, a pious man named **Badram** was accused by some priests that he held to the doctrines of Wycliffe and was brought before the bishop of Norwich. Badram confessed that he believed everything that they said he believed. He was condemned as a stubborn heretic, a warrant was given for his execution, and he was burned at the stake, where he suffered with great faithfulness.

In 1506, a pious man named **William Tilfrey** was burned alive at Amersham, in an enclosed area called Stoneyprat. His executioners forced his married daughter, Joan Clarke, to light the faggots around her father and watch him burn. This same year, the bishop of Lincoln in eastern England condemned a priest named **Father Roberts** for being a Lollard and burned him alive at Buckingham.

In 1507, **Thomas Norris**, a simple man who was poor and harmless, was talking to his parish priest about some questions that he had concerning religion. During the conversation, the priest decided from the questions that Thomas asked that he was a Lollard and reported him to the bishop. Thomas was arrested, condemned, and burned alive.

In 1508, at Salisbury in southern England, **Lawrence Guale** was imprisoned for two years and then burned alive for denying that the bread and wine in the mass became the real body and blood of Jesus when the priest prayed over it. It seems Lawrence had a shop in Salisbury and one day entertained some Lollards in his home. Someone informed the bishop and Lawrence was arrested and "examined;" he held to his beliefs and was condemned as a heretic.

That same year in Chippen Sudburne, **a pious woman** was burned at the stake by a chancellor named Dr. Whittenham, who had tried her as a heretic and condemned her. As her executioners and others left the place where she was burned, a bull broke loose from a butcher and gored Dr. Whittenham through the body. The bull carried Dr. Whittenham's intestines around on his horns for some time, but did not harm any others in the crowd.

On October 18, 1511, **William Succling and John Bannister**, were burned alive at Smithfield. They had formerly recanted their faith in Christ, but returned again to profession of true faith.

During the reign of Henry VII (1485-1509), **John Brown** recanted his testimony of Christ for fear of torture, and as penance had to carry a faggot around St. Paul's cathedral in London. In 1517, he returned to his confession of faith in Christ and was condemned by the archbishop of Canterbury, Dr. Wonhaman, and burned alive. Before chaining him to the stake, Dr. Wonhaman and Yester, bishop of Rochester, tried to make him recant again by having his feet burned in a fire until the flesh fell off and exposed the bones. But this time John Brown held to the truth through the pain and died gloriously for Christ and the truth of God's Word.

On October 25, 1518, **John Stilincen** was arrested, brought before the bishop of London, Richard Fitz-James, and condemned to be burned as a heretic. John had once before recanted his faith in Christ under fear of torture, but when he was chained to the stake at Smithfield before a large crowd, he declared that he was a follower of the teachings of Wycliffe, and though he had been weak enough before to recant his beliefs, he was now ready to die for the truth of God's Word.

In 1519, **Robert Celin and Thomas Matthew** were burned in London. Robert had spoken against image worship and pilgrimages.

In 1532, **Thomas Harding and his wife** were accused of heresy because they denied that the bread and wine turned into the actual body and blood of Christ when the priest prayed over them in the mass. For this, the bishop of Lincoln, in eastern England, condemned them to be burned alive at the stake. They were taken to Chesham in the Pell near Botely and chained to a stake. Faggots were piled around them and set on fire. As the fire rose up, one of the enraged papist spectators struck Thomas in the head with a thick piece of firewood so savagely that his head split open and his brains fell out into the fire. The priests who attended the burning told the people that whoever brought faggots to burn heretics would be given indulgences that would allow them to sin for forty days.

Toward the end of the year, Worham, archbishop of Canterbury, arrested a man named **Hitten**, who was priest at Maidstone in southeast England. Hitten was tortured in prison for several months and often examined by Worham and the bishop of Rochester, Fisher, in an effort to make him recant his reformed beliefs. When they could not, and finally decided to end his suffering, they condemned him as a heretic and burned him alive in front of his parish church as a warning to his parishioners.

Neither simple men, husbands and wives, parish priest, or university professors were safe from the fury of the Roman clergy against those who denied their superstitions and papist doctrines. **Thomas Bilney**, a professor of law at Cambridge University, was arrested for heresy and brought before a council of bishops convened by the bishop of London. They threatened him repeatedly with torture and burning, and created such fear in him that he recanted his beliefs. Soon after, however, he repented with great sorrow. For so doing, he was brought back before the council and condemned to death by burning for being an "obstinate heretic." Before Bilney was burned, he stated that he fully believed in the opinions of Martin Luther.

When chained to the stake, he smiled at all who were there and said, "I have had many storms in this world, but soon my vessel will be on shore in heaven." As the flames roared around him, he stood unmoved and cried out, "Jesus, I believe!" Then he went to meet Him in Whom he believed.

Though the Roman clergy were savage in their cruelty to heretics, they were especially cruel to those who were part of the clergy but were against their superstitions and man-made doctrines. At Barnes, in Surrey in southeast England, a monk named **Richard Byfield** was converted to the true faith by reading Tyndale's English translation of the New Testament. As a result, he also came to believe fully in the opinions of Martin Luther. When this was discovered, he was arrested as a heretic and cast into prison. Because he was a converted Roman *cleric, he was tormented unmercifully by his accusers. To make him recant, he was often confined in the worst dungeon in the prison, where he would almost suffocate from the putrid odors of human waste and stagnant water that nearly covered the dirt floor. Rats and cockroaches were his only companions. At times his jailers would enter his cell and tie his arms behind his back until his shoulders almost dislocated and leave him in that position for days without food or toilet. Other times they would take him to a whipping post and scourge him until there was little flesh left on his back. But still he refused to recant his newfound faith in Christ. So he was taken to Lollard's Tower in Lambeth Palace, where the archbishop had him chained to the wall by his neck and beaten severely once a day by his servants. Finally, as an act of mercy, he was condemned, degraded as Huss had been, and burned at Smithfield, which is just north of St. Paul's Cathedral in London.

It was about that same time, around 1535, that **John Tewkesbury** was arrested for reading Tyndale's English translation of the New Testament, and thus committing an offense against the "holy Mother Church." Faced with threats of torture and burning, he at first said that he did not believe anything he had read that contradicted papist doctrines, but then repented and confessed that he believed the translated Scriptures were true and the papist doctrines were false. For this he was immediately taken before the bishop of London and condemned as an "obstinate heretic." During the time he was in prison before his execution, he was tortured so severely that he was almost dead already when they took him to the stake at Smithfield. There he declared loudly his complete loathing of popery, and stated a strong belief that his cause was just in God's sight.

In 1536, at Bradford-in-Wiltshire in south-central England, a harmless countryman named **Traxnal** was burned alive because he would not acknowledge that the bread and wine actually turned into the body and blood of Christ during the mass, nor would he agree that the pope had supreme authority over the consciences of men and women.

Somewhere near the year 1538, **Nicholas Peke** was burned as a heretic in Norwich in eastern England for the same reason that Traxnal was executed. Three Catholic clergymen, Dr. Reading, Dr. Hearne, and Dr. Spragwell officiated at his burning. When Nicholas had scorched to the point that he was black as tar, Dr. Spragwell hit him on his right shoulder with a long white wand and said to him, "Peke, recant, and believe in the sacrament." Peke replied, "I despise it and you also." Then he lunged forward against his chains and spit blood at Dr. Spagwell, which was a measure of both his contempt and his suffering. Dr. Reading then told Nicholas that he would grant him forty day's indulgence if he would recant his opinions, but Nicholas paid no attention to Reading's foolishness and rejoiced that Christ had counted him worthy to suffer for His name's sake.

Another person burned during the reign of Henry VIII was an old monk named **William Letton** in the county of Suffolk in eastern England. William had spoken out against an idol that was carried in a church procession.

On July 28, 1540, the distinguished **Thomas Cromwell**, Earl of Essex, and the noted politician who proposed the legislation (Act of Supremacy) that in 1534 declared King Henry VIII himself to be Supreme Head of the Church of England, was executed by beheading. His downfall came about this way.

Cromwell had urged the king to marry Anne of Cleves to gain an alliance with her brother, a Protestant leader in western Germany. Henry hated his fourth wife from the beginning, and the Protestant alliance was distasteful to him because he wanted to maintain the principles of the Catholic faith. Although Cromwell was made earl of Essex and lord great chamberlain in April 1540, his enemies persuaded Henry in June that Cromwell was a traitor to both his religion and the king. He was arrested on June 10, condemned without a hearing, and beheaded on July 28, 1540. Before he was beheaded, he was cruelly treated, then made a short speech to the people, and then submitted himself meekly to the axe.

Although the charges against Thomas Cromwell had nothing to do with religion, it's right that this nobleman be ranked among the martyrs, for it hadn't been for his zeal to rid England of popery, he might have retained the king's favor. He also did more for the Reformation in England than any man except Dr. Thomas Cranmer, and for this he earned the wrath of the papists, who plotted against him and brought about his destruction.

About that time, **Dr. Robert** [or Cuthbert] **Barnes, Thomas Garnet**, and **William Jerome** were brought before the ecclesiastical court of the bishop of London and charged with heresy. The three were summarily condemned to be burned, and imprisoned in the Tower of London. Shortly after, on July 30, 1540, they were taken to Smithfield and chained together to a single stake. Dr. Barnes was asked, either at his trial by the bishop or at the stake by the Sheriff of London, for the reports differ, if the departed saints prayed for us. Barnes replied, as so reported, to the sheriff, "Throughout all Scripture we are not commanded to pray to any saints. Therefore I cannot preach to you that saints ought to prayed to, for then I would preach to you a doctrine of my own head. If saints do pray for us, then I hope to pray for you within this half hour." As the fire raged up around the three martyrs, they encouraged each other with unchanging courage that could only come from real faith in Jesus Christ.

Not long after this, a merchant named **Thomas Sommers** and three other men were arrested for reading some of Martin Luther's books. Their punishment was to carry the books to a fire in the market center at *Cheapside, and there throw the books into the fire. The three other men did, but Thomas threw his books *over* the fire so that they weren't burned. For this he was sent back to the Tower of London where he was stoned to death.

During this time, Dr. Longland, the bishop of Lincoln in eastern England, raged so violently against heresy that he burned at the stake **Thomas Bainard** for merely saying the Lord's prayer in English, and **James Moreton** for reading James's epistle in English. He then sent a priest, **Anthony Parsons**, and a man named **Eastwood** and **one other**, to Windsor in south-central England to be examined by the bishop of Salisbury, who only Bonner exceeded as a violent persecutor. The bishop wasted little time in their examinations and condemned all three to be burned.

When they were chained to the stakes, Parsons asked for some water to drink, and when he received it he lifted the cup to his two companions and said, "Cheer up my brothers, and lift up your hearts to God, for after this harsh breakfast we shall have a good dinner in the kingdom of Christ our Lord and Redeemer." When Eastwood heard Parsons' words, he lifted his eyes and hands toward heaven and asked the Lord to receive his spirit quickly.

The executioners had piled faggots and straw around the stakes, and Parsons pulled the straw to him and held it against his chest, and said to those who had gathered to watch the burning, "This is God's armor, and now I am a Christian soldier prepared for battle. I look for no mercy, but through the merits of Christ. He is my only Savior, and I trust in Him for my salvation." The fires were then lit and their bodies burned, but nothing could harm their precious and immortal souls. Their faithfulness triumphed over cruelty, and their sufferings keep them ever in the hearts of those who love the martyrs.

Thus were Christ's godly followers in England persecuted in every cruel and treacherous way that men could devise. For in the parliament that should have protected the good citizens of England, King Henry VIII had made a most blasphemous and cruel act: "Whoever reads the Scriptures in 'Wycliffe's learning' [the mother tongue, English], will forfeit land, cattle, goods, body, and life from themselves and their heirs forever; and be condemned as heretics to God, enemies to the crown, and complete traitors to England." That was man's reward to the true believers in Christ, but their Lord's reward to them was an everlasting crown of righteousness.

10

Persecutions in Scotland

(1527-1558)

Martin Luther's teachings and controversy with the Roman Catholic Church had far-reaching results throughout Europe, Great Britain, and many other places. It stirred up the hearts of many and sent them searching for the truth of God's Word. Among the searchers was a Scotsman named **Patrick Hamilton**. To learn the truth of the Scriptures, he and three companions attended the University of Marburg in west-central Germany, north of Frankfurt. It was

Europe's first Protestant university and was founded by Prince Philip of Hesse, who at that time was a 23-year-old *landgrave. While there, Patrick and his companions became friends with Martin Luther and Philipp Melanchthon, the German theologian who in 1521 wrote *Loci Communes*, the first extensive treatise on Protestant doctrine. The writings and teachings of Luther and Melancthon convinced Hamilton and his friends to leave the papal church and convert to Protestant beliefs.

Now inflamed with true knowledge of faith and godliness, Patrick Hamilton was anxious to return to Scotland and teach his countrymen the right ways of God and Christ as shown clearly in the Scriptures. Taking with him his three companions, he returned home without delay and began to teach wherever he could. Soon, however, James Beaton, the archbishop of St. Andrews, who was an adamant papist, heard of Hamilton's teachings and summoned him to appear before him, which Hamilton did without delay, thinking he would have an opportunity to dispute papist doctrine. But after only a short examination, the archbishop had him arrested and held in the most loathsome part of St. Andrews castle until the next morning, when he was taken before a council of bishops for further examination as a heretic.

The charges read against him were that he had publicly disapproved of pilgrimages, purgatory, prayers to saints, prayers for the dead, the mass, and had denied the infallibility of the pope. Hamilton agreed that all the charges were correct. For this he was immediately condemned to be burned alive, and on the order of the bigoted archbishop the sentence was to be carried out that very afternoon.

When Hamilton was taken to a place of burning only a day after he had willingly met with the archbishop, the crowd that gathered did not believe they were actually going to burn him, but thought it was part of his examination and intended to frighten him into recanting his teachings and returning to the doctrines of the Romish religion. But they soon learned they were mistaken.

When they brought Hamilton to the stake, he knelt down and prayed fervently for some time. When he finished, he was chained to the stake and faggots were piled around him. A bag of gunpowder was then placed in each armpit and set on fire first, but they did not explode and only scorched his arms and face and did not injure him otherwise or start the faggots on fire. So more gunpowder and some dry kindling was brought and set among the faggots and lit. The gunpowder did not explode but did ignite and fire quickly flamed up around Hamilton. As the flames engulfed him, he cried out, "Lord Jesus, receive my spirit! How long will darkness overwhelm this realm? And how long will You allow the tyranny of these men?" Apparently, however, the faggots themselves were green, and after the initial fire died down they burned slowly and caused him great anguish. Yet he bore the suffering with such Christian courage that it was obvious to all the true believers who were watching that the grace of God was much with him in his martyrdom. The year was 1527.

In 1529, a Benedictine monk named **Henry Forest** began to preach that Patrick Hamilton was a martyr and much of what he taught was true. When archbishop James Beaton was informed of this, he had Forest arrested and put into prison. He then sent a friar to hear Forest's confession, knowing that the good monk would speak freely because he thought his confession would be kept secret as it should be. But the archbishop had ordered the friar to report back to him all that Forest confessed, which the friar did, like the treacherous Judas that he was. In his confession, Henry Forest told the friar that he thought that Patrick Hamilton was a good man, and that his teachings could be defended by the Scriptures. This was used by the archbishop as evidence against Forest and he was sentenced to be burned alive as a heretic.

Because Henry Forest was a popular and godly man, the archbishop sought council as to how he should be executed so that the people would not be too much affected. John Lindsay, one of the archbishop's servants, suggested that they execute Forest in a secret place like a cellar, "for," he said, "the smoke from Patrick Hamilton's burning has continued to infect all those on whom it blows." The archbishop agreed with him and had Forest taken to a cellar and there suffocated with a thick pillow held over his face.

In 1534, **David Stratton** [or Straiton] and **Norman Gourlay** [or Guley] cheerfully gave up their lives for the truth of the Gospel. Gourlay was arrested for saying that there was no such thing as purgatory, and that the pope was the antichrist, and that he had no jurisdiction in Scotland. Stratton was arrested on similar charges; he had said that there was no purgatory, only the sufferings of Christ and the tribulations of this world. Straton was a fisherman, and there was also this charge against him: when Master Robert Lawson, vicar [priest] of Eglesgrig, asked for his fish tithes, Stratton tossed them to him out of the boat and some of them fell into the water and swam away. The vicar then accused Stratton of heresy, because by his actions, the vicar said, Stratton was saying that tithes should not be paid to the church.

Gourlay and Stratton were arrested and condemned as heretics by the bishop of Rose. They were burned in a large grassy area between Edinburgh and Leith, for the archbishop intended that the inhabitants of nearby Fife see the fire and be filled with terror and fear at the thought of believing as Gourlay and Stratton did and being burned, also. But there was no fear shown at the stake. Both of the condemned cheerfully gave their souls up to the God that gave them, knowing that through the merits of their great Redeemer they would have a glorious resurrection into eternal life.

In 1538, **Dean Thomas Ferret**, vicar of Dolor and a canon at St. Colm's Inche, preached every Sunday morning to his congregation from the New Testament. This was seldom seen in Scotland because usually only a black friar or a gray friar preached, and almost never from the Scriptures. Therefore the friars became jealous and accused him to the bishop of Dunkeld of being a heretic, and of teaching the mysteries of the Scriptures to the people in their common language, thus making the friars detestable in their sight, for the friars never preached in a language that the people could understand. Furthermore, he did not take the cow and the quality cloth that the people brought to pay for the preaching, and it could make the people think that the friars should do the same.

The bishop summoned Thomas Ferret for examination, during which he told him that he should take the cow and cloth, for it was too much to preach every Sunday without being paid, and that for him not to do so would prejudice the people against the churchmen. Also, that he should preach only those good epistles and good gospels that expressed the liberty of the holy Mother Church.

Dean Ferret said that preaching only on Sundays was not enough, but he would take the cow and cloth from his poor parishioners, and anything else they would give him, and in exchange he would give them anything that he had; and so he and the bishop were in agreement on that. Further, if the bishop would show him the good epistles and good gospels, and the evil epistles and evil gospels, then he would preach the good and omit the evil.

At that the bishop angrily said, "I thank God that I never knew what the Old and New Testament were. I will know nothing but my mass book and my *pontifical. Go your way, and let go of all these fantasies of yours, for if you continue in your erroneous opinions you will be sorry for it, and they will be no way to change the consequences."

Ferret answered, "I am confident my cause is just in the presence of God, and therefore I am not concerned about the consequences." Then he left.

Soon after, a summons was issued by the Cardinal of St. Andrews and the bishop of Dunkeld to Dean Thomas Forret, friars **Keillor and Beveridge**, a priest named **Duncan Simpson**, a layman named **Robert Forrester**, and **several others**. On the day of their appearance before the bishop's council, they were all condemned as heretics and given no chance to defend themselves or recant if they so wished, because it was charged that they were chief heretics and teachers of heresies. Further, there was this against them—most of them attended the wedding of a priest, the vicar of Tulibothy beside Stirling, and ate meat (alleged to be a goose) in Lent at the wedding feast.

And so they were all taken to Castle Hill at Edinburgh and burned alive.

In 1543, **George Wishart**, the Scottish religious reformer who converted John Knox when Knox was a Roman Catholic priest, was teaching at Cambridge University. He was a tall, plain-dressed man, polite and humble, well-traveled, personable, generous to the poor and stingy to himself, who loved to teach and loved God above all things. He ate only two meals a day, fasted one day out of four, and slept on a straw mattress and coarse new canvas sheets, which he gave away whenever he changed them. Because he was quite serious in his teachings of the Scriptures, some people thought he was a severe person, some even disliking what he taught enough to kill him. The Lord, however, was his defense, and usually after he talked with them about their malice and exhorted them to better ways, they were well-pleased with him, and with themselves. Not pleased with him, however, because of his Reformation doctrines, were the Romish clergy, and they were soon to have their way with him.

In 1544, Wishart increasingly desired to preach the true Gospel in his own country, and so he left Cambridge and returned to Scotland. There he first preached at Montrose, and later at Dundee, on the northern bank of the *Firth of Tay. Here he taught on the meaning of Paul's epistle to the Romans and justification by faith as rediscovered by Martin Luther about thirty years before, and he did it with such grace and freedom that the papists were greatly alarmed.

Over the next two years Wishart traveled throughout Scotland, and nearly lost his life several times as the Romish clergy tried to silence him. Once when he was in west Scotland he heard that a plague had broken out in Dundee, and he hurried there to minister to the sick in body and soul. He was, of course, received with joy.

Before he left Dundee to return to Montrose, a popish priest named John Weighton was incited by David Beaton, the archbishop and Cardinal of Scotland, to kill him. According to the story, Weighton hid a dagger under his gown and waited at the bottom of the pulpit stairs for Wishart to come down after he finished a sermon about healing of the soul and body. Wishart, however, saw the priest waiting for him with his hand inside his gown and said to him, "My friend, what is it you want?" and grabbed the dagger and took it from the priest as he tried to free it from his gown. The now terrified priest fell to his knees, confessed his intention, and begged Wishart's forgiveness. Several of the sick who had lingered outside the fence that separated them from those who were well, saw and heard what happened and demanded that the traitor be turned over to them. In their anger they broke through the fence and would have taken the priest, but Wishart held him in his arms and said,

"Whoever hurts him shall hurt me, for he has not harmed me, but has done me much good by teaching me to be more watchful in the future." By this action he calmed the people and saved the life of the evil priest who had tried to kill him.

Soon after Wishart returned to Montrose, Cardinal Beaton had a false letter sent to him as if it were from a well-known friend who owned the Kennier land and estate, asking him to come immediately because he was deathly sick. Along the route to the estate, about a mile and a half from Montrose, Beaton set an ambush of sixty armed men to murder Wishart. But as Wishart and some close companions approached the area, he received a sudden thought that all was not well and he should not continue on his journey. To his companions he said, "God has forbidden me to continue. There is treason ahead. Some of you continue carefully and let me know what you find." When they discovered the ambush set by the cardinal, they returned quickly to Wishart and told him. Wishart said, "I know my life will end at the hands of that bloodthirsty man, but not by being ambushed."

Not long after, in 1546, Cardinal Beaton was told that Wishart was staying with a Mr. Cockburn of Ormiston, in East Lothian in southern Scotland, and asked the governor of that region to take Wishart into custody, which he did but much against his will. Wishart was then taken to Edinburgh and imprisoned in St. Andrews castle.

From there he was summoned to appear the next morning before the Cardinal of St Andrews and his council of bishops on charges of teaching seditious and heretical doctrine. In the morning, the cardinal had one-hundred of his servants dress in battle array as if they were preparing for war rather than escorting someone being tried for preaching the true Word of God. From St. Andrews they marched George Wishart to the Abbey Church in warlike ranks, afraid that the people who so admired and loved

Wishart would try to take him from them, or that he would try to escape, but he followed them meekly to the monastery church. At the door he paused briefly to toss his purse of money to a poor sick man lying on the steps.

When he came inside the church and stood before the cardinal, the sub-prior of the Abbey, named Dane John Winryme, went into the pulpit and gave a sermon on heresy. When he finished, an amply fed priest named John Lander read a lengthy roll of eighteen charges of heresy against Wishart. The charges were filled with curses, blasphemies, and threats, which Lander read with increased rage until sweat ran down his face and he foamed at the mouth and spit out his words. When he finished, he shouted at Wishart, "What do you answer to these charges, you renegade, you traitor, you thief! We have proved them by sufficient witness against you!"

Wishart first knelt and prayed, and then, gently and Christ-like, said, "It is only right that you who are judging me should know what my words and doctrines are and what I have taught, so that I don't die unjustly to the great peril of your souls. Therefore, for the glory and honor of God, for your own well-being, and for the protection of my life, I earnestly request you judges hear me, and I will tell you my doctrines without changing them."

At that, the accusing priest, Lander, screamed, "You heretic, renegade, traitor, and thief! It is not lawful for you to preach. You have taken that authority into your own hands without any authority from the church."

Wishart realized what they intended to do, and made several appeals, but it was no use. They found him guilty of heresy on all eighteen charges and condemned him to be executed by hanging and burning.

On the morning of his execution, the cardinal sent two friars to him in prison. They put a black linen coat on him and tied several bags of gunpowder to various parts of his body. Then they tied his arms behind his back, secured an iron chain around his waist, and led him to the stake by a rope around his neck. To prevent any of Wishart's many friends and admirers from interfering with the execution, Cardinal Beaton had his gunners stand ready at their guns until Wishart was burned and dead. On the way to the stake, one of the friars said to him, "Master George, pray to our Lady, that she may be mediatrix [mediator] for you to her son." Wishart replied, "Stop! Don't tempt me, my brothers. The fire tempts me enough."

At the stake he fell to his knees and three times prayed, "O Thou Savior of the world, have mercy on me. Father of heaven, I commend my spirit into Thy holy hands." Then he prayed for his accusers, saying, "I beseech Thee, Father of heaven, forgive them that have lied against me. I forgive them with all my heart. I ask Christ to forgive them that out of ignorance have condemned me." Then he turned to the people gathered there and said, "For the Word's sake and the true Gospel, which was given to me by the grace of God, I will suffer this day at the hands of men; not sorrowfully, but with a glad heart. For this cause I was sent, that I should suffer this fire for Christ's sake. Watch my face closely. You will not see me change color, for I do not fear this grim fire. I know surely that my soul shall dine this night with my Savior Christ."

Upon hearing this, the hangman knelt before Wishart and said, "Sir, please forgive me, for I am not guilty of your death." Wishart replied, "Come here to me." When he did, Wishart kissed him on the cheek and said, "This is proof that I forgive you, my beloved. Do your work."

Wishart was then hung on the gallows over the fire until his body burned to ashes. When the people saw his great torment, they could not keep from weeping for him and accusing the papists of slaughtering an innocent lamb. Soon after, an angry mob killed the cardinal and occupied his castle. John Knox joined the castle garrison and began teaching the Gospel. Soon Knox became preacher to the revolutionaries. The next year, in July 1547, the Roman Catholics regained the castle with French help, and the defenders were made French galley slaves. In February 1549 Knox was released, and for a time he preached in England and Germany. Later he was pastor of an English congregation in Geneva, Switzerland, where he became a student of John Calvin, the French-born Swiss theologian, who had made Geneva a "city of God." After he returned to Scotland, Knox established Presbyterianism in that country.

The last martyr to die in Scotland was 82-year-old **Walter Mill** [or Milne] in 1558. In his youth, Mill had been a papist and for some time parish priest in the Church of Lunan in Angus. At some point in his life, he went to Germany and there heard the true Gospel. When he returned to Scotland, he set aside all things about the Roman Catholic church, began to teach Reformation doctrine and, though quite old, got married. Soon the bishops of Scotland began to suspect him of heresy. Realizing that he was about to be taken into custody and charged, Mill left his church and hid himself in the country for quite some time. Later the queen allowed him to return to his parish and preach. Nevertheless, not long after he was apprehended by two priests and taken to St. Andrews castle in Edinburgh.

At first Mill was threatened with torture and burning, but when this did not convince him to recant his Reformation beliefs and teachings, he was offered a monk's position and lifetime security in the Abbey of Dunfermline if he would deny the things he had taught, and agree that they were heresy. But he continued to maintain the truth of the Gospel despite their threats and enticing promises.

He was then taken to St Andrews church and put into the pulpit to be accused before the bishops. Because of age and his treatment in prison, Mill was unable to climb the pulpit stairs without help, and the bishops thought he would be too weak to speak loud enough for them to hear him. But when he spoke, his voice rang out with such courage and boldness that the Christians who were present rejoiced while his adversaries were confused and ashamed. Mill knelt in the pulpit and prayed so long that Andrew Oliphant, who had been a priest since the time of Cardinal Beaton, said to him, "Sir Walter Mill, get up and respond to the charges; you're holding my lords here too long." After he finished praying, Walter said, "You call me 'Sir Walter', call me 'Walter,' and not '*Sir* Walter'. I have been one of the Pope's knights far too long. Now say what you have to say."

The examination proceeded in its expected direction, and at the end Andrew Oliphant asked Mill if he would recant his erroneous opinions. He answered, "I would rather forfeit ten-thousand lives than give up a particle of the heavenly principles I received from the sufferings of my blessed Redeemer." Oliphant then pronounced sentence upon him and he was conducted back to prison for execution the next day.

When he was taken to the place of execution, Walter Mill expressed his religious sentiments so strongly and with such keenness of mind for his age and weak condition, that it astonished even his enemies. After prayer, he said to all, "Dear friends, the reason why I am to suffer this day is not because I have committed any crimes, although I consider myself a most miserable sinner before God, but it is for the defense of the faith of Jesus Christ as set forth in the Old and New Testament for us. It is that faith for which godly martyrs have offered themselves gladly before, being assured of eternal happiness. So this day I praise God that

He has called me to be among those servants, and seal up His truth with my life, which I received from Him and willingly offer it back to Him for His glory.

"Therefore, if you wish to escape the second death, do not be seduced by the lies of priests, monks, friars, priors, abbots, bishops, and the rest of the sect of Antichrist. Depend only upon Jesus Christ and His mercy, so that you will be delivered from condemnation and receive eternal life." While he spoke there was great crying and mourning among the people, for they were stirred by his courage and boldness, his steadfastness and faith, and his words inflamed their hearts.

Walter Mill was then lifted up on the stake, and the faggots were lit. As the flames burned him, he cried out, "Lord, have mercy on me! Pray, people, while there is yet time!" And then he left this world to be with his Lord for whom he died.

When the Reformation came fully upon Scotland in 1560, and the Scottish Parliament established Presbyterianism as the national faith, many costly images from papist churches were burned on the site of Walter Mill's martyrdom.

11

The Martyrdom of William Tyndale (1536), John Frith, and Andrew Hewet (1533)

William Tyndale (see Figure 9)

We now come to the story of God's martyr, William Tyndale, who was surely chosen by God to dig up the roots and foundation of the pope's government. Consequently, the great prince of darkness, having malice against Tyndale, left no stones unturned in his efforts to trap Tyndale, betray him, and take his life.

Tyndale was born near the border of Wales in 1494. He was educated at Oxford and Cambridge, and soon after began his life work of translating the Bible into English. When he left Cambridge, he became schoolmaster to the children of a Master Welch, a knight of Gloucestershire in England.

Master Welch served outstanding dinners, and so was often visited by the educated and high-ranking officials of the church. Being a member of the household, Tyndale ate dinner with them and joined in their discussions about such people as Martin Luther, the German theologian, and Desiderius *Erasmus, the Dutch Renaissance scholar and Roman Catholic theologian—and took a hardy part in their discussions about church controversies and questions about the Scriptures.

Since Tyndale was well educated and had devoted himself to studying God's Word, he never hesitated to give them his judgment about scriptural matters in plain and simple words. When they disagreed with him, he showed them in the Bible what the Scriptures said and how they were wrong in their beliefs and doctrines. This happened frequently at the Welch's home, and the local clergy soon grew weary of Tyndale's constant references to the Scriptures and criticism of their doctrines, and began to bear a secret grudge against him in their hearts.

It wasn't too long before the clergy invited Master and Lady Welch to a banquet without Tyndale, and immediately began to expound their erroneous doctrines freely and without resistance. Undoubtedly they planned this in an attempt to turn Master Welch and his wife against Tyndale and back to their doctrines. In this they almost succeeded, for no sooner had Master and Lady Welch returned home, then they began to argue with Tyndale about the things the priests had talked about at the banquet. Tyndale used the Scriptures and began to reason with them how the things they had been told were wrong. Then Lady Welch, somewhat indignantly, said to him, "One of the doctors [of divinity] who was there can afford to spend one-hundred pounds whenever he wishes; and another, two-hundred pounds; and another, three-hundred pounds. So for what reason should we believe you instead of them?"

Tyndale saw that it would do no good to answer her, so after that he talked very little about such matters. He was at that time, however, working on a translation of Erasmus's book, *The Manual of the Christian Knight*, which had been published in 1509, and he gave his master and lady a copy of his translation and asked them to read it. They did, and from then on few of the clergymen were invited to their house for dinner, and when they were invited they were not given the opportunity to expound their papal doctrine freely.

As this continued and the clergy realized that Tyndale's growing influence with the Welch's was the reason for it, they began to gather together and talk against Tyndale in alehouses and other places, saying that what he was teaching was heresy. They also accused him of this to the bishop's chancellor [secretary] and some of the bishop's officers.

As a result, the chancellor ordered the priests to appear before him, and ordered Tyndale to be there also. Tyndale had little doubt that the session was not called for the priests, but to make accusations and threats against him. So on the way he prayed hard and silently to God that He would give him the strength to stand fast in the truth of His Word.

When his time came to appear before the chancellor, he was threatened, reviled, and talked to as though he were a dog. Many things were charged against him, but no one came forth to prove the charges, even though all the priests from the area were there. So Tyndale escaped out of their grasp and went back to Master Welch.

Living near the Welchs was a doctor of divinity and former secretary to the bishop who had been friendly toward Tyndale for some time. Tyndale went to him and explained the many things he saw in the Scriptures that were contrary to papist doctrine and that had caused him his problems with the local clergy and the bishop, for he wasn't afraid to open his heart to this man. Whereupon the doctor said to him, "Don't you know that the pope is the very Antichrist that the Scriptures speak about? But be careful of what you say, for if anyone finds out that you are of that opinion, it will cost you your life."

Not long after, Tyndale disputed with a certain theologian about the truth of the Scriptures until the man cried out in frustration these blasphemous words, "We would be better without God's laws than without the pope."

When Tyndale heard this, his godly zeal burst forth and he replied, "I defy the pope, and all his laws! If God spares my life, it will not be many years before I will cause every boy who works on a farm plowing fields to know more of the Scriptures than the pope does!"

As time passed, the priests increasingly railed against Tyndale and accused him of many things, saying that he was a heretic. The pressure of the attacks became so great that Tyndale went to Master Welch and said that he desired to leave his employ and go to another place. "I am certain," he said, "that I won't be allowed to stay here much longer, and that you won't be able to keep me out of the hands of the clergy, even though I know you would try. But only God knows what harm might come to you if you keep me here, and I would be sorry for that." So Tyndale left with the blessing of Master Welch, and went to London and there preached for a while, as he had done in the country.

Not long after arriving in London he thought about Cuthbert Tonstal, then bishop of London, and especially Erasmus's note in his book in which he praised Tonstal for his learning. He felt that he would be quite happy if he could somehow work for Tonstal. Tyndale wrote a letter to the bishop and then went to see him, taking with him a copy of the oration of Isocartes, the Athenian orator and teacher, which he had translated out of Greek into English, but the bishop gave him various reasons why he had no work for him, and advised him to seek work elsewhere in London. Believing that God in His providence had shut this door for a reason, Tyndale then went to see Humphrey Mummuth, an alderman of London, and asked for help. Mummuth took him into his home, where he lived for about a year. While he was there, Mummuth said, Tyndale lived like a good priest, studying night and day, eating only plain meals and having but one beer with them, and wearing the simplest of clothing.

During that year Tyndale felt an increasing urge to translate the New Testament from Latin into a plainer language. But as he saw how the preachers boasted about themselves and claimed total authority in spiritual matters, and how vain the bishops where in everything they did, and how much he was disliked by them all, he realized that there was no place he could do it in London or England. Soon God provided him sufficient money through Mummuth and some other men so he could leave England and go to Germany, where Martin Luther had just finished translating the New Testament into German (1521), and was working on many tracts and catechisms and a translation of the entire Bible.

After meeting with John Frith, Martin Luther, and other colleagues, Tyndale decided that the only way he could obtain the benefits he wanted from his translation, was to put it in the language spoken by the common people, so that they could read and see the simple plain Word of God. Undoubtedly he was influenced in this decision by seeing Luther's translation and the effect it was having on the German people.

Tyndale knew it wasn't possible to establish the lay people in any truth unless the Scriptures were so plainly laid out before their eyes in their own language that they could understand the meaning of the text. Otherwise, the enemies of the truth would destroy it by using likely but misleading arguments, traditions of their own making that were without scriptural foundations, and by juggling the text and expounding on it in such a way that it was impossible to determine if what they said was the right meaning or not.

He was certain that the chief cause of all the trouble in the Church was because the Word of God was kept hidden from the people, and so for a long time the abominations and idolatries of the hypocritical and self-righteous clergy could not be seen. For this reason the clergy did all they could to keep the Scriptures hidden so that they could not be read at all. And even if someone *could* read them, the clergy so twisted their meaning that the unlearned lay people who despised their abominations could not solve the riddles in their doctrines, even though they knew in their hearts that what the clergy taught them was false.

For this and other reasons, God stirred up this good man to translate the Scriptures into English for the benefit of the simple people of his country. Tyndale began printing his New Testament translation in 1525 in Cologne, Germany, but was interrupted by a legal injunction and completed the printing in Worms in 1526. Soon after, his translation appeared in England. When Cuthbeth Tonstal, bishop of London, and Sir Thomas More, speaker of the House of Commons, saw the translation they were much offended and began to devise ways in which they could destroy what they called "that false, erroneous, translation."

As it happened, Augustine Packington, a textiles merchant, was at Antwerp in the Netherlands on business, and there met bishop Tonstal, who was there because Tyndale had moved there from Worms. Packington liked Tyndale but told the bishop he did not. Tonstal and Thomas More had devised a plan whereby they would buy all of Tyndale's books before they reached England, and he told this to Packington. Packington replied, "My Lord! I can do more to help you in this matter than most of the merchants here, if it would so please you. I know the Dutch men and strangers that have bought Tyndale's books from him to resell them, so if you will give me the money I need, I will buy every book from them that has been printed and is still not sold."

The bishop, thinking he had God "by the toe" and in his control, said, "Do your best, gentle Master Packington. Get them for me and I will pay whatever the cost, for I intend to burn and destroy them all at Paul's Cross church in London."

Upon receiving the bishop's money, Packington went immediately to Tyndale and told him the whole plan, and an agreement was made between them to sell the bishop all the books he could be sold. So the bishop of London had the books, Packington had the thanks, and Tyndale now had ample money to print more books.

After this took place, Tyndale revised and corrected his New Testament and increased its printing so that three times as many books were sent into England. When the bishop learned that more books were appearing in England, he sent for Packington, who was in London on business, and said to him, "How can it be that there are so many New Testaments here? You promised me that you would buy them all."

Packington answered, "I bought all of them that were available, but obviously they have printed more since then. It will probably get no better so long as they have stamps with which to ship the books, so you had better buy the stamps also if you want to be sure." At this answer the bishop smiled, realizing that he had been hoodwinked, and so the matter ended.

A short time after, a George Constantine, who was suspected of certain heresies, was taken into custody by Sir Thomas More, who was now lord chancellor of England. More said to him, "Constantine, I want you to be frank with me about what I'm going to ask you. If you are, I promise you I will show favor to you in all the other things that you are accused of. Across the sea is Tyndale, Joye, and a great many like you. I know they cannot live without help. There are some that help them with money, and since you are one of them and you know where their money comes from. I urge you to tell me who is helping them."

"My lord," Constantine said, "I will tell you the truth. It's the bishop of London who has helped us, for he has given us a great deal of money for New Testaments so he may burn them. He has been and is our only help and comfort."

"I'll keep my pledge," said More, "for I thought that's what it was, and so I told the bishop before he went about doing it."

Soon after, Tyndale translated the Old Testament, and wrote introductions to each chapter that were well worth being read over and again by all who saw them. These books were taken into England by various means, and it cannot be told what a door of light they opened to the eyes of the whole English nation, which before had been shut up in darkness. Tyndale's books, especially the New Testament translation, were of great spiritual benefit to the godly lay people, but of great harm to the ungodly clergy, who were afraid that by the shining beams of truth their deeds of darkness would be clearly seen. So they began to rouse themselves and plan how they might stop Tyndale.

When Tyndale had translated the Book of Deuteronomy, he wanted to print it in Hamburg, Germany, and so started by ship in that direction. But his ship was wrecked on the coast of Holland, and he lost all his books, writings and copies, money and time, and had to start over again. He continued to Hamburg on another ship, and with the help of a Master Coverdale, retranslated all five books of Moses—Genesis, Exodus, Leviticus, Numbers, and Deuteronomy—from Easter until December of 1529, in the house of a pious widow, Mistress Margaret Van Emmerson. After finishing, he returned to Antwerp.

At the end of his English New Testament, Tyndale inserted a letter asking any who read the translation to inform him if they found the least error in it, or if there was any of the translation that they thought was wrong and should be corrected. But the papist clergy, not wanting the book to succeed, cried out against it and said there were a thousand heresies in it, and that it was not to be corrected, but totally done away with.

Some of the clergy said it wasn't possible to translate the Scriptures into English. Some said it wasn't lawful for the lay people to have a New Testament in their common language. Some said it would make all the lay people heretics. And to persuade secular rulers like Sir Thomas More to be on their side, which he already was since he was an unswerving Roman Catholic, they said it would make the people rebel against the king.

These English clergymen, who should have been guides of light to the people, would not translate the Bible themselves or allow anyone else to translate it. All they wanted was to keep the people in darkness and manipulate their consciences with foolish superstitions and false doctrines. In that way they could satisfy their personal ambitions and greedy covetousness, and exalt their own honor above that of any king or emperor—even above Christ Himself.

The bishops and other church officials never rested until the king agreed with them. And so in 1537, a proclamation was hastily written and published under secular authority prohibiting Tyndale's New Testament translation anywhere in England. Not satisfied with that, however, the clergy proceeded to make plans to entangle Tyndale in their nets and take his life from him.

They did it this way.

From examining the records of London, it is obvious that the bishops and Sir Thomas More had in their custody several who had been with Tyndale in Antwerp, and they carefully questioned them to find out all they could about Tyndale, what belonged to him, in whose house he stayed, where the house was, what he looked like, how he dressed when he went out, where he usually went, and where he met with others. When they had learned all these things, they set about to work their ungodly deed.

In Antwerp, William Tyndale had lived about a year in the house of Thomas Pointz, an Englishman who kept a boarding house for English merchants. A Henry Philips, whose father was a merchant and did business in Antwerp, came to the city seemingly on business for his father. He had a servant with him and seemed to be a trustworthy gentleman. Tyndale often ate dinner in a place frequented by merchants, and there he met Philips, who somehow quickly gained Tyndale's confidence and friendship. So much so, that Tyndale had him over to Pointz's house to visit and once or twice to dinner. He even obtained temporary lodgings for Philips at the house, and so trusted him that he showed him his books and other secret things in his study.

Thomas Pointz, however, had no such confidence in Philips and asked Tyndale how he became acquainted with him. Tyndale replied that he was an honest man, well educated, and quite in agreement with his plans. Seeing that Philips had such favor with Tyndale, Pointz said no more, thinking that they probably became acquainted through some mutual friend.

After some time in the city, Philips asked Pointz to show him around the commercial area where he might make some purchases. During their walk they talked about various things, including affairs of the king of England, but nothing was said that made Pointz suspect anything. After awhile, however, Pointz began to understand that Philips was trying to determine whether for money he would help him in a plan he had. Pointz knew that Philips had plenty of money, for several times Philips had asked him for help in obtaining certain things, always of the best, and Philips always said, "I have enough money." The plan and money were eventually discussed, and Pointz agreed to what Philips wanted him to do.

The next day Philips went to Brussels, about twenty-four miles from Antwerp, and brought back with him the procurator-general, who was the emperor's attorney, and several officers of the law. About three days later Pointz went to Barrois, eighteen miles from Antwerp, where he said he had business that would keep him away from his house for four to six weeks.

A few days after Pointz left, Henry Philips came to Pointz's house about midmorning and asked his wife if Master Tyndale was there. When told that he was, he left and positioned the officers he brought from Brussels in the street and around the front door. About noon he came back and went to Tyndale's rooms and asked him to lend him forty shillings, "for," he said, "I lost my wallet this morning on the trip from Mechelen." So Master Tyndale gave him forty shillings, which was easy to get from him if he had it, for he was a trusting man and inexperienced in the deceptive ways of the world. Then Philip said, "Master Tyndale, you shall be my dinner guest here today."

Tyndale replied, "No, I'm going out today to dinner, and you are welcome to come with me and be my guest."

So when it was dinner time, they left Tyndale's rooms to go out. At the front of Pointz's house was a narrow entryway that only one could go through at a time. Tyndale courteously offered to let Philips go first, but Philips made a show of it and insisted that Tyndale go first. Master Tyndale was a short man, and Philips was quite a bit taller. When they got to the door where Philips had positioned the officers in such a way that they could see who came out, he pointed downward toward Tyndale from behind him to let the officers know that he was the one they should arrest. After they put Tyndale into prison, the officers told Thomas Pointz that they felt sorry for Tyndale when they saw how simple and trusting he was.

After Tyndale's arrest, the procurator-general and some officers went to Tyndale's rooms and took away everything that belonged to him, including all his writings and books. They then took Tyndale to the castle of Vilvorde, eighteen miles from Antwerp.

In prison, Tyndale was offered the services of a *procurator to represent him, and an advocator to speak for him, both of which he refused, saying he would speak for himself. During his imprisonment, Tyndale preached so much and well to his jailers and those who came to know him, that they reported that if Tyndale wasn't a good Christian man they had no way of knowing who was.

Although Tyndale answered the questions of his inquisitors truthfully and with good use of reason, no reason was enough to save him from their hate and determination to destroy him and his work. Although he did not deserve to die, he was condemned by reason of a decree made by Holy Roman Emperor Charles V at the Diet of Augsburg in 1530, when the emperor and the Roman Catholics rejected the Protestant position that was presented to the assembly.

On October 6, 1536, in the town of Vilvorde in the Netherlands, William Tyndale, God's first translator of the New Testament into English, was brought to a place of execution, tied to a stake, strangled by the hangman to the point of death, and then burned in fire for doing God's work. As he met the Lord, Tyndale cried with a loud voice, "Lord! Open the king of England's eyes!" (See Figure 10.)

So powerful was Tyndale's doctrine and the godliness of his life, that during the year and a half of his imprisonment, it is said that he converted the jailer and his daughter and several others of his household.

Concerning his translation of the New Testament, because his enemies found so many faults in disagreeable ways and claimed it was full of heresy, William Tyndale wrote from prison to his friend, John Frith, "I call God to record against the day we shall appear before the Lord Jesus, that I never altered one syllable of God's Word against my conscience, nor would I do so this day if all that is in earth, whether it be honor, pleasure, or riches might be given to me."

John Frith

Having mentioned John Frith in our narration of the work and martyrdom of John Tyndale, it is right that we here say a few words about him.

Master Frith was a young man noted for his godliness, intelligence, and knowledge. In the secular world he could have risen to any height he wished, but he choose, instead, to serve the Church and work for the benefit of others and not himself. He studied at Cambridge and there became acquainted with William Tyndale, who planted in him deep roots of the true Gospel and honest piety.

About this time, Thomas Wolsey, the cardinal of York, built a new college at Oxford. Wolsey was appointed papal legate, the pope's direct agent, to England in 1518, and this made him England's most powerful cleric. He also was an ambitious and greedy man, whose church work was more for himself than for others. He financed the building of his new college by closing a number of monasteries and using the money designated for them; he also constructed a palace for himself at Hampton Court on the left bank of the River Thames, just fourteen miles upstream from the heart of London. From 1513 to 1529, he was chief adviser to Henry VIII, but fell from the king's favor when he failed to secure the pope's approval of Henry's divorce from Catherine of Aragon.

For his new college, Wolsey gathered the best of furnishings from church institutions throughout England, and obtained the best professors that were available. Among them was John Frith. At first Wolsey was elated with his professors and the level of education they brought to his college, but then he learned that many of them were meeting to discuss the abuses of the papal church, so he had them arrested for heresy and imprisoned. Naturally, John Frith was one of them.

Not long after his arrest, Frith was released from prison on the condition that he stay within ten miles of Oxford. Rather than stay in a roving prison, however, Frith immediately left England for Europe, where he traveled to Germany and met with William Tyndale and others who had also left England to escape persecution. He stayed away from England for two years, and then secretly reentered the country.

Wearing poor clothing as a disguise, Frith traveled to Reading, just west of London, to meet with the *prior. In

Reading, however, he was arrested as a vagabond—a homeless person—and put in the stocks until he could be identified. Such prisoners were seldom fed, and when Frith became sick from hunger, he asked to see the local schoolmaster, a Leonard Cox.

When Cox arrived, Frith spoke to him in Latin and complained about his confinement. They also spoke to each other in Greek. When they finished, Cox went to Reading's officials and told them that such a well-educated and excellent young man should not be in the stocks. Frith was freed immediately. But his liberty was short-lived, because Sir Thomas More, who was then chancellor of England, had offered a reward for his capture and was searching for him throughout England. Frith continually disguised himself and moved from place to place, but he was finally captured and imprisoned in the Tower of London.

[Ironically, in 1534, Thomas More, who was responsible for the capture and burning of many for heresy, was imprisoned in that same Tower of London for refusing to acknowledge King Henry VIII as supreme head of the Church of England. More was found guilty of treason and beheaded on July 6, 1535. In 1935, the Roman Catholic church declared More to be a saint and canonized him.]

After some time, Frith appeared before the archbishop of Canterbury, and then the bishop of Winchester, to give his defense to the charge of heresy. He also appeared before an assembly of London's bishops. He was examined on two points of heresy: purgatory, and the substance of the communion host and wine. Not coincidentally, he and Thomas More had corresponded several times while he was in prison and argued these same points in their letters.

During his examination by the bishops, Frith stated that he could not agree with them that it was an article of faith that he must believe, under pain of damnation, that when a priest prayed during the mass, the substance of the bread and wine were changed into the actual body and blood of our Savior Jesus Christ, even though their appearance remained the same. And even if this was so, which he did not believe it was, it should not be an article of faith. But as always in heresy charges before the Inquisition, no reasonable defense could change the predetermined sentence of condemnation.

And so John Frith was brought back before the bishops on June 20, 1533, and there condemned to death by burning. On July 4, he was taken to the place of execution, where the solemn ceremony, *sermo generalis*, was first held, and then the faggots were lit around him and several others who were also being burned for heresy. Burning close to Frith was an Andrew Hewet, and a strong wind that day blew the flames from Frith's stake toward Hewet, thereby consuming Hewet quickly and leaving Frith to burn slowly. But even though his agony was prolonged, Frith appeared happy that it shortened the suffering of his fellow martyr.

Andrew Hewet

Andrew Hewet was a twenty-four-year-old tailor's apprentice when he was martyred with John Frith. It came about when he went on a holy day to Fleet Street, toward St. Dunstan's, where he chanced to meet a noted liar, William Holt, who decided after a few minutes of conversation that Hewet believed in the Reformation doctrines. Holt immediately reported his suspicions to certain officers who seached for Hewet and found him in a bookseller's house where he had gone to buy a book. They arrested Hewet and put him into prison.

At his examination before the Chancellor of the bishop of London and the Bishop's Council, Hewet was accused of not believing that the communion host became the actual body of Christ after the Romish priest prayed over it. Hewet agreed that he did not so believe. Asked what he did believe, Hewet replied, "I believe as John Frith believes."

The prosecutor asked again, "Do you believe that the consecrated host is the actual body of Christ, who was born of the Virgin Mary?

Hewet replied, "No, I do not."

The prosecutor demanded to know why he did not believe it. To this Hewet replied, "Jesus himself said, "if any man shall say to you, Lo, here is Christ; or, lo, he is there; believe him not: For false Christs and false prophets shall rise." (See Mark 13:23-22.)

Many of the bishops smiled condescendingly at him, as if he were a foolish child, and then Stokesley, the bishop of London said, "Frith is a heretic, and has already been sentenced to be burned. If you do not recant your opinions, you will burn with him."

Hewet responded, "Truly, I am content with that."

Once more he was asked if he would recant, but Hewet said he would do what Frith did.

So he was taken to where John Frith was and burned at the stake next to him.

12

Work and Persecution of Martin Luther

(1517-1546)

Martin Luther, the son of a Saxon miner, was born in Eisleben, Saxony, on November 10, 1483. The young Luther studied at Magdeburg and Eisenach and then entered the University of Erfurt. When he graduated in 1505, he began to study law at the urging of his father, but in July he abandoned his law studies, renounced the world, and entered the monastery of the Augustinian Hermits at Erfurt. He credited this sudden decision to having been caught in a thunderstorm and knocked to the ground by a bolt of lightning—as he lay on the ground in fear, he realized that his temporal life had little value and only the eternal life of his soul was important.

In 1508, Luther was ordained at the monastery, and in 1509, was sent to the University of Wittenberg where he continued his studies and lectured in moral philosophy. In 1510, Luther visited Rome on business for his order and was shocked to find open corruption among leading church officials. In 1511, he received a doctorate in theology, and was appointed professor of Scripture at Wittenberg.

Although Luther was well acquainted with Roman Catholic scholastic theology, the seriousness with which he took his Christianity and the condition of his soul led him into a severe personal crisis. In the theology that he had been taught, he could not find the answer to his increasing concern as to whether it was possible to reconcile the demands of God's law with human inability to live up to that law. To find his answer he made the study of the Bible the center of his work, and in his studies concentrated on the epistles of the Apostle Paul, especially Paul's letter to the Romans. It was there that he found his answer.

> In the death of Jesus Christ on the Cross, God had reconciled humanity to Himself. Christ was now the sole mediator between God and man, and forgiveness of sin and salvation are effected by God's grace alone, and are received by faith. What was required, therefore, was not a person's strict adherence to the law or the fulfillment of religious obligations, but a response of faith that accepted what God had done in the finished work of Christ. As such faith matured, it would lead to obedience based not on fear of punishment, but on love.

As Luther continued in his studies, he found that Paul's doctrines were radically different than the traditional beliefs and teachings of the Roman church. This affected Luther's personal teachings and they soon began increasingly to turn away from those beliefs and doctrines. Before long he was totally against Roman scholastic theology that emphasized man's role in his own salvation, and against many church practices that emphasized justification by good works. His new understanding of the true Gospel and the finished work of Christ soon led to a clash between him and church officials.

In 1517, Luther had his first direct confrontation with his church over the selling of indulgences. To raise money to build St. Peter's Basilica in Rome, Pope Leo X started selling indulgences to Roman Catholics. These promised partial remission of the amount of time that a person, either the buyer or a loved one, had to suffer in purgatory for their sins. Soon after, some of the more cunning clergy saw the sale of indulgences as a way to raise money for their local churches or themselves. Luther considered himself a good Roman priest, but strongly objected to this practice because it was unscriptural and degraded the forgiving grace of God and the suffering and crucifixion of Jesus Christ.

Luther and Pope Leo immediately clashed over this, but Pope Leo considered Luther's objections to be of little consequences because he had little regard for Luther. So on October 31, 1517, Luther nailed to the main door of the castle church in Wittenberg a list of 95 propositions or theses. Among other things they denied the right of the pope to forgive sins by the sale of indulgences. Almost immediately the list was widely circulated in Germany and caused a great controversy. (See Appendix B for a complete list of the 95 theses.)

On the church side, friars and clerics throughout the region began attacking Luther and his teachings through their sermons and writings. One of them said, "Luther is a heretic, and worthy to be persecuted with fire." He then burned some of Luther's writings and sermons as a symbolic burning of Luther.

Soon after, Maximillian, emperor of Germany, Charles V, Holy Roman emperor and king of Spain as Charles I, and the pope, contacted Frederick III, Duke of Saxony, and demanded that he silence Luther. Frederick did not move immediately, but consulted many educated men on the problem, including *Erasmus. Erasmus answered the duke by saying that Luther had two great faults: he would touch the clerics' bellies, and he would touch the pope's crown. More seriously, the theologian told the duke that Luther was right in his desire to correct errors in the church. He then added this affirmation: "The effect of Luther's doctrine is true."

Later that year, Erasmus wrote to the archbishop of Mentz. In his letter, he stated, "The world is burdened with men's institutions, and with the tyranny of begging friars. Once it was counted a heresy when a man opposed the gospels. But now he is a heretic who is not like the friars, and whatsoever they do not understand is heresy to them. To know Greek is heresy, or to speak more finely than they do, that is heresy."

On August 7, 1518, Hierome, bishop of Ascoli, issued a citation requiring Luther to appear at Rome. Duke Frederick and the University of Wittenberg wrote letters to the pope on Luther's behalf. They wrote a similar letter to Carolus Miltitius, the pope's chamberlain, a German-born believer whom they judged to be somewhat sympathetic to Luther. In their letters they requested that Luther be heard by Cardinal Cajetan in Augsburg instead of Rome. The pope responded by telling Cajetan to summon Luther before him in Augsburg and immediately bring him to Rome, by force if necessary.

In October 1518, Martin Luther went to Augsburg in response to the cardinal's order. He took several letters of commendation with him. He waited in Augsburg for three days until a warrant of safe conduct could be obtained from the Emperor Maximillian. Luther then appeared before Cardinal Cajetan, who demanded three things from him:

1. That he repent and revoke his errors;
2. That he not to revert back to those errors;
3. That he refrain from all things that might trouble the church.

When Martin Luther asked the cardinal what his specific errors were, the cardinal showed him a copy of Pope Leo's papal bull on indulgences and the resulting remission of sins, stated that faith isn't necessary for a person who receives the sacrament, and that the pope was infallible in all matters of faith.

In his written reply, Luther said the pope was capable of error and was only to be obeyed so long as what he said agreed with the Scriptures, and that any faithful Christian has the right to disagree with him and to point out to him his errors from the Word of God. He also stated that no one is righteous and cannot be made so by works, and that anyone receiving the sacraments must have faith in the finished work of Christ. In every case, Luther quoted the appropriate Scriptures to confirm his words.

The cardinal, however, did not want to hear the Scriptures quoted to him in that manner. He ignored Luther's biblical arguments and responded with intellectual and traditional doctrines from his own head rather than from the Scriptures. He then told Luther to go away until he was ready to repent. Luther stayed in Augsburg for three days, and then sent a letter to the cardinal telling him that he would keep silent about the conditions and pardons offered to him if his enemies did the same. He also asked that all points of controversy be referred to the pope for his decision. He then waited another three days, but received no reply from the cardinal. Upon the advice of friends, he left Augsburg and returned to Wittenberg. Before he left, he sent an explanation to the cardinal and an appeal to the pope, which he had posted in public places before he left.

In response to Luther's appeal to him, the pope issued a new edict. He declared that indulgences were a part of the doctrine of the "holy Mother Church of Rome, the prince of all churches," and stated that popes are successors of Peter and, as such, they are vicars of Christ. He stated further that they have the power and authority to release from sin and dispense forgiveness, and to grant indulgences to both the living and the dead—those who remain in purgatory. This doctrine, he said, must be received by all the faithful followers of Christ, and warned Catholics that if they did not accept and practice these doctrines, they would suffer the pain of a great curse, including utter separation from the church.

Luther responded by appealing to the general council of the Roman Catholic Church, protesting this papal edict. When Pope Leo X learned of Luther's complaint to the general council, he sent his chamberlain, the German-born Carolus Miltitius, with a golden rose to be given to Duke Frederick. Miltitius also carried secret letters from the pope to other noblemen in the region. The letters solicited their support for the pope's cause and their rejection of the duke's support for Luther.

Before Miltitius reached Germany, however, Holy Roman Emperor Maximillian I died (January, 1519). Two other prominent leaders immediately contended for the vacant throne: Francis I, king of France; and Charles I, king of Spain. By the end of August, Charles had been elected

German king and Holy Roman emperor, as Charles V, in succession to Maximillian, who was his paternal grandfather.

During the summer of 1519, continued controversy swirled about Martin Luther and his teachings. A formal public debate took place at Leipsic, a city under the dominion of George, Duke of Saxony, one of Duke Frederick's uncles. The debate was between a friar named John Eckius and a doctor of Wittenberg named Andreas Carolostadt. Eckius had attacked certain teachings given by Luther, especially those related to papal pardons. Carolostadt, on the other hand, was strong in his defense of Luther. Duke George promised safe conduct to the participants and their audience. Martin Luther decided to attend the debate, not to take part in it, but simply to listen to what was said.

Despite his intentions to the contrary, Luther was compelled to dispute with Eckius. The particular issue under consideration was the authority of the pope. Luther took his familiar stance regarding decrees from the pope. He stated that unless the papal decrees are backed up by the Scriptures, they are invalid.

Eckius took the traditional line of the church by saying that popes are the successors of St. Peter and, as such, they have full spiritual authority over the church. They are, therefore, Christ's vicars on earth. He strongly stated that the bishop of Rome's authority is firmly grounded in God's law.

The debate continued for five days. Eckius was rude, defiant, and guileful in his approach. He wanted to deliver his adversary into the hands of the pope. He stated his reasons in the following manner: "Forasmuch as the church, being a civil body, cannot be without a head, therefore, as it stands with God's law that other civil regiments should not be destitute of their head, so is it a requirement of God's law that the pope should be the head of the universal Church of Christ."

Martin Luther countered this argument by saying that the Church has a head—Jesus Christ Himself. He stated that He is the only head of the Church. "The Church," he said, "does not need any other head because it is a spiritual body, not a temporal one."

Eckius then quoted Jesus' words as recorded in Matthew's Gospel, "Thou art Peter, and upon this rock will I build my Church" (Matthew 16:18).

Luther explained that this verse is a confession of faith, and that Peter represents the universal Church, not just himself. The rock is Jesus Christ and His Word, not Peter.

Endeavoring to find other Scriptures to support his argument, Eckius quoted Jesus' words from John's Gospel, "Feed my sheep" (John 21:16). He said that these words were spoken by the Lord to Peter alone.

Martin Luther pointed out that after Jesus spoke these words to Peter, equal authority was given to all the apostles, and Jesus commanded them to receive the Holy Ghost, and that the Master then went on to say, "whose sins soever ye remit, they are remitted" (John 20:23).

Looking for additional sources of authority to confirm his position, Eckius pointed to the rulings of the Council of Constance. He cited their adherence to the pope, who, according the council, is "to be supreme head of the church." He said that the general council could not err in such an important matter.

Luther said that certain judgments and the authority of the Council of Constance are to be esteemed, but that other matters related to the council are questionable in that some are simply the judgments of men. He said, "This is most certain, that no council has authority to make new articles of faith."

Reports of this debate, which had no specific conclusion, circulated widely throughout Europe. Eckius remained convinced of his position, while Luther held fast to his belief in justification by faith and that the Scriptures are the chief rule of faith and practice.

In 1520, Luther completed three books in which he declared his views. The first was the *Address to the Christian Nobility of the German Nation*, in which he encouraged the German princes to take the reform of the church into their own hands. The second was *A Prelude Concerning the Babylonian Captivity of the Church*, in which he attacked the Roman church and its theology of sacraments. The third was *On the Freedom of a Christian Man*, in which he defined his position on justification and good works. The friars and doctors of Louvain and Cologne condemned Luther's books as heretical. Luther responded to the condemnation by charging the clergymen involved with being obstinate, violent, malicious, and impious. On June 15, 1520, Pope Leo X issued a bull, *Exsurge Domine,* that gave Luther 60 days to recant, but it had no effect upon him or his doctrines.

In his first book to the nobility of Germany, Luther contended against three main papist premises, which were:

1. No temporal or nonreligious magistrate has any power upon the *spirituality, but these have power over the other.

2. Where any place of Scripture, being in controversy, is to be decided, no man may expound the Scripture, or be judge thereof, but only the pope.

3. No man has authority to call a council except the pope.

He also addressed several other matters in the book: the pride of the pope is not to be permitted, too much money is sent from Germany to the pope, priests should be permitted to have wives, liberty ought not to be restrained in eating meats, willful poverty and begging should be abolished, Emperor Sigismund should have stood with John Huss and Jerome, heretics should be convinced by God's Word and not by fire, the first teaching of children should be centered on the Gospel of Jesus Christ and not on the traditions of the Roman church.

After Charles V was crowned king of Germany and Holy Roman Emperor at Aix-la-Chapelle, Pope Leo sent two cardinals to Duke Frederick. Their mission was to convince the duke to take action against Luther. The cardinals first attempted to win the duke's favor by praising his nobility, leadership, family heritage, and other virtues. Then they made two specific requests in the name of the pope—that he would have all of Luther's books burned, and that he would either send Luther to Rome or have him executed.

The duke responded by saying that the pope's own chamberlain had said that Luther should remain in his domain so that he would not be able to influence Roman Catholics in other lands. He then requested that the cardinals ask the pope to give his permission for *learned theologians and doctors to examine Luther's writings and teachings to determine if he was a heretic. If he was found to be one and would not recant, then the duke would not protect him any longer, but he would until then.

Before the cardinals returned to Rome, they gathered as many of Luther's books as they could find and publicly burned them. When Luther heard about this, he gathered a multitude of students and faculty from the University of Wittenberg and held a public burning of the pope's decrees and the bull that was issued against him. This burning of the documents took place on December 10, 1520.

In January 1521, Pope Leo X condemned Luther for heresy and issued a Bull of Excommunication, *Decet*

Romanum Pontificem, against Luther and ordered Emperor Charles V to execute it. Instead, the emperor called a "diet," or council, at Worms, and in April 1521, summoned Luther to appear before him.

A private audience with the emperor and a few other dignitaries was scheduled in the Earl Palatine's palace. Luther was secretly escorted there, but his appearance before the emperor did not remain a secret for long. A large crowd descended upon the palace in an effort to behold the mysterious Luther. The palace guards were unable to hold them back, and many climbed into the galleries where they could see and hear the proceedings. Once when Luther attempted to speak, Ulrick of Pappenheim commanded him to keep silent until such time as he would be asked to speak.

The representative of the bishop of Treves opened the session by saying: "Martin Luther! The sacred and invincible imperial majesty has enjoined, by the consent of all the estates of the holy empire, that you should appear before the throne of our majesty to answer two main questions: Did you write the books which we have stacked in front of you? Will you recant and revoke them, or will you stand by what you have written?"

Luther answered, "I humbly beseech the imperial majesty to grant me liberty and leisure to meditate so that I may satisfy the interrogation made to me without detriment to the Word of God and peril of my own soul."

After the princes debated his request, Eckius, gave the emperor's decision: "The emperor's majesty, of his mere clemency, grants one day for you to meditate with regard to your answer. Tomorrow, at this same hour, you will give us your answer, not in writing, but in your own voice."

The herald then escorted the reformer to his chambers, where Luther prayed and studied to ascertain God's will concerning the answer he should give.

A large crowd gathered to hear Luther's answer the next morning. Eckius said to Luther, "Answer now to the emperor's demand. Will you maintain all your books which you have acknowledged as yours, or will you revoke any part of them, and submit yourself to the authorities God has appointed over you?"

Martin Luther answered, "Considering the fact that our sovereign majesty and your honors require a plain answer, this I say and profess as resolutely as I may, without doubting [uncertainty] or sophistication [possibly means *a misleading argument*], that if I am not convinced otherwise by testimonies of the Scriptures themselves—for I believe not the pope, neither his general councils that have erred many times and have been contrary to themselves—then my conscience is so bound and held captive by these Scriptures and the Word of God that I will not and may not revoke any manner of thing. It would be ungodly and unlawful for me to go against my own conscience. Hereupon I stand and rest. I don't have anything else to say. God have mercy upon me!"

After the princes conferred again, Eckius said to Luther, "The emperor's majesty requires a simple answer from you, either negative or affirmative, to this question: Do you intend to defend all your works as being Christian?"

Luther turned toward the emperor and the noblemen and pleaded with them to honor his conscience. He implored them not to compel him to go against his conscience, which he said was confirmed by the holy Scriptures. He concluded his response with these direct words: "I am tied by the Scriptures."

As nightfall approached, the assembled dignitaries had not reached a final conclusion regarding Luther. They left the proceedings and had Luther escorted back to his lodging. When the group reconvened, a letter from the emperor was read to the assembly. In effect, the letter stated that even though Luther was wrong in not recanting his position, the emperor would honor his promise to keep him safe. Luther could therefore return home. Before he left, however, Luther was told that he would have to return to the emperor's court in twenty-one days.

A fierce campaign raged against Luther during that time. Bills were posted against him, and throughout the empire the name of Luther was on the lips of all—clergy and laity alike. During the three-week reprieve, the emperor and the pope collaborated on a plan, and the emperor directed that a solemn writ of *outlawry be issued against Luther and all those who took his part, and that wherever Luther could be found he be arrested and all his books be seized and burned. Luther took refuge in the Wartburg castle, where he lived in seclusion for eight months. During that time he translated the New Testament into German and wrote a number of pamphlets.

About this same time, King Henry VIII of England wrote against Luther. He reproved Luther for his position concerning papal pardons, and he defended the supremacy of the bishop of Rome. As a result of Henry's written support, the pope honored the king by giving to him and his successors the glorious title, "Defender of the Faith."

In November 1521, Pope Leo X was stricken with a fever and died on December 1. He was forty-seven. Many suspected that he had been poisoned. His successor was named Pope Adrian VI, a scholar who had been a schoolmaster of Emperor Charles. Adrian was a native German who was brought up in Louvain. He was an educated man whose lifestyle was moderate and gentle, unlike some of his predecessors.

Though Adrian was the first pope to respond to the Protestant Reformation by attempting to reform the Roman Catholic church, he still saw Luther as an enemy of the church and the pope. Shortly after his appointment to the role of pontiff, the emperor called for another assembly of the German states to be held in Nuremberg in 1522. Adrian addressed a letter to the assembly in which he expressed his views regarding Martin Luther. The body of his epistle follows:

> We hear that Martin Luther, a new raiser-up of old and damnable heresies, first after the fatherly advertisements of the see apostolic; then, after the sentence also of condemnation awarded against him, and lastly, after the imperial decree of our well-beloved son Charles V, elect emperor of the Romans and Catholic King of Spain, being divulged through the whole nation of Germany, yet has neither been by order restrained, nor of himself has refrained from his madness, but daily more and more ceases not to disturb and replenish the world with new books, fraught full of errors, heresies, arrogance, and sedition, and to infect the country of Germany, and other regions about, with this pestilence; and endeavors still to corrupt simple souls and manners of men with the poison of his morally evil tongue. And, worst of all, has for his supporters not the common sort only, but also diverse personages of the nobility who have begun also to invade the goods of priests contrary to the obedience which they owe to ecclesiastical and temporal persons, and now also at last have grown unto civil war and dissension among themselves.
>
> Do you not consider, O princes and people of Germany, that these be but prefaces and preambles to those evils and mischiefs which Luther, with the sect of his Lutherans, do intend and purpose hereafter? Do you not see plainly, and perceive with your eyes, that this defending of the truth of the Gospel, first begun by the Lutherans to be pretended, is now manifest to be but an invention to spoil your goods, which they have long intended? Or do you think that these sons of iniquity do tend to any other thing than under the name of liberty to displace obedience, and so to open a general license to every man to do what he pleases?

They who refuse to render due obedience to priests, bishops, and the high bishop of all, and who daily before your own faces make their plunder of church-goods and of the things consecrated to God, do you think they will refrain their hands from the spoil of laymen's goods? Do you think they will not pluck from you everything they can get their hands on?

This miserable calamity will at length have an effect upon you, your goods, your houses, wives, children, dominions, possessions, and those temples [churches] which you hallow and reverence, unless you provide a speedy remedy against the same.

Wherefore, we require you, in virtue of that obedience which all Christians owe to God and to blessed Saint Peter, and to his vicar here on earth, that you confer your helping hands to quench this public fire, and endeavor and study, as best you can, how to reduce the said Martin Luther, and all other deceivers of these disturbances and errors, to better conformity and trade both of life and faith. And if they who are infected shall refuse to hear your admonitions, make provisions so that the part that still remains sound is not corrupted by the same disease. When this morally evil canker cannot with supple and gentle medicines be cured, more sharp salves must be proved, and fiery searings. The putrefied members must be cut off from the body, lest the sound parts also be infected.

In such a way God did cast down into hell the schismatical brethren Dathan and Abiram; and he that would not obey the authority of the priest, God commanded to be punished with death. So Peter, prince of the apostles, *denounced sudden death to Ananias and Sappira who lied to God. So the old and godly emperors commanded Jovinian and Priscillian as heretics to be beheaded.

In the same way, Saint Jerome wished that Vigilant, as a heretic, be given to the destruction of his flesh so that his spirit might be saved in the day of the Lord. So also did our predecessors in the Council of Constance condemn John Huss and his fellow, Jerome, to death, and Huss now appears to revive in Luther. If you shall imitate the worthy acts and examples of these forefathers, we do not doubt but God's merciful clemency will relieve His church.

The princes of the empire responded to the pope's call for Luther's punishment with a letter of their own. Here is a paraphrase of the essence of their response:

We understand that his holiness is afflicted with great sorrow with regard to Luther and his sect. We also recognize that the souls who are influenced by him are in danger of eternal perdition. We share in your sorrow.

Many people in Germany hold views similar to Luther's, and this is why formal punishment of Luther has not taken place heretofore. This would lead to great upheaval, possibly even war, within the empire.

Unless these grievances among the general population can be reformed, there is no hope of harmony in this matter between the secular and the church.

Therefore, we recommend that the pope should, with the emperor's consent, summon a Christian council at some convenient place in Germany as soon as possible. At this council people should be encouraged to speak freely.

We recommend that Duke Frederick would see to it that Luther and his followers not be permitted to write, set forth, or print anything else. And that all preachers

in the duke's dominion be forbidden from preaching any
of Luther's views.

Any ministers who do not comply with this
directive should be punished. Any new books should be
submitted to church authorities for approval before being
sold.

Priests who marry or leave their authorities should
be punished by established church officials.

Immediately thereafter, one of Luther's followers,
Andreas Carolostadt of Wittenberg, stirred up the people
to take actions that provoked the pontiff and his *prelates
even more. Among other things, Carolostadt encouraged
the people to throw down images and statues in Romish
churches. In March 1522, Luther returned to Wittenberg to
restore order against these enthusiastic *iconoclasts who
were destroying altars, images, and crucifixes.

Luther's reforming work during subsequent years
included the writing of the Small and Large Catechisms,
sermon books, more than a dozen hymns, over 100 volumes
of tracts, treatises, biblical commentaries, thousands of
letters, and the translation of the whole Bible into German.

With Philipp *Melanchthon and others, Luther
organized the Evangelical churches in the German
territories whose princes supported him. He abolished many
traditional practices, including confession and private mass.

Luther was sixty-three years old when he died on
February 18, 1546. Melanchthon described the reformer's
final hours as follows:

Wednesday last past, February 17, Dr. Martin
Luther sickened of his accustomed malady, to wit, of
the oppression of *humors in the orifice or opening of

his stomach. This sickness took him after supper, with which he vehemently contending, required withdrawal into a by-chamber, and there he rested on his bed two hours, all which time his pains increased. As Dr. Jonas was lying in his chamber, Luther awaked, and prayed him to rise, and to call up Ambrose, his children's schoolmaster, to make a fire in another chamber; into which, when he was newly entered, Albert, Earl of Mansfield, with his wife, and diverse others at that instant came into his chamber.

Finally, feeling his fatal hour approaching, before nine o'clock in the morning, on February 18, he commended himself to God with this devout prayer: "My heavenly Father, eternal and merciful God, you have manifested unto me Your dear Son, our Lord Jesus Christ. I have taught about Him, I have known Him, I love Him as my life, my health, and my redemption. The wicked have persecuted, maligned, and afflicted Him whom I love. Draw my soul to You."

A few moments passed and then Luther repeated a prayer of commendation three times: "I commend my spirit in your hands, you have redeemed me, O God of truth." He followed his prayer with the recitation of a favorite Scripture: "For God so loved the world, that he gave his only begotten Son, that whosoever believeth in him should not perish, but have everlasting life" (John 3:16). At the finish, he closed his eyes and opened them no more.

Luther's enemies rejoiced at his death, thinking perhaps that his work would die with him. But it did not, of course, for it was based on the truth of the Word of God. And like the Word, Luther's doctrines endured and spread the true Gospel of Jesus Christ throughout the world.

13

The Martyrdom of John Hooper, Bishop of Worchester

(1555)

John Hooper was a student and graduate at Oxford University in England. While completing his study in the sciences, he was stirred with a love for the Scriptures and a fervent desire to gain all the knowledge about them that he could. By combining hours of reading and searching the Scriptures with earnest prayer, the grace of the Holy Spirit soon began to open to him the way of true holiness.

As Hooper grew in God's grace and spiritual understanding, the increasing fervency and piety of his character began to draw the displeasure and hatred of other religious persons at the university, and he was soon compelled to leave. He was then retained to manage the property and affairs of Sir Thomas Arundel, until Sir Thomas learned his opinions about religion and, though favoring Hooper himself, found a way to send him with a message to the bishop of Winchester, whom he thought could do him some good and change his opinions. In any case, he required the bishop to return Hooper to him.

Winchester conferred with Hooper for five days, but saw that he could not do the young man any good, and would not take the good that Hooper could give him, and in accordance with Arundel's request, sent Hooper back to him. The bishop commended Hooper's learning and wit, but from that time bore a grudge against him.

Not long after, Hooper learned that malice and danger were building against him in several quarters, so he left the employ of Arundel, and borrowed a horse from a friend, whose life he had rescued from the gallows a short while before, and traveled to the seaside to cross the channel to France. He stayed in Paris for a short time, and then returned to England, where he was employed by a Master Sentlow until he again was in danger of his life because of his doctrines. Through various means he traveled to Ireland and then through France and on into Germany, where he met a number of learned men at Basil, and especially at Zurich in Switzerland. There he became friends with a Master Bullinger, and there also married his wife who was a Burgundian, and began the diligent study of the Hebrew language.

On January 28, 1547, King Henry VIII died, and his only son, Edward VI became king of England on that day.

Edward was not yet ten years old at the time, having been born to Henry's third wife, Jane Seymour, on October 12, 1537. In his will, Henry had designated a council of 16 to rule England while Edward was a minor, but this arrangement did not last long, and Edward's uncle, Edward Seymour, duke of Somerset, assumed control as protector. Two years later, in 1549, Somerset fell from power and John Dudley, duke of Northumberland, became regent to rule during Edward's minority.

King Edward VI was educated by Protestant tutors and, as a result, favored Protestant reforms in the Church of England. *The Book of Common Prayer* was compiled by Archbishop Thomas Cranmer and first published during Edward's reign.

Shortly after Edward became King, Hooper decided to return to England to help forward the Lord's work to the best of his ability. He thanked his friends in Zurich for their kindness and humanity toward him, and told them that he was leaving. In reply, Master Bullinger said to him:

> Master Hooper, although we are sorry to part with your company for our own cause, yet we have much greater causes for which to rejoice. It is both for your sake, and especially for the cause of Christ's true religion, that you shall now return out of long banishment into your native country again. So not only may you enjoy your own private liberty, but also the cause and state of Christ's Church will get along better because of your return. We have no doubt of it.

> Another cause, moreover, why we rejoice with you and for you is this: that you shall go from exile into liberty, and leave here a barren, sour, and unpleasant country, rude and savage, and go into a land flowing with milk and honey, full of all pleasure and fertility.

Notwithstanding our rejoicing, we have one fear and care that perhaps in your being absent and being so far from us, or else having such an abundance of wealth and blessings in your new welfare, and plenty of all things, and in your flourishing honors even become a bishop, and where you will find so many new friends, that you will forget us, your old acquaintances and well-wishers.

Nevertheless, to whatever degree you may forget and shake us off, yet you can be sure that we will not forget our old friend and fellow, Master Hooper. And if you will please not to forget us, then I pray you let us hear from you.

Hooper responded: "Neither the pleasure of country, nor pleasure of goods, nor newness of friends, will ever induce me to forget you, my friends and benefactors. From time to time I will write to you and let you know how everything is going. But the last news of all I will not be able to write." He took Master Bullinger's hand, "For there I shall have the most pains, and there you will hear that I was burned to ashes."

When Hooper returned to London, he started preaching continuously—most of the time twice a day, and never less than once a day. So many people came to hear his messages that often the church would be so full that those who came late could get in no further than the door. He was earnest in his doctrine, eloquent in his speech, perfect in the Scriptures, and untiring in his efforts.

As he began his life work, so he continued to the end. Neither his labor nor painstaking could break him, promotion change him, or delicious meals corrupt him. His life was so pure and good that no slander could attach itself to him. He was strong in body and mind, and was in every way a perfect minister of the Gospel of Jesus Christ. To many he seemed to be quite severe, and he might have wished to be more popular to people, but he knew what he had to be to best do his work. Once an honest citizen, who had a certain grudge on his conscience, went to Hooper's house for counsel, but when he saw Hooper's somber and grave appearance he did not dare to talk to him because he felt ashamed of himself. So he sought counsel from other men.

Some time after he returned, Hooper was called to preach before the king, and after was made bishop of Gloucester, a position he held for two years. He did so well in that office that even his enemies could find no fault with him. After that, he was made bishop of Worchester.

Even though a considerable reformation of religion had started in the Church of England, the bishops still wore the elaborate apparel that popish bishops wore during certain ceremonies. To Hooper, such ceremonial garments were distasteful because some were worn for superstitious reasons, such as the geometrical cap with four angles that divided the world into four parts, and he requested that the king either discharge him from his bishop's office, or else excuse him from any ceremonies in which the garments were worn. The king granted his request immediately.

Nevertheless, the other bishops stoutly defended the wearing of the ceremonial garments, and said that it was a trivial matter, and the fault was not in the things themselves but in abuses of them. They added that Hooper should not be so stubborn in so light a matter, and that his insistence on having his own way should not be allowed.

This argument between Hooper and the bishops over the wearing of ceremonial clothing caused many good Christians to sorrow, and many of Hooper's adversaries to rejoice. Finally, the bishops got the upper hand and Hooper agreed that sometimes he would attend a ceremony wearing the apparel with the other bishops. When appointed to preach before the king, he appeared in full ceremonial dress, including a four-squared cap that sat awkwardly on his well-rounded head.

When Master Hooper entered into his diocese, he sought every way possible to train up his flock in the true way of salvation. No father in his household, or gardener in his garden, or vinedresser in his vineyard, was more or better occupied than he was in going about his towns and villages to preach to his people. When he was not busy with this, he spent his time listening to public problems, visiting schools, or in private study and prayer. All in his flock were treated alike, whether rich or poor, young or old, well-educated or not. He conducted his life in a way that it might be a light and example to the Church and churchmen, and a perpetual lesson and sermon to the rest.

As a family man, Hooper devoted considerable time to the Christian training of his children. He wanted them to be well educated and well-mannered, and to love the Word of God as he did. If you entered his home, you would imagine you had entered into some church or temple, for all about you there were signs and senses of godly virtue, pious and honest conversation, and reading of the holy Scriptures. There was never any foolishness or idleness, no displays of wealth, no dishonest word, no swearing, only a godly atmosphere.

His handling of finances, both personal and within the church, was above reproach. Except for the basic needs of his family, Hooper used the money from his bishop's office for hospitality to others. Frequently he had banquet-like meals prepared for beggars and poor folks of the region. His servants said that every day he would invite to dinner a certain number of poor people, who were served four at a time with hot and wholesome meals, and then he would speak to them about the Lord's prayer, certain articles of faith, and the ten commandments. Only then would he himself sit down to eat. But all of Hooper's good work soon came to an end.

In November 1552 King Edward VI became ill, and subsequently died on July 6, 1553, three months before his sixteenth birthday. Although John Dudley, duke of Northumberland, tried to divert the succession of the throne to Edward's cousin, Lady Jane Grey, who was a Protestant, he failed, and Edward's half sister Mary, a Roman Catholic, succeeded him as Mary I.

During the later years of the reign of King Henry VIII, when an increasingly Protestant Church of England was brought into being, Mary was harshly treated until she reluctantly agreed with Henry's divorce of her mother, Catherine, and renounced Roman Catholicism under oath. In truth, however, she kept her Catholic faith and never gave it up.

Soon after succeeding to the throne, Mary restored Catholicism to England and reestablished the traditional services and the authority of the pope. A year later she married Philip II, the future king of Spain (1556), son of Holy Roman Emperor Charles V. Together they ruled England for the remainder of her life. It was a rule during which she would earn the epithet of "Bloody Mary" for her persecution and burning of about 300 Protestants for their religious beliefs.

Shortly after her coronation, John Hooper, bishop of Worchester, was one of the first that she summoned to appear before her. Although Hooper knew the evil intents Queen Mary might have toward him—he was warned by many of his friends to get away and take care of himself— he would not leave England. "Once I did flee," he said, "but now I am thoroughly prepared to face what lies ahead. I will live and I will die with my sheep."

Hooper appeared before the queen on September 1, 1553, and was greeted with contemptuous reproach, scorn, and abuse. Nevertheless, he freely and boldly told about his life as a bishop and his doctrines. At the end of the hearing, he was sentenced to prison; not because of his religion, they said, but because he owed the queen money, which, of course, he did not.

On March 19, 1554, Hooper was called to appear before Lord Chancellor Winchester and other commissioners who represented the queen. Winchester asked him if he was married. Hooper answered, "Yes, my lord, and I will not be unmarried until death unmarries me."

For some reason, perhaps because Roman Catholic clergy did not marry, his response was greeted with loud outcries and laughs, and they used gestures that were grossly improper for the place where they were. The bishop of Chichester, Dr. Day, called Hooper a "hypocrite," and lashed at him with angry and scornful words. Bishop Tonstal called Hooper a "beast," and so did a clerk named Smith and others who were there.

Tonstal, bishop of Durham, asked Hooper if he believed in the corporal presence in the sacrament; that is, that Christ's actual body was in the sacrament. Hooper said plainly that there was no such thing, and neither did he believe any such thing. Lord Chancellor Winchester then asked him what authority caused him not to believe in the corporeal presence. Hooper replied, "The authority of God's Word." At that, the clerks were instructed to write that he was married and had said he would not leave his wife, and that he did not believe in the corporeal presence in the sacrament. For these reasons, he deserved being removed from his bishop's office.

On January 7, 1555, while in *Fleet Prison, Master Hooper wrote about his ordeals:

The first of September, 1553, I was committed to the Fleet from Richmond, to have the liberty of the prison. Six days afterward, I paid the warden five pounds sterling in fees for that liberty. Immediately upon receiving the payment, the warden complained to Stephen Gardiner, bishop of Winchester, and then I was committed to close prison, without liberty, for a quarter of a year in the Tower-chamber of the Fleet, where I was treated severely.

Once, by the means of a good and gentle woman, I was given liberty to come down to dinner and supper, but I was not permitted to speak with any of my friends, and had to return to my cell immediately after. Nevertheless, when I came down for dinner, the warden and his wife picked quarrels with me, and then complained bitterly about me to their great friend the bishop of Winchester.

After several months, Babington, the warden, and his wife quarreled with me about the wicked mass, and the warden resorted to the bishop of Winchester and obtained permission to put me into the worst part of the prison, where I have been for a long time in this vile and stinking chamber, with nothing for my bed but a little pad of straw for my mattress, a rotten blanket, and a cloth case with a few feathers in it for my pillow—until God provided good people to send me clean and fresh bedding.

Open sewers run on both sides of this prison, and the stench is unbearable. I am sure they are the cause of the various illnesses I have experienced and am now experiencing.

There are bars and hasps on the door of my cell and chains upon me. I have mourned, called, and cried for help, but even though Warden Babington has known that several times I was near death, and when the poor men of the ward have called for help for me, he has commanded that my cell doors stay locked and that none of his men should come to me, saying, "Let him alone. If he dies, it will be a good riddance."

I paid that same warden twenty shillings a week for my board, and also paid for my man's board, until I was wrongly deprived of my *bishopric, and since then I have paid him as the best gentleman does in his own house, but still he uses me worse and meaner than if I were the lowest person who ever came here.

My aide, William Downton, has also been imprisoned. The warden stripped him of his clothes to search for letters, but could find none except the names of a few good people who gave me money to relieve me in this prison. To cause them trouble, the warden gave their names to Stephen Gardiner, God's enemy and mine.

I have suffered imprisonment for almost eighteen months. My goods, living, family, friends, and comfort have been taken from me. By just account, the queen owes me 80 pounds. She has put me into prison and gives nothing to supply me, and does not allow anyone to come to me with any relief. I am with a wicked man and woman, and I see no remedy, except God's help, but that I will die in prison before I am judged. But I commit my cause to God, whose will be done, whether it be by life or death.

On January 22, 1555, Warden Babington was commanded to bring Master Hooper before the bishop of Winchester and other bishops and commissioners at Winchester's house, at St. Mary Overy's. The bishop of Winchester urged Hooper to forsake the "evil and corrupt doctrine," as he called it, that was preached in the days of King Edward IV, and to return to the unity of the Catholic

Church and acknowledge the pope as head of that church, according to the determination of the whole parliament of England. If Hooper would bow to the pope's holiness, Winchester assured him that he would receive the pope's blessing, and the Queen's mercy, even as he himself and other of his brethren had received it.

Hooper answered that inasmuch as the pope taught doctrine that was altogether contrary to the doctrine of Christ, he was not worthy to be head of the church, and so he would in no way give in to any such illegal authority. Further, he said, the Roman Catholic Church is not the true Church at all. The true Church only hears the voice of her spouse, and flees from the voice of strangers. "However," he said, "if there is any point that I don't know about in which I have offended the queen's majesty, I will most humbly submit myself to her mercy, if her mercy may be had with a safe conscience and without the displeasure of God." The bishop answered that the queen would show no mercy to the Pope's enemies. Whereupon Babington was commanded to return Hooper to Fleet Prison.

On January 28, Winchester and the commissioners sat in judgment at St. Mary Overy's Church and examined Hooper again. After much reasoning and debating, they set Hooper aside and examined a Master Rogers. After the examinations about 4:00 in the afternoon, the bishop directed the two sheriffs of London to conduct the prisoners to the *Compter in Southwark, where they were to remain until 9:00 in the morning to see if they would relent and come home to the Roman Catholic Church.

On their way out of the church door, Master Hooper went ahead with one sheriff, while Master Rogers followed with the other. When Hooper noticed that Rogers was lingering back, he waited until he caught up and said to him, "Come, brother Rogers, must we two be the first to take this matter in hand, and begin to set fire to these dry sticks?"

10111213141516171819202122232425262728293031

"Yes, sir," Rogers replied, "by God's grace."

"Don't doubt but that God will give us strength," Hooper said.

As they continued on, there were so many people in the street, who rejoiced at their steadfastness, that they had trouble passing through them.

The next morning, the sheriffs brought them again before the bishop and his commissioners. After a long and earnest talk, it became apparent to them that Hooper would by no means give in to them, so they condemned him to be degraded, as Huss and Jerome of Prague had been, and read to him his condemnation. Rogers was then brought before them and was also entreated to submit to their demands, but he, too, refused and was likewise condemned. Both men were then turned over to the secular powers, the two sheriffs of London, who took the men to the Clink, a prison near Winchester's house, where they were to remain until night.

After dark, Hooper was led by one of the sheriffs of London and his men, who had many clubs and weapons, through the bishop of Winchester's house, over the London bridge, and through the city to Newgate Prison. Along the way some of the sheriffs men went ahead and put out the candles of the street vendors, who used to sit with them burning at night, in fear that an attempt might be made to take Hooper away from them by force. Or perhaps they were burdened by their evil consciences, and thought that darkness was best suited for such treacherous business.

Nevertheless, many people had heard that Hooper was coming, and came out of their houses with lights and saluted him, praising and thanking God for his holding fast to the true doctrine that he had taught them, and desiring that God would strengthen him to the end. As Hooper passed by, he requested the people to make earnest prayers to God for him, and so went through the market center of Cheapside and was delivered to the keeper of Newgate, where he remained for six days. During that time, no one was allowed to visit him or talk to him except his keepers and those that were given permission.

Several times, Bonner, bishop of London, and others, visited Hooper and tried to persuade him to relent and become a member of their anti-Christian church. They used every means they could devise: twisting the Scriptures and ancient writings to wrong meanings, according to their usual ways; outward gentleness and friendship; many great offers of worldly goods and properties; strong threats; but nothing they said or did moved Hooper from his steadfast faith in Christ and the truth of God's Word.

When they saw that they could not reclaim him so they could use him for their own purposes, they spread false rumors and reports that he had recanted in an effort to discredit him and the doctrines of Christ that he taught. When the false news was spread around it was believed by some of the weaker ones, especially when it was often confirmed by the bishop of London and others, and it wasn't long before Master Hooper heard about the effect the lies were having. He was saddened that some people would give credit to false rumors about him and wrote a public letter:

> The report abroad (as I am incredibly informed) is that I, John Hooper, a condemned man for the cause of Christ, should now, after sentence of death (being in Newgate, a prisoner, and looking daily for execution), recant and renounce under oath that which I have preached up to now.

> And this talk arises from this—that the bishop of London and his chaplains come to see me. I have spoken and do speak with them when they come, for I do not fear their arguments. Neither is death terrible to me. And I am more confirmed in the truth which I have preached up to now, by their coming.

I have left all things of the world, and I have
suffered great pains and imprisonment, but I thank God
that I am as ready to suffer death as any mortal man
may be. I have taught the truth with my tongue and with
my pen up to now, and shortly hereafter I shall confirm
that same truth by God's grace with my blood.

On Monday, February 4, 1555, the jail-keeper told
Hooper to begin to prepare himself because he was going
to be sent to Gloucester to suffer death. Upon hearing this,
Hooper, who was formerly the bishop of Gloucester,
rejoiced exceedingly, lifting his eyes and hands toward
heaven, and praising God that He saw it good to send him
back among the people over whom he was pastor, and there
to confirm with his death the truth that he had taught them.
He did not doubt but that God would give him the strength
to die well for His glory. And immediately he sent to his
servant's house for his boots, spurs, and cloak, so that he
would be ready to ride when he was called.

Four o'clock the next morning, the keeper and others
entered his cell to search for anything he might have written.
Then he was led by the sheriffs of London and their officers
out of Newgate to a place not far from St. Dunstan's church
in Fleet Street, where six of the Queen's guards were
appointed to receive him and conduct him to Gloucester.
There they turned him over to the sheriff, who, with the
Lord Chandos, Master Wicks, and other commissioners,
were appointed to execute him.

In London the Queen's guards took Hooper to the
Angel, where he broke his fast with them, and ate a much
larger meal than he usually did. After the break, he leaped
cheerfully on his horse without help, even though there was
a hood over his head under his hat so that he wouldn't be
recognized. As Hooper traveled joyfully toward Gloucester
with his guards, and it became time to stop for food or rest

or for the night, they always asked him where he usually stopped to eat and rest or lodge along the route between London and Gloucester; and wherever he said, that is where they stopped.

On Thursday, they came to a town in his diocese called Cirencester, fifteen miles from Gloucester, about 11 o'clock in the morning, and there stopped to eat. The woman of the house had always hated the truth, and had spoken all kinds of evil about Master Hooper. But now, knowing the reason why he was going to Gloucester, she showed him all the friendship she could, and in tears confessed that she had often said that if he were ever put on trial he would not hold to his doctrine.

After dinner they continued to Gloucester and arrived there about five o'clock in the afternoon. For over a mile along the road outside the town, people had gathered to see Hooper, and were crying and mourning about his condition. So much so, that one of the guards rode rapidly into town to seek aid from the mayor and sheriffs because they were afraid the people would try to take Hooper from them. The officers and their attendants went to the city gate and commanded the people to stay home, but there was never any indication that a rescue or violence would be attempted.

Hooper was lodged at one Ingram's house in Gloucester, and that night, as he had done every night on the trip, he ate his meal quietly and slept soundly for some time. Then he arose and prayed until morning. He then asked that he be allowed to spend his time in a small room where he could pray and talk with God. So all that day, except for a short time at meals and speaking with whoever the guard allowed to talk to him, he spent in prayer.

One of his visitors, Sir Anthony Kingston, a *knight, who in the past had seemed to be his friend, and was now appointed by the Queen to be one of the commissioners to see to his execution, burst into tears when he was brought into Hooper's room and found him praying. At first, Hooper did not know him, and then Kingston said, "Why, my lord, do you not know me, an old friend of yours, Anthony Kingston?"

Hooper replied, "Yes, Master Kingston, I now know you well, and am glad see you in health, and do praise God for it."

Kingston said, "But I am sorry to see you in this case, for I understand you have come here to die. But, alas, consider that life is sweet and death is bitter. Therefore, seeing that you may have life, desire to live, for life after this may do good."

To this Hooper replied, "Indeed it is true, Master Kingston, I have come here to end this life, and to suffer death here, because I will not deny the former truth that I once taught among you in this diocese and elsewhere. But I thank you for your friendly counsel, although it is not as friendly as I could have wished it. It is true, Master Kingston, that death is bitter and life is sweet. But, alas, consider that the death to come is more bitter, and the life to come is more sweet. Therefore, for the desire and love I have to the one, and the terror and fear of the other, I do not so much regard this death nor esteem this life. I have settled myself, through the strength of God's Holy Spirit, to pass patiently through the torments and extremities of the fire now prepared for me, rather than deny the truth of His Word. In the meantime, I do desire you, and others, to commend me to God's mercy in your prayers."

Kingston said, "Well, my lord, I see there is no remedy for this matter, therefore I will leave. But I do so with gratitude in my heart to God that he permitted me to know you. Through you God appointed to call me back to himself, since I was His lost child."

Hooper replied, "I highly praise God for it, and I pray God that you will continually live in fear of Him."

After these words and many others, Master Kingston left, with bitter tears running down his cheeks. Master Hooper was crying as much, and told Kingston that all the troubles he had sustained in prison had not caused him as much sorrow as their parting.

That same afternoon, a blind boy kept pleading with the guard to see Hooper and was finally allowed to talk to him. Not long before this, the boy had been imprisoned in Gloucester for confessing the truth of God's Word. Master Hooper, after questioning the boy about his faith and the cause of his imprisonment, looked at him tearfully and said, "Ah, poor boy, God has taken your outward sight from you for reasons that are known only to Him. But He has given you another sight which is far more precious, for He has endued your soul with the eyes of knowledge and faith. God give you the grace to pray continually to Him, so that you will never lose that sight, for then you would be blind both in body and in soul."

That same night, Hooper was committed by the guards, their commission having expired, into the custody of the sheriffs of Gloucester, who, with the mayor and aldermen went to Hooper's lodging and took him by the hand. When they did, Hooper said:

> Master mayor, I give most hardy thanks to you, and to the rest of your brethren, that you have taken me, a prisoner and a condemned man, by the hand. To my rejoicing, it is apparent that your old love and friendship toward me is not altogether extinguished. I trust, also, that all the things I taught you in the past are not utterly forgotten. Those things that I taught when I was appointed by the godly King that is now dead to be your bishop and pastor. For this true and sincere doctrine,

which I will not consider as being false and heresy as many other men do, I have been sent here, as I am sure you know, by the Queen's command to die. And I have come here where I taught it, to confirm it with my blood.

Although the sheriffs and those with them were saddened by his words, they were determined to lodge him in the common jail, but the guard pleaded for him and told how quietly, mildly, and patiently he had behaved himself in all ways, and added that any child could guard him as well, and they would rather continue watching over him themselves than have him to taken to a common jail.

So it was decided that he would remain in Robert Ingram's house, and the sheriffs, sergeants, and other officers watched over him that night. Hooper asked if he might go to bed early that night, since he had many things to remember, and so he did at five o'clock in the afternoon and slept soundly until late in the night, and then arose and prayed until the early hours. When he got up that morning, he asked that no one come into his room so that he might be alone until the hour of his execution.

About eight o'clock, on February 9, 1555, Sir John Bridges and Lord Chandos, who had many men with him— Sir Anthony Kingston, Sir Edmund Bridges, and other commissioners who were appointed to see to the execution—came to the house. At nine o'clock Master Hooper was told to prepare himself, for the time was at hand, and he was immediately brought down from his room by the sheriffs, who had with them several clubs and weapons. When he saw the many weapons, Hooper said to the sheriffs, "Master Sheriffs, I am no traitor, and you have no need to make such a work to take me to the place where I must suffer. If you had told me, I would have gone alone to the stake, and have troubled none of you."

It was a market day in Gloucester, and about seven thousand people had gathered to see how Hooper would behave toward death. He was led between the two sheriffs, like a lamb going to the place of slaughter, in a gown belonging to his host, his hat on his head, and a staff with which to steady himself because sciatica pain resulting from his long stay in prison sometimes caused him to stumble. He smiled cheerfully at all whom he recognized, and many said afterward that they had never known him to be so cheerful and healthy looking as he did then.

When they came to his place of execution, Hooper immediately knelt down to prayer since he was not permitted to talk to the people. After he had prayed for a while, a box was brought and put upon a stool, with, it was said, his pardon from the Queen if he would turn from his beliefs and teachings. When he saw it he cried, "If you love my soul, away with it! If you love my soul, away with it!"

When he finished praying, he went to the stake and took off his host's gown and gave it to the sheriffs, asking them to give it back to the owner. He also took off the rest of his clothes down to his jacket and hose, which he would have burned. But the sheriffs would not permit it, such was their greed, and so Hooper obediently removed his jacket, stockings, and first undergarment, which left him wearing only his undershirt. The guard gave him three sacks of a pound each of gunpowder, and Hooper took back one of his stockings and tied his shirt between his legs to hold one of the sacks, and held the other two in his armpits.

Hooper then asked the people to pray the Lord's Prayer with him, and to pray for him, which they did with much crying while he was suffering. He then went up to the stake and an iron hoop was placed around his chest and the stake to hold him there while he was burning. When they offered to similarly bind his neck and legs with two other hoops of iron, he refused them.

In a few moments, the man who was to make the fire came to him and asked for his forgiveness. Hooper asked the man why he should forgive him, that he knew of no offense that the man had committed against him. "O sir!" the man said, weeping, "I am appointed to make the fire." Master Hooper replied, "In that you do nothing to offend me. God forgive you your sins, and do your work, I pray you."

Dried reeds for kindling were put around him, and Hooper took two bundles of them, kissed them, and put one under each arm below the sacks of gunpowder. He then motioned with his hand to where he wanted the reeds placed around him and the faggots placed over them, and pointed out the places were there were not enough of one or the other. When he was satisfied with the placement, the fire was set.

But too many green faggots had been used, almost as many as two horses could carry, and it took some time for the reeds to ignite the faggots. Finally the fire burned around him, but it was a dark and cold morning and there was a strong wind that blew the flames away from Hooper so that he was not touched by the fire. After awhile, a few dry faggots were brought and a new fire kindled with them, for there were no more reeds that could be used. But the fire only burned underneath the faggots and had no power on the outside because of the wind, so it only burned his hair a little and caused his skin to swell. All this time, Hooper prayed, mildly and quietly, as one without pain, "O Jesus, the Son of David, have mercy upon me, and receive my soul."

When the fire from the dried faggots started to die out without igniting the green faggots, Hooper wiped his eyes with his hands and said, with an indifferent loud voice,

"For God's love, good people, let me have more fire!" All this time the lower part of his body was burning, for there were so few dried faggots that the fire did not burn strongly enough to reach his upper body.

After awhile, more dried faggots were brought and a third fire kindled that was stronger than the other two. This fire broke the sacks of gunpowder but they did him little good, neither exploding nor increasing his burning because of the strength of the wind that blew the fire away from him. During this slow burning, Hooper prayed in a somewhat loud voice, "Lord Jesus, have mercy upon me. Lord Jesus, have mercy upon me. Lord Jesus, receive my spirit." These were the last words he was heard to speak.

But even when his mouth was black and his tongue swollen, his lips could still be seen moving in prayer until they shrunk back into his gums. During these moments, Hooper struck repeatedly at his chest, or heart, with his hands until one of his arms fell off, and then continued striking his chest with the other hand while fat, water, and blood spurted out his fingertips. When the flames suddenly flared up in great power, Hooper struck his chest only once more as his strength gave out and his hand stuck to the iron band around his chest. At the same moment, his body fell forward against the band and he gave up his spirit.

Hooper was about forty-five minutes to an hour in the fire. Even so he was like a lamb, patiently suffering the agony without moving backwards or forwards or to the sides—he was in agony unbearable except by God's grace, and yet died as quietly as a child in bed. Now he reigns as a blessed martyr in the joys of heaven prepared for the faithful in Christ before the foundations of the world. For his faithfulness, all Christians are bound to praise God.

14

The Martyrdom of Dr. Rowland Taylor, Parish Clergyman (1555)

Hadley [or Hadleigh], in Suffolk, was one of the first towns in England to receive the true Word of God. Here the Gospel of Christ had great success and took such root that many men and women in the parish of Hadley were extremely knowledgeable about the Scriptures. Some could even be found who had often read the entire Bible, could recite some of St. Paul's epistles by heart, and could give a godly scriptural reply in any controversy. Their children and servants were trained so much in the right knowledge of God's Word, that the town seemed as though it was a university of educated people rather than a town of cloth-making and laborers. What was the most commendable, however, is that they were for the most part faithful followers of God's Word in their living.

All this was due to the efforts of Dr. Rowland Taylor. When he was assigned to the church and its assets in Hadley, he did not turn it over to the care of some farmer and gather in the profits, and set in an unlearned priest to take care of the spiritual needs of the parishioners, as many other bishops did. Instead, he left the archbishop of Canterbury, Thomas Cranmer, in whose house he lived, and moved into the parsonage in Hadley so he could be among the people in his charge.

Taylor was a mild man, humble and without pride. None in his parish were so poor that they could not approach him as a child to a father, and none were so rich that he would not rebuke them when they sinned. His preaching was forceful, firm, and true to the Word of God. He was honest in all things and feared no man when it came to holding fast to the truth of the Scriptures. His wife was an honest, discreet, and sober woman, and their children were brought up in the fear of God and well educated. Altogether, they were a good and godly family and a credit to the name of Jesus Christ.

In his parish, Dr. Taylor was a good shepherd among his flock, watching over them so that they would not be hurt or corrupted by outsiders, and being to them a light in God's house and a candlestick burning brightly for them to imitate and follow. All this he continued doing throughout the reign of that innocent and holy king, Edward VI. But when Edward died in 1553 and his half-sister, "Bloody Mary," succeeded him to the throne of England, the godly Dr. Taylor did not escape the papist violence that overthrew the true doctrine of the Gospel of Jesus Christ, that persecuted with sword and fire all those who would not agree to bow again to the Roman pope as supreme head of the universal Church, and that brought back into the Church of England all the errors, superstitions, and idolatries that were clearly disapproved and justly condemned by God's Word.

In the beginning of this rage of the antichrist, two of Dr. Taylor's parishioners, an attorney named Foster and a tradesman named Clerk, hired John Averth, parson of Aldham and a popish idolater, to hold a mass, with all its superstitious forms, in Hadley's parish church on the Monday before Easter. They obtained entrance to the church building and secretly built up their altar with all its idolatries, but it was broken down by some faithful parishioners who saw them. So the next day they built it up again, and Foster and Clerk brought in Averth with all his implements and garments for the popish pageant, and placed guards with swords and shields around the altar so that Averth would not be disturbed during the mass. Then they gathered a few of the Romish believers and barred the front doors of the church building, but a side door was left unbarred and only latched. They then started their mass.

At that time, Dr. Taylor was in the parsonage, some distance from the church building, praying and studying the Word of God. When he heard the church bells ring, he thought it meant that he was needed at the church, for the bells were often used for that purpose at times other than when church services were being held, and so he went to the church. There he found the church's main doors barred, but entered by the unbarred side door. Inside he saw Averth in his robes, with a broad new shaven crown, ready to begin his popish sacrifice, and many men with drawn swords and shields around the altar guarding him.

Dr. Taylor said to Averth, "Who made you so bold as to enter into this church of Christ and profane and defile it with this abominable idolatry?"

With that Foster raged against Taylor and said, "You traitor! What are you doing here disturbing the Queen's proceedings?"

Taylor answered, "I am no traitor, but I am the shepherd that God, my Lord Christ, has appointed to feed this flock. Therefore I have good authority to be here, and I command you, in the name of God, to get away from this place, and not dare to here poison Christ's flock."

Then said Foster, "You treacherous heretic, will you make a commotion and violently resist the Queen's proceedings?"

Taylor answered, "I am not making a commotion, but it is you papists that make commotions and disturbances. I resist only with God's Word against your popish idolatries, which are against God's Word, the Queen's honor, and tend to utterly overthrow and ruin this kingdom of England."

Then Foster and his armed men took hold of Dr. Taylor and forced him out of the church, and the popish priest proceeded with his Romish idolatry. Dr. Taylor's wife had followed him into the church, and when she saw him violently thrust out of his own church, she knelt down and held up her hands, and with a loud voice said, "I beseech God, the righteous Judge, to avenge the injury that this popish idolater does to the blood of Christ." At that, they forced her out of the church, also, and shut the doors, for they were afraid that the people who were gathering would tear Averth into pieces.

Thus you can see how, without the consent of the people, the popish mass was again set up with battle array, swords and shields, and with violence and tyranny.

A day or two later, Foster and Clerk wrote a letter to Stephen Gardiner, who was bishop of Winchester and Lord

Chancellor, complaining about Dr. Taylor. The bishop responded to their letter by writing to Dr. Taylor and commanding him to come and appear before him within a certain number of days. When Taylor's friends heard about this they were extremely sorry and grieved, for they knew what the result would be, and so they went to Taylor and urged him to flee. But he said to them, "Dear friends, I most heartily thank you for so tenderly caring for me. And although I know that I can look for neither justice nor truth at the hands of my adversaries, I know that my cause is so good and righteous, and the truth so strong on my side, that by God's grace I will go and appear before them and resist to their faces their false doings."

Then one of his friends spoke for all and said, "Master doctor, we think it best that you not do so. You have sufficiently done your duty, and have testified to the truth both by your godly sermons and by resisting the parson of Aldham and those that came here to bring back the popish mass. And since our savior Christ willed and told us that when they persecute us in one city we should flee into another (see Matthew 10:23), we think that your fleeing at this time would be best. That way, you would keep yourself for another time, when the church will have great need of diligent teachers and godly pastors."

"O," said Dr. Taylor, "what will you have me to do? I am now old, and have already lived too long to see these terrible and most wicked days. Flee yourselves, and do as your conscience leads you. For myself, I am fully determined, with God's grace, to go to the bishop, and to his face tell him that what he does to me is insignificant. God will raise up teachers after me that will teach His people with more diligence and fruit than I have done. For God will not forsake His church, even though for a time He tries and corrects us. As for me, I believe before God that I shall never be able to do God as good a service as I may do now. Nor shall I ever have so glorious a calling as I now have, nor so great mercy offered to me for acceptance as God offers me now. Therefore, I beseech you and all my other friends to pray for me. If you will, I don't doubt but that God will give me strength and His Holy Spirit."

When Dr. Taylor's friends saw that he was steadfast and determined to go, they wept openly and commended him to God.

Dr. Taylor and a servant of his, John Hull, traveled to London. On the way, Hull constantly tried to get Dr. Taylor to run away and not go to the bishop, offering to go with him and serve him wherever he went, and even give his life for him in any trouble. But Dr. Taylor would not agree to it and said to him, "O John! Shall I give heed to your counsel and worldly persuasion and leave my flock in this danger? Remember the good shepherd Christ. He not only fed His flock, but also died for His flock. I must follow Him, and with God's grace I will do so."

Shortly after, Dr. Taylor presented himself to the bishop of Winchester, Stephen Gardiner, who was also Lord Chancellor of England. When Gardiner saw Dr. Taylor, he reviled him by calling him an unprincipled man, traitor, heretic, and many other offensive things, as is the Romish custom in such cases. Dr. Taylor listened patiently and then said, "My lord, I am neither a traitor nor a heretic, but a true subject and a faithful Christian man. I have come here as you commanded me, so that I might learn the reason why your lordship has sent for me."

The bishop replied, "Have you come, you villain? Have you no shame that you dare to look me in the face? Do you not know who I am?"

"Yes," said Dr. Taylor, "I know who you are. You are Dr. Stephen Gardiner, bishop of Winchester and Lord Chancellor, and yet only a mortal man, I think. But if I should be afraid of your lordly looks, why are you not afraid of God, the Lord of us all? How dare you not be ashamed to look any Christian man in the face, seeing you have forsaken the truth, denied our Savior Christ and His Word, and acted contrary to your oath and the things you wrote. How will you look when you appear before the judgment seat of Christ and answer to your oath that you made first to King Henry the Eighth, who is well remembered, and afterward to his son, King Edward the Sixth?"

The bishop answered, "Tut-tut, that was as Herod's oath to Salome: unlawful, and so worthy to be broken. I have done well in breaking it, and I thank God that I have come home to our mother the catholic Church of Rome, and that is what I wish you to do."

Dr. Taylor answered, "Should I forsake the true Church of Christ, which is founded upon the true foundation of the apostles and prophets, to approve those lies, errors, superstitions, and idolatries that the popes and their company on this day so blasphemously approve? No, God forbid. Let the pope and his followers return to our Savior Christ and His Word, throw out of the Church the abominable idolatries that he maintains, and then Christian men will return to him. You wrote truthfully against him yourself, and were sworn against him."

"I told you," said the bishop," it was as Herod's oath, unlawful, and so should be broken and not kept. Our holy father, the pope, has released me from it."

Dr. Taylor replied, "But you shall not be so discharged before Christ, Who doubtless will require your oath to be kept, and from Whose obedience no man can pardon you, neither the pope nor any of his followers."

"I see," said the bishop," that you are an arrogant and devious person, and an absolute fool."

"My lord," said Dr. Taylor, "stop using abusive language to me, it is not suitable for one in such authority as you are. For I am a Christian man, and you know that the Scripture says, 'whosoever shall say to his brother, Raca, shall be in danger of the council: but whosoever shall say, Thou fool, shall be in danger of hell fire.'" (See Matthew 5:22.)

Then the bishop said, "You have resisted the Queen's proceedings, and would not allow the parson of Aldham, a very virtuous and devout priest, to say mass in Hadley."

Dr. Taylor answered, "My lord, I am parson of Hadley, and it is against all right, conscience, and laws, that any man should come into my parish and dare to infect the flock committed to me with the poison of the popish idolatrous mass."

At that the bishop became angry and said, "You are a blasphemous heretic, indeed, who blasphemes the blessed sacrament and speaks against the holy mass, which makes a sacrifice for the living and the dead."

Dr. Taylor answered, "No, I do not blaspheme the blessed sacrament that Christ instituted, but I reverence it as a true Christian man should, and confess that Christ ordained holy communion in remembrance of His death and sufferings. Christ gave Himself to die for our redemption upon the Cross. His body was offered there as the propitiatory sacrifice—full, perfect, and sufficient for salvation for all them that believe in Him. This sacrifice, our Savior Christ offered in His own person Himself once for all, and no priest can offer Him any more, and we do not need any more propitiatory sacrifice."

The bishop then called his men and said, "Take this fellow away from here, and take him to the King's Bench. Tell the keeper he is to be confined immediately."

Dr. Taylor knelt down, held up both hands, and said, "Good Lord, I thank You. And, Lord, deliver us from the tyranny of the bishop of Rome and all his detestable errors, idolatries, and abominations. God be praised for good King Edward."

Dr. Taylor was in prison for two years. He spent that time in prayer, reading the holy Scriptures, writing, preaching, and exhorting the prisoners, whoever came to him, to repent and amend their lives.

On January 22, 1555, Dr. Taylor—along with a Master Bradford and Master Saunders, who were also former parish priests—was again called to appear before the bishop of Winchester and the bishops of Norwich, London, Salisbury, and Durham, where he and the other two were again charged with heresy and schism—that is, creating a division in the church. They were required to give a definite answer as to whether they would submit themselves to the Roman pope and renounce their errors. Otherwise, the bishops, according to the laws, would proceed with their condemnation.

When the three men heard this, they answered bravely and boldly that they would not depart from the truth that they had preached in King Edward's day, and neither would they submit themselves to the Romish antichrist. They then thanked God for so great mercy that He would call them to be worthy to suffer for His Word and truth. When the bishops heard and saw their response, they read the sentence of death upon them.

Dr. Taylor was committed to Clink Prison, and when the keeper took him toward the prison, people flocked about to see him. To them he said, "God be praised, good people, for I have come away from them undefiled and will confirm the truth with my blood." He was put in the Clink until it was almost night, and then was taken to the Compter near Poultry. He remained there for about seven days. Then on February 4, 1555, Edmund Bonner, bishop of London, and others came to the prison to degrade him, just as Huss and Jerome of Prague had been degraded many years before.

The next night, the keepers permitted Hooper's wife and his son, Thomas, and his servant, John Hull, to eat supper with him. When they first came in, they all knelt together and he led them in a series of prayers. After supper he gave God thanks for His grace that had given him the strength to abide by His holy Word. Then with tears they prayed together again, and kissed each other. To his son, Taylor gave a Latin book that contained notable sayings of the old martyrs—in the back of it, He wrote:

> I say to my wife, and to my children, the Lord gave you to me, and the Lord has taken me from you, and you from me: blessed be the name of the Lord! I believe that they are blessed who die in the Lord. God cares for sparrows, and for the hairs of our heads. I have ever found Him more faithful and favorable than is any husband or father. Trust in Him by means of our dear Savior Christ's merits: believe, love, fear, and obey Him. Pray to Him, for He has promised to help. Count me not dead, for I shall certainly live, and never die. I go before, and you shall follow after, to our eternal home.

> I say to my dear friends of Hadley, and to all others who have heard me preach, that I depart from here with a quiet conscience concerning my doctrine, for which I pray you thank God with me. For I have, in keeping with my little talent, declared to others those lessons that I gathered out of God's book, the blessed Bible. Therefore, if I, or an angel from heaven, should preach to you any other Gospel than that which you have received, God's great curse be upon that preacher!

> Departing from here in sure hope, without any doubting of eternal salvation, I thank God my heavenly Father, through Jesus Christ my certain Savior.

At two o'clock the next morning, the sheriff of London with his officers came to the Compter and brought out Dr. Taylor and led him without any lights to Woolsack, an inn outside Aldgate. Dr. Taylor's wife had suspected that her

John Foxe, 1587. Figure 1 (see introduction, page ix)

The Supreme Sacrifice:
Jesus Christ, the Lamb of God

Jesus Christ crucified outside Jerusalem

"If the world hates you, keep in mind that it hated me first. If you belonged to the world, it would love you as its own. As it is, you do not belong to the world, but I have chosen you out of the world. That is why the world hates you. Remember the words I spoke to you: ' No servant is greater than his master.' If they persecuted Me, they will persecute you also." John 15: 18-20 (NIV) Figure 2 (see page 4)

The Apostle James (the major) beheaded in Jerusalem, AD 44.
Figure 3 (see page 5)

Matthew the evangelist pinned to the ground and beheaded in Naddayar, Ethopia, AD 60. Figure 4 (see page 6)

The Apostle Andrew crucified at Patras in Achaia, around the year 70. Figure 5 (see page 7)

Thomas, tortured by the natives in Calamina, thrown into an oven, and stuck through with spears, AD 70. Figure 6 (see page 8)

Luke, the evangelist, hung from an olive tree in Greece, AD 93.
Figure 7 (see page 9)

Ignatius, a student under John, devoured by wild animals in Rome, AD 110. Figure 8 (see page 14)

A portrait of William Tyndale. This is the classic accepted portrait of Tyndale, though it is exactly identical to one made of the reformer John Knox some years after Tyndale's death. Fugitives seldom sat for portraits. Figure 9 (see page 121) Courtesy of *Christian History Magazine*, Vol. VI, No. 4, Issue 16, pg. 6.

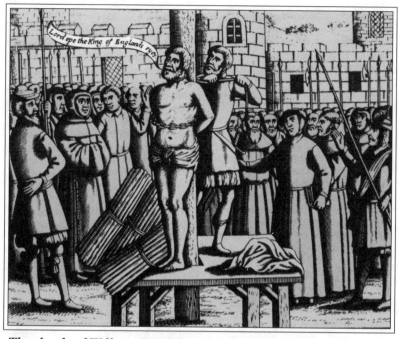

The death of William Tyndale. Figure 10 (see page 133) Courtesy of *Christian History Magazine*, Vol. VI, No. 4, Issue 16, page 16.

Vitalus, buried alive in Ravenna around the year 99. Figure 11
(see page 258)

The decapitation of Wolfgang Binder of Scharding in Bavaria, AD 1571. Figure 12 (see page 258)

Hendrik Pruijt tarred and tied to his ship, and set afire outside Workum, 1574. Figure 13 (see page 258)

John Bret, and Englishman, receives the tongue screw and is burned afterward in Antwerp, 1576. Figure 14 (see page 258)

Matthais Mayr drowned at Wier 1592. Figure 15 (see page 258)

Lai Manping (22) lies dead from beatings inflicted by the Public Security Bureau (PSB) following a raid on a house church meeting in Taoyuan, Shaanxi province. The bloodied offering bag has been thrown on top of him. Chinese authorities are searching for the Christians they believe are responsible for taking this photograph. The PSB has arrested more than 90 Christians in an attempt to cover up the murder (NNI 8/93). Figure 16 (see page 354)

Christian "Wanted Poster." This page, taken from the Muslim magazine 'Takbeer' (Karachi, Pakistan) shows weddings and baptisms involving Muslims who became Christians. It also shows western Christian professionals in Pakistan who witness for Christ.
Figure 17 (see page 354)

The body of Manzoor Masih lies on the street in Lahore, Paki-stan. Manzoor, a Christian under the death sentence from false charges of blaspheming Mohammed, was released by the court and then shot by his Muslim accusers. When Manzoor was ar-rested, the mob stoned her and her children. After her husband's death she said, " Manzoor read the Bible everyday. I compel my children to do also. We are not afraid. I thank God we are Chris-tian, and when we die we will go to heaven. We know that."
Figure 18 (see Page 355)

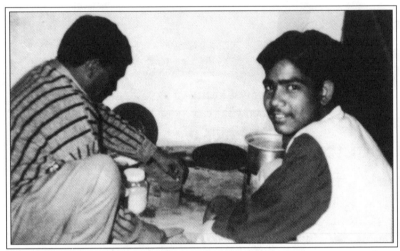

Rehmat Masih and Salamat Masih (no relation) became very close while in prison. They narrowly escaped being killed by fundamentalist gunmen. Rehmat was shot in the stomach three times. Salamat was shot in the hand several times. Figure 19 (see page 355) Courtesy of Open Doors

John Joseph, another Christian found "not guilty" yet was shot through the mouth and neck when gunfire opened, wounding those in the pictures that preceeded, and killing Manzoor. Figure 20 (see page 355) Courtesy of *Voice of the Martyrs.*

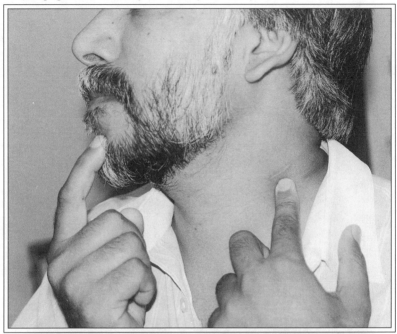

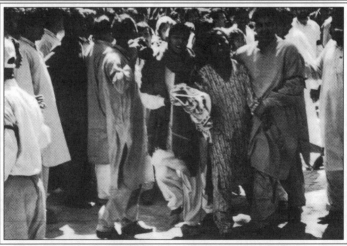

The wife of Manzoor Masih. " . . . We are not afraid when martyrs die. We are happy to face it. Faith will be strong after facing many problems . . . " [see 2 Corinthians 4:17] (A Pakistani Christian Seminary Professor) Figure 21 (see page 355)

A Chinese house meeting where Chinese Christians boldly gather to pray and worship in private homes. Figure 22 (see page 358) Courtesy of Open Doors.

At a glance, one may think this man is facing persecution. It is quite the opposite. This Christian pastor is overcome with emotion when he receives a visiting brother from abroad. Figure 23 (see page 358) Courtesy of Open Doors, August 1996

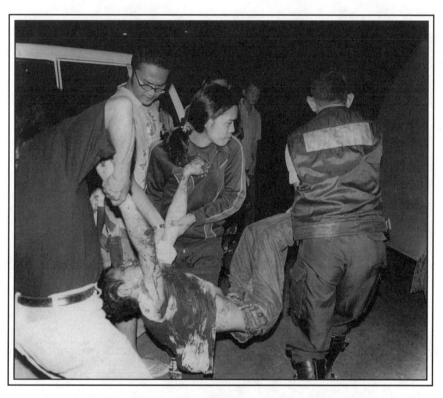

Dominggus Kenjam being carried into hospital.
Figure 24, see page 367
Used by permission of *The Voice of the Martyrs*.

Graham, Timothy and Philip Staines
Figure 25, see page 372
Used by permission of *Gospel Literature Service Publishing*.

Burned Church in India, *Figure 26, see page 372.* Used
by permission of *Gospel Literature Service Publishing*.

The Staines Family
Figure 27, see page 372

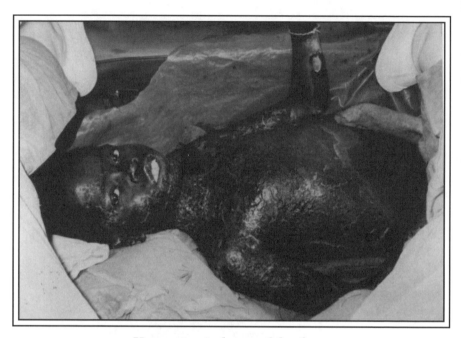

Kamerino's burned body
Figure 28, see page 383
Used by permission of *The Voice of the Martyrs.*

Fourteen-year-old Marina
Figure 29, see page 386
Used by permission of *The Voice of the Martyrs.*

Six-year old Emiliana
Figure 30, see page 386
Used by permission of *The Voice of the Martyrs*.

Rose and her two children
Figure 31, see page 388
Used by permission of *The Voice of the Martyrs*.

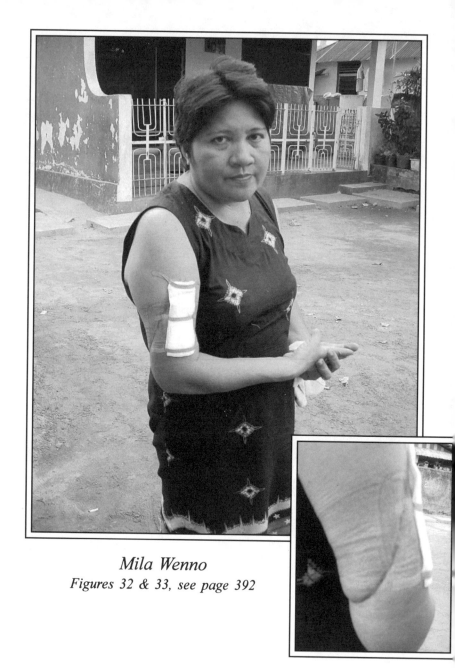

Mila Wenno
Figures 32 & 33, see page 392

Mila's nearly severed arm

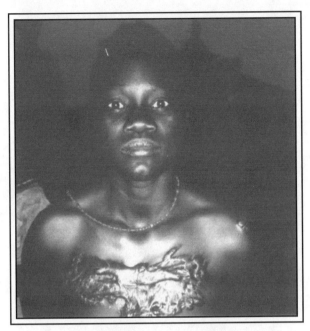

Abuk's wounds from hot knives
Figure 34, see page 395.

Both photos used by
permission of *The
Voice of the Martyrs.*

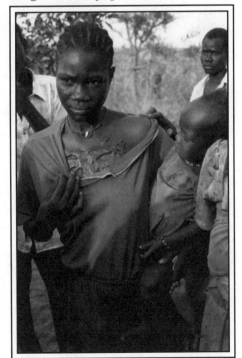

Abuk with her child
Figure 35, see page 395

Figure 36
Used by permission of *The Voice of the Martyrs*.

husband would be moved during the night, and had watched all night from the porch of St. Botolph's church in Aldgate. With her were her two daughters, 13-year-old Elizabeth, who was an orphan the Taylors adopted when she was 3 years old, and Mary, their natural daughter.

Now when the sheriff and his company came near St. Botolph's church, Elizabeth saw them and cried out, "O my dear father! Mother, Mother, Father is being led away."

Mrs. Taylor cried, "Rowland, Rowland, where are you?"—for it was a very dark morning and she could not tell one person from another.

Dr. Taylor answered, "Dear wife, I am here," and stopped. The sheriff's men started to lead him away, but the sheriff said, "Stop for a little, masters, I pray you, and let him speak to his wife," and so they stopped.

Dr. Taylor took Mary into his arms, and then he and his wife and Elizabeth knelt and said the Lord's Prayer. Watching them from a distance, the sheriff and his men began to weep.

After they had prayed, Dr. Taylor stood up and kissed his wife and held her hand and said, "Farewell, my dear wife. Be of good comfort, for my conscience is quiet. God will stir up a father for my children." Then he kissed his daughter Mary, and said, "God bless you and make you His servant." Kissing Elizabeth, he said, "God bless you. I pray you will stand strong and steadfast in Christ and His Word." Then his wife said to him, "God be with you, dear Rowland. I will, with God's grace, meet you at Hadley."

And so he was led to the Woolsack, and his wife followed him. When they arrived, He was placed into a cell, where he was guarded by four attendants and the sheriff's men. As soon as he went into his cell, Dr. Taylor fell upon his knees and gave himself wholly to prayer. The sheriff saw Mrs. Taylor there but would not allow her to speak to her husband again. Nevertheless, he did ask her to go to his house and stay there as if it were her own, and promised her that she would lack nothing, and sent two officers to escort her there. She insisted, however, on going to her mother's house, and so the officers escorted her there and charged her mother to keep her there until they came to get her.

Dr. Taylor remained in the Woolsack until eleven o'clock in the morning, at which time the sheriff of Essex arrived to take charge of him during the next leg of their journey to Hadley. While still within the gated area of the inn, they set Dr. Taylor on horseback and then went out through the gates. Just outside, John Hull waited with Thomas, Dr. Taylor's son. When Taylor saw them he called out, "Come here, my son Thomas." John Hull lifted the child up and set him on the horse in front of his father. Dr. Taylor took off his hat and said to the people who had gathered outside the gates, "Good people, this is my own son." Then he lifted his eyes toward heaven and prayed for Thomas, and then put his hat on the child's head, blessed him, and handed him down to Hull, saying, "Farewell John Hull, you are the most faithful servant any man ever had." With that, they continued their journey toward Brentwood, which is east-northeast of London.

At Brentwood they made a hood to cover Dr. Taylor's head. It had two holes for his eyes so he could see, and a slit for his mouth so he could breath properly. They did this so no one would know who he was, and so he would not speak to anyone, which was their custom with all condemned heretics. They were afraid that if the people heard the martyrs speak, or saw them, the people might be much strengthened by their godly exhortations to stand steadfast in God's Word, and to flee from the superstitions and idolatries of the papacy.

Throughout their journey from London to Brentwood, and then to Chelmsford and Lavenham, which is northeast of London and only a short distance from Hadley, Dr. Taylor was joyful and merry, as if he was going to a most pleasant banquet or wedding. He spoke many excellent things to the men who guarded him, and often caused them to weep when he exhorted them to repent and believe in Christ, and to change their evil and wicked way of living and become godly men. Often he caused them to wonder and rejoice to see him so steady in faith, void of all fear, joyful in heart, and glad to die.

At Chelmsford they met the sheriff of Suffolk who was there to receive him and take him into the region of Suffolk. When they later arrived at Lavenham, a great number of gentlemen and justices upon great horses met them—they had all been appointed to help the sheriff take Dr. Taylor into Hadley. These men, as had all the various ones throughout the journey, exhorted Dr. Taylor to recant his teachings and return to the Romish religion. They promised him a pardon, which they said they had with them, and great promotions, even a bishop's office, if he would accept the pardon. But all their labor and flattering words were in vain. Dr. Taylor refused to give up Christ for the pope.

When they came within two miles of Hadley, Dr. Taylor asked if he could get off his horse, and when permission was given, he leaped down and danced around in great joy. "Why, master doctor," the sheriff said, "what are you doing, are you all right?" Dr. Taylor answered, "Well, God be praised, good master sheriff, never better, for now I know I am almost home. I haven't more than a few steps to go over, and I am right at my Father's house. But, master sheriff, are we going through Hadley?"

"Yes," said the sheriff, "you shall go through Hadley."

Dr. Taylor said, "O Lord! I thank Thee that once more before I die I shall see my flock, whom Thou, Lord, know that I have most heartily loved and truly taught. Lord! Bless them, and keep them steadfast in Thy Word and truth."

When they rode over the bridge into Hadley, a poor man with five small children was waiting for them. When the man saw Dr. Taylor, he and his children fell down on their knees and held up their hands, and he cried with a loud voice, saying, "O dear father and good shepherd, Dr. Taylor. God help and relieve you, as you have many times helped and relieved me and my poor children."

The streets of Hadley were filled with men and women crying over the suffering and loss of their faithful shepherd—they were like frightened sheep about to be attacked by ravenous wolves. They prayed for God's mercy for themselves and for God to strengthen and comfort the man who had watched over them and protected them. Dr. Taylor said to them, "I have preached to you God's Word and truth, and have come here this day to seal it with my blood." As they passed through Hadley's poor district, where Dr. Taylor had ministered so often, he tossed to the poor people the money he had remaining from what charitable friends had given him while he was in prison. It was in this manner that this good father and provider for the poor departed from those for whom all his life he had care and concern.

When they arrived at Aldham Common, the place where Dr. Taylor was to be burned, and he saw the great multitude of people who had gathered there, he asked, "What is this place, and what does it does it mean that so many people are gathered here?" One of men guarding him answered, "It is Aldham Common, the place where you must suffer, and the people have come to see you." Dr. Taylor said, "Thanks be to God, I am indeed at home." With that, he got down from his horse and with both hands tore the hood off his head.

The crown of his head had been scraped, and his hair clipped and cut in a "V" shape as if he were some fool, by the good bishop Bonner when he degraded him in prison. But when the people saw his revered and ancient face, with a long white beard, they burst out weeping and cried out, "God save you, good Dr. Taylor! Jesus Christ strengthen you and help you! The Holy Ghost comfort you!" and many other such wishes. He would have spoken to the people, but the yeomen of the guards were so much about him that as soon as he opened his mouth to speak, one or the other thrust the point of his *tipstaff into his mouth, and would not permit him to speak.

Dr. Taylor then sat down, and when he saw one of the sheriff's men named Soyce, called to him and said, "Soyce, come here and pull off my boots and take them for having done so. You have wanted them for a long time, now take them." Then he got up and took off his clothes down to his undershirt and gave them away. When that was done, he said in a loud voice, "Good people! I have taught you nothing but God's holy Word, and those lessons that I have taken out of God's blessed book, the holy Bible. I have come here this day to seal it with my blood."

Because Dr. Taylor had spoken without permission, Homes, a yeoman of the guard who had used him cruelly on the journey, struck him savagely on the head, nearly knocking him to the ground. Dr. Taylor then knelt down and prayed, and a poor woman who was in the crowd, stepped in and prayed with him. The guards tried to push her away, and threatened to tread her down with their horses, but she would not be removed and stayed and prayed with him.

When they finished, Dr. Taylor went to the stake, kissed it, and climbed into a pitch barrel that they had placed there for him to stand in. He stood with his back upright against the stake, with his hands folded together, and his eyes toward heaven, and continually prayed.

They then bound him to the stake with chains, and the sheriff commanded one Richard Donningham, a butcher in Aldham, to set up faggots, but he refused to do it, saying, "I am lame, sir, and not able to lift a faggot." The sheriff threatened to send him to prison, but he still would not do it. He then appointed Mulleine, Soyce—to whom Dr. Taylor had given his boots, Warwick, and Robert King to set up faggots and make the fire, which they did most diligently. While they were doing it, Warwick threw a faggot at Dr. Taylor, which hit him in the face and cut it open, so that blood ran down. Dr. Taylor said to him, "O friend, I have harm enough, what need was there for that?"

Furthermore, Sir John Shelton was standing near Dr. Taylor and heard him saying the fifty-first Psalm, *Miserere* in English and struck him on the lips. "You knave," he said, "speak Latin. I will make you!"

At last they lit the fire, and Dr. Taylor, holding up both his hands, called upon God, saying, "Merciful Father of heaven, for Jesus Christ my Savior's sake, receive my soul into Thy hands." Then he stood still in the fire without either crying or moving, with his hands folded together before him, until Soyce stuck him on the head with a halberd and split his head open so that his brains fell out and his corpse collapsed into the fire.

15

The Martyrdom of Bishop Ridley and Bishop Latimer

(1555)

These two reverend bishops were martyred together on October 16, 1555. They were excellent men, pillars of the Church, friendly and agreeable in their dispositions, gracious in all ways in their lives, and glorious in their deaths.

Nicholas Ridley

Dr. Ridley was born in Northumberland, began his basic education at Newcastle, and then attended Cambridge University, where his ability for learning promoted him gradually until he was made head of Pembroke College, and he was made a Doctor of Divinity. After returning from a trip to Paris, he was made chaplain to King Henry VIII, who later promoted him to the bishopric of Rochester. From there he was translated to the see and bishopric of London in the time of King Edward VI.

People flocked to the church to listen to his sermons, swarming about him like bees to honey, coveting the sweet flowers and wholesome nectar of the doctrines that he not only preached but demonstrated by his life. He was a bright light to the blind, a heavenly trumpet to the deaf, and a holy voice to the lost sinners. He lived and ministered in such purity that not even his enemies could reprove him in any jot or tittle. Intelligent, wise, artful in dealing with others, Dr. Ridley was such a good, godly, and spiritual man that England may rightly mourn the day that such a treasure was lost.

In person he was an erect and well-proportioned man, forgiving in nature, and with a godly discipline in all his appetites and habits. Each morning he devoted himself to private prayer until ten o'clock, and then took part in the daily prayers that were held in his house by members of his parish. After a midday dinner, he would talk to others or play chess for an hour, and then spend the rest of the afternoon studying or taking care of church business. About five o'clock he would pray for about an hour again, refresh himself at chess for about another hour, and then return to his studying until eleven o'clock, when he would bathe and then retire after praying on his knees for a while as he did in the morning. In short, he was a pattern of godliness and virtue, and tried to make all men and women godly wherever he went.

One example of the affectionate kindness he showed toward everyone, was his treatment of old Mrs. Bonner, the mother of Dr. Bonner, who was the cruel bishop of London in the time of Queen Mary I. Whenever Dr. Ridley was at his residence in Fulham, he always invited Mrs. Bonner to his home for dinner and placed her at the head of his table, treating her like his own mother. He also displayed similar kindness to Bonner's sister and other relatives, and often entertained them in his home with great courtesy and friendship. But when Bonner went over to the side of "Bloody Mary" and was restored to power, he tore everything from Dr. Ridley's sister and her husband, Mr. George Shipside, and would have sacrificed them both if God had not delivered them by means of Dr. Heath, bishop of Worcester.

About September 8, 1552, in his office as bishop of London, Dr. Ridley went early one morning to visit the Lady Mary, who later became Queen Mary I, at Hunsdon where she was staying. There he was gently entertained by Sir Thomas Wharton and her other officers until almost eleven o'clock, when Lady Mary came into the *chamber where they were. Dr. Ridley saluted her grace and said that he had come to do his duty toward her. She thanked him for his pains, and they talked pleasantly together for about fifteen minutes. Lady Mary said she knew him in the court when he was chaplain to her father, and then dismissed him so she could have dinner with her officers.

After dinner, she called Bishop Ridley to her again and they talked for a short time.

Bishop Ridley: "Madam, I came not only to do my duty, to see your grace, but also to offer myself to preach before you on Sunday, if it will please you to hear me."

At this Mary's face tightened and she was silent for a moment, then she said, "My lord, as for this last matter, I pray that you answer the question yourself."

Bishop: "Madam, considering my office and calling, I am bound by duty to offer to preach before your grace."

Mary: "Well, as I have said, I pray that you answer the question yourself, for you know the answer well enough. But if there is no way but that I answer you, then this is your answer. The door of the parish church next to this building shall be open to you if you come, and you may preach if you wish, but neither I nor any of mine shall go and listen to you."

Bishop: "Madam, I trust you will not refuse God's Word."

Mary: "I do not know what it is that you now call God's Word, but it is not God's Word. God's Word was in my father's day."

Bishop: "God's Word is the same in all times, but is better understood and practiced in some ages than in others."

Mary: "In my father's day, you would not have dared to declare as true what you now say is God's Word. And as for your new books, I thank God that I never have read any of them. I never did, and I never will."

After many bitter words against the Reformation form of religion that was then established, and against the government of England and the laws made in the young years of her brother, (which, she said, she was not bound to obey until he became an adult, and then, she declared, she would obey them), she then asked Dr. Ridley if he was a member of the council of bishops. He answered, "No." She said, "You might as well be, the way the council is going nowadays."

She then concluded their discussion by saying, "My lord, for your consideration in coming to see me, I thank you. But for your offering to preach before me, I don't thank you the least bit."

Then Bishop Ridley was taken by Sir Thomas Wharton to the dining room and was given something to drink. After he had drunk, he paused awhile, looking very sad, and suddenly said loudly, "Surely I have done wrong."

Sir Thomas Wharton asked, "Why so?"

Bishop Ridley replied, "I have drunk in this place where God's Word was offered and was refused. Since that was done, if I had remembered my duty, I should have departed immediately, and shaken the dust off my shoes as a testimony against this house." These words were spoken by the bishop with such forcefulness and intensity that some of the hearers later said that their hair stood upright on their heads.

When Edward VI died in 1553 and Lady Mary became Queen Mary I of England, Bishop Ridley was immediately marked for slaughter. But before she attended to the bishop, "Bloody Mary" saw to the execution of Lady Jane Grey and her husband, Lord Guilford Dudley.

Lady Jane Grey was a great-granddaughter of Henry VII and a cousin of Edward VI. Her father was Henry Grey, duke of Suffolk, and her mother was Frances Brandon, a niece of Henry VIII. When Jane was 9-years-old she was placed in the household of Henry VIII as an attendant on Queen Catherine Parr, Henry's 6th wife. Henry died in January 1547, and a few months later Catherine married Lord Seymour, duke of Somerset. She died in September 1547, and Lord Seymour and Jane's father tried to arrange a marriage between 11-year-old Jane and 11-year-old King Edward VI. This scheme to make Lady Jane queen of England failed, and she returned to her father's home. Jane was a brilliant student, and under the guidance of her Protestant tutor, John Aylmer, who later became bishop of London, she learned several languages. At 13, she could read and write Greek; at 15, she also knew Latin, Italian, and French, and was learning Hebrew.

Early in 1553, young King Edward showed signs of fatal consumption [tuberculosis]. Seeing another chance to make Lady Jane, who was a Protestant herself, queen of England and secure power for themselves, her father and John Dudley, the duke of Northumberland, who dominated the government and King Edward, arranged for her marriage to Dudley's son, Guilford Dudley. Northumberland then persuaded King Edward to name Jane his successor in place of Edward's sister Mary, who was the rightful heir to the throne and a known Roman Catholic. Edward died on July 6, and on July 9, Northumberland took Jane before the Privy Council and had her proclaimed queen the next day. The plan fell apart nine days later, however, when the rest of England proclaimed Mary queen.

Jane and her husband, Guilford Dudley, were immediately arrested and imprisoned in the Tower of London and convicted of high treason. That winter, Jane's father, Henry Grey, joined an uprising against Queen Mary. This prompted her to sign Jane's death warrant to prevent any further attempts to make Jane queen. Jane and Guilford were executed on February 12, 1554, seven months after they were arrested.

Guilford was taken out of his cell first and led through the crowd of people and out the *bulwark gate, followed by the sheriff's men, and up Tower Hill to a scaffold. There he was beheaded with an ax. About an hour later, Lady Jane was taken from her cell and led in the same manner to the central *keep within the prison, and there also beheaded with an ax.

Lady Jane was widely praised for her beauty and learning, and was obviously not herself a conspirator but rather an innocent victim of a political plot to put a Protestant queen on the throne. On the scaffold, Jane declared she had not wanted the crown, and she would die "a true Christian woman." She was 16 years old when she was executed.

In the meantime, Bishop Ridley and several others were also imprisoned in the Tower of London. Then about March 10, 1554, Nicholas Ridley, bishop of London, Thomas Cranmer, archbishop of Canterbury, and Hugh Latimer, once bishop of Worcester, were taken from the Tower to Windsor, and from there to Oxford University to debate with the doctors of divinity and other learned men about the presence, substance, and sacrifice of the sacrament. The articles they were to debate were these:

1. Whether the natural body of Christ is really in the sacrament after the words spoken by the priest;

2. Whether after the words of consecration any other substance remains in the sacrament other than the body and blood of Christ;

3. Whether in the mass there is a propitiatory sacrifice for the sins of the living and the dead.

After hearing these read, Dr. Ridley said without delay that they were all false, and that they sprang out of a bitter and sour root. His answers were sharp, witty, and knowledgeable. He was asked whether or not he would dispute the articles. He said that so long as God gave him life, He would not only have his heart, but also his mouth and pen to defend His truths. But he required time and books before he could answer properly. They said he would dispute on Thursday, and until then he would have the books he needed. Then they gave him the articles, and told him to write what he thought of them that night. Dr. Ridley later wrote a report about what occurred at the examination.

The report and narration of Master Ridley, concerning the misordered disputation brought against him and his fellow prisoners at Oxford:

Never since I was born have I seen anything handled more vainly or with greater disorder than the debate against me in the schools at Oxford. Truly, I would never have thought it possible to have found among men, said to be knowledgeable and educated in this area, any who were so brazen-faced and shameless, so disorderly and vain, and who conducted themselves more like stage players putting on a play rather than serious doctors who were there to debate.

It's no great marvel, seeing that those who were the moderators and overseers of the others, and who should have given good examples in words and seriousness, gave worse examples above all the others. By their actions they blew the trumpet to the rest as a signal to rave, roar, rage, and cry out. By this, good Christian reader, it is clear that they never sought for any truth of principles or beliefs, but only sought the glory of the world and their own bragging victory.

A great part of the time allowed for the debate was uselessly used up with shameful rebuffs and reviling taunts, with hissing and clapping of hands, all so they could get the people's favor. I was greatly grieved in my heart when I saw all these things, and protested openly that such excessive and outrageous disorder was inappropriate for those schools and for men of learning and dignity, and that those who did those things were only showing the slenderness of their cause. My humble complaint, however, was so far off from doing any good at all, that I was forced to listen to rebukes, rebuffs, and taunts that no honest person could stand to hear spoken against even an evil and miserable ruffian without blushing.

At the beginning of the debate, when I tried to state my answer to the first proposition in a few words, even the doctors themselves cried out, "He speaks blasphemies! He speaks blasphemies!" And when on my knees I heartily begged them that they would grant to hear me to the end of my statement, the moderator cried out loudly, "Let him read it! Let him read it!" But when I tried to read again, there was immediately so much shouting, so much noise and disorder, so much confusion of voices, crying, "Blasphemies! Blasphemies!" that I cannot remember ever hearing or reading about anything like it. Except, perhaps, that one in the Acts of the Apostles in which Demetrius the silversmith and others of his occupation stirred up when they cried out against Paul, "Great is Diana of the Ephesians! Great is Diana of the Ephesians!"

The cries and disturbances of those against me were so strong that I was forced to stop the reading of my statements, even though they were short.

After this, Ridley, along with Latimer and Cranmer, were sent to the common prison at Barcardo. There Ridley was separated from them and placed in the house of a man named Irish, where he remained until the day of his execution on October 16, 1555.

Hugh Latimer

Hugh Latimer was born about 1485 at Thurcaston (or Thurkesson) in the county of Leicester. Latimer was born and reared there until he was about four years old, at which time his parents, who were wealthy farmers, seeing how intelligent he was, determined to have him well educated and trained in knowledge of good literature. In the common schools where he lived, Latimer did so well that at age fourteen he was sent to Cambridge University. There he continued in ordinary studies, and then concentrated on studying theology, the kind the ignorance of that age allowed, and was a zealous observer of the Romish superstitions of the time. He was ordained a priest in about 1510, and in his speech given when he received his Bachelor of Divinity in 1522, he spoke angrily against the blessed reformer Melanchthon, and openly attacked good Mr. Stafford, who was a divinity lecturer at Cambridge.

It was surely God's grace that moved the Cambridge reformer, Thomas Bilney, who was burned for heresy in 1532, to go to Latimer's study and ask him to hear his confession. Latimer willingly agreed, thinking perhaps that Bilney might be returning to the Roman Catholic religion. But during the confession, Latimer was so affected by Bilney's faith in Christ that he began to question him about it, and, by the work of the Holy Spirit, was converted immediately to the true faith. He gave up his studies of the Romish religion and became a blessed scholar of Reformation doctrines. Like the Apostle Paul, he who had been a persecutor of Christ became one of the Lord's most ardent and active advocates—and before Dr. Stafford died, they were blessedly reconciled.

After his conversion, Latimer worked eagerly for the conversion of others, and became a public preacher and a private instructor in the university. Many times he taught about the absurdity of praying in Latin, and of not allowing the Scriptures to be printed in English and so withholding God's revelations about salvation from the people who were to be saved by belief in them. In a sermon given about Christmas 1529, Latimer spoke about the common use of the season, and gave the people Christmas cards that had written on them Scriptures in English from the fifth, sixth, and seventh chapters of Matthew. He told them that they should live in accordance with those Scriptures not only at Christmas but every day, and that it was with the heart and not ceremonies that they serve God. By so doing, he quietly overthrew any eternal ceremonies that did not give glory to God's holy Word and sacraments.

The Sunday before Christmas day, Mr. Latimer went into the church and had the bells rung as he entered the pulpit, then he exhorted and invited all who were there to serve the Lord with inward heart and true affection, and not with outward ceremonies. The Lord, he explained, should be worshipped and served in simplicity of the heart and truth. In that was true Christianity, and not in the outward deeds of the letter only, or in the glittering show of man's traditions, of pardons, pilgrimages, ceremonies, vows, devotions, voluntary works, extra works, *foundations, *oblations, the pope's supremacy—all these are either needless where the other is present, or else are of small value in comparison.

It would take a long time to tell what a stir this preaching caused in Cambridge, but it was not long before strong criticism was directed toward Latimer from several of the resident friars and heads of the college houses. First came Buckenham, the head of the Black Friars, who declared that it was not expedient that the Scriptures be in English, because the ignorant might be brought into danger of leaving their occupation or run into some other inconvenience. For example, the farmer might hear this in the Gospel, "No man, having put his hand to the plow, and looking back, is fit for the kingdom of God" (Luke 9:52), and might, perhaps, stop his plowing. Likewise, the baker, when he hears that a little leaven corrupts the whole lump of dough (see Galatians 5:9), "may perhaps leave our bread unleavened, and so our bodies shall have no added seasoning." Also, the simple man, when he hears in the Gospel, "if thine eye offend thee, pluck it out, and cast it from thee" (Matthew 18:9), may make himself blind and so fill the world full of beggars.

When Latimer heard about Dr. Buckenham's sermon, he came to the church to answer the friar, and a large crowd from the town and the University came also to hear him, along with doctors and other graduates. Buckenham attended, also, with his black-friar's hood around his shoulders, and sat directly in front of Latimer underneath the pulpit. As Latimer talked, Buckenham sunk lower and lower into his hood, for Latimer struck his nonsense so violently and with such scholarly logic that he never again dared speak out against Latimer from the pulpit.

Later a grey friar and doctor named Dr. Venetus, also railed and raged against Master Latimer, calling him a mad and brainless man, and telling the people not to believe him. Once more Latimer went to the pulpit to respond to the accusations, with the same results as with Buckenham. In fact, he so confused and befuddled Dr. Venetus that he drove him not only out of having any confidence in his accusations, but also clean out of the university.

Whole swarms of friars and doctors from throughout the university came against Latimer on every side, preaching and barking against him. Then Dr. West, bishop of Ely, preached against him at Barwell Abbey, and prohibited him from preaching again in the churches of Cambridge University. In spite of that, the Lord provided for him. Dr. Barnes, head of the Augustine friars, licensed him to preach in his church of the Augustines. So for three years, Mr. Latimer continued to advocate openly the cause of Christ, and so eloquent where his sermons that even his enemies confessed the power of those talents he possessed. During that time, he and Master Bilney used to spend much time together, often walking in the fields and along a small hill, which was soon called "Heretics' Hill."

About this time, Latimer and Bilney visited the prisoners in the Cambridge Tower or Castle, and there met a woman who was accused of killing her child, which she plainly and steadfastly denied. The two searched out her story, and found that her husband did not love her and had been looking for some way to get rid of her. Their child had been sick with tuberculosis for almost a year, and during a harvest, when the woman's husband was away working, the child died. She looked for neighbors to help bury the child, but they were all working somewhere in the harvest, and so with a heavy heart she was forced to bury the child by herself. When her husband came home, he accused her of murdering the child. This was her trouble, and Mr. Latimer, after investigating the matter and her carefully, believed that she was not guilty. Immediately after, he was called to preach before King Henry VIII at Windsor. After his sermon, the King sent for him, and talked to him as to a friend. Finding such an opportunity, Mr. Latimer knelt down and explained the whole matter to the King, and begged him to pardon the woman. The King graciously granted the pardon, and had it written out and given to Latimer to take home with him.

This kindly act of Latimer's, along with several like it, only served to increase the anger of his adversaries. Shortly after, he was summoned to appear before Cardinal Wolsey for heresy, but because he was a strong supporter of the king's supremacy, in opposition to the pope's, he was highly favored by Thomas Cromwell, Earl of Essex, who, later in 1534, proposed the legislation that established the monarch as head of the established church, and Dr. Buts, the king's physician. With their help he escaped the cardinal's claws and was made parish priest in the diocese of Sarum at West Kingston in Wiltshire.

Here he preached so strongly against purgatory, the immaculacy of the Virgin Mary, and the worship of images, that he was summoned to appear before William Warham, archbishop of Canterbury, and John Stokesley, bishop of London, on January 29, 1531. In London, he was put to great trouble and had to appear before the bishops three times a week for several weeks. During this time he was not able to take care of his duties in his diocese. Finally, he wrote to the archbishop and told him that because of certain infirmities he could not appear whenever they commanded him to, and reproved them for keeping him from his duties for no just cause but only for preaching the truth against vain abuses that had crept into religion.

Nevertheless, the bishops required him to agree to several articles that stated he would conform to certain accustomed practices in the church. There is reason to believe that, after repeated weekly examinations, he did so agree, since from that time he did institute certain practices in his church that involved no important article of faith. In addition, those practices that he could not avoid, but which he felt should be freed from superstition, he modified so that they were harmless to his flock. For example, he charged his ministers to say specific words when they gave the holy water in baptism, and the holy bread in communion, to the people.

Words to be spoken in giving Holy Water:

Remember your promise in baptism;

Christ His mercy and blood-shedding:

By Whose most holy sprinkling,

Of all your sins you have free pardoning.

Words to be spoken in giving Holy Bread:

Of Christ's body this is a token,

Which on the Cross for your sins was broken.

Therefore of your sins you must be forsakers,

If of Christ's death you will be partakers.

It is believed that Dr. Latimer would have brought more things to pass if there had been enough time, for he knew that the holy water and holy bread not only had no basis in the Scriptures, but were full of profane *exorcisms [see definitions of *exorcism* and *exorcise* for 16th century use] and *conjurations that were contrary to the truth and knowledge of the Gospel.

Dr. Latimer was delivered from the bishops this time through the favor and power of King Henry VIII, before whom he often preached and who was much influenced by the things he said and the Scriptures he quoted. Additionally, through the efforts of Dr. Buts and Lord Cromwell, King Henry advanced Latimer to the office of bishop of Worcester, where he taught for several years, both from the pulpit and from his life.

In 1539, King Henry VIII, who had never adopted Protestant doctrines, instituted his *Six Articles Act*, which Archbishop Cranmer had opposed when it was debated in the *House of Lords. The passage of the Act was a triumph for Bishop Stephen Gardiner, who wanted to preserve the basic tenets of the Roman Catholic faith within the Church of England, and the conservative bishops, who also favored the traditional Roman Catholic views. At the same time, it was a defeat for Archbishop Cranmer and Thomas Cromwell who favored the Reformation views, and wanted to do away with all popish doctrines and practices in the Church.

The *Six Articles Act* upheld the Roman Catholic doctrine of transubstantiation, the celibacy of priests, the observation of vows of chastity, the holding of private masses, confessions to a priest, and the needlessness of the laity receiving both the bread and wine in communion. The Act was popularly called, "the six stringed whip."

The Six Articles Act

1. It was affirmed "that in the most blessed Sacrament of the altar, by the strength and efficacy of Christ's almighty word (it being spoken by the priests) is present really, under the form of bread and wine, the natural body and blood of our Savior Jesus Christ, conceived of the Virgin Mary; and that after the consecration there remains no substance of bread or wine, nor any other substance, but the substance of Christ, God and man.

2. Communion in both kinds [bread and wine] is not necessary for the laity.

3. Ordained priests are not to be married or marry.

4. Monastic vows of chastity or widowhood by men or women are to be continued and observed.

5. Private masses are approved.

6. Auricular [spoken] confessions to a priest are expedient and necessary and are to be retained.

(All but the last were deemed to be ordained by God's Word.)

For those not observing the six articles, there were severe penalties:

Article 1. Those who contradicted or despised the blessed Sacrament would be guilty of heresy and condemned to be burned, and all their goods and lands forfeited.

Articles 2-6. Those who preached, taught, or obviously held opinions contrary to articles 2 to 6 inclusive, would be condemned to a felon's death, without benefit of clergy. For a first offense of holding contrary opinions, punishment would be imprisonment and loss of all property; for the second offense, punishment would be death. Those who contemptuously or obstinately refused confession, or abstained from receiving the blessed Sacrament at the accustomed time, would be imprisoned and fined; a second offense would be punished by a felon's death. Any man or woman who married, having advisedly avowed chastity, would suffer a felon's death. The marriages of clergy who had avowed chastity or widowhood were declared null and void, and those clerics who failed to put away their wives or who married in the future would be declared felons and suffer a felon's death.

In addition, the *Six Articles Act* gave the Church of England commissioners the power to destroy books that contained material contrary to the Act, and it decreed that parish priests were to read the Act periodically in their churches. The Act was repealed in 1547 when Edward VI became king, but it was temporarily revived during the reign of Mary I.

Although Henry VIII reformed the government of the church soon after he declared himself to be Supreme Head of the Church of England, he refused to allow any changes to be made in its doctrines. Before his divorce from Catherine of Aragon, he had opposed the teachings of Martin Luther in a book that had gained him the gratitude of the pope and the title "Defender of the Faith"—a title the monarch of England still bears. And now, after separation from Rome, Henry persecuted with equal violence the Catholics who adhered to the government of Rome, and the Protestants who rejected its doctrines.

When the *Six Articles Act* was instituted, Dr. Latimer and others, among them Shaxton, bishop of Salisbury, threw off their Romish garments and renounced their *bishopric. Latimer then went to London for treatment for injuries that he received when a tree fell upon him, nearly killing him. While there he continued preaching and was soon arrested under the penalties of the *Six Articles Act* and imprisoned in the Tower of London.

Latimer remained a prisoner in the Tower for eight years until the coronation of King Edward VI in 1547. When released he returned to the Lord's work in Stamford and many other places, preaching twice every Sunday and often on the weekdays. He was about sixty-two years old when Edward became king, and still suffered from the injuries he sustained when the tree fell upon him, yet he worked at spreading the Gospel as much as a man half his age. Every morning, winter, and summer, he got up about two o'clock to spend several hours studying his Bible and books written by other reformers. Whether from some inward revelation, or from his personal understanding of coming changes in the government in England, he often said that preaching the true Gospel of Christ would cost him his life, and he cheerfully prepared himself for that moment.

Soon after King Edward's death in 1553, Latimer, now about sixty-eight years old, was summoned to appear before the council of Bishops in London. On his way he traveled through Smithfield where he jokingly said that Smithfield had often groaned for him. When he appeared before the council he was taunted and mocked by the papist bishops and cast into prison in the Tower of London. There he remained for almost a year, nearly dying of the cold through the winter, and being continually harassed and cruelly mistreated by the lordly papists, who thought then their kingdom would never fall. Through it all, Latimer was patient and cheerful and overcame all their merciless treatment of him by the strength of the Lord's grace.

In March 1554, Latimer was transferred to Oxford, along with Bishops Ridley and Cranmer, to dispute the charges brought against him by Stephen Gardiner, bishop of Winchester. This is the same Stephen Gardiner who was once master of Trinity Hall at Cambridge, and later was secretary to Cardinal Wolsey and worked for Henry's divorce from Catherine of Aragon. He was first appointed bishop of Winchester by King Henry VIII, and in 1535 wrote a treatise, *On True Obedience*, in which he defended the monarch's supremacy over the Church of England. Most likely he was also the author of Henry's Six Articles. After Edward VI became king, Gardiner was removed from the royal council and his bishopric and was imprisoned. When Mary I became Queen, Gardiner was reinstated as bishop of Winchester and was made lord chancellor. He then turned from his stated belief in the monarch's supremacy and once more affirmed papal supremacy over the Church of England.

At Oxford, Latimer, along with his fellow prisoners, was condemned and committed again to prison, where he stayed from April to October. During that time, the prisoners spent most of their time in godly conversations, fervent prayer, or fruitful writing. Latimer, because of his weak condition, wrote less than the others, but conversely he spent more time in prayer. Sometimes he knelt for so long that he wasn't able to get up without help. His prayers concerned three principal matters:

1. Since God had appointed him to preach the Gospel, He would give him sufficient grace to remain steadfast until he gave his life for it.

2. That God in His mercy would restore His Gospel to England once again.

3. That God would keep Princess Elizabeth safe, and make her Queen of England to comfort His comfortless realm.

That Latimer's first prayer was answered is amply testified to by his death outside the Bocardo gate at Oxford when his tormentors were about to set fire to him and he lifted his eyes to heaven and said, "God is faithful, Who does not allow us to be tempted above what we can bear." His last two prayers were answered when Queen Mary I died on Nov. 17, 1558 and the reign of Queen Elizabeth I began.

The Burning of Nicholas Ridley and Hugh Latimer

The night before the execution of Ridley and Latimer on October 16, 1555, Dr. Ridley said to Mrs. Irish, the keeper's wife who brought them their supper meal and wept as she served it, "Though my breakfast in the morning will be somewhat sharp and painful, yet I am sure my supper in the evening will be most pleasant and sweet."

The place of burning was on the north side of Oxford, opposite Baliol College. Dr. Ridley wore a furred black gown, much as he often wore as a bishop, a velvet furred piece around his neck, a velvet night-cap upon his head with a corner cap on top of it, and a pair of slippers on his feet. Mr. Latimer had on a worn, coarse, woolen frock, a buttoned cap and kerchief on his head, and a new long shroud that hung down over his stockings to his feet. The sight of them stirred the hearts of many who thought of the honor they once had and the severe affliction that had befallen them.

When they passed Bocardo, Dr. Ridley looked up toward the window where the former archbishop of Canterbury, Thomas Cranmer, was held, hoping to see him, but at that moment Cranmer was busy disputing with friar Soto and others, and he could not be seen. Looking back, Ridley saw Latimer behind him and said, "Oh, there you are." To which Latimer answered, "Yes, and I'm following after you as fast as I can." Dr. Ridley held both hands up to heaven, and then when he saw how cheerful Latimer was, he hurried to his side, embraced him, and kissed him, saying, "Be of good heart, brother, for God will either make the fire less painful, or strengthen us so that we can endure it."

With that he went to the stake, knelt next to it, kissed it, and prayed fervently. Behind him, Mr. Latimer also knelt and prayed, calling upon God for them both. A Dr. Smith then preached a short sermon against them, quoting the Apostle Paul, "if I give my body to be burned, and have not charity, it profiteth me nothing," and urging them to recant and come home to the Roman church, and so save their lives and souls.

Dr. Ridley then asked Mr. Latimer, "Will you first answer the sermon, or shall I?" Latimer replied, "You answer first, I pray you." "I will," said Ridley. When the sermon ended, they knelt together facing Lord Williams of Thames, to whom Ridley said, "I beseech you, my lord, even for Christ's sake, that I may speak but two or three words." Lord Williams asked the mayor and vice-chancellor if he should allow Ridley to speak, but the bailiffs and the vice-chancellor, Dr. Marshal, hurried over to Ridley, put their hands over his mouth, and said, "Mr. Ridley, if you will revoke and recant your erroneous opinions, you will not only have the liberty to speak, but you will save your life as well."

"Not otherwise?" asked Ridley.

"No," said Marshall.

"Well," said Ridley, "so long as there is breath in my body, I will never deny my Lord Christ and His known truth. God's will be done in me."

They were then commanded to make themselves ready. Dr. Ridley removed as much of his clothing as he could and gave it to various friends in the crowd that had come to see them. Mr. Latimer, having nothing worth giving, asked for help in removing his stockings, and was soon stripped to only his shroud. Strangely, though in his clothing he had appeared as an old and withered man, now he stood straight and upright, a venerable and fearless man, as pleasing in appearance as any godly father could be.

Ridley held up his right hand and said, "O heavenly Father, I give unto Thee most hearty thanks, for that Thou has called me to be profess Three, even unto death. I beseech Thee, Lord God, have mercy upon this land of England and deliver her from all her enemies."

The executioner than circled Dr. Ridley and Mr. Latimer with a chain and fastened it to the stake. As he nailed in a staple, Dr. Ridley took the chain in his hand and said, "Good fellow, knock it in hard, for the flesh will have its way." Then his brother brought a bag to tie around his neck. Ridley asked what it was, and he said, "Gunpowder." "Then," said Ridley, "I take it to be sent of God; therefore I will receive it as being from God." He then asked if he had any for his brother, meaning Mr. Latimer. His brother said he did, and Ridley replied, "Then give it to him quickly, lest it be too late." So his brother tied a bag of gunpowder around Latimer's neck, also.

Faggots were then placed around them, kindled with fire, and one laid at Ridley's feet. When Latimer saw it, he said, "Be of good cheer, Ridley, and play the man. We shall this day, by God's grace, light up such a candle in England, as I trust, will never be put out."

When Ridley saw the fire flaming up toward him, he cried with a wonderful loud voice, "Lord, Lord, receive my spirit!" On the other side of the stake, Latimer cried as forcefully, "O Father of heaven, receive my soul!" Then he stroked his face with his hands, and, so it seemed, washed them a little in the fire, and soon died, apparently with little or no pain.

For Ridley, however, the fire was not burning as it should. The faggots had been laid heavy upon the *gorse [spiny shrubs] that was used for kindling and piled too high, so the fire burned first underneath and was held there by the top layers of wood. When Dr. Ridley felt the fire burning his underparts, he asked, in Christ's name, that they allow the fire to come upon him. His brother-in-law misunderstood what he said, and trying to relieve him of his pain, heaped more faggots upon him and buried him in them completely. This caused the trapped fire underneath to burn more fiercely and burn through the lower part of his body before it touched his upper body. This caused Ridley to plead repeatedly that the fire be allowed to come upon him, saying, "I cannot burn." This, indeed, seemed to be true, for even after his legs were consumed, the side that the people could see was untouched, and even his shirt was not singed. Yet even in this torment, he did not forget to call on God, saying "Lord have mercy upon me," and intermingled these words with his cry, "Let the fire come upon me, I cannot burn."

He remained in this agony until one of the guards realized what was happening to him and used the hook at the blade of his halberd to pull off the top faggots. When Ridley saw the fire flame up, he twisted himself over to the side where the fire was until it reached the bag of gunpowder around his neck. When the gunpowder exploded, he stirred no more.

Hundreds of the onlookers were moved to tears by what they had witnessed, for there were none, who were not totally empty of all humanity and mercy, who would not have grieved at the fire that raged upon their bodies, and especially the agony that poor Ridley suffered.

Well, dead they are, and the world gave them its reward for their work. But the reward they have in heaven will be declared on the day of the Lord's glory when He comes with all His saints.

16

The Martyrdom of Archbishop Cranmer

(1556)

Thomas Cranmer was one of the principal figures in the English Reformation. He was born in Arselacton, Nottinghamshire, on July 2, 1489, and was well-educated throughout his childhood. After his basic education, he studied at Cambridge University, where he was ordained a priest in 1523, and was given a fellowship to Jesus College. There he married, and as a result lost his fellowship and left Jesus College to be a university teacher at Buckingham College. He lodged his new wife at a nearby inn called the Dolphin, whose landlady was a relative of hers, and because he often visited there, some popish merchants spread the rumor that he worked at the inn attending to the horses.

Not long after, his wife died in childbirth and Cranmer returned to Jesus College where he had again been granted a fellowship.

In a few years, Cranmer was promoted to professor of theology at Jesus College, and was commonly appointed one of the school heads to examine candidates for Bachelors or Doctors of Divinity degrees. It was Cranmer's practice to judge qualifications of the candidates by their knowledge of the Scriptures rather than the writings of ancient fathers of the church, and so many popish priests and friars, who did not study the Bible, were rejected, while others improved themselves in knowledge of the Scriptures because they knew it was the only way they could pass Cranmer's examination. As a result, he was much hated by some for his insistence on adherence to the Scriptures, and much thanked by others because they had been forced to advance themselves in knowledge of God's Word.

In the summer of 1529, a plague [probably bubonic] struck Cambridge, and Cranmer left to stay at the home of a Mr. Cessy, the father of two of his students, at Waltham Abbey. Around that time, and for a period of about three years, the controversy of King Henry VIII divorcing his wife, Catherine of Aragon, was foremost in everyone's mind throughout England and had not yet been resolved.

Shortly before his coronation in 1509, Henry married Catherine, who was the daughter of Ferdinand II and Isabella I of Spain. She had previously been the wife of his older brother, Arthur, who died in 1502, thereby making Henry heir apparent to the throne. The new marriage was happy for almost twenty years, but by 1527, Henry was displeased with her because she had not borne him a son to continue the Tudor line. There was also the matter of his infatuation with his wife's maid, Anne Boleyn. So having a double reason for wanting to set aside his wife, Catherine, Henry convinced himself that the reason he had no male heir was that his marriage to her was not pleasing to God because Leviticus 20:21 stated, "If a man shall take his brother's wife, it is an unclean thing: he hath uncovered his brother's nakedness; they shall be childless."

[This verse does not mean the *widow* of a dead brother, for if it did it would contradict the *levirate* law, which required a brother to marry his dead brother's widow so that his name would not be lost in Israel (Deuteronomy 25:5-10). It was also known as the law of the *kinsman redeemer*. This is the theme of the *Book of Ruth* (Ruth 2:20; 3:2, 9-13; 4:1-11), and is the law that the Sadducees used when they confronted Jesus' doctrine of a resurrection (Matthew 22:23-33). Leviticus 20:21 forbids taking the wife of *a brother who is still alive*. This is the law that John the Baptist referred to when he told Herod the tetrarch that it was not lawful for him to have his brother's wife, because his brother, Philip, was still alive (Mark 6:14-17). For reasons not explained in Foxe's original book, and perhaps known only to those involved, the law was wrested to King Henry's benefit and interpreted to mean also a dead brother's wife.]

Based on his interpretation of Leviticus 20:21, King Henry VIII ordered his chief minister, Cardinal Wolsey, to approach the papacy for a decree that his marriage to Catherine was invalid and that he was free to marry again. Cardinal Wolsey, who was the archbishop of York and had been appointed in 1518 as the pope's representative in England, reluctantly accepted personal responsibility for the success of Henry's appeal to Pope Clement VII in Rome. Catherine opposed the annulment, however, as did her nephew Charles V, Holy Roman Emperor and king of Spain. Because Charles dominated Italy during this period, Pope Clement was unable to grant Henry's request and so procrastinated over the annulment and unwittingly brought about the English Reformation.

In 1529, a divorce trial held in London was adjourned without a decision. In anger at the delay Henry dismissed Cardinal Wolsey from the position of Lord Chancellor that he had held since 1515. In an attempt to appease Henry's expected wrath, Wolsey had previously given Hampton Court Palace to him, and now he asked the king to take over all his possessions and retired to his archbishopric of York. In 1530, Wolsey was arrested and summoned to London to answer a charge of treason, but died on the way on November 29 in Leicester.

When Cranmer was at Waltham in the summer of 1529, it happened in God's providence that King Henry left London to stay at Waltham for a night or two. Among those with him were Stephen Gardiner, then secretary to Cardinal Wolsey, and a Dr. Fox, who was an almoner [a person responsible for distributing alms]. Both of these gentlemen, who were supporters of Henry in his quest for a divorce, stayed at Mr. Cressy's home where Cranmer was lodged.

At supper one evening, the two men, who were well acquainted with Cranmer, asked him what he thought about the king's cause. Cranmer replied that in his opinion they made more trouble by legal engagements against the church law than they needed to. "I think it would be better, " he said, "to decide by the Word of God the question as to whether a man may marry his brother's wife or not. By this the king's conscience could be quieted, and there would not be the frustrating delays year after year that prolong the time. There is but one truth in the question, and the Scriptures will show it clearly if handled properly by learned men in the universities, and that could be as well done here in England, as it could be in Rome. You would by this way have made an end to this matter long ago."

The two men liked Cranmer's response and were eager to share it with the king, who was about to send to Rome for a new commission to ponder the question. The next day the king traveled to Greenwich in southeast England on the Thames River. His mind was still much unsettled, and he wanted an end to this long and tedious matter. Hoping for some new help, he called Dr. Stephen and Dr. Fox to him and asked them, "What now, my masters, shall we do in this infinite cause of mine? A new commission must be secured from Rome, and when this matter will end, only God knows. I do not."

Dr. Fox answered, "We believe that there is a better way that can be arranged for your majesty. Dr. Cranmer suggested that we put the question to the test of God's Word in the universities rather than turning to Rome again."

"Where is this Dr. Cranmer?" the king asked.

"He is still at Waltham."

"Good," said the king, "I want to speak with him, so send for him immediately. He seems to have the answer to the problem. If I had known of this plan two years ago, it would have saved me much money, and I would been have rid of this anxiety."

Dr. Cranmer was sent for, but when he got to London he quarreled with Stephen and Fox because he said they had gotten him involved in a problem that he had no chance to study. Therefore he asked them to make excuses for him to the king so that he would not have to meet with him. But it was no use, the more they made excuses for Dr. Cranmer's absence, the more the king scolded them; and so no excuse did any good, and Cranmer was required to come to the king's court and talk with him.

"Master doctor," the king said, "I ask you, and because you are my subject, I charge and command you to set aside all your other business, and to make some effort to help the progress of my cause according to your plan, as much as you able to do so, so that I might soon understand the end that I can expect. For I proclaim before God and the world that I do not seek to be divorced from the queen, if by any means I might morally be persuaded that our marriage is not against any of the laws of God. For there is no other cause that would ever move me to seek such a thing. Neither was there ever a prince who had a more gentle, obedient, and loving companion and wife than the queen is, nor did I ever imagine a woman better than her in every way. If this doubt had not risen, I assure you that for the virtues alone that she has, besides high regard of her noble ancestry, I would be well contented to remain with her, if it was the will and pleasure of Almighty God."

Dr. Cranmer asked the king to commit the examination of this matter by the Word of God to the best educated men of the universities of Cambridge and Oxford. "Excellent words," said the king, "and I am satisfied with that. Nevertheless, I especially want you to write your thoughts about the matter."

After the king left, Cranmer wrote without restraint what he thought about the king's question, and added that the bishop of Rome, the pope, did not have the authority to do away with the Word of God.

After reading what Cranmer wrote, the king asked him, "Will you stand by this before the bishop of Rome?"

"That I will do by God's grace, if your majesty sends me there."

"Good, said the king, "I will even send you to him in the safe office of an ambassador."

And so by Dr. Cranmer's handling of this matter at the universities of Cambridge and Oxford, it was concluded that the marriage of a man to his brother's widow was *not* lawful according to the Word of God, and King Henry and his wife should be divorced.

As a result, in 1530 Dr. Cranmer was appointed ambassador to Rome, along with Dr. Stokesley, the earl of

Wiltshire, Dr. Carne, Dr. Bennet, and others. At that time, Pope Clement VII was at Bologna in north-central Italy, and there they appeared before him. Clement wore the usual rich clothing of his office and had sandals on his feet. As was customary, he presented his foot to them to be kissed, but Dr. Stokesly refused and remained standing, which encouraged the rest to keep themselves from such idolatry. At that moment, however, a spaniel belonging to Dr. Stokesly was directly in front of the pope, and seeing the pope's big toe he both licked it and bit at it, whereupon the pope yanked his sacred foot away and kicked at the dog with his other foot.

Somewhat insulted, the pope demanded to know the reason for their mission to see him. They presented to him Dr. Cranmer's written opinion about King Henry's marriage, and said they had come to Rome to defend that opinion, and that according to the Word of God no man should marry his brother's wife, and the pope had no authority to do away with the Scriptures. The pope treated them courteously and said he would give them his decision shortly and dismissed them. They never saw him again.

While the others returned to England, Dr. Cranmer went to see the Holy Roman Emperor, Charles V, on King Henry's behalf, and convinced him that the opinion he had written was in keeping with the Scriptures. He also went to Germany in 1531 to win the support of the Protestant princes. While there, despite his priestly orders, he married the niece of Andreas Osiander, a Lutheran theologian, whom he met at Nuremberg. He left his new wife with Osiander when he returned to England, and then after awhile sent for her privately. She remained with him until 1539 when Henry instituted his Six Articles, and then he was compelled to return her to Germany to stay with friends for a time.

In 1529, King Henry had angrily swept Cardinal Wolsey from his office as Lord Chancellor. Sir Thomas More, a stout Roman Catholic, was made Lord Chancellor in his place. In 1532, More resigned that position for what he said were reasons of ill health, but it was probably because he was in violent disagreement with what he considered to be the government's interference with the church in Rome.

After More's resignation, King Henry appointed a new chief minister, Thomas Cromwell. Not long after, Cromwell proposed that England break with the papacy so that the archbishop of Canterbury could grant Henry his divorce. Legislation to this effect was passed by Parliament in 1533. As a result Henry was free to marry Anne Boleyn, and the Church of England was established as an independent national church, no longer in communion with the Roman Catholic church or the pope.

On March 30, 1533, shortly after Cranmer returned to England, he was appointed archbishop of Canterbury, an office formerly held by Dr. Warham, who before he died recommended Dr. Cranmer to take his place. On May 23, Archbishop Cranmer declared that the marriage of Henry and Catherine had been invalid from the first, and within five days he pronounced legal the marriage of Henry and Anne Boleyn, which had been performed secretly the preceding January. In September, Anne Boleyn bore Henry a daughter, Elizabeth. Elizabeth was declared heir to the throne in place of Catherine of Aragon's daughter, Mary, who was now regarded as illegitimate.

Like Catherine, however, Anne Boleyn failed to bear Henry a son and he soon lost interest in her. In 1536, after the stillbirth of a boy, he had her arrested and tried for adultery. When she was found guilty, their marriage was invalidated by Archbishop Cranmer. She was subsequently beheaded on May 19, 1536. Eleven days after her execution,

Archbishop Cranmer officiated at the marriage of King Henry to Jane Seymour, who had been Anne Boleyn's maid of honor when she married the king. Although Cranmer had been Anne Boleyn's friend, it was dangerous to oppose the will of the carnal tyrannical monarch. It was also politically expedient to do whatever he requested.

Jane Seymour did bear the son Henry wanted— Edward, who would be king of England after Henry died. But she lived only twelve days after his birth and died on October 24, 1537.

Henry's fourth wife was Anne of Cleves. They were married in 1540. Anne was a member of a Protestant ruling family from Germany. Thomas Cromwell, the king's top minister, negotiated the marriage because he feared a Catholic alliance against England and wanted to gain diplomatic support from Lutherans on the Continent. Cromwell had led Henry to believe that Catherine was very beautiful, but when he saw her he discovered that he had been tricked. Additionally, the Protestant alliance was distasteful to him—he wanted to maintain the principles of the Catholic faith—and unnecessary as well. So he insisted on a divorce almost immediately. Archbishop Cranmer invalidated the marriage at Henry's request. At the same time, Cromwell's conservative enemies, especially Thomas Howard, duke of Norfolk, took advantage of Henry's displeasure with Cromwell and convinced him that Cromwell was a traitor to both his religion and the king. Consequently, Cromwell was arrested June 10 for treason and heresy, condemned without a hearing, and beheaded in London on July 28, 1540.

The king then married Catherine Howard, who was Thomas Howard's niece. By 1542, however, he was tired of her and brought charges of unchastity against her—meaning she was morally impure and immodest. Archbishop Cranmer played a leading role in the proceedings against her. She was found guilty of the charges and beheaded shortly after in that same year.

Henry's last wife, who miraculously survived him, was Catherine Parr. Her most notable achievement was convincing Henry to show more kindness to his daughters, Mary and Elizabeth. After Henry's death in 1547, she married Baron Seymour of Sudeley, brother of Edward Seymour, 1st duke of Somerset. She died in childbirth in 1548. None of Henry's last three wives bore him children.

On the political side, Archbishop Cranmer's actions seem to have had more than a note of compromise in them, but on the reformed church side there was no compromise. He was perhaps more responsible than any other person for the advancement of the Reformation in England. He worked vigorously in seeing to the removal of all popish superstitions and errors from the Church of England, and supported the English Bible translations of 1537-40. Between 1536 and 1540 he was involved in dissolving all the monasteries and nunneries in England. When their properties were confiscated by the government, he and other men of the Church worked to have their many goods and properties used for the poor and for building schools, but Henry granted the estates to noblemen who would support his policies. When Henry instituted his Six Articles in 1539, Cranmer opposed them as strongly as he could; in this he was supported by the bishops of Sarum, Worcester, Ely, and Rochester. The beheading of Lord Cromwell—a good friend of Cranmer's—in 1540 stunned him and set back the Protestant cause considerably. It marked a change in the tide of the Reformation in England. And from about this time until the time of Edward VI, Archbishop Cranmer fought several charges that were brought against him.

In 1544, the archbishop's palace at Canterbury was burned, and his brother-in-law and others died in the fire.

Often God intends such afflictions to humble us, for Cranmer could no longer boast of any great happiness, since he now was harassed constantly by either political, religious, or natural crosses. Stephen Gardiner, bishop of Winchester, had brought charges against Cranmer before, and now he charged him again with heresy, and informed the king that he should not tolerate teachings in his realm that were contrary to his Six Articles, that it would result in the same commotions and uproars that were taking place in parts of Germany because of Martin Luther's teachings. The king was Cranmer's friend, however, and gave him his signet ring as a sign that he would defend him.

When Cranmer was brought before the Council of Bishops in London, he presented them with the king's ring, which meant he was putting the matter of his defense in the king's hands. The Council fell apart in confusion, and when they went to the king about the matter, he not only declared that the archbishop was among those who had the best influence upon others in his realm, but sharply rebuked his accusers for the malicious false statements they made to injure his reputation.

There now being peace between England and France, King Henry VIII and the French king, Henry the Great, were both anxious to have the Mass abolished in their respective kingdoms, and Cranmer set about to accomplish this great work. But the death of Henry VIII in 1546, temporarily stopped the work.

When King Edward VI was crowned, Archbishop Cranmer delivered a charge at his coronation that will forever honor his memory for its purity, freedom, and truth. Soon after, Edward appointed Cranmer to continue his work in removing the mass from all church services in England. Until Edward became king, Cranmer did not seem to have a thorough knowledge of the Eucharist, for he had in the past agreed with the papist that there was the real presence of Christ in the consecrated bread and wine. But after spending some time conferring with Bishop Ridley, he took upon himself the defense of the Reformation doctrine concerning the Eucharist, and effectively refuted the error of the papists who say that those who take communion eat the natural body of Christ.

During Edward's reign, Cranmer worked for the glorious Reformation with unabated zeal, even when he was seized with a severe fever in 1552, from which it pleased God to deliver him so that he might testify by his martyrdom the truth of that seed that he had diligently sown. Among other great works that Cranmer accomplished during Edward's time was the creation of the first *Book of Common Prayer* in 1549, its revision in 1552, and the creation of the confession of 1553 called the Forty-two Articles—which were the basic summary of belief of the Church of England, and which taught justification by faith. The *Book of Common Prayer* contained the order of worship of the Church of England. Archbishop Cranmer's goal was to remove the papist prayer books that were in Latin, and produce a book in English that would be true to the example of the early church, Scriptural in content and spirit, and an instrument for uniting the church and the realm. The new book contained daily services of morning and evening prayer, baptism, and the Lord's Supper and services for confirmation, marriage, churching of women, visitation of the sick, and burial. Ordination rites were added to the book in 1550. He also put the English Bible into parish churches throughout England.

Just before King Edward VI died in July 1553, John Dudley, duke of Northumberland, persuaded him to name Lady Jane Grey, Dudley's daughter-in-law, as heir to the throne. To this the Council of Bishops and the king's legal advisers agreed and signed the king's testament to this effect. They then sent for Archbishop Cranmer and asked him if he would sign the testament also. But he said that it was contrary to King Henry's testament in which the king had stated that Mary should be his heir, and that he signed that testament and could not now sign this contrary one. He further stated that he was judge of no one, but was responsible for his own conscience and would not sign without speaking first with the king himself. Edward told him that the nobles and his lawyers had advised him to name Lady Jane his heir, and so with much anxiety Cranmer signed.

[Here again there seems to be compromise on the part of Archbishop Cranmer. This established spirit or attitude of compromise would soon cause him great anguish of heart and soul. Perhaps in this there is a lesson for us in that compromising in minor things will invariably cause us to compromise in major things.]

When King Edward died, Archbishop Cranmer was exposed to all the wrath of his enemies. Many of those who had agreed to the accession of Lady Jane Grey were forgiven with a simple fine, except for the Duke of Northumberland and the Duke of Suffolk, both of whom were beheaded, and Archbishop Cranmer. He was accused in parliament and judged guilty of high treason. Although he wanted to ask for pardon from Queen Mary, she refused to see him. He then sent a humble letter to her, explaining the reason that he signed Edward's testament in favor of Lady Jane, but there was no reply. Queen Mary was bitter about Archbishop Cranmer's part in Henry's divorcing her mother, and, having retained her papist beliefs during her brother's reign, she resented Cranmer's changing England's religion from Roman Catholic to Protestant.

In early 1554, Cranmer wrote to the Council of Bishops, and entreated them to obtain a pardon from the queen for him. The letter was delivered to a Dr. Weston, a member of the council, who read it and returned to Cranmer.

Not long after, a rumor was circulated that Archbishop Cranmer had performed a popish mass to gain the queen's favor, but he publicly denied the charge, and in writing justified his forty-nine articles of faith. Mr. Scory, bishop of Chichester, read the statement and asked the archbishop if he could have a copy of it. Scory then lent it to a friend of his who had many copies made and distributed abroad. Soon every *scrivener's shop was making copies and selling them. Some of the copies reached members of the Bishop's Council, and Cranmer was commanded to appear before them.

When he appeared, a bishop of the Queen's private council said to him, "My lord, there is a letter circulating in your name, in which you seem to be distressed that the mass has been set up again. I do not doubt but that you are sorry that this letter has gone abroad."

Cranmer replied, "I do not deny that I am the author of that letter. I had a mind to put it on the door of Paul's Church, and on the doors of all the churches in London, with my seal on it." When they saw his steadfastness, they dismissed him.

Not long after, he was arrested and sent to the Tower of London and condemned for treason, but since the queen had discharged others accused of the same crime, she released him from that charge and charged him with heresy, which pleased the archbishop because the cause was now not his own but Christ's—not the Queen's but the Church's. In March 1554 he was removed from the Tower and sent to Oxford University with Bishops Ridley and Latimer. He was about 69 years old at the time, having been born around 1485.

After the public debate in Oxford between the doctors of Oxford and Cambridge and the three bishops, Cranmer, Ridley, and Latimer, they were judged to be heretics and committed to the mayor and sheriffs of Oxford. But since the sentence of heresy was illegal because the power of the pope had not yet been reestablished in England, a new commission was sent from Rome, and a new process set up to legally convict these three godly men.

On Thursday, September 12, 1555, eighteen days before the ecclesiastically legal condemnation of Ridley and Latimer, Dr. Cranmer was brought to the church of St. Mary to appear before the new commission, which consisted of the pope's representative, Dr. Brooks, and the Queen's representatives, Drs. Story and Martin. The archbishop acknowledged the authority of Drs. Story and Martin, but protested his having to appear before a representative of the Romish pope. This offended Bishop Brooks, and he told Cranmer that it would be appropriate for him, considering the authority he represented, to properly and respectfully acknowledge his position. Cranmer replied that he had taken a solemn oath never to consent to the admitting of the bishop of Rome's authority into the kingdom of England again, and that he meant by God's grace to keep that oath. Therefore he would not give any sign or token that might indicate that he consented to accepting such authority.

During the lengthy examination that then took place, Dr. Cranmer's answers and remarks were of such a nature that at the end Dr. Brooks said to him, "We came here to examine you, but I think you have examined us."

Foolishly, Cranmer was then cited to appear before the pope in Rome within eighty days, which he said he would do if the Queen would send him and pay his way, since he was now too poor to pay his own way. He was then returned to prison. Within twenty days after, contrary to all reason and justice, the pope sent a letter to the Queen to degrade Cranmer and remove him from his office of archbishop and remove from him all symbols of that office. So on February 14, 1556, a new commission was appointed, and Thirlby (or Thirleby), bishop of Ely, and Bonner, bishop of London, were *deputed to sit in judgment at Christ Church in Oxford.

Bonner, who for some years had been against Cranmer and now rejoiced to see his degradation, first read a statement against him:

> This is the man that has always despised the Pope's holiness, and now is to be judged by him. This is the man that has pulled down so many churches, and now has come here to be judged in a church. This is the man that condemned the blessed sacrament of the altar, and now has come here to be condemned before that blessed sacrament hanging over the altar. This is the man that like Lucifer sat in the place of Christ upon an altar to judge others, and now has come before an altar to be judged himself.

Bonner went on with his pompous repetition, beginning every sentence with "This is the man," until at last Bishop Thirlby pulled at his sleeve to stop him, and later said to him at dinner that he had broken his promise to him, for he had earnestly asked him to treat the archbishop with reverence.

Bonner's speech having been ended, they proceeded with degrading Archbishop Cranmer. First they attempted to take Cranmer's *crosier from him, which he held fast to and refused to release. In imitation of the example of Martin Luther, he then pulled a written appeal out of his left sleeve, and gave it to them and said, "I appeal to the next General Council." In reply, Thirlby, the bishop of Ely, said to him, "My lord, we have been commissioned to proceed against you."

They then put ragged clothes on him to represent the dress of an archbishop, and then stripped him of those clothes and his own gown, and put on him a worn and ragged gown of a parish attendant. A barber then clipped his hair all around his head, and Bonner roughly scraped the tops of his fingers where he had been anointed. Lastly they put a *townsman's cap on his head, and delivered him to the secular powers. All this Cranmer bore without moving or speaking. When they finished, they returned him to prison.

During the nearly three years he had previously been imprisoned, Dr. Cranmer was treated with the utmost harshness because of the many popish enemies he had made as archbishop, but the severity of his treatment only made him more determined to stand fast in his beliefs. So his enemies now tried a different course and removed him from prison and placed him in the house of the dean of Christ Church, where he was treated with every indulgence. This was such a contrast to his hard imprisonment, that it threw him off his guard. It's possible also that because of his open, generous, nature he was more easily seduced by kind treatment than by chains and threats. How often when Satan finds one of his schemes blocked, he devises another, more subtle, one—and what is more enticing than smiles and good fellowship after years of hate and abuse?

So it was with Cranmer. His enemies promised him his former splendor and position, as well as the Queen's favor, if he would simply recant—and all this was offered in the face of his certain burning at the stake. Cranmer began to hope that he would not only have his life, but would be restored to his ancient office of archbishop, and that there would be nothing in the kingdom that the Queen would not easily grant him, whether it was riches or dignity. But if he refused, there was no hope of health and pardon, for the Queen was determined that she would have Cranmer a catholic or no Cranmer at all.

To make his road to apostasy easier, his seducers first gave him a document written in general terms that essentially meant little, so Cranmer willingly signed it. Having taken that first step, the second step was easier, and so when he was given five more consecutive documents that each increasingly explained the first document, he signed each of them—and each became easier to sign. Finally, the recantation document that they really wanted Cranmer to sign was placed before him, and with the habit of signing having been formed, he signed it. It read:

> I, Thomas Cranmer, late archbishop of Canterbury, do renounce, abhor, and detest all manner of heresies and errors of Luther and Zuinglius, and all other teachings which are contrary to sound and true doctrine. And I believe most constantly in my heart, and with my mouth I confess one holy and Catholic Church visible, without which there is no salvation. Therefore, I acknowledge the bishop of Rome to be supreme head on earth, whom I acknowledge to be the highest bishop and pope, and Christ's vicar, unto whom all Christian people ought to be subject.
>
> As concerning the sacraments, I believe and worship in the sacrament of the altar the body and blood of Christ, being contained most truly under the forms of bread and wine—the bread, through the mighty power of God, being turned into the body of our Savior Jesus Christ, and the wine into His blood. In the other six sacraments, also, (alike as in this) I believe and hold as the universal Church holds, and the Church of Rome judges and determines.
>
> Furthermore, I believe that there is a place of purgatory, where departed souls are punished for a time, for whom the Church does godly and wholesomely pray, like as it does honor saints and make prayers to them.

Finally, in all things I profess, that I do not believe differently than what the Catholic Church and the Church of Rome holds and teaches. I am sorry that I ever held or thought differently. I beseech Almighty God, that of His mercy He will condescend to forgive me whatever I have offended against God or His Church, and also I desire and beseech all Christian people to pray for me.

All those who have been deceived either by my example or doctrine, I require them by the blood of Jesus Christ to return to the unity of the Church, that we may be all of one mind without schism or division.

To conclude, as I submit myself to the Catholic Church of Christ, and to the supreme head thereof, so I submit myself unto the most excellent majesties of Philip and Mary, king and queen of this realm of England, etc., and to all other their laws and ordinances, being ready always as a faithful subject ever to obey them. God is my witness that I have not done this for favor or fear of any person, but willingly and of my own conscience for the instruction of others.

The Apostle Paul wrote, "Let him that standeth take heed lest he fall" (1 Corinthians 10:12), and this was a fall indeed. The papists rejoiced in their triumph, and all true Christians sorrowed in their defeat. Rome had what it wanted, and Cranmer's recantation was immediately printed and distributed so that it would have maximum effect upon the astonished Protestants. But God soon worked against the designs of the papists through the degree to which they carried their unappeasable persecution of Cranmer. All this time, Cranmer was not certain that he would live, although the bishops had promised him that he would.

The Queen, meanwhile, having now come to her time of revenge, received his recantation with joy, but she would not relent from her determination to put Cranmer to death. And Cranmer was increasingly suffering from a guilty conscience. It was love of life and fear of pain and death that caused him to recant, but now he was the joy of every papist and the contempt of every Gospel Christian—the knowledge of this pressed upon him with great force and anguish. On one side was praise, on the other side scorn, on both sides danger—he could neither die honestly nor dishonestly live.

To drink the full measure of Cranmer's blood, the Queen wrote to Dr. Pole [or Cole] and commanded him to prepare, as it were, a funeral sermon for Cranmer, to be delivered at St. Mary's Church in Oxford on March 21, just before his burning. Cranmer was not to be made aware of this until it was too late. Soon after, Lord Williams of Thame, Lord Chandos, Sir Thomas Bridges, and Sir John Brown, along with other worshipful men and justices, were commanded in the Queen's name to be at Oxford on the same day with their servants and attendants to prevent any commotion that Cranmer's death might cause.

Dr. Pole visited Cranmer the day before his execution, and inquired if his faith in the Roman Catholic doctrine still held. Cranmer replied that by God's grace he would daily be more firmly settled in the Catholic faith. Pole did not tell him that he was to be burned the next day. The next morning, March 21, 1556, Pole visited him again and asked him if he had any money, and when Cranmer said he did not he gave him fifteen crowns to give to the poor—and exhorted Cranmer to remain steady in his faith. Undoubtedly Cranmer now began to suspect what was happening and began to prepare himself.

About 9 A.M., Bishop Bonner and others of the Queen's commissioners and the sheriffs, took Cranmer from Bocardo Prison to St. Mary's Church. He was still dressed in the torn, dirty, clothes they put on him at his degradation, and the sight of him so dressed caused many to grieve for him. St. Mary's was filled with rejoicing Roman Catholics and grieving Protestants, both expecting to hear the reasons for Cranmer's apostasy. At the front of the church they placed him on a low, shabby stage that was erected opposite to the pulpit. There he knelt and turned his face toward heaven and prayed fervently to God.

In his sermon, Dr. Pole said that Archbishop Cranmer committed atrocious crimes and deluded many, and that his conversion back to the true church was undoubtedly the work of Almighty God. At the end of his sermon, he exhorted Cranmer to take his death well, and assured him that for those who die in His faith God would either abate the fury of the flame or give strength to stand it. These words were probably the first certainty that Cranmer had that he was going to burn even though he had recanted. Pole then asked the archbishop to give a sign of the reality of his conversion, and said to the people, "Brethren, lest anyone should doubt of this man's earnest conversion, you shall hear him speak before you." Then he turned again to Cranmer and said, "Master Cranmer, openly express the true profession of your faith, that all may understand that you are a catholic indeed."

"I will do it," said the archbishop, and then asked the people to pray for him, saying that he had committed many grievous sins, but that there was one awful sin that weighed heavily upon his mind, and he would speak of it shortly.

All the while he spoke, Cranmer wept bitterly, often lifting up his eyes and hands toward heaven and then letting his hands drop heavily to his sides, as if he was not worthy to worship God or even live. Before he spoke, however, he fell to his knees and poured out the anguish of his tormented soul:

O Father of heaven! O Son of God, Redeemer of
the world! O Holy Ghost, three persons all one God!

Have mercy on me, most despicable coward and miserable sinner. I have offended both against heaven and earth, more than my tongue can express. Whither then may I go, or whither may I flee? To heaven I am ashamed to lift up my eyes and in earth I find no place of refuge or relief. To Thee, therefore, O Lord, do I run. To Thee do I humble myself, saying, O Lord, my God, my sins are great, but yet have mercy upon me for Thy great mercy. The great mystery that God became man, was not wrought for little or few offenses. Thou didst not give Thy Son, O Heavenly Father, unto death for small sins only, but for all the greatest sins of the world, so that the sinner return to Thee with his whole heart, as I do at present. Therefore, have mercy on me, O God, whose virtue is always to have mercy. Have mercy upon me, O Lord, for Thy great mercy. I crave nothing for my own merits, but for Thy name's sake, that it may be hallowed thereby, and for Thy dear Son, Jesus Christ's sake. And now therefore, O Father of Heaven, hallowed be Thy name.

And with many more good words he prayed. Then he rose and said he wanted to give them some godly exhortations by which God might be glorified and they strengthened in their faith. He spoke at length about the danger of loving the world, about obeying their rulers, about loving one another, and about those who were rich giving to the poor. He then quoted the first three verses from the fifth chapter of the Book of James and spoke briefly about them. Then he said:

Inasmuch as I have come to the end of my life, on which hangs all my life past and all my life to come, either to live with my master Christ forever in joy or else to be in pain forever with the wicked in hell, and since I presently see before my eyes either heaven ready to receive me or else hell ready to swallow me up, I shall therefore declare to you my true faith and how I believe, without hiding anything, for now is no time to conceal whatever I have said or written in times past.

First, I believe in God the Father Almighty, Maker of heaven and earth. And I believe every word and sentence taught by our Savior Jesus Christ, His apostles and prophets, in the New and Old Testament.

And now I come to the great thing that so much troubles my conscience, more than any thing that I ever did or said in my whole life, and that is the distribution of a writing that is contrary to the truth, which I now here renounce and refuse. These things were written with my hand contrary to the truth that I believed in my heart, and written for fear of death and to save my life, if it might be. That includes all such bills or papers that I have written or signed with my hand since my degradation, in which I have written many untrue things.

And inasmuch as my hand has offended and written contrary to my heart, my hand shall first be punished— for when I come to the fire it shall first be burned.

As for the pope, I refuse him, as Christ's enemy, and antichrist, with all his false doctrine.

When he finished this unexpected declaration, amazement, shock, and indignation ran through the church. The pope's followers were completely frustrated in their attempt to use the archbishop to destroy the faith and steadfastness of the true Christians. Like Samson, Cranmer destroyed more of his enemy with his death than he did in his life. Throughout the church voices began to rise in protest, and when he attempted to speak more about the sacrament and the papacy, some of them began to cry out, yell, and wail—especially Pole who shouted out, "Stop the heretic's mouth and take him away!" Cranmer was pulled roughly from the platform and led to the fire by several friars who reviled and taunted him all the way to the place where Nicholas Ridley and Hugh Latimer were burned five months before. The archbishop did not answer their insults and threats but spoke to the people as much as he could, encouraging them to hold fast with Christ.

At the place of burning he knelt and prayed, then arose and removed his clothing to his undergarments, and stood quietly while an iron chain was tied around him and the stake. Kindling was laid around him and over those the faggots. Two friars who had been of those who had first convinced him to recant, tried to get him to do so again, but he was now steadfast and immovable in his faith in Christ and His Word. So they set fire to the wood.

When the fires flamed up around him, this true man of God, who for a moment had weakened but then gloriously returned to the truth, did what he had foretold he would do. He stretched out his right arm and held his hand in the flames, steady and unshrinking, until it was burned black as cinders. While it burned, he frequently exclaimed, "This unworthy right hand."

The pain and death that he had feared seemed now as nothing to him, and his body remained as unmoved in the flames as the stake to which he was tied. So long as his voice allowed him, he repeated "This unworthy right hand," and used often the words of the martyr Stephen, "Lord Jesus, receive my spirit." When the flames roared greatly around him, nearly hiding him in their fury, he gave up the ghost—and met his Lord.

17

The Fires of Smithfield

(1410-1556)

About the year 1103, which was the third year of the reign of Henry I, the youngest son of William the Conqueror, the hospital of St. Bartholomew was founded in Smithfield—now a district of London north of St. Paul's Cathedral—by means of a minstrel named Rayer, who belonged to the king. It was later finished by Richard Whittington, who was then alderman and mayor of London. For well over a hundred years, Smithfield was the place where *felons and other transgressors of the king's laws were executed.

John Brady, *Artificer

On Saturday, March 1, 1410, during the reign of King Henry IV, a tailor named John Brady was questioned by Thomas Arundel, archbishop of Canterbury, about whether there was the actual presence of Christ in the consecrated sacrament. Brady replied that it was impossible for any priest to speak words and make the wine and bread the body of Christ. When the archbishop saw that Brady would not change his belief, and considered that he had started convincing others to believe the same, he condemned Brady as an open and public heretic and turned him over to the secular powers.

These things took place in the morning, and the king's *writ to burn Brady came that afternoon. He was immediately taken to Smithfield and put into an empty barrel and bound with iron chains to a stake. Dried wood was then put around him. As he was thus standing, it happened that the king's eldest son, who would succeed to the throne as Henry VI, was there and tried to find some way to save his life. In the meantime, the *prior of St. Bartholomew's brought a consecrated Eucharist in a solemn procession, preceding it with twelve torch bearers, and showed it to the condemned man and demanded to know what he believed about it. Brady replied that he knew full that it was hallowed bread, but not Christ's body. At those words they put fire to him.

When the innocent soul felt the fire, he cried, "Mercy!" Most likely he was calling upon the Lord, but his cry was so horrible sounding that when the Prince heard it he commanded the fire to be quenched, and asked Brady if he would forsake his heresy. If he would, the Prince said, he would give him all he needed to live—a yearly *stipend out of the king's treasury, enough to support him.

But this valiant champion of Christ, paid no attention to the Prince's words, and refused all offers others made to him, for he was determined to suffer any kind of torment, no matter how painful it was, rather than acknowledge so great idolatry and wickedness. Therefore the Prince commanded that he be put to fire again. Even so, Brady held steadfast and persevered invincibly to the end.

William Sweeting and John Brewster

These two men had been tried for heresy once before, judged guilty, and sentenced to wear, on penalty of burning, miniature painted faggots as badges denoting that they were heretics for as long as their *ordinary appointed. When they stopped wearing the badges, they were arrested again and charged for that crime, for their beliefs contrary to Rome's teachings about the sacrament, for reading forbidden books, and for having as companions certain persons suspected of heresy. They were burned together on October 18, 1511.

John Stilman

In 1518, John Stilman was charged for publicly speaking against worshipping images and praying to them and giving them offerings—also for denying the actual presence of Christ in the consecrated Eucharist, and for highly praising John Wycliffe and declaring that he was a saint in heaven. After being judged guilty and condemned by the Council of Bishops, he was delivered to the sheriffs of London and burned at Smithfield.

John Lambert

Lambert was born and brought up in Norfolk, studied at Cambridge University, became proficient in Latin and Greek, and then left England because of the violence of the times and went to Europe and stayed there for about a year with Tyndale and Frith. During that time he became chaplain to the English House [somewhat like an Embassy] in Antwerp, Belgium. While there he was troubled by Sir Thomas More and by a man named Barlow who carried accusations against him to England. Not long after Lambert was taken by English officials from Antwerp to London, and brought for examination before Warham, the archbishop of Canterbury. Shortly after, however, the archbishop died and Lambert was free for quite some time. He returned to London and there worked teaching children Greek and Latin. Then, in 1538, he heard a sermon preached by Dr. Rowland Taylor in St. Peter's Church.

After the sermon Lambert went gently to Dr. Taylor to talk to him about the matter of the sacrament of the body and blood of Christ, which Taylor had spoken about in his sermon, but mostly in agreement with Romish beliefs. Wanting to answer Lambert's disagreements and questions to his satisfaction, Dr. Taylor conferred with a Dr. Barnes [this may have been the same Dr. Barnes that was burned for heresy on July 30, 1540], but Barnes apparently did not totally agree with Taylor's views at that time, or did not want to join the controversy between him and Lambert. Soon, what started as a private debate became a public matter, and Archbishop Thomas Cranmer sent for Lambert and forced him to defend his beliefs openly. At this time the archbishop did not yet agree with the Reformation doctrine of the sacrament, but later he was an earnest professor of it. In this continual debate, it is said that Lambert appealed to London's bishops and to King Henry VIII himself.

Finally, the king called an assembly of bishops and others and appeared before them dressed all in white. On his right hand sat London's bishops, and behind them the famous lawyers, clothed all in purple. On his left hand sat the peers of the realm, justices, and other nobles in the proper order of their noble standing. Behind them sat the attendants of the king's private quarters. The manner and form of what was now a judgment of Lambert, was terrible enough to make even an innocent person ashamed or uneasy. The look on the king's face, his cruel expression with his brows drawn severely together, did much to increase this terror, and plainly declared that the king's mind was filled with indignation. He looked sternly at Lambert, and then turned to his councilors and called forth Dr. Sampson, bishop of Chichester, and told him to tell the people why they were assembled.

When Sampson finished his oration, the king stood up, leaned on a cushion covered with white cloth, and turned toward Lambert with his brows forced into a fierce scowl, as if threatening something painful, and said, "Ho! good fellow, what is your name?"

The humble lamb of Christ knelt on one knee before the king and replied, "My name is John Nicholson, although many call me Lambert."

"What," said the king, "you have two names? I would not trust you, having two names, even if you were my brother."

"O most noble prince," replied Lambert, "your bishops forced me, as if it was necessary, to change my name."

They talked for some time in this way, and then the king commanded Lambert to declare what he thought concerning the sacrament of the altar. Speaking first for himself, Lambert thanked God that He had so influenced the heart of the king that he would not consider it beneath himself to hear and understand religious controversies.

At this the king angrily interrupted Lambert and said, "I did not come here to listen to my own praises rendered in my presence, so briefly go on with the matter without any more ceremony. Answer the question concerning the sacrament of the altar—what do you say, is it is the body of Christ, or do you deny it?"

Lambert replied, "My answer is like that of St. Augustine, that it is the body of Christ, in a certain way."

King Henry said, "Do not answer me out of St. Augustine or any other authority, but tell me plainly whether *you* say it is the body of Christ or not.

Lambert said, "Then I deny that it is the body of Christ."

"Mark well!" King Henry said, "For now you shall be condemned by Christ's own words, 'This is my body.'" Then he commanded Archbishop Cranmer to prove the error of Lambert's assertions, which Cranmer attempted to do with many words and Scriptures. Altogether it would take too long to repeat the arguments of every bishop, and there is no reason to do so, since there was no power in any of them, for they were all contrary to the true Word of God.

At last, when the day was passed and torches were being lit, the king, wanting to end this debate, said to Lambert, "Who do you say now, after all the great efforts you have put forth, and all the reasons and instructions of these knowledgeable men, are you now satisfied? Will you choose to live or die? What do you say? You have free choice."

Lambert answered, "I give and submit myself entirely to the will of your majesty."

"Commit yourself to the hands of God," the king said, "and not to mine."

"I commend my soul to the hands of God," said Lambert, "but my body I entirely give and submit to your clemency."

Then said the king, "If you do commit yourself to my judgment, you must die, for I will not be a patron to heretics." Turning to Thomas Cromwell, he said, "Cromwell! read the sentence of condemnation against him."

Cromwell read the sentence, and Lambert was immediately taken to Smithfield for burning. As with all such executions, many of London's citizens gathered to watch—some as friends, some as enemies—along with the official witnesses. Because of their church and government positions, and because they officiated at Lambert's trial, the archbishop of Canterbury, Thomas Cranmer, and the king's chief minister, Thomas Cromwell, were among the officials there to witness Lambert's burning.

Of all those burned at Smithfield, none were so cruelly and mercilessly handled as this blessed martyr. After his legs had burned to stumps, his tormentors withdrew most of the fire from him so that only a small fire burned beneath him, and then two of them stood on each side and impaled his upper body with the *pikes on their halberds and held him up so that he could not fall into the fire.

Lambert hung helplessly that way as many of the people groaned and cried with pity. Then the fat in his fingertips caught fire and he lifted up his hands toward heaven and cried to the people, "None but Christ, none but Christ." At that his tormentors let him down again from their halberds, and he fell forward into the fire and there gave up his life for Christ.

Mistress Anne Askew, Daughter of Sir William Askew, Knight of Lincolnshire

Here in Anne Askew's own words are her account of her examinations for heresy, which she wrote at the request of certain faithful men and women.

The First Examination before the Inquisitors, 1545

Christopher Dare examined me at Sadler's Hall, and asked me why I had said I had rather read five lines in the Bible than hear five masses in the Temple church. I confessed that was what I said, not to express disapproval of the epistle or the Gospel, which are somewhat read in the mass, but because the one greatly edifies me and the other does nothing at all. He then charged me that I had said if an evil priest ministered, it was the devil and not God. My answer was that I never said any such thing. But this was what I said: that whoever it was that ministered to me, his evil condition could not hurt my faith, for it was in spirit that I received the body and blood of Christ. He then asked me what I said concerning confession. I answered that my meaning was, as St. James said, that every man ought to acknowledge his faults to others, and each to pray for the other. Then he sent a priest to me to ask if I did not think that private masses helped the souls of the departed. I said it was great idolatry to believe more in the masses than in the death that Christ died for us.

Then they took me to the Lord Mayor, and he charged me with one more thing, which I never said, but which they did—whether if a mouse ate the host he received God or not? I did not answer but only smiled.

Then the bishop's chancellor rebuked me, and said that I was much to blame for speaking the Scriptures. For St. Paul, he said, forbade women to speak or to talk about the Word of God. I told him that I knew Paul's meaning as well as he did, which is in 1 Corinthians 14 and says that a woman ought not to speak in the congregation by the way of teaching—and then I asked him how many women he had seen go into the pulpit and preach. He said he had not seen any. Then I said that he ought to find no fault in poor women unless they had violated the law.

I was then taken to the *Compter, and there remained for eleven days, with no friend admitted to speak with me.

The Sum of My Examination Before the
King's Council at Greenwich

They said it was the king's pleasure that I should turn the matter over to him. I answered them plainly that I would not do so, but if it were the king's pleasure to hear me, that I would show him the truth. They said it was not right for the king to be troubled by me. I said that Solomon was considered the wisest king that ever lived, yet it did not displease him to hear two poor common women—much more should his grace hear a simple woman and his faithful subject.

The Lord Chancellor asked my opinion about the sacrament. I said this, "I believe that as often as I receive, in a Christian congregation, the bread in remembrance of Christ's death, and do it with thanksgiving according to the holy practice that He instituted, I receive with that the fruits, also, of His most glorious passion." The bishop of Winchester directed me to make a direct answer. I said I would not sing a new song in a strange land. The bishop said that I spoke in parables. I said it was best for him, "for if I show the open truth, you will not accept it." I told him I was ready to suffer all things at his hands, not only his rebukes, but all that should follow besides—yes, and all that gladly.

My Lord Lisle, my Lord of Essex, and the bishop of Winchester demanded earnestly that I confess the sacrament to be flesh, blood, and bone of Christ. Then, I said, that it was a great shame for them to counsel me contrary to their knowledge.

Then the bishop said he would speak to me as a friend. I said, "So did Judas when he betrayed Christ." Then the bishop wanted to speak to me alone. But that I refused. He asked me why. I said that in the mouth of two or three witnesses every matter should stand.

Then the bishop said that I would be burned. I answered that I had searched all the Scriptures, yet I could not find that either Christ or His apostles put any creature to death. "Well, well," I said, "God will laugh your threatenings to scorn."

Then I was sent to Newgate Prison.

My Handling Since My Departure from Newgate Prison

From Newgate I was sent to the sign of the Crown, where Master Rich and the bishop of London, with all their power and flattering words, tried to persuade me away from God, but I did not consider their shining pretenses. After that Nicholas Shaxton came to see me and counseled me to recant as he had done. I said to him that it would have been better for him if he had never been born. Then Master Rich sent me to the Tower of London, where I remained until three o'clock in the afternoon.

About then Rich and one of his council came to see me and charged me to obey them and tell if I knew any wealthy woman who believed as I did. I told them I knew none. They said the king had been informed that I could name a great many. I answered that the king was as well deceived in that matter as he was false in other matters.

They then commanded me to tell them how I was financially cared for in the Compter, and who willed me to stick to my opinion. I said that there was no creature that strengthened me, and as for the help I had in the Compter it came by means of my maid. As she went about in the streets, she moaned about my condition to the apprentices she saw working and they, by her, sent me money, but who they were I never knew.

They said that they were various gentlewomen who gave me money—but I did not know their names. Then they said there were various ladies that had sent me money. I said that there was a man in a blue coat who delivered ten shillings to me, and said that my Lady of Hertford sent it. Also another in a violet coat gave me eight shillings, and said my Lady Denny sent it. Whether it was true or not, I could not tell.

They then put me on the *rack because I did not confess any ladies or gentlewoman that were of my religious opinions, and there they kept me for a long time. And because I laid still and did not cry out, my Lord Chancellor and Master Rich took pains to rack me with their own hands until I was nearly dead.

Then the Lieutenant had me removed from the rack. Involuntarily I fainted, and then they revived me. After that I sat on the bare floor for two long hours reasoning with my Lord Chancellor, who with many flattering words tried to persuade me to give up my opinion. But my Lord God, (I thank His everlasting goodness) gave me grace to persevere, and will do so, I hope, to the end.

I was then taken to a house and laid in a bed, with as weary and painful bones as ever had patient Job. I thank my Lord God for the rest. The Lord Chancellor then sent me word that if I would give up my opinion I would want nothing, but if I would not I would immediately be sent to Newgate, and soon be burned. I sent him word again that I would rather die than break my faith.

The day of her execution being set, this good woman was brought into Smithfield in a chair, for she could not walk because of her torture on the rack. At the stake they tied her body tightly with a chain to hold her up. They were so many people there that fences were put up to hold them back. Upon the bench at the front of St. Bartholomew's Church were the church and government witnesses—Wriothesley, Chancellor of England, the old Duke of Norfolk, the old Earl of Bedford, the Lord Mayor, and various others. Before the faggots around those being burned that day was set on fire, one of those on the bench heard that there was gunpowder about the condemned and became afraid that it might explode and wood and fire would come flying around the bench. But the Earl of Bedford explained to him that the gunpowder was not laid upon the faggots, but only upon their bodies, and that to rid them early of their pains.

Then Lord Chancellor Wriothesley offered Anne Askew the king's pardon if she would recant. But she answered that she had not come to Smithfield to deny her Lord and Master. Thus the good Anne Askew, being enveloped in flames, as a blessed sacrifice to God, died in the Lord in 1546. Behind her she left a remarkable example of faithfulness for all Christians to follow.

Seven Martyrs Suffering Together

There were so many martyrs burned at Smithfield and other places that there is not enough room in this book to tell all of their stories, or even name them all. It could be as well said about the martyrs as John said about Jesus, "And there are also many other things which Jesus did, the which, if they should be written every one, I suppose that even the world itself could not contain the books that should be written. Amen" (John 21:25).

To name only a few, for only God knows the many, there was **Thomas Man, John Lacels, John Adams, Nicholas Belenian, John Bradford, John Leaf, John Philpot, Thomas Loseby, Henry Ramsey, Thomas Thirtel, Margaret Hide, Agnes Stanley, John Hallingdale, William Sparrow, Richard Gibson, Henry Pond, Reinald Eastland, Robert Southam, Matthew**

Ricarby, John Floyd, John Holiday, Roger Holland—
and the seven who were burned on January 27, 1556.

On that day in 1556, during the reign of Queen Mary
I, **Thomas Whittle**, priest; **Bartlet Green**, gentleman;
John Tudson, artificer; **John Went**, artificer; **Thomas
Browne**; **Isabel Foster**, wife; **Joan (Warne) Lashford**,
maid; were burned together. Only bits and pieces of some
of their stories have come down to us.

Thomas Whittle was most cruelly treated by Bonner,
the bishop of London, who beat him repeatedly in the face
until he could hardly be recognized. To a friend, Whittle
wrote, "The bishop sent for me in the porter's lodge where
I had slept all night on a straw-filled mattress laid on the
ground. Never before have I had such a painful night of
sickness. When I came before the bishop, he asked me if I
would have come to mass that morning if he had sent for
me. I answered that I would have come to him at his
commandment, "but as to your mass," I said, "I have little
affection." He was greatly displeased at this answer and
said I would be fed with bread and water. As I followed
him through the great hall, he turned back and beat me with
his fist, first on one cheek and then the other. Then he put
me into a little salt-house, where I stayed for two nights
without any straw or bed. I slept upon a table, and, I thank
God, I slept soundly."

Strengthened with the grace of the Lord, Whittle stood
strong and immovable and was brought to the fire with the
other six.

Bartlet Green was of a good family and was educated
at Oxford University. While there he often attended the
lectures of Peter Martyr and saw the true light of Christ's
Gospel. On January 15, 1556, he was arrested and
condemned for heresy. As he was being taken to Newgate
Prison, two friends met in hopes that they could somehow
comfort their persecuted brother. But their hearts were so

filled with friendship and love for Green that all their could do was weep. Green said to them, "Ah, my friends! is this the comfort you have come to give me, in this the time of my heaviness? Must I, who needs the comfort ministered to me, now become comforters of you?"

When Green was scourged with rods by Bishop Bonner, he greatly rejoiced. Yet his extreme modesty was such that he never mentioned the scourging, lest it might seem that he was glorying in himself. Just before his burning, however, he did tell his friend Mr. Cotton about it.

Thomas Brown lived in the parish of St. Bride's in Fleet Street, and because he did not attend the masses at his parish church, he was apprehended by the constable of the parish and taken to Bonner. He was then taken to Fulham and required to go into the chapel to hear mass, but he refused and went out into a wooded area and knelt among the trees. For this he was greatly accused by Bishop Bonner who said to him, "Brown, you have been before me many times, and I have toiled with you to win you from your errors. Yet you, and those like you, say that I go about to seek your blood."

To this Brown answered, "Yes, my lord, indeed you are a bloodsucker, and I wish I had as much blood as water in the sea for you to suck." So Bonner condemned him to be burned.

Joan (Warne) Lashford was the daughter of one **Robert** (or John) **Warne**, a cutler, who was persecuted for the Gospel of God and burned; and then was burned his wife, **Elizabeth**; and after her, their daughter Joan.

Elizabeth Warne, whose husband had already been burned as a heretic, was arrested on January 1, 1555, while meeting for prayer with nine others in a house in Bow Churchyard, London. She was imprisoned in the Tower until

June 11, and was then transferred to Newgate Prison, where she remained until July 2. On July 6, the ten prisoners were all brought before Bishop Bonner—so many were being persecuted at that time that they could no longer be judged separately. The names of the nine were **George Tankervil, Robert Smith, Thomas Fust, Thomas Leyes, John Wade, Stephen Wade, George King, William Hall,** and Joan (Warne) Lashford. The charges against them were not believing in the actual presence of the body of Christ in the consecrated Eucharist, not attending masses and speaking out against them, and speaking out also against the traditional Romish ceremonies and sacraments. Elizabeth was brought before the bishop several times and when threatened with burning told him, "Do with me what you will, I will not deny Christ. If I am in error, so was He." On July 12, 1555, she and eight of the other nine were condemned as heretics and were burned the following month at Stratford-le-Bow.

The tenth person not condemned and burned at that time was her daughter Joan. She was released for a period of time and arrested again a few months later. During the time that her father was in prison and later her mother, Joan ministered to them as well as she was able. At the time of her second arrest she was twenty years old and known to be of the same doctrine as her parents. When examined by Bishop Bonner, she fearlessly declared that she would neither attend a popish mass nor confess her sins to a priest. She was burned at the stake six months after her mother.

Five Unknown Stories

While searching for illustrations for the *New Foxe's Book of Martyrs,* we found five copper engravings depicting the martyrdom of five Christian men—Vitalus, Wolfgang Binder of Scharding, Hendrik Pruijt, John Bret, and

Matthias Mayr. Only scant information was available to us at the time. Nevertheless, we decided to include the engravings because the ways in which they were tortured and put to death typify the ways in which thousands of other martyrs were tormented and executed. There is this also: they deserve to be remembered.

Vitalus (see Figure 11)

Vitalus was buried alive in Ravenna, Italy, around the year A.D. 99.

Wolfgang Binder of Scharding (see Figure 12)

Binder was beheaded in Bavaria, Germany, in 1571.

Hendrik Pruijt (see Figure 13)

In 1574, outside *Workum, Hendrik Pruijt was tarred and tied to a small boat. Then he was set on fire and the boat pushed out into the water.

John Bret (see Figure 14)

In Antwerp, Belgium, in 1576, John Bret, an Englishman, had his tongue bored through with a red-hot nail, and was afterward burned at the stake. Although the available information did not say, it was normally those who preached Reformation doctrines of the Gospel of Jesus Christ who had their tongues mutilated.

Matthais Mayr (see Figure 15)

In 1592, in Weir (town not found), Mayr's hands were tied behind his back and he was let down into the water at the end of a pier and drowned.

18

The Saint Bartholomew Day Massacre

(1572)

On August 24, 1572, there began a mass killing of the Huguenots, who were French Calvinist Protestants, by the Roman Catholics. It originated in Paris and spread throughout France for two months until almost **one-hundred-thousand Protestants** were killed and the Huguenots were nearly extinguished from the face of the earth. It all started at a wedding celebration.

Charles IX, king of France from 1560 to 1574, proposed a marriage between his 19-year-old sister, Margaret of Valois, and 19-year-old King Henry of Navarre. Henry, who in 1589 would become King Henry IV of France, was raised by his father as a Calvinist and was leader of the Huguenots. Charles thought that by this marriage he could settle the antagonism between the Roman Catholic majority in France and the Protestants, whose armies under the leadership of Admiral Gaspard de Coligny had several times defeated the French royal army and won a shaky truce.

Gaspard de Coligny was born in Chatillon-sur-Loing, France, on February 16, 1519. He had a brilliant military career, and in 1552 was appointed admiral of France. His brother, Francis d'Andelot, was a Calvinist, and through his influence Coligny converted to Calvinism after his capture in the Battle of St. Quentin in 1557.

When King Henry II was killed accidentally in a jousting tournament in 1559, Coligny joined himself with the prince of Conde (prince de Conde), Louis I, to lead the French Huguenots, and demanded religious tolerance from the new king, Charles IX, who was a Roman Catholic. Although Coligny tried to obtain a peaceful solution to the religious troubles between the Roman Catholic government and the French Protestants, civil war broke out. In 1569, Louis I was killed at the battle of Jarnac when the duke of Anjou's army defeated the Huguenots. Coligny then became head of the Protestant armies.

Shortly after a defeat at Moncontour, Coligny marched his army across France and defeated the royal army at Arnay-le-Duc in June 1570. As a result of this victory, he was able to obtain a truce from the king, but he waited more than a year before risking an appearance at the king's court. Once there, however, he quickly gained favor with the 21-year-old King Charles IX, and often counseled Charles in matters of the kingdom.

As the friendship and confidence between Charles and Coligny grew, Catherine de' Medici, the queen mother, saw it as a threat to her ambitions. Since the death of Henry II, her husband and Charles's father, she had wielded great power over Charles and wanted to hold on to it. But Coligny's counsel was beginning to weaken that power.

The wedding of Margaret of Valois and King Henry of Navarre was publicly celebrated in Paris on August 18, 1572, with the cardinal of Bourbon officiating. After the ceremony, a great dinner was held. It was attended by the king and queen mother, the bishop of Paris, many Roman Catholics prelates, and every high-ranking official in France who could attend, both Catholic and Protestant.

Four days after the wedding, on August 22, 1572, as Admiral Coligny was coming from a meeting of the French Council, he was wounded in both arms by an assassin who was hired by Catherine and members of the Guise family. While being treated, he said to a minister who was with him, "O my brother, I now know that I am dearly loved by my God, since I am wounded for His most holy sake." Although the minister advised him to leave Paris at once, Coligny, who had been a soldier almost his entire life, choose to stay.

At first, Charles swore to avenge the attempt on Coligny's life and immediately ordered an investigation to learn who the assassin was and who had hired him to kill Coligny. Fearing that such an investigation would expose her role in the assassination plot, Catherine, with the help of intimate associates, worked upon the fears and religious prejudices of her son and persuaded the young king that it was all part of a Protestant plot to start an uprising, and that he should immediately order the deaths of all the Huguenot leaders before they could act against him. Now fearful for himself, the king agreed with their suggestions, including the death of Coligny, his friend and counselor. Catherine and her associates quickly planned a general killing of all Huguenots. Most of the Huguenot leaders from throughout France were already in Paris for the wedding, and none were to be left alive. The first to die would be Coligny. Henry, the third duke of Guise (Henri, 3d duc de Guise), was to see to his death.

At midnight on August 24, 1572, the feast of St. Bartholomew, a signal was given and the slaughter of the Huguenots began. The wounded Coligny was attacked in his own home by a group led by the duke. A German named Besme [or Bemjus], who was a servant in the Guise's house, plunged a sword through Coligny's chest and threw him, still alive, out of a window into the street. There, another of Guise's men chopped off Coligny's head as he lay at the duke of Guise's feet. Besme later said that he had never seen a man die more valiantly than the admiral.

Still raging against Coligny though he was dead, the savage papists cut off his arms and private members, dragged his armless body through the streets for three days, and then hung him upside down by his heels outside the city. Along with him they murdered every Protestant leader they could find, great and honorable men like the admiral's son-in-law, **Count de Teligny** [or Telinius]; **Count de la Rochefoucault** [or Rochfoucault]; **Antonius**; **Clarimontus**; the **marquis of Ravely**; **Lewis Bussius**; **Bandineus**; **Pluvialius**; **Burneius**; and **many others**. But this did not satisfy their lust for blood, it only increased their ungodly appetite, and they began to slaughter the common Protestants, hunting them down like animals day and night. In the first three days, nearly **ten-thousand bodies** were counted in Paris alone.

They threw the bodies into the Seine River until the water was red as blood. The butchery was so continuous that along the street gutters in Paris blood ran like water after a rain storm. So furious was the rage of the murderers that they killed even those Roman Catholics whom they believed were weak in their diabolical religion. Soon the massacre spread throughout all of France and continued until October. It was as if an unholy plague had gripped the papists until they were more animal than human in their zeal to kill every Protestant in France. No one tried to stop them, and there was no punishment no matter how many they killed.

In Orleans, just 70 miles from Paris on the Loire River, **a thousand men, women, and children** were slaughtered. At Lyon, about 250 miles southwest of Paris at the junction of the Rhone and Saone rivers, **eight hundred** were massacred. Children and parents clinging to each other in love and fear were killed without regard of sex or age. **Three hundred** who sought refuge in the bishop's house were murdered, and the impious monks would not allow their bodies to be buried. In Rouen, 70 miles northwest of Paris on the Seine River, and in Toulouse, 370 miles south of Paris, and in many other cities throughout France, when they heard of the massacre of the Huguenots in Paris and that it had been approved by the king, they shut the gates to the city or posted guards so that no Protestant could escape while they hunted them down, imprisoned them, and then barbarously murdered them. In Rouen alone, **six thousand** were killed.

In the province of Anjou in the Loire River Valley, they slew a minister named **Albiacus**, and raped and murdered **many women**. Among them was **two sisters** whom they abused in front of **their father** after tying him to the wall so that he was forced to watch. When they finished, they killed the three of them.

In Bordeaux, even though it was the capital of the English-held province of Aquitaine on the Atlantic coast, a hell-bound monk, who often preached that the papists should kill all Protestants, so stirred up the Roman Catholics that **264 Protestants** were cruelly killed.

In Blois, 91 miles southwest of Paris, the duke of Guise allowed his soldiers to kill **all the Protestants they could find** and take their property. No one was spared regardless of sex or age, and **every young woman** was raped by the soldiers before she was butchered or drowned in the Loire River. They did the same thing in a city called Mere, where they also found a minister named **Cassebonius** and threw him into the Loire River where he drowned. In every city and village they came to, whether large or small, well-known or virtually unknown, they acted with the same barbaric savagery.

In a place called Turin [not Turin, Italy], **the Protestant mayor** gave them a great deal of money for his life. After taking his money, they beat him with clubs, stripped him naked, and hung him upside down with his head and chest in the river so that he had to keep jerking himself upward out of the water to keep from drowning. When they tired of this spectacle, they cut open his stomach, pulled out his intestines, and threw them into the river. Then they cut out his heart and carried it around the city on a spear.

At Penna, **300 were slaughtered** after they had been promised safety. At Albia on the Lord's day, **45 were killed**. At Nonne the citizens fought for some time until they were guaranteed they would not be harmed, only their properties would be seized. But once the papists entered the town they **slew everyone regardless of age** with brutal savagery and set the houses on fire. **A woman and her husband** were dragged from their hiding place and she was raped several times in front of him. Then they put a sword in her hands and held her hands around the hilt while they forced the blade into her husband's stomach. When that fiendish deed was finished, they killed her also.

In the village of Barre, these servants of Satan cut open the stomachs of **small children** and pulled out their intestines, which they then chewed upon in insane rage. At Matiscon they cut off the arms and legs of **numerous victims**; some they then killed and others they let bleed to death. For the savage entertainment of themselves and others like them, they often threw Huguenots, both men and women, from a high bridge into the Loire River while exclaiming, "Did you ever see a person jump so well?"

It is impossible to tell of all the forms of savagery inflicted upon the Protestants during the two months of this horrible massacre. But one example will suffice for all.

The **wife of Philip de Deux** was pregnant and being attended by a midwife because she was about to give birth. The papists broke into their house and killed **Philip** in his bed, and then, ignoring the pleadings of the midwife, plunged a dagger into his wife's stomach. She staggered from the house to a barn and climbed up into the corn loft, hoping to hide from the butcher's there and deliver her child before she died. But soon they found her and stabbed her in the stomach again and cut it open. Then they threw her from the hayloft to the ground below. When she struck the ground on her back with great force, the child burst out of her open womb. Immediately one of the Catholic ruffians caught up the child, stabbed it, and threw it in the river.

As a second witness of the truth of this massacre of the Huguenots, here is a letter written by a sensible and educated Roman Catholic:

> The marriage of the young king of Navarre with the French king's sister was celebrated with great splendor. All the affections, the assurances of friendship, all the promises sacred among men, were abundantly given by Catherine, the queen mother, and the king. During the celebration, the wedding guest thought of nothing but enjoying festivities, plays, and masquerades.
>
> Then, at twelve o'clock at night, at the beginning of St. Bartholomew, the signal was given. Immediately all the houses of the Protestants were forced open at

once. Admiral Coligny, alarmed by the uproar, jumped out of bed just as several assassins rushed into his bedroom. Leading them was Besme, a servant in the family of the Guises. This miserable person plunged his sword into the admiral's chest and also cut him in the face.

Henry, the young duke of Guise, who stayed at the bedroom door until the horrid butchery was done, called aloud "Besme! is it done?" Immediately after, the ruffians threw the admiral out of the window, and he was killed at Guise's feet by another ruffian who cut off his head.

Count de Teligny, who had married Coligny's daughter ten months before, was also killed. He was such a handsome man that the ruffians who first moved to kill him were struck with compassion, but others who were more barbarous pushed past them and murdered him.

In the meantime, all of Coligny's friends were assassinated throughout Paris. Men, women, and children were indiscriminately slaughtered and every street was strewed with dying Protestants. Priests ran through the streets holding a crucifix in one hand and a dagger in the other and warned the leaders of the murderers to spare neither relatives or friends.

Tavannes, the marshal of France, an ignorant and superstitious soldier, rode his horse through the streets of Paris, crying to his men, "Shed blood! Shed blood! Bleeding is as wholesome in August as in May." In his son's written memories of his father, we are told that when Tavannes was dying and made a general confession to his priest, the priest said to him in surprise, "What! no mention of St. Bartholomew's massacre?" To which Tavannes replied, "I consider it an action worthy of reward and praise that will wash away all of my sins."

Only a false spirit of religion can inspire such horrid sentiments.

The newly wed Henry of Navarre and his wife were asleep in the king's palace; all of his servants were Protestants. **Many of them were killed** in bed; others ran through the palace hallways and rooms trying to escape, some even into the king's antechamber. The young wife of Henry, fearful for her husband and herself, jumped from her bed to run to the king's bedroom to throw herself at her brother's feet and ask for protection. But when she opened her bedroom door, several of her Protestant servants rushed into the room for refuge. Soldiers came into the room past her and killed one who was hiding under the bed. Two others were wounded with halberds and fell at her feet, covering them with their blood.

Count de la Rochefoucault, a young nobleman who was greatly in the king's favor, and who had a certain happiness in his conversation and could speak with a great deal of humor, had spent a pleasant evening with the king and his court attendants until eleven o'clock. The king felt some remorse about Rochefoucault because he was a Protestant, and urged him two or three times not to go home but to spend the night in the Louvre, where he knew he would not be found. But the count said he must go home to his wife, and so the king urged him no more and said privately to his attendants, "Let him go. I see God has decreed his death." Two hours later the count and **his wife** were murdered.

Many of the poor victims fled to the banks of the Seine for refuge, and some swam over the river to the suburbs of St. Germain [or Germaine]. From his bedroom window in the royal palace, the king could look down upon the river and see the swimmers trying to escape. One of his servants had prepared a rifle for him and he killed several of those in the river. The queen mother was undisturbed by all the slaughter, and often looked down from her balcony and shouted encouragements to the murderers and laughed at the dying groans of the victims.

Some days after this horror in Paris took place, the French parliament tried to make the massacre seem less serious and justify it by putting the blame on admiral Coligny and accusing him of a conspiracy against the king, which no one believed. They then sought to defile his memory by hanging his body by chains in public view. The king himself went to see this shocking spectacle. When one of his court attendants advised him to withdraw, complaining of the corpse's stench, he replied, "A dead enemy has a good smell." The massacres on St. Bartholomew Day are painted in the royal exhibition hall of the Vatican in Rome, with the inscription: *Pontifex, Coligny necem probat,* which means, "The Pope approves of Coligny's death."

This horrible butchery did not occur only in Paris. Orders were issued from the king's court to all provincial governors to kill all Huguenots within their provinces. As a result, about **one-hundred-thousand Protestants** were massacred all over France. Only a few governors refused to obey the order. Montmorrin, the governor of Auvergne in central France, wrote to King Charles and said, "Sire: I have received an order under your majesty's seal to put to death all the Protestants in my province. I have too much respect for your majesty not to believe that the letter is a forgery. But if, God forbid, the order is genuine, I have too much respect for your majesty to obey it."

In Rome, the joy over the St. Bartholomew Day massacre was so great that they declared a day of festivity and jubilee. Those who celebrated the day and expressed gladness in every way they could devise were given many indulgences. The man who first carried the news of the massacre to Rome was given 1000 crowns by the cardinal of Lorraine for his ungodly message. In Paris. the king also commanded that the day be kept with every demonstration of joy, for he believed that the whole race of Huguenots had been exterminated, and with them all Protestants in France. But the true Gospel of Christ cannot be exterminated from any country—only God can remove it.

It is appropriate that we end this narration of the St. Bartholomew Day massacre by telling what happened to young King Henry of Navarre, whose wedding gave opportunity for the massacre, and whose life was spared.

There are those who say that he was saved from death by the queen mother because she wanted to keep him alive as security for herself against any Huguenot attempts on her life, and that she thought also that perhaps she could use him to convince the Huguenots who escaped to surrender. Others say that Henry escaped the massacre by letting it be thought that he had renounced the Protestant faith. And there are those who say he was spared but forced to convert to the papal church; and that not long after, he renounced his conversion so he could resume leadership of the Huguenot armies.

After the massacre was over, King Charles was greatly disturbed by it and fell into a great melancholy and remained that way until he died two years later of a fever. He was succeeded by his brother, Henry III. As king of France, Henry III immediately made peace with the Huguenots. This enraged the Roman Catholics who then formed a powerful league of Catholics, led by the house of Guise, to oppose the king.

In 1585 the league forced Henry III to ban Protestantism again and tried to exclude Henry of Navarre from the succession to the throne of France. Because the league still distrusted the king, in May 1588 they caused an uprising that expelled him from Paris. The league and the pope then declared that Henry

III was removed from office and no longer king. In December 1588, Henry retaliated by having Henri, duc de Guise, and his brother, the Cardinal de Guise, murdered.

When he was declared deposed, Henry III made an alliance with Henry of Navarre, and in 1589 they began a military advance on Paris. But Henry III was assassinated by a Roman Catholic fanatic, Jacques Clement, at St. Cloud.

Before his death, King Henry acknowledged Henry of Navarre to be his successor. In addition, Henry of Navarre claimed the throne by right of his descent from King Louis IX through Louis's son, Robert of Clermont. Also, Henry's wife, Margaret of Valois, was the daughter of Henry II.

The powerful Roman Catholic league refused to recognize him, and were backed in this by King Philip II of Spain. Henry tried to overcome them by military force and regain the throne in Paris, but failed in his attempts, so in 1593, he converted to Catholicism. This gave him the support he needed to capture Paris, which he did in 1594. It is reported that he justified his conversion by saying, "Paris is worth a mass." By 1598, Henry IV, as he was now named, was in complete control of the French empire.

Immediately after assuming full control of France, Henry IV issued the *Edict of Nantes*. This edict ended a half century of war and gave the Huguenots equal political rights with the Catholics; the right to live freely anywhere in France; freedom of private worship in their own homes; and freedom to worship in public in certain places, but not in the king's court nor within fifteen miles of Paris. It also granted them a few strong places as "cities of refuge" where they could flee from persecution and be safe, if they could reach them. One such place was the municipality of La Rochelle in western France on the Bay of Biscay. The Edict of Nantes remained in force until 1685 when it was revoked by Louis XIV.

During his reign as king of France, Henry IV, the former Henry of Navarre, dedicated himself to bettering the living conditions of the citizens of France, and with exploration in the New World. He died on May 14, 1610, when he was assassinated by a religious fanatic as he was riding through Paris.

Section II

The Next Three Centuries

19

Persecution of Anne Hutchinson, Mary Dyer, Margaret Wilson, Madame Jeanne Guyon, and Miguel de Molinos

During the next three-hundred years, the number of Christians killed for their faith decreased rapidly, as did general systematic persecutions based on government or religious policies. The world was changing rapidly, becoming something different than what it had been, becoming civilized and mechanized—so torturing, burning, and hanging people for their religious beliefs was, in general, no longer tolerated. It was out of date.

In the timelines of history, the 1600s were the time of the triumph of science; the time of Johannes Kepler, Galileo Galilei, Francis Bacon, Robert Hooke, Sir Isaac Newton; the time when scientist were discovering never-before-seen outer worlds with the telescope, and never-before-seen inner worlds with the microscope. It was the time of *Don Quixote, Paradise Lost,* and *Pilgrim's Progress.* By the mid-1600s the Reformation was firmly established in many countries, and an uneasy peace settled over most, but not all, of the Church.

The 1700s were the time of reason, rights, and revolutions. It was the time of Daniel Boone, Benjamin Franklin, Captain James Hook, and Catherine the Great. It was also when the shame of slavery began to reach its height. During this century more than 2000 slave ships sailed regularly from Liverpool, England, to West Africa. About six-million Africans lost their freedom during this century, and tens of thousands died during what was known as the "Middle Passage" from Africa to the West Indies. Ship owners herded as many as possible into the airless, disease-ridden holds of their ships, and once ashore many were branded or maimed to prevent escape. Those who rebelled were often beaten nearly to death or hanged. Most of the six-million slaves were sold in the Americas. Paradoxically, on July 4, 1776, the Declaration of Independence was approved by the Continental Congress in Philadelphia. It declared "that all men are created equal, that they are endowed by their Creator with certain unalienable Rights, that among these are Life, Liberty, and the pursuit of Happiness."

The 1800s were the time of the machine age. It was the time of Napoleon Bonaparte, Florence Nightingale, Karl

Marx, Harriet Beecher Stowe, Samuel Finley Breese Morse, and Alexander Graham Bell. It was also the time of Nat Turner, Dred Scott, *Uncle Tom's Cabin*, John Brown, Abraham Lincoln, and the Civil War.

Tucked in among those bustling years, however, as the world changed so radically, were religious persecutions against Christian groups and individuals that few had time to notice, and even fewer had time to care. Consequently, only a meager number of stories and records have come down to us. But we know, because of the nature of the Beast, and because "all who live godly in Christ Jesus will suffer persecution," that these few stories are only a reflection of the tip of the iceberg. In this chapter are the stories of four of the women who were persecuted—three of them martyred—and one man. In the next chapter are the stories of five of the men.

Anne Hutchinson, 1591-1643

Anne Marbury Hutchinson was born in Alford, Lincolnshire County, England, in July 1591, and was baptized on July 20th. She was the third oldest of thirteen children of an English clergyman, Francis Marbury, who was twice imprisoned by ecclesiastical authorities for preaching against the tenets of the established Church of England. Marbury had graduated from Christ College, Cambridge, and was licensed to preach soon after. At the time of his first arrest, he was parish priest in Northampton. When he was released, he was forbidden to revisit the church in Northampton, but he still refused to stop speaking out against the Church of England and was arrested again.

Although Anne had no formal education she learned much by listening to her father and his friends discuss religion and government. When she was fourteen, her father was appointed to St. Martin's Church in London. In 1612, when she was twenty-one, she married William Hutchinson, her childhood sweetheart, in St. Mary Woolchurch in London, and they returned to Alford to live. They remained there for twenty-one years. During that time, Anne gave birth to fourteen of her children—only one died in infancy, which was an unusual record for the times.

In spite of her busy life as wife and mother, Anne was active in religious affairs. Often she made the 24-mile trip to Boston, Lincolnshire, to listen to John Cotton, who was rector of St. Botolph's Church. Cotton was a graduate of Cambridge University, an ordained Anglican priest, a strict Calvinist, and a leading proponent of Puritanism. His rigorous Calvinism eventually brought him into conflict with church authorities, and in 1633 he was forced to leave England. With the Hutchinson's eldest son, Edward, he emigrated to the Massachusetts Bay Colony in New England, where he became minister of the only church in Boston. Anne was a devoted follower of Cotton and sought his counsel many times. Because the Hutchinsons and Cotton were good friends, the Hutchinsons had planned to sail with Cotton, but Anne was pregnant with her fourteenth child at the time, and so they decided not to sail until the summer of the following year.

Several times Anne had been arrested for speaking out about her Puritan beliefs, and so she broke with the Church of England long before they sailed for America. Since the break, she had traveled wherever she could to listen to any minister that might be teaching the truth of God's Word. Once she said, "The Lord did *discover to me all sorts of ministers and how they taught." She was also an avid student of the recently published (1611) King James version of the Bible.

Anne was strongly influenced by discussions she heard about Antinomianism, which opposed moral rules and law in favor of obedience to the inner guidance of the Spirit.

At the time of the Reformation a few followers of Martin Luther had taken his concept of justification by faith alone to mean that the law had no bearing on the life of a Christian. Anne's view was, "just because you observe the letter of the law is not proof that you are good in your heart." Whatever her concept of Antinomianism, her life was blameless and of the highest moral standards—God was her life.

When her fifteenth child was born in the *Massachusetts Bay Colony in March 1636, she gave it the biblical name of Zuriel (Numbers 3:35), which means "My work is God."

Boston was then a farming town with a population of about one thousand. Soon after arriving there, Anne opened her home to large classes of woman and began to teach them the things that she had learned in her search for spiritual truth. Some say that as many as eighty woman attended her meetings in their large farmhouse, which was on the corner of School and Washington Streets, just across from the home of the colonial governor, John Winthrop.

Anne ministered healing with considerable success to both the spirit and the bodies of those who came—she was especially successful with sick babies, probably because of the great compassion she had for them. In the harsh life of women in early New England, Anne was a soothing and comforting voice that taught them how to draw upon God for the strength and grace they needed. Like the Quietists who were stirring in Europe, she taught them that the Holy Spirit within a person controls the right actions of that person, and that if a person's heart is filled with the true grace of God, that person cannot go astray.

At the outset, Anne had accepted Puritan teachings, but gradually she began to disagree with *orthodox Puritanism. Brilliant, expressive, and well versed in the Bible and theology, she denied that keeping religious laws was a sign of godliness and insisted that true godliness came from an inner working of the Holy Spirit. She also came to believe that persons under a "covenant of grace," especially as shown in the New Testament, could speak directly with God.

Even though the women of Boston were being helped by Anne, the fact that she was a woman preaching to other women, and was doing it independently in her home, soon began to raise the hackles of the male clergy in the established religions. Contributing to these increasing protests was the fact that Anne often criticized the preaching of the clergy, who frequently taught that salvation was only possible by obedience to certain laws. Anne believed that the Lord dwelt within each individual, and that faith alone would win salvation. This was in opposition to the teachings of the Puritan fathers. At one point Anne referred to some of the clergy as, "a company of legal professors who do nothing but continually go over the law that Christ has abolished."

In December 1636, a group of opposing clergymen called upon her to try to convince her to deny her beliefs— among them, to her surprise, was her English minister and friend John Cotton. Cotton had supported her at first, but now he was publicly renouncing her teachings. Anne's replies to their questions and criticisms were frank and harsh, which only served to increase their antagonism toward her. Her enemies soon began to compare her with Jezebel of the Old Testament, while her friends compared her to Priscilla of the New Testament. Like Priscilla did with Apollos, Anne was trying to expound the Scriptures more accurately to the women who came to her for help, but the very men who had come to America to escape persecution in England were now her persecutors.

Anne's teachings were branded as the heresy of antinomianism, and the colonial government moved to discipline her and her numerous followers in Boston. When one of her supporters, Henry Vane, defeated Governor John Winthrop in 1636 and became governor of the colony, the Puritans fought back and the following year returned John Winthrop to the governorship. Under Winthrop's leadership, a synod of ministers condemned Anne's doctrines in August 1637. In November she was brought to trial by the governor in a gloomy church in New Towne, on the Charles River opposite Boston, and was found guilty of sedition and contempt.

During her trial she spoke of having come to New England because the Lord spoke to her. The prosecutor asked her, "How did you know it was God that spoke to you and not Satan?" She replied, "How did Abraham know that it was God who told him to offer his son? I, too, knew by the voice of God's Spirit to my soul."

Though scripturally correct, Anne's answer only antagonized her enemies who now thought she was placing herself too high—perhaps above them. So they condemned her. Governor Winthrop made the announcement: "You are banished from our colony as being a woman not fit for our society."

Anne said, "I want to know why I am being banished."

Winthrop replied, "Say no more—the court knows why, and is satisfied.

Among other things, Anne had been condemned for "holding two public teachings every week in her house, and for criticizing most of the ministers, except Mr. Cotton, for not preaching a covenant of free grace."

Anne's health was poor because of the wear on her body from giving birth to so many children—she was now carrying her sixteenth and last, taking care of her large household, and continual ministering to all who came to her. Included in her banishment was four month's imprisonment, but since the Massachusetts Bay Colony did not have a prison at that time, and she could not travel in the winter because of her health, she was confined in nearby Roxbury in a home that belonged to a relative of one of the ministers who had accused her.

In March 1638, she was brought to trail again, this time by the Puritan church for holding unorthodox opinions. The proceedings were held in her own First Church of Boston, which was pastored by a John Wilson. Every settler high and low, and from far and wide, including Governor Winthrop, crowded into the small church. Missing, however, were her main supporters—the women she had taught and counseled in her home. Some had been banished from the colony, some had left the colony in disgust over the persecution of Anne, and some were plain afraid to be known as her supporter or friend. The only ones with Anne were her son Richard and her son-in-law, Thomas Savage.

The trial took several days. During it her pastor, John Wilson, spoke strongly against her to the assembly, as did her former counselor and friend, John Cotton. On the final day, Wilson apparently, or deliberately, misinterpreted a statement Anne made and scornfully said to her, "You say you can commit no sin?"

Anne replied, "If my heart is right I cannot sin."

"And is your heart right?"

Anne answered, "I am trying to make it right."

A prepared confession was given to her and she was instructed to read it out loud, but she read it in a barely audible voice, with her head bowed. The confession contained little more than that she had misinterpreted the Bible and that she had made unkind remarks about the clergy. For these Anne asked for prayer and said that the root of her faults was the height and pride of her spirit. In response to her remarks, one of her accusers shouted, "You have stepped out of your place. You have been a husband instead of a wife, a preacher instead of a hearer, and a magistrate instead of a subject." Another said, "You have set yourself in the place of God so that you would be exalted and admired and people would follow you. Your sin has found you out."

Her former friend, John Cotton turned the reading of her expulsion from the church over to her pastor, John Wilson. In an ecclesiastical voice, Wilson intoned, "In the name of the Lord Jesus Christ, and in the name of the church, I do cast you out. I do deliver you up to Satan. I do account you from this time forth to be a heathen and a Publican and so to be held by all the brothers and sisters. I command you in the name of Christ Jesus and of this church as a leper to withdraw yourself out of this congregation."

Anne's only reply was, "The Lord judges not as a man judges. Better to be cast out of the church than to deny Christ."

Within two days after being cast out of the First Church of Boston by her Puritan pastor, Anne was ordered by Governor Winthrop "to be gone within a week from the Massachusetts Bay Colony." Heavy with her sixteenth child, Anne traveled to Aquidneck, Rhode Island, where her husband and other family members had already gone to set up a new home for her. But her worn and tired body could not sustain the life of the baby she carried, and it was born dead.

With her family and a small group of followers, Anne settled at Pocasset, which is now Portsmouth, Rhode Island. There, Roger Williams helped them to purchase land from the Indians. Williams, who was a staunch Puritan, had himself been expelled from Massachusetts in 1635 for his "strange religious opinions" and "very dangerous ideas," and had traveled to the Rhode Island area and founded Providence—so naming it "for God's merciful providence unto me in my distress."

Once their new farm house was built, Anne renewed her teaching and healing ministries, with nearly the same results she had in Boston. But her troubles were far from over, for her Massachusetts Bay persecutors would not leave her alone and sent a delegation to Rhode Island to inquire about her and warn the Puritan churches there about her doctrines. Anne's husband, William, was now chief magistrate of Rhode Island, and they even tried to influence him against his wife. But William told them, "I am part of my wife more than I am the church. Anne is a dear saint and a true servant of God." Then they asked permission to talk to the congregation in her home church in Portsmouth, but her pastor refused them. So the persecutors showed up at the Hutchinson home, claiming they had come from the Lord and the church. Anne said to them, "Which Lord do you mean? There are lords many and gods many, but I acknowledge but one Lord. Your church is not the true Church of Christ."

Her persecutors then threatened to have the titles to their properties in Rhode Island invalidated, and threatened to forcibly take her back to Boston and there imprison her and subject her to the humiliation of public lashing. This was later done to her older sister Katherine Scott, who was the mother of many children and a sober and godly woman. All of this so terrorized the Hutchinsons that they planned to leave Rhode Island and move further into the wilderness. Unexpectedly, as they were making preparations to leave, William died.

Now without the help of her husband, Anne hurried her preparations and left her home of four years and traveled to New Amsterdam, where she felt the Dutch would protect from her religious persecutors in the Massachusetts Bay Colony. It was a long and dangerous journey—one hundred and thirty miles by land, or traveling by water in a crude craft that hugged the coastline. She choose the water and arrived at Long Island with her family in the late summer of 1642. There she choose a home site at Vredeland, which is near what is now Pelham Bay in New York, even though she had been told that hostile Indians were killing white settlers in that area. Anne believed that if they treated the Indians here as well as they had the Indians in Rhode Island, she and her family would be as safe. The following summer, however, in August or September, the Indians killed her and everyone on the farm—**Anne's three daughters and two sons, a son-in-law**, a house servant, and a farm hand.

Now there are those who might say that Anne and her family were not martyrs, that they were not put to death specifically for their faith in Christ. But consider that if this first woman preacher in New England had not been hounded for her religious beliefs by the Puritans in Massachusetts Bay Colony, she and her family would not have been living in the New Amsterdam wilderness, and they would not have been killed by hostile Indians. The clergy drove her out because she dared to believe differently than the established church, and then they would not allow her a place to live, only a place to die.

Mary Dyer [or Dyar], 1610-1660

Mary Dyer was a Quaker martyr. On June 1, 1660, she was hanged on Boston Commons by the Puritans for preaching Quaker doctrine. Like Anne Hutchinson, who was an associate and friend, her persecution for her religious beliefs helped the cause of religious tolerance in America.

Mary was raised in England, and she and her husband, William, emigrated to Boston in 1635. They joined the First Church of Boston, and there Mary met Anne Hutchinson, who would have a great influence upon her religious beliefs. During Anne's trial in 1638, Mary was one of the few who stood by her, and when Anne was banished from the Colony and went to Rhode Island, Mary and her family followed.

When news of the Hutchinson family massacre reached Providence, Mary gave a moving funeral address for her in the church they had both attended. Naturally, their common Puritan enemies insisted that Anne had infected Mary with her insidious errors of doctrine.

In *1651, Mary's husband traveled with Roger Williams to England when Williams went there to confirm his colony's land grant. Mary went with her husband and stayed for four years, even though he returned to Rhode Island in 1652. During her stay she joined the Society of Friends, commonly known as Quakers. Before Mary returned to America in about 1655 or 1656, Quakers had already reached Boston and stirred up the antagonism of the clergy and the Puritan authorities by their beliefs even more than Anne Hutchinson did.

The principal points that the Massachusetts Bay people had against them were these:

1. In their public meetings they worshipped in "a manner most agreeable to their consciences," and not according to orthodox church tradition.

2. They refused to pay tithes, which they considered to be a Jewish ceremony that was abolished by the coming of Christ.

3. They were against wars and fighting.

4. They would not take oaths because Jesus said, "Swear not at all" (Matthew 5:34).

5. They refused to pay their share of building or repairing buildings for a worship that they did not approve.

6. They would not remove their hats to show honor or respect for a man.

7. Their insistence on the use of "thee" and "thou" when addressing a single person.

8. Their missionary zeal in publishing what they believed to be the truth, sometimes even in places appointed for national public worship.

When Mary's ship docked at Boston, it was her intention to simply pass through the city on her way to Rhode Island. But shortly after leaving the ship, she and a Quaker woman with her, **Ann Burden**, who came to America from England to settle her husband's estate, were arrested and imprisoned. There were now enough people being arrested so that the Massachusetts Bay Colony had been forced to build themselves a prison. When Mary did not arrive in Rhode Island when she was due, her husband inquired about her and learned that she was in prison in Boston. He went there immediately, but wasn't able to gain her release until he swore under oath that she would not remain in any town in Massachusetts Bay Colony, and she would not speak to anyone in the colony's jurisdiction on their journey home.

Since Mary Dyer and Ann Burden were arrested so immediately, and without apparent reason, it's probable that they reached Boston about the time that the General Court of the Massachusetts Bay Colony enacted a decree against Quakers on October 14, 1656.

At a General Court Held at Boston, the Fourteenth of October 14, 1656

Whereas, there is a cursed sect of heretics, lately risen up in the world, which are commonly called Quakers, who take upon them to be immediately sent from God, and infallibly assisted by the Spirit, to speak and write blasphemous opinions, despising government, and the order of God, in the Church and commonwealth, speaking evil of dignities, reproaching and reviling magistrates and ministers, seeking to turn the people from the faith, and gain proselytes to their *pernicious ways: this court taking into consideration the premises, and to prevent the like mischief, as by their means is wrought in our land, does hereby order, and by authority of this court, be it ordered and enacted, that what master or commander of any ship, *bark, *pink, or *ketch, shall henceforth bring into any harbor, creek, or cove, within this jurisdiction, any Quaker or Quakers, or other blasphemous heretics, shall pay, or cause to be paid, the fine of one hundred pounds to the treasurer of the country, except it appear he *want true knowledge or information of their being such; and, in that case, he has liberty to clear himself by his oath, when sufficient proof to the contrary is *wanting: and, for default of good payment, or good security for it, shall be cast into prison, and there to continue until the said sum be satisfied to the treasurer as *aforesaid.

And the commander of any ketch, ship, or vessel, being legally convicted, shall give in sufficient security to the governor, or any one or more of the magistrates, who have power to determine the same, to carry them back to the place from where he brought them; and, on his refusal so to do, the governor, or one or more of the magistrates, are hereby empowered to issue out his or their warrants to commit such master or commander to prison, there to continue, until he give in sufficient security to the content of the governor, or any of the magistrates, as aforesaid.

And it is hereby further ordered and enacted, that what Quaker soever shall arrive in this country from foreign parts, or shall come into this jurisdiction from any parts adjacent to it, shall be forthwith committed to the House of Correction; and, at their entrance, shall be severely whipped, and by the master thereof be kept constantly to work, and none allowed to converse or speak with them, during the time of their imprisonment, which shall be no longer than necessity requires.

And it is ordered, if any person shall knowingly import into any harbor of this jurisdiction, any Quakers' books or writings, concerning their devilish opinions, shall pay for such book or writing, being legally proved against him or them the sum of five pounds; and whosoever shall disperse or conceal any such book or writing, and it be found with him or her, or in his or her house and shall not immediately deliver the same to the next magistrate, shall forfeit or pay five pounds, for the dispersing or concealing of any such book or writing.

And it is hereby further enacted, that if any persons within this colony shall take upon them to defend the heretical opinions of the Quakers, or any of their books or papers, shall be fined for the first time forty shillings; if they shall persist in the same, and shall again defend it the second time, four pounds; if notwithstanding they again defend and maintain the said Quakers' heretical opinions, they shall be committed to the House of Correction until there be convenient passage to send them out of the land, being sentenced by the court of Assistants to banishment.

Lastly, it is hereby ordered, that what person or persons soever, shall revile the persons of the magistrates or ministers, as is usual with the Quakers, such person or persons shall be severely whipped or pay the sum of five pounds.

This is a true copy of the court's order as attests:

Edward Rawson, Secretary

About a year after she was imprisoned, which would be in late 1657 or early 1658, Mary and two other Quakers went into the colony of New Haven to preach. When detected, they were immediately expelled. It seems that the colonies of New Plymouth, New Haven, and even the Dutch settlement of New Amsterdam where Anne Hutchinson had sought refuge, were copying and passing the laws that were enacted against the Quakers by the Massachusetts Bay Colony. The Quakers now had few places where they could preach their doctrines, and almost as few places where they could go, without being persecuted.

On October 14, 1657, the General Court of the Massachusetts Bay Colony passed an even tougher law against the Quakers, this one having penalties of imprisonment and physical mutilation. The other colonies and New Amsterdam followed their lead and passed similar laws.

At a General Court Held at Boston, the Fourteenth of October, 1657

As an addition to the late order, in reference to the coming or bringing of any of the cursed sect of the Quakers into this jurisdiction, it is ordered that whosoever shall from henceforth bring, or cause to be brought, directly, or indirectly, any known Quaker or Quakers, or other blasphemous heretics, into this jurisdiction, every such person shall forfeit the sum of one hundred pounds to the country, and shall, by warrant from any magistrate be committed to prison, there to remain until the penalty be satisfied and paid; and if any person or persons within this jurisdiction, shall henceforth entertain and conceal any such Quaker or Quakers, or other blasphemous heretics, knowing them so to be, every such person shall forfeit to the country forty shillings for every hour's entertainment and concealment of any Quaker or Quaker, etc., as aforesaid, and shall be committed to prison as aforesaid, until the forfeiture be fully satisfied and paid.

And it is further ordered, that if any Quaker or Quakers shall presume, after they have once suffered what the law requires, to come into this jurisdiction, every such male Quaker shall, for the first offense, have one of his ears cut off, and be kept at work in the House of Correction, until he can be sent away at his own charge; and for the second offense, shall have his other ear cut off; and every woman Quaker, that has suffered the law here, that shall presume to come into this jurisdiction, shall be severely whipped, and kept at the House of Correction at work, until she be sent away at her own charge, and so also for her coming again, she shall be alike used as aforesaid.

And for every Quaker, he or she, that shall a third time herein again offend, they shall have their tongues bored through with a hot iron, and be kept at the House of Correction close to work, until they be sent away at their own charge.

And it is further ordered, that all and every Quaker arising from among ourselves, shall be dealt with, and suffer the like punishment as the law provides against foreign Quakers.

Edward Rawson, Secretary

Apparently this law did not sufficiently deter the Quakers from practicing and preaching their doctrines, and the following year, on October 20, 1658, the General Court of the Massachusetts Bay Colony passed another law that added the threat of death to the previous law. This law, also, was copied and passed by the New Plymouth and New Haven colonies, and the Dutch settlement at New Amsterdam.

An Act Made at a General Court Held at Boston, the Twentieth of October, 1658

Whereas, there is a pernicious sect, commonly called Quakers, lately risen, who by word and writing have published and maintained many dangerous and horrid tenets, and do take upon them to change and alter the received laudable customs of our nation, in giving civil respects to equals, or reverence to superiors; whose actions tend to undermine the civil government, and also to destroy the order of the churches, by denying all established forms of worship, and by withdrawing from orderly Church fellowship, allowed and approved by all orthodox professors of truth, and instead thereof, and in opposition thereunto, frequently meeting by themselves, insinuating themselves into the minds of the simple, or such as are at least affected to the order and government of church and commonwealth, whereby several of our inhabitants have been infected, notwithstanding all former laws, made upon the experience of their arrogant and bold obtrusions, to disseminate their principles amongst us, prohibiting their coming into this jurisdiction, they have not been deferred from their impious attempts to undermine our peace, and hazard our ruin.

For prevention thereof, this court does order and enact, that any person or persons, of the cursed sect of the Quakers, who is not an inhabitant of, but is found within this jurisdiction, shall be apprehended without warrant, where no magistrate is at hand, by any constable, commissioner, or selectman, and conveyed from constable to constable, to the next magistrate, who shall commit the said person to close prison, there to remain (without bail) until the next court of Assistants, where they shall have legal trial.

And being convicted to be of the sect of the Quakers, shall be sentenced to banishment, on pain of death. And that every inhabitant of this jurisdiction, being convicted to be of the aforesaid sect, either by taking up, publishing, or defending the horrid opinions of the Quakers, or the stirring up mutiny, sedition, or rebellion against the government, or by taking up their abusive and destructive practices, viz. denying civil respect to equals and superiors, and withdrawing from the Church assemblies; and instead thereof, frequenting meetings of their own, in opposition to our Church order; adhering to, or approving of any known Quaker, and the tenets and practices of Quakers, that are opposite to the orthodox received opinions of the godly; and endeavoring to disaffect others to civil government and Church order, or condemning the practice and proceedings of this court against the Quakers, manifesting thereby their complying with those, whose design is to overthrow the order established in Church and state: every such person, upon conviction before the said court of Assistants, in manner aforesaid, shall be committed to close prison for one month, and then, unless they choose voluntarily to depart this jurisdiction, shall give bond for their good behavior and appear at the next court, continuing obstinate, and refusing to retract and reform the aforesaid opinions, they shall be sentenced to banishment, upon pain of death. And any one magistrate, upon information given him of any such person, shall cause him to be apprehended, and shall commit any such person to prison, according to his discretion, until he come to trial as aforesaid.

Edward Rawson, Secretary

The first Quakers arrested and tried under this new law were **William Robinson**, a merchant from London, England, and **Marmaduke Stevenson**, a farmer from Yorkshire, England who had come to Boston in September 1659 to visit and encourage *Friends in New England. Also arrested and tried were Mary Dyer and **Nicholas Davis**, who were in Boston visiting Friends who were in prison. All of them were sentenced to banishment, on the pain of death.

William Robinson, however, was considered to be a teacher of Quaker doctrine, and so was also sentenced to be whipped severely. The constable was commanded to find a strong man to do it, and Robinson was taken into the street and stripped to the waist. His hands were then put through holes in the *carriage of a large cannon and held there by a jailer. The executioner then gave him twenty strokes with a heavy corded whip. Shortly after he and the other prisoners were released, and banished from the colony, as shown in the following warrant:

> You are required by these, presently to set at liberty William Robinson, Marmaduke Stevenson, Mary Dyar, and Nicholas Davis, who, by an order of the court and council, had been imprisoned, because it appeared by their own confession, words, and actions, that they are Quakers: wherefore, a sentence was pronounced against them, to depart this jurisdiction, on pain of death; and that they must answer it at their peril, if they or any of them, after the fourteenth of this present month, September, are found within this jurisdiction, or any part thereof.

> *Edward Rawson, Secretary*

All of the banished Quakers left Boston, but Robinson and Stevenson did not feel free to leave completely, and so they went only as far as Salem, which was still in the jurisdiction of the Massachusetts Bay Colony, to visit and build up their friends in the faith. Not long after, they were apprehended and put into prison in Boston, with their legs chained to the wall. Hearing that they and other Quakers were in prison, Mary Dyer returned to visit them. While she was standing outside the prison talking with a Quaker named Christopher Holden, who was asking about a ship bound for England, where he intended to return, she was recognized and taken into custody.

Having broken their banishment, Robinson, Stevenson, and Dyer had, according to the law under which they were banished, forfeited their lives. On October 20, 1659, they, and several other Quakers, were brought before John Endicot, who was then governor of the Massachusetts Bay Colony. Endicot asked them why they had returned to his jurisdiction after being banished from it. They replied that they had returned in obedience to the Lord who had told them to do so, and that the law by which they had been banished was unjust. Endicot commanded the jailer to pull off the men's hats, and then said that they had made several laws to keep Quakers away from the Colony, and neither whipping, imprisoning, cutting off ears, or banishing them on pain of death, would keep them away. He further stated that it was not his desire nor theirs that they should be put to death. But he followed that statement by saying to William Robinson, Marmaduke Stevenson, and Mary Dyer, "Give ear, and listen to your sentence of death. You should go from here to the place from where you came [prison], and from there to the place of execution and there be hanged till you are dead." Mary Dyer replied, as they all did, "The will of the Lord be done." Several other

Quakers in the court that day were imprisoned, whipped, and fined.

Because this was the first hanging of Quakers for their beliefs, and the first hanging of a woman, there was a great outcry to prevent the execution of Mary Dyer and the two men, but the date for the triple hanging was officially set for October 27, 1659. Like thousands of martyrs before her, Mary thanked the Lord that He counted her worthy to suffer for His name.

While she was in prison, her husband, William, wrote a letter from Rhode Island to Governor Endicot begging clemency for "My Deare Wife," and one of her sons made a personal appeal to the governor on her behalf. These were to effect a last minute reprieve for her.

On the day of the execution, they took Mary, William, and Marmaduke to Boston Common, there to hang them from a great oak tree. Mary's arms and legs were tied, and her long skirt was bound tight around her ankles. She was set upon a ladder, and the hangman's noose was placed around her neck. Next to her were the two men. At the last moment, a reprieve for Mary came from the governor and she was untied and taken down from the ladder. The ladders under William Robinson and Marmaduke Stevenson were then pulled from under them, and they were hung by their necks until they were dead.

Mary was told that she could have a full reprieve from all punishment if she would promise not to preach Quaker doctrines anymore, but she refused and wrote a letter to the General Council so stating that. She was again banished from the Massachusetts Bay Colony and returned to her home in Rhode Island. She remained there for only a short while, however, and soon went to Long Island where Anne Hutchinson had gone. There she thought much about the persecution of Quakers in the Massachusetts Bay Colony, and determined to fight the unjust laws against them, even if it meant giving her life to overcome it.

Not much more than six months after she had been sentenced to die, Mary showed up in Boston again, and began to preach to all who would listen. She was immediately arrested, brought before Governor Edicot's court, and sentenced to hang on June 1, 1660.

This time Boston Common had a hanging scaffold, and as Mary climbed the steps to the platform, John Wilson, her former pastor at the First Church of Boston, and one of the Puritan ministers who had persecuted Anne Hutchinson, told her that if she would repent of her errors, she would be released. This was the same thing that was often done during the burning of martyrs in England and elsewhere in the previous century—the persecuting clergy offering their victims a last-minute reprieve if they would recant their beliefs.

Mary's reply to him was irrevocable: "No, I cannot, for in obedience to the will of the Lord God I came, and in His will I abide faithful to the death." She was then hung by the neck until she was dead, and her body was buried in an unmarked grave at the place where she was executed.

Margaret Wilson, 1668-1685

Margaret Wilson's family were covenanters in Scotland.

Covenanters were *dissenters who bound themselves by oath or covenant to maintain *Presbyterian forms and doctrines in Scotland. In 1637, when King Charles I of England tried to impose the Anglican prayer book and enforce church rule by bishops in Scotland, whose population was predominantly Presbyterian, the Scottish Covenanters rebelled. This led to the Bishops' Wars between England and Scotland, which in turn led to the

English Civil War, which consisted of three wars from 1642 to 1651. On one side were the royalists, or Cavaliers; and on the other side were the parliamentarians, or Roundheads.

In the Solemn League and Covenant of 1643, the Scots pledged their support to the English *parliamentarians in the English Civil War with the hope that Presbyterianism would become the established church in England. This hope was not fulfilled. After the monarch was restored in 1660, following the death of Oliver Cromwell in 1558, the restored monarch King Charles II brought back the *episcopacy (rule by bishops) and denounced the covenants as unlawful.

The Scottish Covenanters revolted against this form of church in Scotland three times (1666, 1679, 1685), with each revolt being more harshly repressed than the previous one. When Roman Catholic King James II was overthrown in 1688, and the Dutch Protestant William III became King, he reestablished the Presbyterian church in Scotland.

During the last revolt of the covenanters, Margaret Wilson's family carried on a constant guerrilla warfare against the enemies of their church. Her father, Gilbert Wilson, was a farmer in Glenvernock. There they hid and cared for covenanting preachers, who were being hunted down and executed, and magnified the Lord at every opportunity. In February 1685, seventeen-year-old Margaret was hiding with several covenanters from English soldiers who had been pursuing them. After a time they ran out of food, and she left their hiding place and made her way through the bitter winter cold to her home to get food and warm clothing. Before she could return, however, she was apprehended and locked up in the "Thieves' Hole," where they kept the worst kinds of criminals. She was left there for almost two months, and then taken to another prison and badgered day and night to change her beliefs. But she steadfastly refused.

Margaret's youngest sister, Agnes, had also been caught about that time. She and Margaret were sentenced to be flogged through the streets of Wigtown by the public hangman. They were then to be taken to a place designated and executed. Gilbert Wilson paid 100 pounds sterling for the release of Agnes, who was absolved of her crime because of her age, but Margaret had to pay for her crime of aiding the Covenanters, or swear an oath of allegiance to the king of England.

Near Wigtown, there was a stream called Bladnoch that was fed by the ocean—it was almost empty when the tide went out, and several feet deep when the tide came in. Much like along the Fundy coast in Nova Scotia, where the tides often reach more than fifty feet and rush up small streams so fast that small boats filled with tourists can ride the rushing wave.

On the morning of her execution, while the tide was out, a stake was driven in the bottom of Bladnoch stream and Margaret was tied to it. Along the shore the townspeople gathered, ready to rush in and untie her the instant she relented and swore oath.

The tide came in and quickly reached up to Margaret's waist. Her voice rang out, "To You, O LORD, I lift up my soul. O my God, I trust in You; Let me not be ashamed; Let not my enemies triumph over me" (Psalm 25:1-2).

Someone had given her a Bible, and she opened it and read out loud from the eighth chapter of Paul's epistle to the Romans. It's the chapter that says, "The Spirit itself beareth witness with our spirit, that we are the children of God: And if children, then heirs; heirs of God, and joint-heirs with Christ; if so be that we suffer with him, that we may be also glorified together. For I reckon that the sufferings of this present time are not worthy to be compared with the glory which shall be revealed in us." The chapter ends with these words:

*Who shall separate us from the love of Christ? shall
tribulation, or distress, or persecution, or famine, or
nakedness, or peril, or sword?*

*As it is written, For thy sake we are killed all the
day long; we are accounted as sheep for the slaughter.*

*Nay, in all these things we are more than
conquerors through him that loved us.*

*For I am persuaded, that neither death, nor life,
nor angels, nor principalities, nor powers, nor things
present, nor things to come,*

*Nor height, nor depth, nor any other creature, shall
be able to separate us from the love of God, which is in
Christ Jesus our Lord.*

When the water reached Margaret's arms, she tossed
the Bible onto the bank of the stream and prayed. Her
tormentors, who were now in boats near her, urged her to
relent, telling her that she was a young girl and if she would
just pray for the king and swear allegiance to him they
would release her. She replied that she would never take
the oath but she would pray for his salvation. One of the
men pushed her head under water and held it there for some
time, and then released it. As Margaret gasped for breath,
people on the shore shouted, "Margaret, won't you take
the oath?"

Instead she prayed, "Lord, give these men repentance
and save their souls."

One of the men cursed at her and said, "We don't want
your prayers. Just take the oath."

She replied, "I'll take no sinful oath."

For some reason, the officer in charge ordered her
lifted from the stake, apparently thinking that she was going
to swear the oath. When the people saw her released, many

of the covenanters were heartbroken and cried out, "She has taken the oath. She has taken the oath."

But Margaret said plainly and loudly so that all could hear, "I will not swear allegiance to an earthly king. I am one of God's children, and I will not take a sinful oath."

At that she was lowered back on the stake and left there as the tide continued rolling in and she could be seen no more.

Madame Jeanne Guyon 1648-1717

Someone once said that only two people had ever truly manifested the inner life of Christ—one was the Apostle Paul, and the other was Madame Jeanne Guyon. John Wesley said about her, "We may search many centuries before we find another woman who was such a pattern of true holiness." Another wrote that Madame Guyon had been persecuted by her church "because she loved Christ too much."

Madame Guyon was born in Montargis, France, of Roman Catholic parents. Her maiden name was Jeanne Marie Bouvier de la Motte. When two and a half years old she was sent to the Ursuline Seminary in Montargis; at four she was placed with the Benedictines; at ten she was sent to a Dominican convent. At the convent she found a Bible that had somehow been left in her room, and spent hours reading it. When she was fifteen, her family moved to Paris, and Jeanne began to move into French society. She was a beautiful young girl and attracted many men, which increased what seemed to be natural vanity. At sixteen, she married Jacques Guyon, a wealthy man twenty-two years older than her.

Although like all young brides Jeanne dreamed of a happy marriage, hers was anything but that. Her husband was sick most of the time, and her mother-in-law, who lived

301

with them, hated her and did everything she could to turn her son against his new bride. Because she had lived with her son before he married Jeanne, she continued to have charge of the house, gave the servants precedence over Jeanne, and forced her to perform humiliating tasks. Nothing Jeanne did was right no matter how hard she tried. But she never complained. She saw it all as God using her afflictions to make her inwardly holy and full of His life. She constantly read Thomas à Kempis book, *Imitation of Christ*, and gave up as many vanities as her young heart would let her.

At twenty she gave up dancing and going to plays and parties. The life of Christ had grown so strong within her that she now wondered how she could have ever enjoyed those worldly pastimes. But her vanity would not let go of her, and she often told of how she would spend hours before her mirror tending to her face and hair. She prayed time and again that God would do something to rid her of this ugly thing that she could not get rid of herself. Then, she said, God in his mercy sent her smallpox. When she recovered, her beautiful face that so held her vanity captive was covered with pockmarks. Now she had nothing to be vain about, and she rejoiced that God had set her free. He decreased her external beauty, but at the same time He increased her inner beauty so that at times she seemed almost to be caught up to heaven.

When Jeanne was twenty-eight, her husband died. He had been sick most of the twelve years of their marriage. Before his death, Jeanne knelt at his bedside and begged his forgiveness for anything she had done that had wronged him. He replied, "It is I who have done wrong rather than you. It is I who beg your pardon. I did not deserve you." She was left with three children, two sons and a two-month-old daughter. Her eldest son and her eldest daughter had died from diseases. She was also left a large estate and so always had sufficient money to care for herself and her children and to give to others, which she did generously.

During the years that followed, Jeanne moved more and more into the inner life. She increasingly believed that the Christian life consisted not of rules, regulations, and rituals, but of the life of Christ in the soul of a human being. Christianity was "Christ in you, the hope of glory." If Christ truly and dynamically lived within us, Jeanne decided, than the place to find him was inward, not outward. That would mean giving up everything of the world, and submitting everything to Christ. Absolute surrender became her goal. She wrote, "When self dies in the soul, God lives; when self is annihilated, God is enthroned." Thus she increasingly turned from outward religion to inner religion. She gave up the activities of her church for contemplation, and gave up vocal prayers for silent communication with Christ within her.

When she was about thirty-four, she placed her children in religious schools and began to travel and teach the inner life. She traveled throughout France and Switzerland, teaching wherever God led her. During this time she also wrote to many people, counseling them and leading them gently in the way of the inner life.

Much of Madame Guyon's teachings was based upon the *quietism doctrines of **Miguel de Molinos,** a Spanish Roman Catholic priest, with whom she often corresponded. In 1675 Molinos wrote his views in his *Spiritual Guide*, which was well received by many who read it, even Pope Innocent XI. But opponents of the pope and of Molinos' views, accused Molinos of heresy and immorality. Some of his accusers even went so far as to say that because he was a Spaniard, he was descended from a Jewish or Mohammedan race, and that he might carry in his blood, or in his education, some seeds of those religions. They insinuated that he was no real Christian at all, but an enemy to the Christian religion, and he intended to erase from the minds of true Christians a sense of the mysteries of Christianity. This foolishness was given little credit at Rome, but, nevertheless, an order was sent to examine the registers of the place where Molinos was baptized.

In 1685, Molinos was arrested by the Inquisition on charges of heresy and immorality. Many of his followers were arrested with him, but the majority of them renounced his teachings and were released. But though Molinos had for years held the highest reputation in Rome, he was now treated as the worst heretic. After spending some time in prison, he was again taken before the Inquisitors to answer to a number of articles brought against him from his writings. When he appeared in court, he was wrapped in a heavy chain and a lit candle was put into his hand while two friars read aloud the charges against him. Although he refuted each charge beyond any argument, he was found guilty and condemned to life imprisonment.

Several times in prison he was tortured most cruelly, until finally he broke down and signed a confession admitting that he had done wrong. Because of the severity of his torments and his age, his body gradually grew weaker and he died in 1696, at the age of sixty-eight.

Another noted Christian of the times with whom Madame Guyon corresponded was François de Salignac de la Mothe Fénelon, archbishop of Cambrai. Unlike Molinos, Fénelon learned almost all he knew about the contemplative life from Jeanne Guyon's letters and from personal conversations with her. They were close and staunch friends for twenty-five years. When Madame Guyon's enemies tried every means to destroy her, Fénelon remained loyal and refused to side with them against her.

He wrote, "It would be infamous weakness in me to speak doubtfully in relation to her character, in order to free myself from oppression."

The oppression that Fénelon was referring to came from his former friend and mentor, Jacques Bénigne Bossuet, a French Roman Catholic Bishop and writer. In 1697 Fénelon wrote a book, *Maxims of the Saints*, that expressed his approval and views of the contemplative life. Bossuet immediately attacked it as inconsistent with traditional Christian teachings. The two prelates appealed to Rome to settle the argument, and Bossuet won. In 1699, Pope Innocent XII condemned parts of the book. Soon after, Fénelon was exiled to his diocese by Louis XIV, who had not only sided with Bossuet but was also offended by a political novel Fénelon wrote that year.

As Madame Guyon's teachings became more popular and widespread, church leaders began to charge her with heresy because some of her teachings were different than church doctrine. The Roman church taught that any relationship with God and Christ had to be through the rituals and sacraments of the church, but she taught that each person could directly communicate with God in her inner being, and that was best done by laying aside the rituals and religious activities of the church and living the contemplative life. Such a thing could not be allowed. Taken to its logical conclusion, it would destroy any need for the established church. There was also the problem that she was advocating giving up worldly pleasures, denying self, and living a truly holy life—this offended the pleasure-loving King Louis XIV and his nobles, and the pleasure-loving clergy. So they began burning her books, stealing her mail, and harassing her every way they could. In one town, a priest gathered up every one of her books and burned them in the town square. But a local merchant bought 1500 copies and distributed them throughout the town after the priest left.

Finally, charges of heresy and immorality were brought against her and she was arrested. She was accused of having immoral relations with her spiritual adviser, Father Lacombe, who had traveled with her party, which consisted of her young daughter and her nurse, and two servants. After Jeanne's arrest, Father Lacombe was also arrested, put into prison, and then transferred to a hospital for the insane. Prior to his arrest and imprisonment, he had not had mental problems, but now he was in such a mental state that he signed a paper confessing misconduct with Madame Guyon while he was with her party.

Jeanne spent the next seven years of her life in prison. In 1695, she was sent to the state prison in Vincinnes, a city of north-central France east of Paris. Then on August 28, 1696, she was confined in a monastery in Vaugirard, near Paris. Two years later, in September 1698, she was taken to the Bastille, which was used primarily to house political prisoners. She stayed in the Bastille for four years. During her last two years there, she could not have visitors, speak to anyone, or write letters. A maidservant who insisted on staying with her throughout her imprisonment died in the Bastille. It was during her second year there that Jeanne wrote this short poem: "I ask no more, in good or ill, but union with Thy perfect will." Later, in writing about her prison experiences, she wrote:

> Thou, O my God, increased my love and my patience in proportion to my sufferings. . . . All our happiness, spiritual, temporal, and eternal, consists in resigning ourselves to God, leaving it to Him to do in us and with us as He pleases.

During the winter of 1701, Jeanne became ill because of the cold and damp conditions in the Bastille. Louis XIV, knowing he could no longer justly keep her in prison, released her for six months so that she could recover, and banished her to Blois, one hundred miles southwest of Paris, where her son, Armand Jacques Guyon, lived. Later the king renewed her release for six months more, and then indefinitely. But she was never really free because she could not leave Blois, and the king could put her back into prison anytime he wished.

But being confined to one city did not stop Jeanne from teaching and helping many to find the peace and joy of the inner life, for thousands traveled to Blois to listen to her and be taught by her. She also wrote hundreds of letters, and her autobiography during that time. Though still a prisoner, she was more free in Christ than those who imprisoned her.

Madame Jeanne Guyon died on June 9, 1717, at the age of sixty-nine, and was buried at Blois in the Church of the Gordeliers. She left behind more than sixty volumes of writings that for almost three-hundred years have encouraged Christians to seek the deeper life, the inner life of Christ in them, the hidden life of the heart and spirit. The truths she wrote about her relationship with Christ have become spiritual classics, and greatly influenced not only her contemporary Archbishop Fénelon, but such Christians as John Wesley, Hudson Taylor, Jesse Penn Lewis, Adoniram Judson, Hannah Whithall Smith, Fanny Crosby, and Watchman Nee. Many of the leaders of great Christian revivals were touched by this humble woman of God who was persecuted and imprisoned by her government and her church because "she loved Christ too much."

20

Persecution of Donald Cargill, John Bunyan, George Fox, William Carey, and Robert Thomas

Donald Cargill, Scottish Covenanter, Martyred 1681

The Scottish Covenanters were Presbyterians who were devoted to maintaining Presbyterianism as the sole religion of Scotland. Early covenants, the written documents which bound them to their cause, supporting the Presbyterian form of Protestantism were signed in 1557 and in 1581.

When Charles I was made King of England, Scotland and Ireland in 1625, he tried to impose the Anglican Church on Scotland. In 1638, the covenant of 1581 was revived, and those who signed it added a vow to   establish

Presbyterianism as the state religion of Scotland. Over the next twenty-two years there were many changes in the ruling heads of England, and then, in 1660, King Charles II was restored to the throne. He denounced all Scottish covenants as unlawful, restored the episcopacy—rule by bishops—on Scotland once more, and declared himself the head of the church in Scotland. The Covenanters refused to accept any human as the head of the Church of Christ, and declared that Christ alone was the head of His Church. During the years from about 1660 to 1688, they revolted three times and each time were harshly defeated by overwhelming English forces. During those years, many Covenanter pastors and lay people were hunted down, cruelly treated, and killed.

As the controversy raged throughout Scotland about who was the head of the Church—the king or Jesus Christ— the dividing line became clearly drawn. In November 1662, one of the Covenanter pastors, Donald Cargill, was banished from Scotland. But he stayed away only a short time and then returned, to spend most his remaining life hiding from English forces. He and other Covenanter pastors would come out of hiding only long enough to preach the Gospel in as many towns as they could before being detected, and then would go back into hiding. Once, in June 1679, Cargill was severely wounded during an encounter; another time, in July 1680, he was abandoned when his companions thought he had been killed; but both times he escaped to preach some more.

On November 22, 1680, a large reward was offered for his capture, dead or alive. On the advice of other Covenanters, Cargill left Scotland and took refuge in England. Then in April 1681, he returned to Scotland to preach Christ and encourage the Covenanters where he had preached before. On July 10, he preached one of his finest sermons in a parish in the county of Lanarkshire in southern

Scotland, where the Covenanters had fought several battles against English forces.

The next morning, while he was still sleeping, the home where he was staying was broken into and he was seized and taken immediately to Glasgow in western Scotland, on the Clyde River. There he and **several other Covenanters** were tried and sentenced to death for believing and declaring that Jesus Christ was the true head of His Church. They were beheaded on July 27, 1681. As Cargill mounted the ladder on the scaffold, he said, "The Lord knows I go up this ladder with less fear and anxiety than I ever entered the pulpit to preach."

For reasons unknown, the executioner trembled exceedingly and did not sever Cargill's head with one blow. He swung frantically at Cargill's neck several times until finally Cargill's head was separated from his body, and he stood before the Lord that he had so honored by his life and his death.

Seven years later, when Roman Catholic King James II was overthrown in 1688, the Dutch Protestant William III became King and reestablished the Presbyterian church in Scotland.

John Bunyan, Puritan, 1628-1688

It has been said that after John Milton, author of *Paradise Lost*, John Bunyan was the greatest literary genius produced by the Puritan movement in England. Bunyan was born in Elstow, England, in November 1628. Educated briefly in the local school, Bunyan early became a *tinker like his father. Throughout his youth he was constantly repenting for the sins he committed. Though he was never a drunkard or sexually immoral like many of the young men of his day, he confessed that he was often guilty of "cursing, swearing, lying, and blaspheming the holy name of God." His conscience was also bothered by dancing and playing a game called *tipcat [or tip cat], especially on Sunday after church services. One Sunday, after hearing a sermon on the evil of breaking the Sabbath, he was playing tipcat on the village green, and heard a voice say to him, "Wilt thou leave thy sins and go to heaven, or have thy sins and go to hell?" About that time he also overheard some poor women in Bedford talking. "Their talk was about the new birth, the work of God in the hearts. They were far above my reach."

During the English Civil War, Bunyan served in the parliamentary army from 1644 to 1647. While in the army, a fellow soldier standing guard next to him was shot in the head—that served to increase Bunyan's concern about his sins and the condition of his soul. After leaving the army, Bunyan married. His wife's name is unknown, but when they were married she brought with her two little books on Christianity that awakened his interest in religion. In 1653, he joined a *Nonconformist group that met in St. John's Church in Bedford. Although it was a Congregational church, it practiced water baptism, and so was considered by many to be a Baptist church.

Before long, Bunyan was preaching in the villages around Bedford with such great fervor and eloquence that people flocked to hear him. When Charles II was recalled to the throne in 1660 and restored the supremacy of the Church of England, and English and Scottish Nonconformists and Presbyterians were again persecuted, Bunyan was arrested for disobeying the laws prohibiting Nonconformist meetings and was thrown into the prison in Bedford. There he remained for twelve years, with only brief intervals of freedom. Anytime he desired he could have gained his permanent freedom by promising not to preach Nonconformist doctrine. But to the offer he always replied, "If you let me out today, I will preach again tomorrow."

About his arrest and imprisonment, he wrote, "Before I went down to the justice, I begged of God that His will be done; for I was not without hopes that my imprisonment might be an awakening to the saints in the country. Only in that matter did I commit the thing to God. And verily at my return I did meet my God sweetly in the prison."

Although he suffered a great deal because of the wretched condition of the prisons in those days, the hardest thing to bear was the thought of his family's suffering and his separation from them. His first wife had died, and just before his arrest he had married again. His second wife cared for his four small children, one of them a blind daughter whom he adored.

While he was in prison, Bunyan supported himself and his family by making tagged shoelaces. When not doing that, he read the two books he had brought with him—the *King James Bible* and John Foxe's *Book of Martyrs*, preached to the other prisoners, and wrote religious books and papers. By studying the contents and literary styles of the King James Bible and Foxe's book, Bunyan began to write religious tracts and pamphlets. It is said that he "lived in the Bible until its words became his own." In 1666, he wrote his spiritual autobiography, *Grace Abounding to the Chief of Sinners.* In this book he chronicled his many battles with Satan and "the merciful working of God" on his sinful soul, which resulted in his salvation and the acceptance of his divine call to preach to other sinners.

In 1672, King Charles II suspended the laws against religious dissenters, and Bunyan was released. Three years later he was again put in prison for six months for illegal preaching. It was during this imprisonment that he wrote the first part of *The Pilgrim's Progress,* the story of Christian's journey to the celestial city—it was published in 1678. This book is acknowledged to be the first novel ever written.

Bunyan later wrote *The Holy War*, published in 1680, which would have been his greatest work if he hadn't written *The Pilgrim's Progress*. He also wrote the second part of *The Pilgrim's Progress*, which was the story of Christiana's pilgrimage—it was published in 1684.

It was certainly not Bunyan's intent to write a literary masterpiece when he wrote *The Pilgrim's Progress*. He knew almost nothing about literature other than the *King James Bible*, a few Christian books, and Foxe's *Book of Martyrs*. He simply had a message he wanted to give to his people, and wrote it in a way and a language that he felt they could understand. Writing the story was not difficult. Bunyan knew the main character and his spiritual struggles well, for he himself was "Christian" and the struggles were his.

During the last years of his life, John Bunyan remained with his beloved congregation in Bedford, where he found his greatest happiness in ministering to his people. But he frequently preached in neighboring towns, and even in Noncomformist's churches in London. He became so well know as a national leader and teacher that he was often called "Bishop Bunyan."

In 1688, on a journey to London to reconcile a father with his son, he was caught in a drenching, cold rain. Within hours a violent fever seized him. He died in London on August 31. He was buried there in a church cemetery called Bunhill Fields.

George Fox, 1624-1691

George Fox was born in July 1624, at Drayton, in Leicestershire. His parents were Puritans. As a boy, George was extremely religious. When he was 19, he became suddenly and irrevocably disgusted by the sinfulness of many Christians. It happened while he was at a fair with two Puritans. He was invited to join a drinking session, but although he paid for his round of drinks, he touched nothing because he was shocked at the difference between their religious profession and their moral behavior. That night, he felt that he was divinely called to a spiritual life and left his family and went off alone. It was September 9, 1643, just two months after his nineteenth birthday.

For three years Fox searched for true spiritual perfection, but could not find it no matter where he went or what ministers or religious people he talked to. It wasn't until after much meditation, lonely nights of prayer, and intense study of the Bible, that he came to the conclusion that God was to be found only within the soul of each individual. This he was more certain of than anything in his life, for God Himself had spoken to him. "When all my hope was gone," he wrote in his Journal, "so that I had nothing outwardly left to help me, nor could tell what to do, then, Oh then, I heard a voice which said, 'There is one, even Christ Jesus, that can speak to thy condition,' and when I heard it my heart did leap for joy."

In 1647, he began his ministry as an itinerant preacher traveling from village to village. He preached his new belief of the *Inner Light* and soon won many converts. "Christ has been too long locked up in the mass and the Book," he proclaimed, "let Him be your prophet, priest, and king. Obey Him." Fox believed, as the Puritans did, that the formal practices of the Church of England violated the spirit of Christianity. He taught that people can worship God directly without help from clergy. His followers refused to attend the services of the Church of England or to pay tithes for its support. They refused to take oaths. They were frugal and plain in dress and speech. Fox also taught his followers that all people were equal and they should not consider

315

one person superior to another, that they should not swear allegiance to an earthly king, and that they should not take up arms and kill. Fox challenged the Church to return to a pacifist policy.

England was torn by civil war, however, and the authorities did not like this sect that claimed equality for all and refused to take up arms or swear allegiance. Hundreds were jailed. It was while he was in prison that Fox wrote his Journal and pamphlets supporting his beliefs.

Fox's first imprisonment was in 1649 at Nottingham for interrupting and rebuking a minister in St. Mary's who was expounding the authority of the Scriptures—he was arrested for "brawling in church." A year later, he was jailed at Derby on a trumped-up charge of blasphemy. When he was sentenced in 1650 by Justice Gervase Bennet, Fox warned the judge to "tremble at the Word of the Lord." The quick-witted Bennet contemptuously called Fox and his followers "quakers," and this incident, together with what were sometimes agitated movements during times of revelation in their meetings, caused that name to stick to them.

During this time the Quakers were a much persecuted people. They were beaten by angry mobs, imprisoned for not paying tithes, driven away for preaching their doctrines, prosecuted for disturbing public worship. It is estimated that Quakers were imprisoned over two thousand times, and that more than **thirty-two** of them died during their imprisonment. Fox himself was jailed in 1653, in 1656, and then spent three years in prison from 1664 to 1666.

Despite continued persecution, however, the Society of Friends, as it was now called, grew in size and strength, especially in northwestern England. In 1666, although weakened by hardship and the effects of his recent lengthy imprisonment, Fox began to devote most of his time to the organization of the Quakers as a church. He had married

Margaret Fell, a widow ten years his senior who was one of his converts, and she was of great assistance to him in the increased work of the new church.

In 1671, Fox traveled on a missionary journey to North America and the West Indies. When he returned to England in 1673 he was again imprisoned, this time for two years. This was the last time. The rest of his life Fox remained relatively free from persecution. He died in London on January 13, 1691.

William Carey, 1761-1834

William Carey was an English Baptist missionary and linguist who taught himself several languages so he could better understand the Scriptures and teach them in other countries. He learned Greek so he could study the New Testament in the original language, and then taught himself French and Dutch, and developed a working knowledge of Latin and Hebrew.

Carey was baptized in the Church of England but joined the Baptists in 1783 and began to preach. During his first eight years as a preacher, he received no salary and supported himself by working as a shoemaker. There was little missionary work done in those days, since many thought that the Great Commission had been given to the apostles alone. When Carey brought up the subject at ministerial meetings, he was often told that "God alone" would convert the heathen in pagan countries. When he first talked of going to the mission field himself, his wife was strongly against it, but later agreed to go with him. In 1791, he published a book that became the source of the modern missionary movement. It had the long title of *An Enquiry Into the Obligation of Christians to Use Means for the Conversion of the Heathen.* In it he detailed the scriptural teaching about the Great Commission and outlined a plan for missions.

With encouragement from what became the Baptist Missionary Society, Carey sailed in 1793 with his family to India and settled near Calcutta. Not long after he arrived there, the British government and private companies came against his missionary efforts and threatened to kick him and his family out of the country. But he stayed through the threats and through the hardships. He received little money from England, and supported himself and his family by working on an indigo plantation. His five-year-old son, Peter, died of dysentery, and his wife went insane. She screamed constantly and had to be bound in a secluded room so that she wouldn't harm herself. She remained that way for twelve years until she died. In addition, a missionary companion he brought with him, John Thomas, squandered all their money.

Nevertheless, Carey mastered the languages of eastern India, and translated the New Testament into Bengali in 1801, and the Old Testament in 1809. Altogether, he translated portions of Scripture into thirty-four languages, the entire Bible into six languages, and partial translation of the Bible into twenty-four languages. He also wrote grammars and dictionaries in Sanskrit, Marathi, Punjabi, and Telugu. For years he fought against the Hindu custom of burning wives alive at their husbands' funerals, and, in spite of strong government opposition, succeeded in having the practice of *Suttee* abolished in 1829. William Carey died on June 9, 1834. The strength behind his accomplishments could be summed up in his classical exhortation from Isaiah 54:2-3, "Expect great things from God; attempt great things for God."

Robert Thomas, (Korea) killed 1866

Robert Thomas was ordained on June 4, 1863, in a little church in Hanover, Wales. The next month, he and his wife were sent to Shanghai, China, by the London

Mission Society, where his wife died soon after they arrived.

In 1866, after having evangelized for a few months in the southern part of Korea, Thomas traveled on the American ship, General Sherman, up the Taedong River, which runs from Namp'o on the Yellow Sea northward past P'yôngyang, the capital of what is now North Korea. In a shallow part along the river, the ship was grounded on a sandbar. Korean soldiers on shore, not having seen many vessels of this type on the river, became suspicious and scared, perhaps thinking there were foreign soldiers on board. They boarded the ships waving long knifes at the passengers and crew and started killing many of them.

When Thomas saw that he was going to be killed, he held out his Korean Bible to them and said in that language, "Jesus, Jesus." His head was cut off and thrown into the river. Though some may say his mission voyage was a failure and a waste of a young life, God does not perceive things the way we do, and His ways are not our ways.

Twenty-five years after Thomas's death, an American visitor stayed at a small guest house in the area where Thomas was killed, and noticed strange wallpaper in the main room. The paper had Korean words and numbers printed on it. When he asked the owner of the house about it, the owner told him about Thomas being killed there, and said that he had taken the Korean Bible that Thomas held out to the soldiers and used the pages to cover his walls. For twenty-five years, he said, many had come to his house to "read the walls" where Thomas's Bible was preserved.

Section III

Modern Martyrs

21

The Past Century

The word *martyr* has the sound of antiquity about it. It's a word for the days of Jesus and the early Church, for the days when pagans roared across Europe, for the days when barbarity within the Church burned its noblest saints. It's a word for a time long past, for yesteryear, for days of yore, for some day other than our modern day. But the word *martyr* is more applicable to our day, to *today*, than to any day in the history of the world. During this century alone, more Christians have been killed for their faith than in all the previous centuries combined. *Selah*. Think deeply of that for a moment.

Boxer Rebellion

The century began with the Boxer Rebellion in China. Although the rebellion was motivated by the political and economical exploitation of China by various Western powers, it was the Christian missionaries and the Chinese Christians who suffered the full force of the Boxer's vengeance. It started in 1899 when a secret society of Chinese called the Righteous and Harmonious Fists—named Boxers by the Western press because they practiced boxing skills that they believed made them impervious to bullets—began a campaign of terror against Christian missionaries in the northeastern provinces of China. Officially, the Boxers were denounced by the Chinese government, but they were secretly supported by many of the royal court, including the Dowager Empress Cixi (Tz'u-hsi). The terrorist activities of the Boxer society gradually increased through 1900. By May of that year, Boxers were wandering the countryside and attacking Western missionaries and Chinese converts to Christianity wherever they could find them. During the summer, Boxers rampaged in Peking, burned down churches and the houses of Westerners, and killed all the Chinese Christians that had not been able to flee the city.

Among the missionaries caught in the Boxer rampage in China, were **Jonathan Goforth** and his wife **Rosalind**. One day at their mission station at Changte they received a much delayed message from the American Consul in Chefoo, saying, "Flee south. Northern route cut off by Boxers." The Chinese Christians at the station helped them to pack necessary goods on a cart and urged them to leave immediately, for no missionaries at that time were being left alive by the Boxers. Fighting between Western troops and the Boxers had increased in and around the Chinese capital of Beijing. On June 18, 1900, there was a general uprising and Dowager Empress Cixi ordered that all foreigners be killed.

On June 27, the Goforths left their missionary station and headed south. With them were their four children, three men, five women, one boy, and three servants. The days were hot and the nights cold, and they slept on the ground whenever they dared to stop. Just outside the village of Hsintien, a large crowd of men attacked them with knives, stones, clubs, and guns. The backs of the animals pulling the carts were broken, and Jonathan Goforth was struck down with the blunt edge of a sword, nearly breaking his neck. As he fell and held his arm up to protect himself, it was slashed to the bone in several places. When he struggled to his feet, he was struck unconscious with a club. As he regained some consciousness, in God's providence, a rider galloped through the crowd to where their carts were and was thrown from his horse. The thrashing horse now formed a barrier between the attacking men and the missionary party. As Jonathan dazedly got to his feet, a man stood over him as if to strike him with a club, but instead whispered, "Get away from the carts." When they moved away, their attackers ignored them and started fighting among themselves over the goods in the carts.

Eventually the Goforths received help from some of the villagers and were taken into the village and locked in a small hut for their safety. Jonathan's wounds were attended to and they were given water and food. The next afternoon, a member of their party came to the hut and told them that no one had been killed, but one member had been seriously crippled. As they were sent on their way the next day, they learned that their rescuers were Muslims who had been fearful that they could not face God if they had joined in destroying the missionary party.

After the Chinese had suffered several humiliating defeats, a peace treaty was signed on September 7, 1901, and the Boxer Rebellion was over. In the two years that the Boxers rampaged, they killed approximately 250 missionaries and nearly 30,000 Christian Chinese.

During the first quarter of the twentieth century, there was no systematic persecution of Christians. Then in 1924, Joseph Stalin gained control of the Union of Soviet Socialist Republics (USSR) and the communistic form of government was fully established. Over the years, atheistic Communism spread throughout the world, especially after World War II, during the period of 1945 to 1975. From the beginning, the Communists persecuted Christians, destroyed their churches, imprisoned them, tortured them, and killed them. During the height of Communism worldwide, an average of *330,000 Christians were killed every year.

After the dissolution of the USSR in 1991, the number of Christians killed each year fell off radically, but are still at staggering numbers. According to the *1997 *World Christian Encyclopedia*, between 155,000 and 159,000 Christians are killed for their faith throughout the world every year. This number increases slightly each year, but apparently for demographic reasons—population increase—and not because of increased persecution. These numbers account only for those Christians who are *killed* for their faith, and do *not* include those who are persecuted but not killed. Hundreds of thousands of Christians are persicuted each year in addition to those who are killed.

Although there are still a few Communist countries, such as Cuba and China, where Christians are still being persecuted, it is now the Muslim countries that are responsible for most of the Christians who are being killed for their faith.

In China today, it is said that there is no official government policy of persecution, and that it is not illegal to be a Christian. Yet Christians continue to be harassed and arrested by the police. Underground churches are sought out and their meeting places destroyed. Though the Chinese constitution guarantees religious freedom, the Government of China does all it can to prevent non-registered religions from being practiced. Chinese Christians still live close to the years when they were openly persecuted in what was then called *Red China*.

In the Muslim countries, there is usually no official policy for persecuting Christians, most of them state that there is freedom of religion in their country. Nevertheless, they don't discourage persecution, and don't punish those who attack Christians, not even if the Christians are killed. In fundamentalist Muslim countries, persecution of non-Muslim religions, especially Christianity, continues as a government policy.

During the two World Wars and the difficult years between them, little attention was paid to religious persecutions in the world—the world had hardly paid attention to the Jewish holocaust in Nazi Germany. Even those who did try to report persecutions, like those who tried to report Nazi persecution and slaughter of the Jews, could find no organizations that would listen to them, and no organizations that would keep reports of the persecutions. Only in the last part of this century have such organizations come into existence.

One of the leading organizations that is gathering information about martyrs around the world and providing help for them is ***The Voice of The Martyrs (VOM).** It was founded in 1967 by **Pastor Richard Wurmbrand**, who spent fourteen years in Romanian prisons for his faith, and is directed in the United States by **Tom White**, who spent seventeen months in a Cuban prison for the same reason. They provided us with the map at the front of this book, which shows where Christians are suffering today, and provided us with most of the stories that follow of martyrs in this century. The stories in this chapter are from the early seventies to the late eighties. The ones in the next chapter are from the last seven years. These stories are only a few of the thousands that have been recorded in the last thirty years.

Soviet Union, 1966

The following facts are from a copy of a letter written by Brother and Sister Slobda from Dubradi village, in the county of Vitebsk, to the Soviet premier, Aleksei Nikolayevich Kosygin. The letter tells how a local court ordered their daughter **Galia**, age 11, and their son **Alexander**, age 9, to be taken away from them because they had raised them in the Christian faith. For two years the children were kept in an atheistic boarding school that was so unsanitary the children were infested with lice. The legs of Galia swelled to almost twice their size, and twice both children were sick with lung disease, possibly tuberculosis. After two years of detention, the children ran away from the school back to there home.

Soon after, the authorities came to the Slobda home to take the children back. Galia and Alexander climbed on a couch and wept terribly. Police officer Lebed, who came to the house, couldn't bear the cries of the children and left without them. A few days later the children attended school as normal. The director of the school called Galia into his office. Police officer Lebed was waiting for her and grabbed her and carried her out to his police car. She fought so fiercely that once Lebed fell to the floor, but he never let go of her. On the way, Galia kept calling, "Men, men, help!" But, of course, no one helped her. Another Christian girl, **Shura**, was also thrown into the same car. She had been taken by the school nurse to the clinic to take some medicine; there, other police officers were waiting to grab her, also. Neither child was returned to their parents. After that, Alexander remained at home and was not sent to school.

Soviet Union, 1968

Report of a Christian courier who carried messages in and out of the Soviet Union and on one trip got into a Soviet camp to visit Christian prisoners:

> I saw the wife of a Christian martyr, who left many children behind. She looked amazingly young, although she had grown-up children. I asked her for an explanation. She answered, "Suffering has renewed my youth." Another Christian told me, "We would like an easing of our conditions, but not full ceasing of the oppression. We fear that liberty would make us lose the burning love [of Christ]." Another one said, "We, when we think of the cloud of witnesses in the spiritual skies, are happy that the part of sky which is the most cloudy is over the Communist countries. We are happy to give the greatest number of martyrs."

The Bamboo Curtain, 1969

An eye-witness report was received about the deaths of several Christians in a Communist labor camp.

A young girl was bound hand and foot and made to kneel in the center of a circle of people who were commanded to stone her or be shot. Several Christians refused and were immediately shot. The girl died under a hail of stones—her face shining like that said of St. Stephen when he was stoned. Later, one of those who threw the stones, broke down and received Christ as Savior.

A young man was hung on a cross like Christ. During the six days before he died, he prayed constantly out loud that his persecutors would be forgiven and receive Christ.

Five students were forced to dig five deep holes. They were then put in the holes and dirt was thrown on them by other prisoners. As they were buried alive they sang Christians hymns.

For refusing to stop preaching about Christ, **Evangelist Ni-Tio-Sen** had his eyes gouged out, and his tongue and both hands cut off. He was then sent to a prison in Shanghai.

Romania, 1970

In January 1970, Pastor Wurmbrand of VOM wrote this, "I quote from a book of **D. Bacu**, called *Piteshti*, the name of a prison in Romania":

> The guards beat us. On the floor there were only urine and blood. But not only the guards beat us. Christians who had become renegades under tortures were put to beat their former friends. A friend, the best whom I had had before the arrest and in whom I believed blindly, hit me with fury in my face. I was not able to say a word, not even to ask him something. I believed it was a nightmare, the collective madness. The beatings lasted three or four hours, once every nine hours. After this, the beaten were stripped naked and made to lie under the beds.
>
> A prisoner has been compelled to make in one night 1000 *genuflections. Normally, a man cannot make more than 50.
>
> You were obliged to stand at attention the whole day, without the right to move even a muscle. A concentrated look toward the ceiling, serenity on your face, were considered signs of secret prayer. You were brought back to reality by being powerfully struck on your leg with a stick.

Pastor Wurmbrand continued, "Some Christians recanted under the torture. They became the worst torturers of their former fellow-believers, even of their relatives."

China, 1970

In August 1970, it was reported that **Vladimir**, a Christian, was arrested in Shanghai. In prison they put iron tubes around his legs and tightened them with screws. Then they beat on the tubes with a hammer until the vibrations broke the bones in both legs. All this to make him confess to imaginary crimes against the government. He did not confess. Several Communist police officers then went to his home and one of them, a woman, held Vladimir's baby in his hands and told Vladimir's wife, "If you don't sign an accusation against the prisoner [her husband], we will smash the head of the child." She refused, not believing any human being would do that. The woman police officer smashed the baby's head against the wall several times, killing it. The mother went mad and grabbed a knife from a table and stabbed the officer. The other police officers shot and killed her.

Natalia Gorbanevskaia, 1970

A poet, **Natalia** wrote a book published secretly in the Soviet Union—it appeared in France under the title, *At Noon in Moscow*—in which she expressed the longing for liberty by the people of the Soviet Union. The book starts with the Scriptures, "The Holy Ghost witnesses in every city, saying that bonds and afflictions *abide me. But none of these things move me, neither count I my life dear unto myself, so that I might finish my course with joy" (Acts 20:23-24).

Not long after, Natalia was arrested and put into an insane asylum, since Communists consider that anyone who loves freedom or Christ insane. In the Soviet Union there were many such asylums, and many went in sane and came out insane.

They were not places to make the insane mentally well, they were places to make the mentally well insane. Often Communist police disguise themselves as doctors so they could torture their prisoners by using drugs and medical devices.

The asylums were huge buildings that house thousands of prisoners. There were no walls between the cells, only rows of iron bars. Often 100-200 prisoners were put into one cell. The floors were made of planks with spaces between them. Day and night you hear every sound: prisoners walking, crying, coughing, sneezing, snoring, raging, cell doors slamming, toilets flushing, thousands of sounds of thousands of prisoners. There was never silence, never peace, only the sound of madness. Only a strong faith in Christ could keep the madness out of your soul.

A Letter Smuggled Out of the Soviet Union in 1971 by an Imprisoned Member of the Underground Baptist Church

Thank you for the parcel. The officers took counsel from each other several days what to do with the parcel, then in the end the order came that I could receive it on the condition that I should write back, "Please don't send parcels more than four times a year." I answered, "I can write this, but what the others will do I don't know." My beloved, I must confess that I miss nothing. The Lord has given me a good appetite so that I am satisfied even with the food which no pig would eat. We are bent to the earth with gratitude that so many pray for us, as we have heard from you that it happens. Yes, our well-being depends on this.

My hair becomes gray, I have more and more wrinkles on my face, I have to work in great heat. My work is at an oven in which brooms are dried. I work 18 hours a day, from 5 in the evening until 8 in the morning. During this time I have to be entirely naked, but still the sweat can be gathered with buckets from my body. You have to wipe yourself continually.

Is the oak in our garden still growing? ["Oak" was the nickname of one of the leaders of the underground church. So the brother was asking if the work was continuing.]

Another Letter from a Different Prison in the Soviet Union, 1971

The pressures which are used against us here and which are repugnant to the flesh, cause men to lose completely their honor and to become worse than animals. But those same things are useful and unavoidable, for those who love God, in order to become godly. Therefore, we have no motives to complain. It is true that the desire after our dear ones is so great that we are sick with love for them, but in this we can change nothing.

Recently we were brought before a court. It was proposed to us to walk crooked ways [renounce faith in Christ] in order to have it better in the future. One of the judges said, "Is all the pain you have had to endure not enough to have produced in you a change of mind?" I answered, "I have passed through no pains. Prison is a place in which I have learned very many good things, and which has made me to be more decided in faith. You will not be able to understand this riddle because you do not believe in Him."

I will be appointed now as the gardener of the prison, and I would be very happy to receive from you some seeds of flowers. I would like to smell the fragrance of flowers which come from you, who show me so much love.

> When you look forward, everything is dark and horrifying, but we can say, "Until here, God has helped." So He will help us as we go forward.

Soviet Union, 1972

Russian **Pastor Serghei Golev** spent 22 years of his life in prison, was released for a while, and then at age 82 was put into prison again. His wife went to see him, but was forbidden to visit him because it was discovered that he had a New Testament hidden in his cell. She was only allowed to see him from a distance through the barbed wires in the yard. When he came into the yard she could see that he was crying. She shouted at him, "I never saw you weeping. Strengthen yourself. Soon everything will end." From behind the barbed wire he answered, "I got tired." But seeing and hearing his wife returned his strength to him.

Later, several Christian brothers discussed in their cell how they would like to die. One said, "I wish to die while serving the Church; let her bury me." Another said, "I desire to be with my family, to bring my children to faith and then to die." Pastor Golev, who had had that one moment of weakness, said, "I wish to die in prison. Here I passed my best years. Right from here to the Lord—this is my prayer."

Albania, 1973

The **bishop of Durazzo** was locked in a round iron cage the size of his body. The inner walls had spikes that pressed into his flesh. The cage was then rolled through the streets until he died from the pain and loss of blood. **Franco Gjini**, *abbot of Mirdizia, was kept in a 9 x 9 concrete cell for 68 days. Several times pieces of wood were driven under his fingernails. Toward the end he was given electric shocks. Then he was shot. As he went to the place of his execution, he encouraged other prisoners to stay strong in their faith.

Peter Koskava, a priest, was told by the Communists, "Speak against God and save yourself." He answered, "I consecrated my life to Christ. I cannot speak against Him, only against you, the oppressors." Soon after, he was executed. An old priest named **Slako** was beaten to death on the street because he prayed out loud. Just before **De Macai**, a priest, was shot, he cried, "Long live Christ the King!"

Cuba, 1973

A Christian prisoner was asked to sign a statement containing accusations against other Christians that would have led to their arrest and imprisonment. He said, "The chain keeps me from signing this." The Communist officer said, "But you are not in chains." The Christian prisoner replied, "I am bound by the chain of witnesses who throughout the centuries gave their lives for Christ. I am a link in this Chain. I will not break it."

> St. Thomas Aquinas, after calling martyrdom the greatest proof of perfect love for Christ, said, "Words pronounced by the martyrs before authorities are not human words, the simple expression of a human conviction,but words pronounced by the Holy Spirit throuh the confessors of Jesus

Soviet Union, 1974

Trofim Bondar was a Russian Baptist who was sentenced to three years in prison in 1971 for using his home for prayer meetings. He was 72. At the age when others are enjoying retirement, he was enjoying hard labor because he loved the Lord. In the prison camp, Bondar continued witnessing for

Christ, so they gave him injections to weaken him physically. When he was released in December 1974, he could no longer talk intelligently. Soon after, he became totally paralyzed and died within a few weeks.

Czechoslovakia, 1975

When **Victor Korbel** entered the Czechoslovakian army, he took with him his Bible and Durer's drawing, "The Praying Hands," saying, "This will remind me what I should do every day." The Easter Monday after he entered the army, his parents had an underground church meeting in their home. Suddenly the doorbell rang and two army officers entered and said, "We've brought your son home." He was in a coffin—they had not been notified that he was dead. Victor's sister sat down at the piano and played, "Jesus, Lover of my Soul." The parents wept over the coffin and said, "Thy will be done."

Later they received a letter from one of Victor's army friends. He wrote:

We shall never forget the last days we spent with him. He used to read to us from the Bible, and he spoke about God. On Good Friday, he asked us to go with him to church. We all said that we would be glad to, but that we needed permission. "I'll try to get it," said Victor. The officer got mad at him. We could hear his cursing. He accused Victor of poisoning us with religious propaganda. We were not allowed to leave the barracks. Next morning, Victor was found dead in the courtyard. He had been shot.

Romania, 1975

Florea died in Gherla Prison in Romania. He had been beaten until both arms and legs were paralyzed because he refused to do slave labor on the Lord's day. The Communists would not take him to a hospital to be treated, but left him in his prison cell where there was no running water, no bedding, nothing with which the other prisoners could help him. They had to spoon-feed him, but they did not have a spoon, so they used their fingers. Yet he was the most serene and joyful among them. His face shone. When the other prisoners sometimes sat around his bed brooding about their sorrows and complaining that their future was so bad, he would say, "If the outlook is bad, try the uplook."

After one of the prisoners was released, he went to see Florea's family. He told Florea's nine-year-old son about his father, and that his father had told them he wanted his son to grow up to be a good Christian man. The boy replied, "I would rather become a sufferer for Christ like my father."

A Christmas Love Letter—Soviet Union, 1975

A Christmas letter written by the Russian Christian writer, **Alexander Petrovagatov**, who spent 30 years in prisons and concentration camps for his faith, was smuggled out of the Soviet Union and released in 1976. This is what he wrote:

On Christmas Eve I remember all men, independent of their faith and color, of their social position or level of education. I remember men in power and those who suffer in jails and camps, the rich and the poor, the strong and the weak, those who have risen to peaks and those who have fallen into the abyss, the sick and the healthy, the persecuted and the persecutors. Foremost, I think about those who I only recently left after having been with them in prison and camps for almost thirty years.

On our festive table there is a small Christmas tree, apples, grapes and other dainties. In my heart words ring like a bell: Can you eat all these things while at least one man is hungry? Can you sleep in a warm bed, when somewhere a prisoner is not allowed to lie down even on the cold concrete?

Garlands ornament my Christmas tree while the heavy chains of slavery and barbed wire surround the camps. I do not write only about Soviet camps and prisons; I think also about those who have no freedom in other countries. I think about all those who do not eat and drink this night, who cannot look at the most sparkling star which made Christ known to the wise men because the prison windows are covered with planks.

I greet, on Christmas day, our eagles and doves— mothers and wives, brides and those who could not become brides—my sisters who take the Cross for the Word of God, for truth, for righteousness, for faithfulness toward God and love toward men.

Christmas greetings to all the persecuted, the suffering, to all those who seek light. Christmas greetings to all persecutors and oppressors, to all those who curse and confiscate.

Christmas greetings to Helen Zagriazkina, who betrayed me seven years ago. I visited the church in which you were a leader. I wished to see you face to face, but was told that you don't work anymore. But do you ever pray? Pray, pray.

All men, prisoners and guards, men of the secret police and patrol officers, secretaries or the Communist central committees and presidents—pray while it is not too late. There will be no second birth of Christ. There will be a second coming. "Behold, I come soon," says the Lord. Soon, very soon.

China, 1977

In Kiangsi, China, two Christian girls, **Chiu-Chin-Hsiu and Ho-Hsiu-Tzu**, and their pastor, were sentenced to death. As on many such occasions in Church history, the persecutors mocked and scorned them for being so foolish as to die for an unseen God. Then they promised the pastor that if he would shoot the girls they would release him. He accepted.

The girls waited patiently in their prison cells for the moment of their execution. They prayed quietly together. Soon guards came for them and led them out. A fellow-prisoner who watched the execution through the barred window of his prison cell, said that their faces were pale but beautiful beyond belief, infinitely sad but sweet. They were placed against a wall, and their pastor was brought forward by two guards. They placed him close in front of the girls and put a pistol into his hand.

The girls whispered to each other, then bowed respectfully to their pastor. One of them said:

> Before being shot by you, we wish to thank you heartily for what you have meant to us. You baptized us, you taught us the way of eternal life, you gave us holy communion with the same hand in which you now have a gun. May God reward you for all that you have done for us. You also taught us that Christians are sometimes weak and commit terrible sins, but they can be forgiven again. When you regret what you are about to do to us, do not despair like Judas, but repent like Peter. God bless you, and remember that our last thought of you was not one of indignation against your failure. Everyone passes through hours of darkness. We die with gratitude.

They bowed again to their pastor, closed their eyes, and stood silently waiting.

The pastor had obviously hardened his heart—he raised the pistol and shot them. No sooner had they fallen to the ground, then the Communist guards put him against the wall for immediate execution. As they shot him, no one heard words of repentance, only the sound of screaming.

Afghanistan, 1981

A Dutch couple named **Barendsen** were missionaries to Afghanistan, which had been taken over by the Communists. After several harrowing experiences, they returned home to the Netherlands for a short furlough. Just before they headed back, they were asked if they were afraid to return to Afghanistan. They replied, "We know only one great danger—not to be in the center of God's will." Not long after returning, they were taken prisoners by Afghanistan Communists, tied to chairs, and cut to pieces. At the graveside during their funeral in Holland, their five-year-old son said out loud, "I forgive the men who killed my mother and father."

Martyrs Killed by Communists and Muslims, Various Places, 1981

British Adventist missionaries **Ann and Donald Lale** were killed by Communists in Zimbabwe.

Schel kov and **Baholdin** of the Seventh-day Adventist church were killed in a Soviet Union prison.

Romanian Orthodox Christians **I. Cusha and D. Bacu** died under torture in prison. Among other things, they had been forced to eat feces and drink urine.

Professor G. Manu died of illness in the Romanian prison, AIUD. He had been offered medicine only on condition he sign a statement denying his faith—he refused.

The American Coptic Association reported that in June, ten Christians were killed in Cairo, Egypt. One named **Mina** was stoned to death, and another named **Jad** was killed with a sword. **Kamel Marzuk** and his family, along with a priest named **Girgis**, were wrapped in kerosene-soaked mattresses and burned to death.

Romania, 1982

Romanian uniformed and secret police in Ploesti forced their way into the homes of accused Bible distributors, beating the occupants and confiscating Bibles, religious literature, U.S. currency, food, and western-made goods. Informed sources— including family members who witnessed the searches—say the "Nazi-style raids" were executed with a brutality not seen in Romania since the end of World War II.

Silviu Cioata and **Costel Georgescu** were the most recently reported victims. Two uniformed and three secret police officers spent over 5 hours combing Cioata's apartment in Ploesti. Officers confiscated Bibles and other evidence. Cioata was arrested after the search. His family has not seen him or heard from him since; they say the police refuse to divulge his whereabouts. Georgescu was arrested the same day. Sources in Ploesti say officers forced their way into Georgescu's home, where he was severely beaten, and then taken away. There is no further word about him.

Eight other Brethren Church members from Ploesti were interrogated the same day by the secret police. They were questioned about a large shipment of Bibles confiscated from a Romanian ship in Turnu Severin. During the last week of September, 1981, Romanian police arrested ship captain **Piru Virgil** and burned 13,000 Bibles.

Lebanon, 1984

According to the Catholic Information Center in Beirut, Druze militia and Syrians, armed and supported by the Soviets, burned 17,200 homes of Christians of all denominations, plus 85 churches, monasteries, and Christian schools. A total of 1,220 Christians are reported dead or missing. Those found had been tortured and mutilated—cut to pieces by axes, roasted over fire, sawed in two, or had their throats cut. Most of the women had first been raped.

Nicaragua, 1985

In Nicaragua, **Brother R_____**, who was a Sunday school superintendent of the Assemblies of God, was jailed and tortured for six months by the Communist Sandinistas. In prison his hands were chained behind his back and he was lifted in that position until his arms pulled out of their sockets. He was beaten and tortured for days, until his genitals swelled to the size of a softball. The flesh on his buttocks was burned with an electric cable, and his skull was cracked by blows from rifle butts.

Brother R_____'s cell had no furniture, and he was forced to sleep on the concrete floor, which was deliberately covered with water. Often while he was asleep, the guards would sneak up and apply live electric wires to the wet floor, which would cause jolts of electricity to surge through his body. They would then laugh hilariously as Brother R_____ tried to find some place in his cell to escape the electric current. He seldom did.

During interrogations, Brother R_____ was forced to drink salt water. Later, in an attempt to quench the terrible thirst this caused, he would lap water from his cell floor.

Miraculously, Brother R_____ survived and was released. Not long after he and his family escaped to Honduras, where a Christian mission helped them with food and rent as they started a new life.

Soviet Union, 1987

Galina Viltchinskaya, a courageous young Christian poet, was freed by numerous interventions from Christians abroad after only three years in jail, even though she had been given a long sentence. To compensate, however, the Communists arrested her mother, 54-year-old **Zinaida**, and sentenced her to 12 years in prison in Gomel. They put her in a cell with some of the worst murderers in the prison. When her family was finally allowed to see her, they hardly recognized her—she had lost 55 pounds.

In the Gomel prison it was strictly forbidden to share even a piece of bread with another prisoner, which made friendship impossible. Eventually, each prisoner viewed the others as enemies, and treated them as such. "But," said Zinaida, "God taught me to love such people, too, and to reply to evil with good."

Zinaida could only pray at night when the other prisoners in her cell were asleep, for when they were awake there was constant cursing, foul language, and blaspheming. During the day, Zinaida had to work outdoors without decent shoes or clothing, even when the cold was severe, so she developed tremendous arthritic pains in her arms and legs, and they trembled continuously.

The last time her family was allowed to visit her, she told her children, "In such difficult moments, I think about how Christ suffered for me, and this gives me power to bear everything. I gave my life fully into the hands of the Lord. He knows in what ways to lead me. My hope is only in Him. He sees that I am at the end of my tether. I wait for Him to help."

Soviet Union, 1987

Valentina Savelieva, a Russian Baptist, who was recently released after five years in prison, wrote:

> We were often knee-deep in the mud. Our coats and boots were never dry, and we had to keep our coats on all night because it was so cold—the temperature was seldom above 41 degrees [Fahrenheit]. The walls and ceilings of our cell were covered with ice, and with

so many prisoners breathing during the night the ice would sometimes melt and drip water on us. We never seemed to get dry. There were not enough blankets to keep warm, and not enough mattresses, so many of us had to sleep on the dirt floor. When we awakened in the morning, we had to be careful not to rise too quickly, for our hair was frozen to the dirt. It was impossible to remain free from lice. Everyone was sick, and many died of tuberculosis. Food was scarce and hardly eatable, and often our food was stolen. The prison was full of demon-possessed criminals, who cursed day and night. They wanted to destroy my faith.

For prayer, the Christians often gathered in the snow to avoid hearing the obscene conversation of the thieves and murderers who were in their cells. When strengthened through prayer, the Christians would then return to their cells and tell those same prisoners about Christ. Valentina was moved through five jails, and used each one to spread the Gospel.

Nicaragua, 1989

The Nicaraguan Commission on Human Rights reported that prisoners, which included many who were arrested for being Christians, were kept without water in tin-roofed trucks that were allowed to stand in the sun for up to five days. Sometimes prisoners were hung by their hands on walls for two or three days without food or toilet. Often a prisoner was forced to stand day and night on a chair with a noose around his neck. When interrogated, there was always a knife held to the prisoners throat or a gun held to his temple. Sometimes the prisoner did not come back from the interrogation. Thomas Borge, Nicaragua's Minister of Interior

Affairs, was invited to lecture at the national convention of West Germany's Evangelical Church, where he was loudly cheered.

Soviet Union, 1990

Sophie Botcharova and a few young people were converted in the underground Baptist Church of Elektrostal. Authorities were not concerned about this church so long as it consisted of only of the elderly, but when the youth joined it the persecution began. The police would go wherever the Sunday church meeting was being held, disrupt the services, and arrest the leaders, who were always given heavy fines some of the elderly sisters became frightened and began to resent the presence of the young people. At the same time, the young people began to realize that they were a burden to the church.

So when asked, Sophie and most her friends joyfully accepted the task of working in an underground printing facility, which eventually published 400,000 pieces of Christian literature. Several of the older brethren, and even some of the young people, refused to help because they said they did not have the necessary skills. Sophie replied, "I cannot accept this as a reason to refuse. Nobody can have fewer abilities than I. God does not seek talent, but souls ready for sacrifice. He gives the abilities. I experience this."

The working conditions at the printing facility were oppressive. They had only one small room, and in that room they had to make space for the printing press, for storing large quantities of paper, for a kitchen, and sleeping room for eight people. The one window in the room was darkened and sealed so that no one could look into the room or enter through the window. Consequently, there was little fresh air and no way anyone could get a normal amount of rest.

Recently, after 12 years of working in those conditions, Sophie died of lung cancer. Her last words were: "The world does not exist for me anymore. Gardens bloom around me. I am raptured by this supernatural beauty. I wait for my Lord."

China, 1990

Amelio Crotti, who had been a prisoner in China wrote about his experiences. Among other things he wrote this:

> From my cell I heard a mother speak soothing words to her child of five, whose name was **Siao-Mei**. She had been arrested with the child because she had protested against the arrest of her bishop. All the prisoners were indignant at seeing the suffering of the child. Even the prison director said to the mother, "Don't you have pity on your daughter? It is sufficient for you to declare that you give up being a Christian and will not go to church any more. Then you and the child will be free."

> In despair, the woman agreed and was released. After two weeks she was forced to shout from a stage before 10,000 people, "I am no longer a Christian."

> On their return home, Siao-Mei, who had stood near her when she denied her faith, said, "Mummy, today Jesus is not happy with you."

> The mother explained, "You wept in prison. I had to say this out of my love for you."

> Siao-Mei replied, "I promise that if we go to jail again for Jesus I will not weep."

> The mother ran to the prison director and told him, "You convinced me to say wrong things for my daughter's sake, but she has more courage than I."

> Both went back to prison. But Siao-Mei no longer wept.

Lebanon, 1991

Mary Khoury was 17 when Damour, her village in Lebanon, was raided by Muslim fanatics who were bent on converting everyone to Islam by force. She and her parents were given one choice: "If you do not become a Muslim you will be shot."

Mary knew Jesus had been given a similar choice: Give up His profession of being the Son of God and the Savior of the world, or be crucified. He chose the Cross. So she replied, "I was baptized as a Christian and His word came to me: 'Don't deny your faith.' I will obey Him. Go ahead and shoot." A Muslim who had just killed her father and mother shot her and left her for dead.

Two days later the Red Cross came into her village. They found Mary and her family where they had been shot—she was the only one alive. But she was now paralyzed, the bullet had severed her spinal cord. Her paralyzed arms were extended and bent at the elbows, reminiscent of Christ at His crucifixion.

At first Mary was depressed. Then the Lord spoke to her and she knew what she must do with her paralyzed life. "Everyone has a vocation," she said. "I can never marry or do any physical work. So I will offer my life to the Muslims, like the one who cut my father's throat, stabbed my mother while cursing her, and tried to kill me. My life will be a prayer for them."

China, 1991

Ngen Do Man was a Chinese evangelist for three years and won over 200 souls for the Lord. Her daughter said her favorite Bible verse was Joshua 24:15—"And if it seem evil unto you to serve the LORD, choose you this day whom ye will serve; whether the gods which your fathers served that were on the other side of the flood, or the gods of the Amorites, in whose land ye dwell: but as for me and my house, we will serve the LORD." On January 26, Ngen Do Man was on her way to share the Gospel at a house meeting when she was accosted by several violent anti-Christians and stabbed thirteen times. She died instantly.

Nigeria, 1992

In Kaduna and many other places, a Muslim mob went on a rampage against Christians, killing and burning. **Rev. Tacio Duniyo; Musqa Bakut** and his sons, **Bawa, Bije, and John Wesley**; and 300 laypeople were killed. Before killing the elderly Duniyo, the Muslims gouged out his eyes and cut through his mouth to his chin. They also cut open Bije's mouth. This was punishment for their using their mouths to preach the Christian Gospel. In addition, Pastor Duniyo's church and twenty-five Christians in it were burned,

The fanatics cut off **Pastor Selchun's** right hand. When it fell to the ground he raised the other one and sang, "He is Lord, He is Lord. He is risen from the dead, and He is Lord. Every knee shall bow and every tongue confess that Jesus Christ is Lord." His wife and sister stood near him and prayed.

In Zaria the rioters stormed the jail and killed any prisoners and jailers who could not identify themselves as Muslims. They even killed men who claimed to be Muslims but could not recite passages from the Koran.

Vietnam, 1992

Le Thi Loi's husband, a Christian pastor, was executed in a rice field after being accused of subversion against the government, tried, and found guilty. After his death, the government sent her a bill for her husband's execution, the court "trial," the coffin, the burial, and the bullet that killed him. The total was $4,000, which would take her years to repay. If she did not, she would be imprisoned.

Pakistan, 1992

Tahir Iqbal died in prison for his faith. A Muslim by birth, he received a Bible from a friend and was converted as he read it. Then he began to witness to others, especially to children. On December 7, 1990, Iqbal, a paraplegic, was arrested when a Muslim clergyman denounced him for insulting the prophet Mohammed by underlining passages and writing in the margins of the Koran. In Pakistan this crime is punishable by death. Put into prison, Iqbal, who was confined to a wheelchair, suffered deteriorating health while his lawyers sought every legal means available to obtain his release. Nevertheless, Iqbal remained imprisoned in Kotlakhpat Central Jail in Lahore until his death. Aware that he could be executed for his "crime," Iqbal said, I'll kiss my rope but I will never deny my faith." No official reason was given for his death. He was quickly and quietly buried.

Letters from Bangladesh About *Ramadan, 1993

Marzina Begum: I became a Christian with my son and two daughters in June 1993. My husband is a farmer and he is the one who told me about Jesus. When evangelists came to our area and we learned more about Jesus, twenty-five other people became Christians, too.

When Ramadan came, the village people came and tried to force us to celebrate the Muslim day. When we refused, they beat my husband and even broke his leg. Then they stole our two cows. One of our village leaders wanted to take me and forcibly marry me. When this happened, I left my husband and children with my father and fled to the protection of the ____ ____ [name of place left out of original printing of letter for safety reasons]. After Ramadan is over, I will return, but I don't know what to expect.

Fagu Miah: I heard the Gospel when some men were preaching at Anowar's house. After the meeting they talked to me and my wife and four daughters. We decided to become Christians. For the past two years, we have been faithful to Christ. The new Christians from our village meet together for prayer and fellowship every day.

When Ramadan started, the village people [Muslims] tried to make me fast with them. They beat me and then they destroyed my house. They also stole my money and tools. Because I am a farmer, this is very hard for me to deal with. I am 48 years old. The situation was so bad I left the children with my brother and come with my wife to [Name Withheld].

Hafizur Rahaman: In April 1993 I was introduced to some evangelist by my friend, Salim. We heard the Gospel and asked questions. Eventually, my wife and I along with our three daughters and one son, received Jesus as our Lord. For the past two years we have been faithful Christians. Every Sunday we have a prayer fellowship in our area.

When Ramadan started, the village people beat me up so badly that I lost hearing in both of my ears. They also took my rickshaw from me, so now I cannot support my family. Then we fled to [Name Withheld]. After prayer, some hearing returned to my left ear, but I still cannot hear anything with my right ear.

China, 1994

The Public Security Bureau (PSB) attacked a house church in Taoyuan, Shaanxi province. During the arrest they ordered the Christians to stop singing, but they continued to sing even louder. An American citizen in the group was tied up and placed in another room. He heard a Christian woman in the courtyard: "She was screaming. From what I could hear, she was terribly beaten." Two women tried to escape but were pulled back into the house. Christian sister **Xu Fang** later reported, "Two of us sisters were placed on the stove and a large millstone of over 130 pounds was placed on our backs while they beat us with rods. They also . . . ripped open our pants . . . using the most cruel method to beat our private parts." A photograph in a newspaper of one of the Shaanxi Christians shows massive scars and bruises around the lower back and buttocks area, and large holes where chunks of flesh were ripped out of the buttocks.

The Chinese government, in a letter from the Chinese Ambassador to Britain, confirmed the death of a Christian, **Lai Manping** (see Figure 16), during the Shaanxi "incident," but justified it by stating that the house church was an "illegal gathering." Lai Manping was just twenty-two years old, and died from a beating he received during the raid. The PSB has arrested more than 90 Christians in an attempt to cover up this murder. Not long after this, PSB officials and several leaders of the "official church" toured the USA and stated that there had been no persecution of Christians in China since the "revolution."

Pakistan, 1994

Four Pakistani Christians—**Salmat, Rehmat, Gul**, and **Manzoor *Masih**—were acquitted of blasphemy charges, due in large measure to hundreds of protest letters from Christians around the world. Many of those acquitted remain in hiding or leave Pakistan if they can, because the government cannot protect them once they are released and are in public places— it also makes little effort to do so, and makes no effort to stop the printing of "Wanted Posters." Figure 17 shows a poster printed in the Muslim magazine *Takbeer* in Karachi. The poster shows weddings and baptisms involving Muslims who became Christians. It also shows Western Christian professonals in Pakistan who witness for Christ. The magazine threatens them and lists their names, addresses, and telephone numbers so that they can be persecuted.

Shortly after Salmat, Rehmat, Gul, and Manzoor were released, Manzoor was gunned down on the streets of Lahore by Muslim fundamentalists who protested his acquittal (see Figure 18)—they used automatic weapons in their attack. With him were Rehmat, who was shot in the stomach three times; Salamat, who was shot several times in the hand; and another Christian who had previously been acquitted, **John Joseph**, who was shot through the mouth and neck (see Figures 19 and 20). **Manzoor's wife and children**, who were attacked by a mob and stoned after he was arrested, remain faithful to the Lord. After his death, his wife (see Figure 21) said, "Manzoor read the Bible every day. I compel my children to do also. We are not afraid. I thank God we are Christian, and when we die we will go to heaven. We know that."

In 1995, Salamat and Rehmat left Pakistan for their safety.

Nigeria, 1995

In the town of Potiskum, a Christian believer, **Azubuike**, was stoned and macheted almost to death by Muslims. Another Christian was beheaded. His head was then placed on a stick and carried around the town by a Muslim who repeatedly shouted, "Allah Akbar! Allah Akbar!" (God is great!) This happened when about 5000 Muslims, mostly young *Koranic students, invaded Potiskum with the same shouts.

The Muslims burned nine churches to the ground, and killed several Christians, among them **Pastor Yahaya Tsalibi** and **Brother Ezra Turaki**. Another 165 Christians were injured. Bibles, books, cars, trucks, and equipment that belonged to the Christians and the churches were set on fire.

Malo Garba was accosted by Muslims and told to recite the Koran, when she refused they struck her in the face several times and broke all her teeth and damaged the bones in her face so severely that it required two operations to repair the damage.

Indonesia, 1996

Stenley was a recent graduate of Palembang Bible School of Geredja Pantakosta, and was eager to go to the mission field on the remote island of Mentawai, Indonesia, where the inhabitants mix witchcraft and the occult with Islam. Once there, he preached the Gospel boldly, and told the Muslims to burn their idol that contained a rolled up scroll from the Koran. One day a Muslim did exactly that, and when other Muslims in the area heard about it, they were enraged and reported Stenley to the police. He was arrested and put into prison.

When Pastor Siwi of the Palembang Bible School received word that Stenley had been arrested, he went to Mentawai to see him. Stenley, however, was not at the jail where he was supposedly being held, he had been transferred to another prison. It took several days for Pastor Siwi to find Stenley, and when he did, he learned that Stenley had been severely beaten on the head and was in a coma. The last time Pastor Siwi saw Stenley he said to him, "Stenley, this is Pastor Siwi. Can you hear me?" Tears rolled down Stenley checks, but he wasn't able to speak. A few hours later he was dead.

Stenley's beating and death so affected the people in his hometown, that five of the Christians enrolled in the Palembang Bible School, and eleven Muslims received Christ as their Lord and Savior. In the middle of the night on which Stenley died, seven of the Bible School students gathered for prayer and then woke the school superintendent and requested that they be sent to preach the Gospel on the island of Mentawai where Stenley was martyred. Shortly after Stenley died, the Muslim official who beat him, drowned with his family while on a boat trip during a storm.

Iran, 1996

Pastor Mehdi Kibaj was accused of apostasy—denial of the Muslim faith and blasphemy against Mohammed. He was imprisoned in a cramped hole with no room to stretch his legs. While he was in prison, his wife, Azizeh, was threatened with stoning. She divorced him and was forced by the government to marry a Muslim.

Then Pastor Kibaj was condemned to death. To the surprise of all, however, he was freed within a month. A few months after his release, a *fatwa* against him appeared in a Tehran newspaper, calling for his execution. Soon after, he was found dead in a park. He was sixty-five. His four children remain faithful to Christ. The spiritual condition of his wife is not known.

China, 1996

A house church in the village of Xiangshan, Beixing Township, Huadu City, in the province of Guandgong in southern China, was raided for the fourth time by the Public Security Bureau (PSB) officials. In this raid, the PSB arrived at church leader Yang Qun's home on July 26 and detained her 17-year-old son, **Jiang Guoxiong**.

According to the report, Jiang, who was under the age of legal responsibility in China, was severely beaten on the head, face, and body, and was restrained with thumbcuffs, a device regarded internationally as an instrument of torture. As of the time of this writing [1996], Jiang remains in prison and reportedly preaches boldly to his fellow prisoners. His imprisonment occurred because **Yang Qun** continues to open her home as a meeting place for Christians.

See Figure 22 for a photograph of Chinese Christians who boldly meet in a private home to pray for their country, other Christians, and themselves. Figure 23 shows the joy of a Chinese pastor who is overcome with emotion when he receives a visit from Christians from abroad. Only the hearts of the saints who live under daily persecution know how much it means to them when others understand their plight and reach out to them with the love of Christ and help them in their struggle.

Indonesia, 1996

Since 1991, approximately 280 Christian churches in Indonesia have been attacked, burned, demolished, and closed. One of the worst attacks came on Sunday, June 9, 1996, when ten Christian churches were attacked simultaneously in and around the city of Surabaya in southern Indonesia. Surabaya is the capital of East Java Province, and is the second largest city in Indonesia, after Jakarta. About 5000 Muslims took part.

8 A.M. During the Sunday school service, hundreds of shouting people destroyed the Bulak Banteng church building. They used *clurits, clubs, stones, and hammers. Two houses and one church apartment were also damaged. Several church members were injured, including a church leader who was beaten, kicked, and clubbed while his attackers screamed, "Indonesia is Islam. You know that!"

9:30 A.M. Hundreds of people destroyed the Kristen Kemah Injil Kalvari Church in Bulak Banteng. Evangelist Wesson Solaiman was hit on the back of the head three times, and required several stitches to close the wound. Several of the women church members were handled indecently during the attack.

10:10 A.M. Approximately 1000 people destroyed the Jatisrono church building. The attack lasted about 30 minutes.

10:30 A.M. A mob destroyed the Patekosta Tabernakel Church in Wonosari.

10:50 A.M. The Bukit Sion Church was attacked by about 500 people who marched in with teenagers as their shield, followed by bikers and two trucks, which they used to carry off their loot.

11:20 A.M. The Firman Hayat Church in Jalan Tenggumung was attacked by about 1500 people after the Sunday service.

11:30 A.M. The Jawi Wetan Christian Church was attacked. It's pastor reported: "On Sunday, June 9, 1996, we celebrated the Unduhunduy, or Harvest Day. After the service was over, eight people from the congregation stayed over to clean the sanctuary. At 11:30 A.M., about 500 people walked in with planks of wood, iron crowbars, and rocks in their hands. They came through and wrecked the front and side gates and the church doors. Then they smashed all the windows on the first and the top floors, and demolished all church accessories. They also smashed the roof, the ceiling, and the lights. Practically, they destroyed everything inside the church building. Evidently not satisfied with the results, they beat up the eight people who were cleaning the church building."

11:45 A.M. The HKBP church building in Jalan Sidotopo was destroyed by a crowd of about 1200 people. One church member was severely beaten about the head. During the violence, several items were stolen from the church, and the members were molested and robbed.

11:45 A.M. The Batak Protestant Christian Church is attacked. It's pastor reported: "Having received the news at 10:45 A.M. about the vandals destroying Church Cahaya Kasih, one of our members asked for help from the police via a hand phone. Before the police arrived, however, the mob arrived at the church at 11:45 A.M., and suddenly vandalized the church. There were about 1200 vandals. The first group consisted of 300 people in which the majority were children. Ten minutes later the second group, consisting of about 400 teenagers arrived. The rest were adults.

"They first threw things at the windows and the church's roof outside until they were damaged. The second group that arrived forced the gates open and all the vandals came in with wooden clubs and crowbars in their hands. They broke all the window glass and destroyed the doors. They destroyed everything in the church, including the congregation's Bibles and song books.

"One of our members tried to stop them by saying, 'It is enough, enough, everything has been destroyed.' Because of this he was attacked by an overwhelming number of vandals and beaten severely on the head."

Pakistan, 1996

On October 14, in a village near Multan, **Ayoob and Samson Masih** were attacked and beaten by a Muslim mob, and then arrested for blaspheming Mohammed. Their families were forced to leave their homes and cattle to find safety.

A few days later, 23-year-old Samson was released from police custody and again attacked by the mob. This time he was so badly beaten on the back, chest, and head that he had difficulty talking. Twenty-eight-year-old Ayoob remained in police custody, and though he was seriously injured by the mob and in much pain, he was "happy and praising the Lord."

Sources claim that Ayoob's blasphemy charges came from a conversation he had with a Muslim. According to another Christian, Ayoob was reading his Bible outside his house, and a Muslim started making fun of him. They exchanged several opinions on religion, and the Muslim reported Ayoob to the local authorities and accused him of blaspheming Mohammed.

According to the Pakistani newspaper, *Daily Khabrain*, a group of Muslims in Arif Wala held a rally and demanded that Ayoob be sentenced to death by hanging. Christian leaders in Pakistan held a countering rally and sent a petition to the Lahore High Court for his release from prison and acquittal of all blasphemy charges. At the time of this writing, February 1997, Ayoob was still in prison.

Indonesia, 1996

Pastor Ishak Christian, his wife, daughter, niece, and a church worker when burned to death as three thousand Muslims ran amok in a church-burning spree in Situbondo, East Java. Traveling by motorcycle, rioters torched seven churches in Situbondo, as well as two Christian schools and an orphanage, then spread out to neighboring cities. By the time police restored order, a total of 25 places of worship had been burned in seven cities. This incident constituted the worst outbreak of violence perpetrated by Muslims against Christians in Indonesia in recent years, and brought the number of churches burned in 1996 alone to over 50.

Sudan, 1997

During the past thirty years, about three million people have been killed in Sudan because of their religious beliefs—

particularly Christians or members of animist religions—
according to Ulrich Delius, an expert on Africa from the German
Society for Endangered Peoples. Causes of death include
starvation, war, massacres, and mass deportations.

The 29 million Arabian Muslims who live in the north of
the country make up 64 percent of the population. One-fifth of
the population is Christian, while the remaining 16 percent is
animist. The Christians live primarily in southern Sudan, and
are trying to protect themselves against forced Islamization by
the government.

In 1989, Sudan was taken over by Muslim extremists and
declared an Islamic state. In 1992, the military junta in Khartoum
declared a "holy war" against non-Muslims. More than 1.8
million Christians—men, women, and children—living in the
capital city of Khartoum have had their homes destroyed by
the Muslim government—since 1992 over 250,000 homes have
been bulldozed. Thousands have been forcibly moved to refugee
camps just outside the city. Food is used as a weapon by the
Sudanese Muslim government to force Christians to convert to
Islam. Houses are marked with an X to signify that they are to
be destroyed, usually because Christians live there.

In the south it is even worse. Ulrich Delius told IDEA, a
German news service, "The annihilation of the southern
Sudanese is one of the worst genocidal crimes of the present
day. Whole villages have been liquidated, entire Christian
congregations have been burned to death in their churches. Most
[non-Muslim] southern business leaders have been killed, and
countless people from southern Sudan have been tortured to
death."

Government soldiers have committed massacres among
the civilian population. "Soldiers plunder the villages, rape the
women, and torture or kill the men," said Delius. "Some of the
victims have been burned alive, while others had their ears or

genital organs amputated. More than 10,000 [non-Muslim] women and children have been kidnapped and sold as slaves at local markets."

Sudan's mastermind behind this Islamic movement, Dr. Hassan Al Turabi, ominously declared that "those in power who would like to stop this movement [Islam] have no future whatsoever." Sudan's government has isolated their country internationally, most likely to hide their flagrant human rights violations, which they either deny or justify, or perhaps to keep out foreigners who would sympathize with the "enemy" of their government—Christians. In a formal ceremony, Sudanese soldiers swear on the Koran to uphold Muslim law.

Sudan, 1997

In Sudan, fifteen children sick with malaria followed their Muslim master through the rough terrain. After hours of walking through the swamps and mud, and climbing over rocks in the 110-degree heat, they met six Christian men—three Africans and three white men, one of them **Kevin Turner** from **The Voice of Martyrs** in America. The men offered to purchase the children from the slave trader, and after haggling over the price, he gave in. He had ten other children that he wanted to sell on this trip, but they were too sick to survive the long walk to his slave markets.

One of the slaves was a 16-year-old girl who had been owned by two different men. Forced to have sexual relations with them, she had a child by each of them, one two years old, the other just a baby that she carried with her that day. Every day these fifteen children had been forced to memorize the Koran. If they did not learn as much as was expected of them that day, they were not given any food. Since the food they did receive was barely sufficient to sustain them, all fifteen were gradually starving to death. Until that day they thought they would be slaves until they died. But some Christians cared enough for them to pay the price for their freedom, just like them Jesus paid to set them free.

Pakistan, 1997

Pakistan's so-called "black law" has struck again, with the arrest of still another member of the Christian minority, **Ayub Masih**. Accused of blasphemy against the prophet Mohammed, Ayub faces execution. A church source in Lahore confirmed that Muslim riots and processions against Masih's alleged blasphemy had taking place in various cities of the region.

As of this year, more than a dozen Christians have been prosecuted under Pakistan's harsh blasphemy law, enacted five years ago. This is Law 295C, which prohibits blasphemy of the Koran and the prophet Mohammed. Anyone found guilty of this law is automatically sentenced to death by hanging.

Although none of the Christians have been convicted to date, some were imprisoned for many months without bail while their cases were being "deliberated." Five of these Christians were murdered by Muslim extremists after they were released, and another four fled the country to obtain religious asylum abroad. In almost every case of a Christian being released, a *fatwa* is declared against the Christian and published in a public newspaper. Often "wanted" posters are placed about the city pleading for the death of the person, and death threats are called out on the loudspeaker from the minaret at the local mosque.

Indonesia, 1997

On January 30, anti-Christian riots erupted in Indonesia for the third time in four months. Four churches were burned, one totally, by Muslim mobs in the city of Rengasdenklok, 31 miles east of Jakarta, the capital city. The riots began when rumors spread that a local Chinese Christian businessman had complained that the Muslim evening prayers were "too noisy." His house and shop were destroyed by the mob, which then moved on to Christian churches.

Pakistan, 1997

On February 5, in Shanti Nagar in Punjab Province, a rumor surfaced alleging that Christians had destroyed a Koran and thrown its loose pages into a mosque shortly after evening prayers. Within 24 hours, the Muslims had joined forces in the surrounding villages and gathered an army of 30,000 intent on revenge. The inflamed Muslims went on a rampage, burning down churches and destroying the houses and shops of Christians. A Christian leader visited Shanti Nagar the following morning and reported, "Every house is burned out, the town is looted, all the vehicles are burnt, and they have destroyed the water tanks, the electricity system, everything."

Twenty Christians were hospitalized and one brother, **Feroz Masih**, died from his injuries. Two young girls were missing and believed to be held by Muslim terrorists. At one point, approximately 1000 Christian men, women, and children were taken into a nearby field to be executed. Fortunately, the Pakistani army arrived before the massacre took place. Nearly 15,000 Christians are now homeless and have lost all their personal property. They have no food, no water, no place to sleep, and nothing to wear except the clothing they wore while watching their town burn. Damage to the Christians was reported to exceed $2.5 million in American dollars.

It was later discovered that members of the Pakistani police were responsible for destroying the Koran and had falsely accused the Christians in the name of Islam.

Sudan, 1998

Abraham was a 26-year-old Sudanese pastor. He started

a church in the southern district of war-torn Sudan, and it grew to over four-hundred active members.

Like many congregations in the Sudan, the church members had no Bibles, there was only a ragged and worn New Testament that Abraham had been given many years before. The spiritual life and growth of the congregation centered around that book—it was most precious to them all, especially to Abraham.

That New Testament was God's way of bringing Abraham to Jesus Christ. Many years before, the red-covered book was given to Abraham by some young people on an outreach mission to the Sudan area where Abraham lived. Members of the group tried to witness to Abraham and his family, but he did not respond to the gospel. He did, however, keep the New Testament they gave him.

For the next several months, Abraham read the New Testament through and through and through again. After about a year, he gave himself and his life to Christ. Not long afterward, he felt that God was calling him to the ministry, and left home to attend a seminary. When he finished his schooling, he returned to his village and began building a church, person by person, and heart by heart.

In war-ravaged Sudan, where civil strife has raged for nearly eighteen years now, it isn't easy or safe to be a Christian pastor—or a Christian. Churches have been burned time and again, some with the Christians still inside them. Sudan's Islamic government is on a mission to convert every person in the country to Islam. Those who won't convert are beaten, tortured, and often killed. Young women are taken as Islamic concubines. Young boys are sold as slaves. Others are sent to Muslim schools where they are forced to memorize the Koran in Arabic, which takes seven to nine years.

Said one survivor of a destroyed Christian church in Sudan, a man named André, whose entire back and left arm were badly burned in the fire. "I was praying in our church with ninety-nine other believers. The Islamic government soldiers came and bolted the doors of our church shut. Then they set the church on fire. We could not escape. I crawled under the bodies of my brothers and sisters [in Christ] who had fallen to the floor from the smoke and flames, and hid there. The soldiers kept watching until the church burned to the ground, and then left us all for dead. I was the only one who survived."

In the midst of all this danger and persecution, Pastor Abraham labored for the Lord, shepherding his flock of four-hundred literally in the valley of the shadow of death. And he did it with an always joyous smile and a warm heart.

Then Islamic government soldiers rode into his village on horseback and opened fire on men, women, and children. They looted, burned, and killed—and left as quickly as they had come. Just four days prior to their attack, an organization that ministers to the persecuted church had brought a supply of Bibles in the Dinka language for Pastor Abraham's congregation—the first they ever had. But the soldiers burned them all, included Abraham's ragged New Testament that he valued as much as his life.

In the end they took that, too, for in the debris left after the bloody attack, members of Pastor Abraham's church found his bullet-riddled body.

Sudan, 1998

Nine-year-old James Jeda watched as Islamic soldiers killed his father, mother, and four brothers and sisters. They did not kill him, but took him as a prisoner. He thought they were going to make him a slave to them, which was a common practice. So that evening when they old him to gather wood for a fire, he assumed they were getting ready to cook something for their supper.

When the fire was burning at its highest, the soldiers asked James if he had seen or knew of any rebel soldiers in the area. He told them he did not. Then they told him that he must become a Muslim and accept Mohammed as God's prophet and bow down to Allah.

Still in shock from seeing his parents and brothers and sisters killed, James told them with all the courage that he could muster that he couldn't do that. "I am a Christian," he said, his voice trembling.

Enraged, the soldiers picked him up and threw him violently into the fire for which he had gathered wood. They watched him for a few moments as the flames engulfed him, and when they did not see him moving they thought he had been knocked unconscious or was already dead and packed up their weapons and left.

James wasn't dead, however, Somehow he withstood the terrible pain for a few moments, and when the flames roared up around him he rolled out of them away from the soldiers and ran off into the bush before they could see him.

The front of James's stomach is terribly scarred where he laid in the flames for those few moments, and his right arm is partially deformed due to the heat of the fire. You can easily see the places on his body where the doctors grafted skin over his third-degree burns.

He still grieves over the death of his parents and brothers and sisters, and still feels the pain of his loss, and of being all alone in the world. When you look into his eyes you can see a young boy who has suffered things that most children never imagine even in their worst nightmares.

Yet he has a ready, joyous, smile. Especially when he proudly proclaims, "I am a Christian."

Indonesia, 1999

On December 15, Dominggus Kenjam, a 20-year-old Bible student, was asleep in his dormitoryat the Doulos Bible School in Jakarta, the capital of Indonesia on the northeast coast of the main island of Java. Suddenly he was awaken by shouts of "Allah Ahkbar! Allah Ahkbar!"[1] Before he could escape, several Muslims broke into the room, grabbed him, and beat him nearly unconscious with their fists and clubs. Writhing in agony on the floor, Dominggus heard the Muslims say to each other, "We will allow the women to live. The men must die."

Forcing himself to his feet, Dominggus tried to run out of the room and away from his attackers, but he was struck by the semicircular blade of a sickle across the back and right side of his neck, nearly cutting off his head. This time he fell unconscious to the floor. Apparently thinking he was dead, his attackers left him lying in a pool of his own blood.

Some time after his attack, when he had started to mend from his horrendous wound, Dominggus said that his spirit left his body that night, and was carried by angels to heaven. As it was, he looked behind him and could see his body lying motionless on the floor with blood all around his head and still running from the deep cut across the back and side of his neck.

Amazingly, he said, he felt no fear or pain. Just a tremendous peace that he had never felt before as he was carried to what he believe would be his new life in heaven. But when he reached there, he said, Jesus met him and told him that he was to return to earth Jesus said to him, "It is not time for you to serve Me here."

Back in his body, Dominggus heard the voices of the emergency medical workers that had arrived at the Bible school to take care of the many Bible students that had been attacked.

---

[1] "God is Great!" But the God the Muslims worship as Allah is not the God of the Bible.

Thinking that Dominggus was dead, they were preparing to take him to the morgue. Not knowing, however, whether he was a Christian or a Muslim, they were discussing whether to take his body to a Christian or a Muslim morgue.

Not wanting to go to any morgue, but especially not to a Muslim one, Dominggus prayed to God for enough strength to speak. The strength came, and he hoarsely cried out as loud as he could, "I am a Christian."

Realizing now that this dead student they were preparing to take to a morgue was alive, the medical workers rushed him to the hospital. (See Figure 24) Seeing the extent of his wound, the hospital doctors could hardly believe that he was still alive, and they were certain that if by some miracle he managed to survive he would be severely handicapped—mentally and physically.

But today, Dominggus is fully recovered, and only the permanent scar around the back and side of his neck remains. And like many who have suffered for Christ, he has a renewed faith and message of forgiveness. The incident, he says, has brought him much closer to God, and for the first time in his life he is actively praying for his Muslim neighbors, and especially for those who attacked him.

"If I ever meet them one day," he says, "I will tell them about Jesus. And Jesus said we are to forgive our enemies, so I have forgiven them."

Dominggus continues in Bible school, and without question the Lord has great plans for him in his work for the kingdom of God.

India, 1999

Graham and Gladys Staines were Australian missionaries at the Mayurbhanj Leprosy Mission in Mayurbhanj, India, southwest of Calcutta. The Mission has two centers, one for treatment and one for rehabilitation. The facilities include dormitories for men and women, an occupational training center, and a chapel. About 80 patients normally live at the Mission, and there is a continuous flow of out-patients. The Staines worked in the treatment center. They lived in an old house within the Mission compound with their three children, Esther (14), Philip (11), and Timothy (7).

In January, Graham took his two sons with him on an annual trip to a leprosy hospital that he was in charge of in Manoharpur, a tiny village nestled in the remote hills of Keonjhar, about 155 miles north of the Orissa state capital of Bhubaneswar. Orissa had the highest incidences of attacks against Christian churches in India—some 60 attacks between 1986 and 1998. Graham was aware of this, and also that some of the tension had found its way to Manoharpur, But he wasn't worried. He had decided a long time before to follow Christ wherever He led him to minister to lepers, and Manoharpur was one of the places.

There is no electricity or running water in the village of Manoharpur, and no modern conveniences. At night, Graham and his two sons slept in the back of their Willys station wagon, which had more than enough room for them, and comfortable bedding, which they carried on their trips to these remote areas.

The boys always enjoyed the trips with their father, and he enjoyed having them along. They had already developed a love for these simple people and the lepers that their parents treated. Graham hoped that someday they would follow in his footsteps and join their parents in this work to which they had devoted their lives. India was now his and Gladys' home and always would be. They loved the people of India and could not imagine living and working anywhere else.

God had brought them here, and God poured His love through them as they ministered to the lepers and treated their sores. One former leper said about the Staines:

"Our world was darkness. We always faced death. None of the religious leaders bothered to give us even one meal. When we begged for alms, they would throw stones at us and chase us away. We were untouchables. These religious leaders used to tell us that we deserved leprosy because of our sins in our previous birth-because of our karma. And we were left to die in the jungles all alone, like worms. But then came Staines Dada and his friends. They stretched forth their hands of mercy to us and to the Leprosy Home. There we saw the love of God.

"Dada and his wife would personally wash our sores and dress the wounds with medicines and when we were cured, they would teach us some skills, and give jobs to us. . . . Philip and Timothy, what loving kids, they used to come and play with us lepers, the outcasts of society."

At this point, the young woman, Sarida, was overcome with grief and unable to speak any longer.

On this particular night in Manoharpur, January 23, Graham fixed the bed in their station wagon not long after dark and they all climbed in to settle down for the night. It had been a hard day, and they were all tired—the boys more from running around the village and playing with the other children than from work, though they always willingly helped their father when he needed them. Before they went to sleep, they did what they always did on these trips, talked about Jesus for a while, and then each said a prayer. Graham loved to hear his boys pray, especially Timothy who still prayed in the innocence and simplicity of a young child.

Not far from their station wagon, about 300 yards, a group of young men were playing drums and enjoying a traditional Indian dance. The rhythmic beat of the drums helped Graham and his two sons fall asleep quickly and soundly. Tomorrow was going to be another busy day.

But there wouldn't be any tomorrow for them.

At about 11 P.M. on January 22, a group of radical Hindus

led by a man named Dara Singh left Jamadwar and headed for Manoharpur. Singh was no stranger to the police, having been arrested several times for initiating violence.

At about 12:20 A.M. on January 23, Singh and his mob arrived at Manoharpur. They approached through the fields, armed with axes and tridents (three-pronged spears). They had just one pre-determined target, the Staines station wagon where Graham and his two young sons slept. As they got near the vehicle, they started screaming as loud as they could.

Singh struck first, swinging his axe at the tires and slashing them open so the vehicle could not move. The others broke open the windows and struck at the Staines, beating all three unmercifully with their fists and clubs. Graham received the worst beating as he tried to shelter the children with his body. After beating all three nearly unconscious, the raging mob then repeatedly stabbed them—thrusting their tridents through the broken windows time and again in a wild frenzy.

Then Singh piled straw under the vehicle and set it on fire. In seconds, the station wagon was engulfed in flames. Through the broken windows Graham could be seen holding his two young sons close to him. Anyone who knew him was certain that the one name he would be speaking over and over as the flames consumed them was Jesus.

The murderers watched as the three in the vehicle were roasted alive. Someone ran up with a bucket of water to try to douse the flames and was chased away. Dr. Subhankar Ghosh, a close friend of Graham remembers vividly every moment of that terrible night.

"We had dinner with the Staines around 9 P.M., and they went to sleep in their station wagon, parked near the church, at about 9:45. I was sleeping in one of the huts, only about 300 feet from the church. [Just after] midnight, we were woken up by some strange shouts and screams, and I peeped through the side window. I couldn't believe what I saw. I heard shouts, screams, beatings, breaking of doors. There were 50-60 people with burning torches in their hands . . . shouting 'beat, beat' around the station wagon.

"Soon they started smashing the windows of the jeep with bars and sticks. The frenzied mob blocked Graham from escaping with his children. There were brutally beaten. Then suddenly I saw the jeep in flames. I knew my dear friends would be burned into ashes. The attackers had already blocked the doors of the village huts so that no one could get out and help the Staines. A few who did get out and questioned the mob were threatened [with beatings and burning themselves].

"The villages said the attackers were shouting 'Victory, Dara Singh.' The attackers also burned another jeep, parked nearby, and its driver was beaten and chased away. After an hour, the furious militants fled the scene.

"[We freed our doors and raced outside.] We couldn't believe what we saw. We were numbed. Graham was an embodiment of Christian love and compassion. And his children—tender, cheerful, who used to play with the lepers and their children! Is there no limit to man's wickedness?"

Hasda, the driver of the station wagon and a co-worker with the Staines for over 20 years, gave his report of the burning.

"I was woken up by the screams of some people. There were about 50-60 men around the jeep where Saibo and children were sleeping. They were smashing the vehicle with staves and stones. Some carried tridents also. Then I saw somebody putting a bundle of straw under the vehicle and setting it on fire. I brought water and tried to put out the fire, but some of them caught me and beat me hard and chased me away.

"I ran to Murmu's hut and informed him, and he ran to call the village chief. When I returned to the vehicle, what I saw was most tragic. Fire had devoured the two vehicles, and my Saibo and little Philip and Tim [were] turned into ashes. I am sorry I couldn't do anything to save my Saibo and the little ones. My parents were cured lepers and inhabitants of Rajabasa rehabilitation center. I was born there. The Staines treated me like their son. Philip and Tim used to play with my children [and] take them on their cycles. The future of the mission is [now] in God's hands. Our Lord is able."

Also at Manoharpur that night was Gilbert Venz, a visiting friend of the Staines from Australia, who had accompanied Graham to the village. He also remembers vividly what happened.

"The village had turned in for the night, but at about 12:30 midnight, what seemed like a large group of men began raising a commotion in the street outside. They were screaming, 'Don't come out, we will kill you.'

"I was indoors and we found that the door had been blocked from outside. Graham and the kids were sleeping in the jeep."

Because he was trapped inside, Venz didn't know the station wagon had been set on fire. But he kept hearing the terrifying noise of the mob. Later, as he heard the shouting subside, someone freed the door and he rushed out and ran towards the station wagon. He found only a burned out, smoking, shell—and three bodies charred beyond recognition, locked in a tight embrace. In life and in the agony of their deaths, Graham and his sons had been inseparable. (See Figures 25, 26, 27)

A number who fled the raging mob said they saw a wide beam of bright light shining down on the burning station wagon. "I do believe," said Gladys Staines, "that my husband and children were specially strengthened by my Lord and the angelic hosts from heaven."

Asked if she would now leave India and their work with the lepers, she replied, "Never. My husband and our children have sacrificed their lives for this nation. India is my home. I am happy to be here. I hope to die here and be buried along with them."

Indonesia, 1999

In January, a Bible camp was held at the Station Field Complex at Pattimura University on the island of Ambon. Just as the camp was closing, a raging Muslim mob raced toward it, attacking those who were preparing to leave and those still in the camp. (See also the story of Roy Pontoh.)

When those in the camp heard the shouts and chants of the mob, they hid wherever they could. Assistant Pastor Hendrick P.H. Pattiwael took his wife and young children and hid in a room in one of the buildings. But it was no use, the mob searched every building, forcing every Christian out into the open where they could vent their fury upon them.

When Pastor Pattiwael heard the mob shouting and racing through the building where he was hiding with his family, he came out of the room, leaving his wife and children in hiding, and convinced the Muslim's that he was the only one there and led them away from the room.

Inside the room, Mrs. Pattiwael heard her husband cry out with a loud voice, "Jesus, help me!" Then she heard the mob leaving, and all was quiet. She waited in the room for several hours, and only came out when she was certain the mob had left the camp. But though she looked throughout the University grounds, she could not find her husband. It was not until several days later that she learned that the Muslim mob had beaten and stabbed her husband to death.

She learned of his death from the police, who came to where she was staying and took her to the home of her husband's family, where they had taken his body when it was found. There she saw her husband lying in a coffin, his body full of bruises and stab wounds in his chest, shoulders, arm, and abdomen—all speaking of a slow, torturous, death at the hands of the vicious mob, venting their hate on him for his faith in Jesus Christ, and for his refusal to bow to their Allah.

When Mrs. Pattiwael saw her husband's body she was

shocked, and felt that God had not protected him. For some time she was bitterly disappointed that God had allowed such a thing to happen to him, and could not understand it. But it wasn't long before she somehow began to know within herself that her husband's sacrifice was precious in God's eyes: "Precious in the sight of the LORD Is the death of His saints" (Psalm 116:15).

She remembered also that a few days before her husband's death he asked her, "Do you love Jesus?" She, of course, said she did. But then he went on to tell her that if she loved Jesus, but loved her husband or family more, then she was not worthy of God's kingdom. Then he said to her, as if he somehow knew what was soon to happen to him, "I am ready to die for Jesus."

Mrs. Pattiwael has come to believe that God gives His children the best, even during difficult times—and that He is absolutely in full control of our lives. When a Christian worker from the United States asked her what Christians in free countries should do, she said, "Seek God more earnestly, so they can stand [firm with Jesus Christ] in the midst of trouble."

Pakistan, 1999

Sharif Masih and his family lived in a small house that he rented on a farm where he worked for an yearly salary of only $100. Each year he was forced to borrow money from his employers just to provide enough food to feed his family. This amounts to a form of legal slavery, for the loans ensure employers that their workers have to work for them for years without end, because they can never repay any of the principle on the loans. The only other recompense he received for a year's work was $50 worth of grain a year.

Sharif has only daughters. His youngest, Zeba, who was 12 at the time, was a Christian. To help with the family income, Zeba agreed to take a job as a servant girl with a local Muslim family.

Because she is a beautiful and sweet-spirited girl, Zeba's employers thought she might make a good wife for one of their young Muslim men. In an attempt to convert Zeba to the Muslim faith, her employer began trying to teach her Koranic verses, demanding that she memorize them. She refused.

Enraged at her refusal, her employer and other servants beat her with sticks and their fists, kicked her, and spat upon her. They even had her arrested for alleged crimes against the state, which were dismissed for lack of proof.

When Zeba's parents learned of the cruelty inflicted on their twelve-year-old daughter by her employers, Mrs. Masih immediately went to the home to ask why they would harm her little girl. .

Mrs. Maish was beaten by Zeba's employers and their Muslim servants. Then she was doused with gasoline and set on fire. Although rushed to the hospital by others who saw the incident, she did not survive.

But that was not the end of the tragedy. Zeba's oldest sister, Aseema, was unable to bear the grief and hopelessness that had descended upon her family, and went into shock and never recovered. She literally died of a broken heart not many weeks after her mother.

In Pakistan, Christians are less than the lowest class of citizens, and need daily the prayers of their brothers and sisters in Christ all over the world.

Since this senseless tragedy occurred, concerned Christians have arranged to have Zeba trained in English, in tailoring, and in basic business training, so that she will never again be forced to work as a servant girl in a Muslim household. In addition, money was contributed this year, 2001, to pay off her father's debt to his employer so that he can find better employment for a higher wage.

"Then the King will say to those on His right hand, 'Come, you blessed of My Father, inherit the kingdom prepared for you from the foundation of the world: 'for I was hungry and you gave Me food; I was thirsty and you gave Me drink; I was a stranger and you took Me in; I was naked and you clothed Me; I was sick and you visited Me; I was in prison and you came to Me.

"Then the righteous will answer Him, saying, 'Lord, when did we see You hungry and feed You, or thirsty and give You drink? 'When did we see You a stranger and take You in, or naked and clothe You? 'Or when did we see You sick, or in prison, and come to You?'

"And the King will answer and say to them, 'Assuredly, I say to you, inasmuch as you did it to one of the least of these My brethren, you did it to Me.'" (Matthew 25:34-40, NKJV)

Indonesia, 1999

In January, Christian children and teenagers attended a Bible camp at the Station Field Complex at Pattimura University on the island of Ambon. (See the story of Assistant Pastor Pattiwael.) When the camp was over, cars were to take the laughing, rejoicing, children and young people back to their homes, but there were many of them and not enough cars. So Pastor Mecky Sainyakit and three other Christian men left for Wakal village to rent more transportation.

On their way to the village, they were stopped by a mob of Muslims, who pulled them from their car and attacked them. Pastor Mecky and one of the other men were stabbed to death—the other two men escaped. The raging mob then burned the bodies of the two Christian men they had just brutally murdered.

Back in the Bible camp at the University, the children and young people became frightened when they heard shouts of death and Muslim chants coming toward them. They rushed around trying to find hiding places, but when the mob reached the University they forced many of them out into the open. One of them was fifteen-year-old Roy Pontoh.

Roy was terribly frightened, trembling with fear, but not so frightened that he would renounce his faith in Jesus Christ when he was threatened with death by the mob. And when they told him that he must become a Muslim, a soldier of Allah, the teenager mustered all the courage he had and with a quivering voice declared, "I am a soldier of Christ."

Hearing those words, an enraged Muslim attacker swung a sword at Roy's stomach, knocking out of his hands a Bible that he held out in front of him. Then he swung his sword again, and sliced through Roy's stomach, ripping it open. Just before he died, Roy said one final word that had eternal meaning and truth in it: "Jesus."

The mob then dragged Roy's body away and throw it into a ditch, like it was the body of a dead animal. Four days later his family found his body, took it home, cleaned it, and gave Roy a Christian burial. Although often torn by grief, Roy's Christian parent's are proud that their young son's faith in Jesus Christ stood firm and strong.

22

Martyrs Today - This Century

Indonesia, 2000

A large group of school kids on the island of Haruku have lost one or both parents because of recent waves of persecution against Christians.

Fourteen-year-old Maria Nenkeulah says tragedy struck her family when her mother and father left her at home to baby-sit her younger siblings one night in January.

"I waited for them until ten o'clock and wondered why they hadn't come back," Maria said.

Maria's parents didn't return because they had been hacked to death by a radical Muslim mob. Their bodies were found buried beneath some banana leaves at the bottom of the village water well.

Maria finds it difficult to forgive. She remains bitter against those responsible for killing her mother and father. "I still don't know whether I can forgive them or not because they have killed my parents." Maria said.

Maria's six younger brothers and sisters are now split up and living with various relatives. Maria asks Christians everywhere to pray for her. "Pray that God will give me the ability to eventually care for my brothers and sisters," she said. And also give her the grace to forgive those who killed her mother and father.

Nigeria, 2000

Thirty-five year-old Saratu Turundu loved teaching Sunday school at Rehoboth Church in Kaduna, Nigeria. She was unmarried and had no children of her own, so she gathered all the children in her Sunday School class into her heart with all the love she had. It was a big heart with room for many others. Friends and relatives said she often demonstrated the love of Christ by showing great compassion and concern for both Christians and Muslims in the Muslim-dominated community.

Then in February, ravaging Muslim mobs attacked Christians and burned their homes, businesses, and churches. Though many were frightened by the violence and hate against them, and fled the village, Saratu was not afraid. When one mob came to her beloved Rehoboth Church to set fire to it, her brothers urged her to flee into the woods, but she would not run away and defied the mob, though it did no good.

Then she went to her nearby apartment and knelt on the floor to pray for the Christians. Angry Muslims poured several containers of gasoline over the outside walls of the building around her apartment, and then set it on fire. Unable to get out of the apartment because of the smoke and flames, Saratu burned to death.

Her younger brother, Pastor Zakari Turundu, says his sister was murdered because she was a Christian. "I saw my sister's dead body in her room," he said. The fire was so hot that "she was burned to ashes."

Rehoboth Church was burned nearly to the ground, but church members continued to attend services inside the charred walls of the sanctuary. All of the church records, Sunday School material, and Pastor Zakari's books were destroyed in the fire.

Pastor Zakari says he forgave those who were part of the violence and bloodshed that day in Kaduna. "I've released my bitterness and anger to the Lord," he says. "I'm just praying for them now, asking God to use me to reach out to them." Considering the love she had for others, his martyred sister, Saratu, would certainly agree with that prayer and be pleased with it.

Sudan, 2000

Muslim forces had been roaming the area around the small village for days, and the Christian villagers were afraid to even leave their homes to get food. Ten-year-old Kamerino hadn't eaten for many days, and though the hunger pains had stopped, he knew that if he did not get food for himself and his grandmother soon they would both starve to death. The Islamic army had already taken the life of his parents, and now there was a good chance that they would take his if he went out looking for food. But what choice did he have? So he and three nearby friends made plans to go out early the next morning and search for food.

His grandmother reluctantly agreed to let him go, with the understanding that he and his friends would come back that same day.

The four boys left early the next morning, just after dawn. But in their desperation to find food they became careless, and ran into a large group of Islamic soldiers. A Muslim officer yelled at the boys and commanded them to come to him. Fearing for their lives, or of being sold as slaves or made Muslims, the boys ran into a small nearby field and hid in the tall grass. They remained silent as the soldiers called repeatedly to them to come, and stayed low when the soldiers searched through the grass. When they heard the soldiers leave the field, the boys hoped they were giving up and going away.

But the soldiers were enraged at the thought of three small boys outwitting them, so they surrounded the small field and set it on fire. As the flames encircled the field and burned toward them, the boys kept moving toward the center of the flames, but eventually the circle of fire was too close to them, and they had few choices left. Three of the boys ran out of the field as rapidly as they could, hoping to dodge the soldiers and get away. But it was no use. They were quickly and easily caught—their fate, whether it was to be killed or made slaves or Muslims, was sealed.

Kamerino chose to stay in the field, curling himself up into a small ball as the fire ate at him. After the field burned to the ground, the Muslim soldiers searched the scorched ground for the fourth boy. They found Kamerino's motionless body, curled up on the ground, burned from head to toe. Assuming he was dead, they left the area with their three young prisoners.

Several days later, a missionary team bringing blankets and other items to the southern Sudanese Christians, drove north to the village of Kit, just fifty miles from the Islamic front. That evening they showed the Jesus film, distributed most of their supplies, and started the trip back the next morning. A few miles outside Kit they came upon a Sudanese military camp, and stopped to distribute some blankets they had left to the wives and children of the soldiers who were fighting on the front lines. They then sat down for a few moments to talk to some of the military officers.

While they were talking, a Sudanese woman tapped one of team members on the shoulder and said, "Please come quickly. Please come to see this little boy. He has skin problems."

Not certain of what the pleading women meant by "skin problems," the team members followed the woman into a tiny room in a small cement structure. They were no lights or windows in the room, so one of them turned on his flashlight and began shining it along the floor. On one side of the room, they saw a young boy lying on the cement floor on a small, green, piece of plastic. His body was covered with a tattered blanket. He stared up into the beam of light with pain-filled eyes, but did not make a sound.

Two of the team members knelt next to the boy and gently lifted the blanket. Hundreds of flies covered his body and hovered around the room. His skin was blistered and cracked, and smelled of burn flesh. A purple dye stained parts of his body where someone had vainly tried to treat his burns. It was Kamerino. Somehow God's grace had brought them to him. (See Figure 28)

When Kamerino did not return to the village with his friends that day, his grandmother asked some of the villagers to go out and search for him. They found him trying to get home. Somehow he had managed to get to his feet after the Islamic soldiers left and start back toward the village.

He could not have walked very far before they found him, however. His chest was so badly burned that he had trouble breathing, and his feet were so deeply burned that they could hardly bear the weight of his small body.

Kamerino was brought back to the village, put in the small room, and left to whatever treatment his grandmother could get for him. If he was going to survive, it would be up to his own ability to do so. But there was little hope that he would make it, for the villagers had no way to transport him the nearly fifty miles south to the Christian hospital in Nimule. It had been eight days since the Islamic soldiers had set the field on fire and burned Kamerino nearly to death in it.

After being told what happened to Kamerino, the team members rearranged their belongings in the truck, grabbed the green plastic by the corners and lifted the boy into the truck bed and secured him in as well as they could. They then assured Kamerino's grandmother, who had called them to his aid, that they were taken her grandson to the hospital, and that he would get proper medical treatment.

Able to understand and speak only a little English, and confused by the speed with which everything was happening, Kamerino was too scared to talk, but every time the truck hit a rough spot in the road, he would scream from the pain in his burnt flesh. Unfortunately, the road to Nimule was crude and the truck constantly bounced and rolled back and forth.

Although the Sudan is filled with death and suffering, and thousands die yearly at the hands of the Islamic army or from disease and starvation, the only thought in the minds of those in the truck was getting the young Sudanese boy, whose body had nearly been completely destroyed by flames of hatred, to the safety and care of the Nimule Christian hospital.

At the hospital, Kamerino was gently lifted out of the truck bed and placed upon a stretcher by Christian nurses and carried into the hospital room to begin his treatment. As of this writing he is well on his way to complete recovery, although he will always bear in his body the marks of persecution.

An e-mail inquiry to The Voice of the Martyrs about his present circumstances brought back this reply:

Kamerino is now living in an orphanage and has been assigned to the care of a Christian lady there. We praise God that she is a Christian. He says that when he is older he wants to go and try to find his family and for them to be together again. In the horrible tragedies of that country so many family are separated, we are praying that one day Kamerino will be united with his family.

Indonesia, 2000

One of the worst incidents in Indonesia in 2000 occurred on the small island of Kasiui—about two hours by boat from Ambon—during the month of Ramadan, the Islamic holy month of fasting and prayer, when approximately 1000 armed radical Muslims, or Jihad warriors, set out to persecute the local Christians. (See **Ramadan** for information about the Islamic holy month and related violence.)

On November 25, they began to burn homes and rounded up nearly 200 Christians and took them to a village mosque. When word reached the nearby villages, the Christians fled to the forest to protect their families. The jihad (holy war) warriors continued their assault by burning homes, schools, and all the Bibles they could find.

The warriors then waited in hiding outside the pilfered villages for another five days until the Christian families, thinking they had left, came out of the forest. When they did, the armed Muslims surrounded them and forced them to the mosque where the other Christians were still being held.

During the assaults, seven Christian villagers were killed, along with two schoolteachers who were beheaded after seeking the protection of a local Muslims who were thought to be more moderate. The head of one of the schoolteachers was put on a pole outside the mosque as a warning to the other Christians who were being held captive.

With approximately five-hundred Christians now held captive, the jihad warriors proceeded to douse them with water to "cleanse" them in a Muslim ritual. A fourteen-year-old girl, Marina(See Figure 29), cried violently when she was doused with water as a symbol of being purified in order to accept Islam, because she thought that being put through the ritual meant she had renounced Jesus Christ. Later, she was forcefully circumcised by Muslim women.

After dousing the Christians with water, the armed Muslims surrounded them and began to recite Islamic prayers and Koranic verses, demanding that the Christians recite them also. Those who refused were beaten and forced to stand in a nearby field for hours without food or water.

After the dousing, the Christians were forced back into the mosque in groups to complete their "conversion" to Islam.

Then they were told, "If you do not agree to be cut down below, we will cut you up above, referring to forced circumcisions of the men, women, and children. The Christians did not doubt the threats of the jihad warriors, and had only to look at the severed head of the local schoolteacher to know what they meant by "we will cut you up above."

Over a period of two days, the Muslims went from house to house and circumcised as many as ten Christians at a time with a single razorblade. No one was given antiseptic, painkillers, or even bandages—only a small piece of cotton was placed on the men's wounds. Before the assault was over, more than six-hundred Christians, including fifty children, were forcibly circumcised. The victims were told they had to undergo circumcision if they were to be considered "real" Muslims.

More women than men were circumcised, and even small children were cut. A six-year-old girl named Emiliana was restrained while her genitals were forcibly butchered. She was too young and embarrassed to fully understand or talk about her experience. (See Figures 29)

Thomas Rusin, 30, says he was told that he must "follow the Muslim way or be killed." He says he did not fight his armed attackers. "I felt scared because I hadn't faced this problem before," he said. "I was in bed for two days and could not walk."

Thomas Rusin's wife, Ester talked openly about her forced circumcision. She says two Muslim women held her hands down and then cut her genitalia with a razor blade. Nevertheless, she says her hateful attitude against her attackers changed after she turned to prayer. "I feel better and I forgive them for all that they've done to me," Ester said.

But Ester's husband, Thomas, and many of the other men are not yet received the grace they need to forgive their attackers. Some of them have even turned to retaliating against the Muslims who forcefully circumcised them.

All Christians everywhere need to pray much that our persecuted brothers and sisters in Christ will be given the grace of God that alone can enable them to forgive those who persecute them so viciously.

Nigeria, 2000

In the Northern states of Nigeria, the Islamic Sharia Law (the laws and punishments dictated by the Koran, such as the amputation of a hand for stealing were instituted), was adopted, affecting both Muslims and non-Muslims. Christians protested the adoption of the law, and were violently attacked by radical Muslims and others. In February, 260 Christians churches were destroyed, and more than 460 Christians were killed in the riots. At the time of this writing, many others are still missing and unaccounted for. Many of the Christian men were mutilated with knives, killed, and their bodies dumped into wells.

One Christian pastor's wife, Rose, told of her harrowing experiences during the Sharia riots. Her oldest daughter was at school. When Rose realized that violence had broken out against the Christians, she locked her two pre-school children in their house, telling them not to open the door for anyone except her. She then set out on a bicycle to her daughter's school to get her.

On the way, she ran into a radical Muslim mob. They told her that women were not to ride bikes, and threatened her. Thankfully, one of them intervened on her behalf and she was allowed to go on without being harmed—but without her bicycle. She walked more than a mile among the Muslim mobs, but was not hurt.

"God helped me," she said. "God did not let them do anything to me. He was in complete control."

When she finally got to the school, she found that her daughter wasn't there, but had been taken with other school children to a military base for safety. Rose then walked to the base and found her. They then returned home where the younger children were waiting—frightened but safe.

The next day, her husband left the house to attend a Christian gathering. It was the last time Rose saw him alive. He was killed when a Muslim mob attacked the gathering. Several days later, his body was recognized and identified by Christian friends just before it was going to be buried in a mass grave. Rose is grateful that today her husband has a grave that his children can visit. (See Figure 31)

In the month's since her husband's murder, Rose has drawn great comfort from the Scriptures, especially the Book of Acts. "The same God," she said, "allowed Stephen to be stoned [and killed], and allowed Peter to escape from prison. God has been faithful, and His grace has been sufficient [for me]." She continues to work in the church her husband pastored, and to raise her three children.

Two spared

During the riots in which Rose's husband was martyred, a young boy, Joshua, watched as the radical Muslims killed his father. As they prepared to kill his mother, also, she pleaded with them to kill her young son first, so he would not be left alone to wander the streets and beg. The Muslims looked at Joshua, who was only two years old, and then at the mother. After a short discussion, they left the woman's house without harming either her or Joshua.

Ramadan

Ramadan is the Islamic holy month of fasting. One of the basic institutions, or five pillars, of Islam, Ramadan is the ninth month on the Islamic calendar. The Islamic calendar is based on a lunar cycle, and the month begins and ends with the official sighting of the new moon. During the month-long fast, able-bodied adults and older children fast during the daylight hours from dawn to dusk.

Ramadan related violence

While violence remained a near constant reality in Algeria throughout the 1990s, the most acute outbreaks of fighting routinely occurred during the annual Islamic holy month of Ramadan. From the inception of civil war in 1992, an average of more than 600 people were killed during Ramadan in each year of civil war.

Ramadan-related violence proved particularly brutal during 1997 and 1998. During the 1997 month of Ramadan, which began in early January according to the Western calendar, Islamic militants launched a widespread campaign of terror, vowing to detonate fifty bombs during the course of the holy month. Several hundred people were killed as a result of this campaign, and hundreds more died in massacres conducted throughout the countryside.

In 1997-98 the month of Ramadan began with the single bloodiest reported massacre to date in the civil war, as the Armed Islamic Group (GIA) conducted a series of massacres in four villages near the western Algerian town of Relizane, some 180 miles (290 kilometers) west of the capital city of Algiers. Various unofficial sources placed the death toll from the night-long massacre at 412.

That massacre began the most brutal of the Ramadan-related violence during the course of the civil war, as more than 1,000 people—mostly civilians—were killed in massacres conducted by pro-Islamic guerrillas during the first week of the holy month.

China, 2000

Pastor Li De Xian was a arrested again in April, the very day the United States submitted an article to the United Nations calling for censure of China due to human rights abuses. Pastor Li has been arrested thirteen times in six months for "illegal preaching" in Hua Du.

Several times in the past the officials in Hua Du had stated that they did not want to arrest Pastor Li, but their orders were coming from a higher authority. Only recently has it been learned that the "higher authority" giving them the orders to arrest Li is the Religious Affairs Bureau of Guangzhou.

When the pastor was taken to prison, he was immediately put into chains. Unlike other prisoners, his jailors chained his ankles not once but twice. Steel cuffs were first put around his ankles and screwed tight against them by bolts on both sides. Then a second set of cuffs was put around his shins just above the cuffs on his ankles—also squeezed tight against his leg by bolts.

Then a long steel bar with a ring in the center was fastened between the cuffs on his ankles, spreading his legs farther apart then his shoulders. He was then handcuffed and his hands forced down to the bar and chained to the ring. In that bent over position his shoulders were just inside his knees, and he could not straighten up to relieve the pressure on his back. His jailors left him that way without a word as to why he was being tortured or how long it would last.

By the second day, the pain from his shoulders down to his lower back was agonizing. He was certain that if they left him in that position much longer, his back would be permanently damaged.

At the end of three days, during which he had no food or water except what was given to him by other prisoners, his hands were released and he was able to straighten up. After a few days the pain in his back left. He was thankful that there was no permanent injure.

Since his hands were now free, Pastor Li was forced into doing manufacturing work assigned to the prison—ironically, it was assembling Christmas lights that were going to America. The irony is that many Americans who purchased the lights for their Christmas trees were undoubtedly Christians decorating their home for the holiday season to celebrate the birth of Christ, never suspecting that the lights they were using for that purpose were assembled in a Chinese prison by a Christian pastor who had been arrested for preaching Christ.

Li needs glasses to read, and he had none in the prison, so he could not see very well to assemble the small Christmas lights. The lights had to be assembled, and they gave him a quota of a minimum of 4000 lights a day. Any day he failed to meet his quota, he was whipped. His work day started at six each morning, and did not end until eleven each night—a seventeen-hour day.

After two weeks, Pastor Li was released with a stern warning that he was not to preach again in Hua Du. But he continues to preach, and never speaks ill of those who so often arrested him and caused him great suffering.

"I will preach [the gospel of Jesus Christ] until I die," Li has vowed. Standing firmly with him through all the persecution are his wife and son, who are both under constant surveillance by the authorities.

391

Indonesia, 2001

Mila Wenno is a forty-three year-old Christian nurse. She and her husband, Stefanus, were on their way to church on their motorbike over the same route they had taken for twenty years without incident. But on January 21, a group of twenty radical and angry Muslims were blocking the road.

The mob had been brought to the island where the Wennos lived from another island, so that they could not be easily identified. Each member of the mob was armed with either a rifle or machete. Seeing the mob of Muslims ahead, Stefanus believed the best way to avoid trouble was to continue through them without stopping.

But it was no use. One of the Muslims swung the end of his rifle like a baseball bat and struck Mila in the head, nearly knocking her from the bike, and forcing her to grab her husband to keep from falling. While Stefanus was trying to keep the motorbike under control to get away from the now shouting and chanting Muslims, another man swung his machete at Mila and sliced through the muscle and bone of her right arm just above the elbow, leaving the arm hanging from her shoulders by a few inches of flesh. (See Figures 32,33)

Although Mila's arm was saved, she no longer has any feeling in her hand and forearm because of the severed nerves, and the arm is virtually useless.

Amazingly, Mila's attitude is not one of sadness and bitterness because of the persecution, but rather one of joy. When questioned about the incident, Mila smiled joyously and said, "At first I felt terrible and sad, but this was God's will. It has drawn me closer to Him, and I know He will bless me and my family."

Mila and her husband Stefanus were among 876 Christian families left homeless that terrible day after radical Muslims burned most of their village. Many of the villagers—3,493 people—sought refuge in the jungle nearby, where they have constructed temporary homes and shelters and will live until they feel it is safe to return to their permanent homes. When that will be, or it if ever will be, they have no way of knowing. But they continue to pray and hold steady in their faith in Christ.

Sudan, 2001

Sudan in East Africa is currently experiencing an onslaught of persecution. The Muslim government of Khartoum in the North has declared a jihad, or holy war, against the mostly Christian South. Omar Hassan al-Turabi, an Islamic leader, has stated that anyone who opposes Islam "has no future."

Muslim students are recruited out of universities and told that they can keep whatever they pillage if they join the war against non-Muslims. Since 1985, approximately two million have perished due to the genocide. Because of the war, famine has plagued the country as people are unable to plant and harvest. Families in the South are terrorized—fathers killed, mothers raped, and children sold into slavery.

Yet in the midst of these atrocities, the body of Christ in Sudan remains strong, worshiping their Savior and leading others to Him.

An elder of the Church of Christ was arrested in 1998 in Kadugli for distributing Bibles. He was beaten by the police so brutally that he almost died. Another man had his hands burned while in police custody following his arrest for preaching in a public place.

"In reality, it is very difficult and dangerous to preach the gospel or distribute Christian literature and Scriptures in Sudan, especially outside the church buildings," said the leader.

"Permissions to build new schools or churches are refused. We are not even allowed to help orphans, although Muslims receive permissions with no problem," said another church leader.

Pakistan, 2001

Jhang Amjad and Asif Masih, two Pakistani Christians, were sentenced to life in prison for violating Section 295-B—Pakistan's anti-blasphemy law. Both were arrested and jailed more than two years ago for allegedly setting fire to a copy of the Koran, the Islamic Holy book.

Amjad and Masih were sentenced in Sessions Court in Jhang, Pakistan, March 20th. Both men suspected the Sessions Court judge was under pressure from radical Muslims to hand down the maximum sentence possible under Pakistani law.

On March 19th, the attorney for Amjad and Masih argued that the men had been falsely accused of burning a Koran. He presented the judge with an undamaged Koran and claimed that it was the book the two had been accused of burning. The judge admitted that the book appeared undamaged after he examined it, but sentenced both men to the maximum sentence, life in prison anyway.

After the sentencing, a representative from an organization that ministers to persecuted Christians stated, "The lives of two innocent men and their families have been forever altered simply because they are Christians."

Sudan, 2001

Although this atrocity occurred several years ago, it is included here because the Christian martyr who was brutalized by Islamic soldiers still carries the marks of her suffering in her body. Those marks are no less than the marks that the apostle Paul referred to when he said, "From now on let no one trouble me, for I bear in my body the marks of the Lord Jesus"

(Galatians 6:17). And this Christian woman could well be ranked with those disciples who rejoiced "that they were counted worthy to suffer shame for His name" (Acts 5:41).

Her name is Abuk. She lives in the war-ravaged country of Sudan, where a jihad, or holy war, against the mostly Christian south has raged for nearly two decades. At the time of the atrocity, Abuk lived with her family in a small village near the frontlines of a battle being fought at that time.

One morning just after dawn, Islamic soldiers raided her village. Most of the villagers fled before the marauding soldiers, but Abuk was not able to get away in time. Several soldiers abducted her and told her that she had to go with them. She refused. They then told her that she must convert from Christianity to Islam by immediately renouncing Christ and accepting Mohammed as the chief and last prophet of God. She again refused.

Enraged at her refusals, the soldiers savagely tore off her clothes and tied her up. After starting a fire, they put their large knives into it until they were red hot, and then stabbed, sliced, and mutilated Abuk's upper chest, shoulders, and back. (See Figures 34,35) Fighting to hold back her screams of pain even as she heard herself screaming, Abuk prayed to Jesus for the strength to withstand the agonizing torture and not deny or turn from Him.

When Abuk would still not renounce her Christianity, the soldiers beat her unconscious and left her to die of her wounds. Sometime later, she regained consciousness, and stumbling, falling, and often crawling, she made her way to the other villagers to get help.

Though its been several years since she was tortured for her Christianity, Abuk still suffers from her massive wounds. She is almost in constant pain from them, and because of a lack of proper medical help where she lives, there is often infection in many of the scars she carries on her body.

Abuk has a strong faith in Jesus Christ, and would undoubtedly suffer again for Him. But like any of us would be, she is always strengthened when Christians come to her village to bring supplies, to encourage them, and to tell them that their brothers and sisters in Christ throughout the world are praying for them.

Appendix A

Word Changes and Definitions

1651 (The records differ, some say Mary Dyer went to England in 1650, some say 1651, and some say 1652. Since three major encyclopedias agree that Roger Williams went to England in 1651 to have his colony's charter confirmed, we have chosen 1651 as the year Mary accompanied her husband and Williams to England.)

330,000 (World Christian Encyclopedia, © 1997 by Global Evangelization Movement {published by Oxford University Press, NY, NY, 10016}.)

abash (make ashamed or uneasy; disconcert)

abbot (the superior of a monastery)

abide (await)

abscond (to leave quickly and secretly and hide oneself)

absolution (the formal remission of sin imparted by a priest, as in the sacrament of penance)

ado (fuss - trouble - bother)

aforesaid (said before)

aggrieved (feeling distressed, afflicted)

Alcoran (Koran)

ambassage, or embassage (*Archaic - Middle English*: office or function of an ambassador)

Angevins (Angevin: of or relating to the House of Anjou, especially as represented by the Plantagenet kings of England descended from Geoffrey, Count of Anjou.)

animadversion (strong criticism)

antichamber (antechamber - a small room serving as an entryway into a larger room, such as a bedroom)

antipope (a person claiming to be or elected pope in opposition to the one chosen by church law)

arrant (completely such)

artful (skillful in accomplishing a purpose, especially by the use of cunning or craft)

artificer (a skilled worker, a craftsman, or craftsperson)

asperity (severity; rigor; harshness of manner; ill temper or irritability)

assoil (to absolve, pardon)

assuage (to make something burdensome or painful less intense or severe)

augment (make greater)
axletree (a crossbar or rod supporting a vehicle, such as a cart)

B

barbarity (cruel or savage act)
bark (*Nautical:* a sailing ship with from three to five masts, all of them square-rigged except the after mast, which is fore-and-aft rigged—a small vessel that is propelled by oars or sails)
behold (to look upon, gaze at)
belike (*Archaic:* probably; perhaps)
benefice (*Ecclesiastical:* a church office endowed with fixed capital assets that provide a living, or the income from such assets)
bereave (to deprive)
beseem (*Archaic:* to be appropriate for; befit)
besought (past tense of beseech: to request or implore)
bethinking (reminding or remembering)
bill (a billhook—halberd or similar weapon with a hooked blade and a long handle)
billet (a short, thick piece of wood, especially one used as firewood)
bishopric (the office or rank of a bishop; the diocese of a bishop)
bruit (to spread news of, to repeat)
buckler (a small, round shield either carried or worn on the arm)
bull (an official document, often an edict, issued by the pope and sealed with a bulla)
bulla (a round seal affixed to a papal bull)
bulwark gate (a gate in the fortification walls)

C

caitiff (a despicable coward; a wretch)
calumny (a false statement maliciously made to injure another's reputation)
canon (a member of an assembly of priests serving in a church)
Canterbury, archbishop (the archbishop of Canterbury is *primate of all England)
carp (find fault in a disagreeable way)
carriage (a wheeled support or frame for carrying a heavy object, such as a cannon)
catechumen (someone being taught the principles of Christianity)
chamber (a room where a person of authority, rank, or importance receives visitors)
chamberlain (an officer who manages the household of a sovereign or a noble; a chief steward — a high-ranking official in various royal courts.)
Cheapside (A street and district in the City of London, England. It was the market center of medieval London and the site of the Mermaid Tavern, a

gathering place for Elizabethan poets and playwrights.)
chid (*chide*: to scold, express disapproval)
cleric (a member of the clergy)
cloked (not in current dictionaries)
clurits (knives shaped like a crescent moon)
Compter (Prior to the 17th century, spelled *Counter* or *Countour*. From 17th century on also unofficially spelled *Coumpter*. Originally the office, courts, or hall of justice. Later, the prison attached to it, especially a prison for debtors in such cities as London and Exeter. Over the years, several such places were named Compter. For example, in London from the 15th century there was the *Poultry Compter,* taken down in 1817, the *Bread Street Compter,* which was succeeded by the *Wood Street Compter,* which, in turn, was succeeded by the *Giltspur Street Compter,* which was closed in 1854.
conduce (to contribute or lead to a specific result)
conjuration (the act or art of conjuring; a magic spell or incantation)
conjure (to summon [a devil or spirit] by magical or supernatural power)
constancy (steadfastness, as in purpose or affection; faithfulness)
constantest (not in current English dictionaries)
constantness (not in current dictionaries)
contemned (to view with contempt; despise)
contemning (viewing with contempt, despising)
contumacy (obstinate or contemptuous resistance to authority; stubborn rebelliousness)
contumelious (rudeness or contempt arising from arrogance; insolence—an insolent or arrogant remark or act.)
conversant with (familiar, as by study or experience)
costermongers (*Chiefly British*: those who sells fruit, vegetables, fish, or other goods from a cart, barrow, or stand in the streets)
countryman (a man who lives in the country or has country ways)
courtier (an attendant at a royal court
crosier (a staff with a crook or cross at the end, carried by or before an abbot, a bishop, or an archbishop as a symbol of office)
culpable (deserving of blame or censure as being wrong, evil, improper, or injurious)
cure (*Ecclesiastical*: spiritual charge or care, as of a priest for a congregation—the office or duties of a curate)
cutler (one who makes, repairs, or sells knives or other cutting instruments)

D

denounced (to condemn openly as being evil or reprehensible—Middle English *denouncen* to proclaim)
demeanor (way a person behaves)
deputed (appointed or authorized as an agent or a representative)

descanted (commented at length; discoursed)

dignities (the ceremonial symbols and observances attached to high office)

dignity (a high office or rank)

diocese (the district or churches under the jurisdiction of a bishop; a bishopric)

discomfiture (frustration or disappointment — lack of ease; perplexity and embarrassment — *Archaic*: Defeat)

discover (*Archaic*: To reveal or expose)

discretions (judges, or those sitting in judgment)

disdain (to regard or treat with haughty contempt; despise. To consider or reject as beneath oneself)

dispraise (disapproval; censure)

disputation (the act of disputing; debate - an academic exercise consisting of a formal debate or an oral defense of a thesis)

dissenters (see nonconformists)

divine (theologian)

doating (not in current dictionaries)

dolor (sorrow, grief)

durst (*Archaic*. a past tense and a past participle of dare)

E

ecumenical (the term *ecumenical* comes from the Greek word *oikoumenos*, meaning "household of God")

eftsoons (soon)

elector (one of the German princes of the Holy Roman Empire entitled to elect the emperor)

embassy (a mission to a foreign government headed by an ambassador; a staff of diplomatic representatives headed by an ambassador)

episcopacy (a system of church government in which bishops are the chief clerics)

epithet (a term used as a descriptive substitute for the name or title of a person)

Erasmus, Desiderius (b.1466? - d.1536) (Dutch Renaissance scholar and Roman Catholic theologian who sought to revive classical texts from antiquity, restore simple Christian faith based on the Scriptures, and eradicate the improprieties of the medieval Roman church. His works include *The Manual of the Christian Knight*, published in 1503, and *The Praise of Folly*, published in 1509.)

espied (to catch sight of something distant, partially hidden, or obscure)

essay (make an attempt at; try)

exorcise (the word *exorcise* is first recorded in English in a work composed possibly before the beginning of the 15th century, and in this use *exorcise* means "to call up or conjure spirits" rather than "to drive out spirits," a sense first recorded in 1546, which may have been so recorded in Foxe's original book.)

exorcism (the act, practice, or ceremony of exorcising)

F

faggot (sticks, twigs, or branches tied together into bundles and placed around the stake)

fain (*Archaic*: obliged or required)

fatwa (religious edict, proclamation, usually for someone's execution)

fautor (probably *faitour* - *Archaic*. An impostor; a deceiver)

felicity (great happiness, bliss)

felon (*Archaic*: an evil person)

fetters (chains)

firth (*Scottish*: a long, narrow, inlet of the sea)

Fleet Prison (a jail that stood at Fleet rivulet [or river] in London; from the 12th century it was the king's prison and it held many noted persons)

folly (foolishness; lack of foresight, understanding, or sense; foolish actions or results)

forasmuch as (insomuch as, since, because of the fact that)

forsook (left altogether, gave up)

fortuned (*Archaic*: To endow with wealth. *Obsolete*: To ascribe or give good or bad fortune to—*Archaic*: To occur by chance; happen.)

foundations (funds for the perpetual support of an institution; an endowment)

Friends (members of The Society of Friends—Quakers)

froward (stubbornly contrary and disobedient; obstinate)

G

gainsay (declare false, deny)

galley (a ship propelled by sails and oars, and used as a merchant ship or warship in the Mediterranean)

gaol (*Chiefly British*: jail)

genuflections (genuflect: to bend the knee or touch one knee to the floor or ground, as in worship)

gibbet (a device used for hanging a person until dead; a gallows)

glaverers (not in current dictionaries)

glozing (flattering)

gorse (any of several spiny shrubs)

gridiron (a flat framework of parallel metal bars normally used for broiling meat or fish)

H

halberd, also halbert (a weapon of the 15th and 16th centuries having an axlike blade and a steel spike mounted on the end of a long shaft)
haply (by chance or accident)
heresiarch (someone who originates or is the chief supporter of a heresy or heretical movement)
holpen (a past participle of help — helped)
House of Lords (also called Lords—the upper house of Parliament in England, made up of members of the nobility and high-ranking clergy)
humors (probably a body fluid, such as blood, lymph, or bile.)
hurdle (a frame or sledge on which condemned persons were dragged to execution)

I

iconoclast (someone who attacks and seeks to overthrow traditional or popular ideas or institutions - someone who destroys sacred religious images)
ignominious (marked by shame of disgrace; deserving disgrace)
impugn (to attack as false or questionable)
induce (to influence or persuade someone to a certain course of actions)
infallibility (*Roman Catholic Church* - incapable of being in error in expounding doctrine on faith or morals)
intrepid (resolutely courageous; fearless)
inveigh (to give way to angry disapproval; protest angrily and strongly)
Islam (a monotheistic religion characterized by the acceptance of the doctrine of submission to God and Muhammed as the chief and last prophet of God)
Isocartes (or Isocrates—Athenian orator and rhetorician whose letters and pamphlets are a valuable source of ancient Greek political thought. 446-338 B.C.)

K

keep (stronghold or jail)
keepers (jailers)
ketch (*Nautical*: a two-masted fore-and-aft-rigged sailing vessel with a mizzenmast stepped aft of a taller mainmast but forward of the rudder)
knave (devious, deceptive, unprincipled person, crafty)
knight (a medieval gentleman-soldier, usually high-born, raised by a sovereign to privileged military status after training as a page and squire — a man holding a nonhereditary title conferred by a sovereign in recognition of personal merit or service to the country.)
koranic students (those Muslims studying the Koran)

L

landed (consisting of land or real estate)
landgrave (a nobleman in medieval Germany who had jurisdiction over a particular territory, also used as his title)
learned (possessing or demonstrating profound, often systematic knowledge)
lineage (ancestry)
list *(Archaic*: to be disposed; choose — a desire or an inclination)
Lollard (Middle English word, taken from the Middle Dutch word *Lollaerd*, meaning *mumbler, mutterer, heretic.*)
lowering (to appear dark or threatening, such as the sky)

M

magnanimity (the quality of being magnanimous)
magnanimous (courageously noble in mind and heart)
marry (*Archaic*: used as an exclamation of surprise or emphasis)
Masih (a name new Pakistani Christians adopt to signify their faith, even as many Muslim converts adopt the name Mohammed.)
Massachusetts Bay Colony (The Massachusetts Bay Company was a joint stock trading company chartered by the English crown in 1629 to colonize a large area in New England that extended from 3 miles north of the Merrimack River to 3 miles south of the Charles River. Within months it was taken over by a group of Puritans, under the leadership of John Winthrop, who wanted to establish a religious community in the New World. The first colonists sailed from England in 1630 and established the Massachusetts Bay Colony, with its center at Boston.)
mattock (a digging tool with a flat blade set at right angles to the handle)
Melanchthon, Philipp. (Originally Philipp Schwarzerd. b.1497 - d.1560. German theologian and a leader of the German Reformation. A friend of Martin Luther, he wrote *Loci Communes*, published in 1521. It was the first extensive treatise on Protestant doctrine.)
mercer (a dealer in textiles)
misliked (disliked, disapproved)
Miter (*Ecclesiastical*: the liturgical headdress and part of the insignia of a Christian bishop.)
Mohamet (Mohammed or Muhammed or Muhammad)
Muhammad or Mohammed, 570?-632. (Arab prophet of Islam. At the age of 40 he began to preach as God's prophet of what he claimed to be the true religion. Muhammad established a theocratic state at Medina after 622 and began to convert Arabia to Islam.)
Muslim (a believer in or adherent of Islam)

N

nether (located beneath or below; lower or under)

nonconformists (In England and Wales, Nonconformists are Protestants [Presbyterians, Methodists, Baptists, Congregationalists, Quakers, and others] who do not belong {conform} to the established Church of England. The term originated in the 17th century, when it was used alternately with "Dissenters.")

O

oblations (the act of offering something, such as worship or thanks, to a deity; a charitable offering or gift)

opprobrious (expressing contemptuous reproach; scornful or abusive; bringing disgrace; shameful or infamous)

oracle (*Theology*: a command or revelation from God)

ordinary (a cleric, such as the residential bishop of a diocese, with ordinary jurisdiction over a specified territory)

orthodox (adhering to the accepted or traditional and established faith, especially in religion — adhering to the Christian faith as expressed in the early Christian ecumenical creeds)

ostler (variant of hostler — a person who is employed to tend horses, especially at an inn.)

outlawry (the act or process of outlawing or the state of having been outlawed)

overpass (overlook or disregard; go beyond, surpass)

P

palatine (a soldier of the palace guard of the Roman emperors, formed in the time of Diocletian—soldier of a major division of the Roman army formed in the time of Constantine I—used as a title for various administrative officials of the late Roman and Byzantine empires—a feudal lord exercising sovereign power over his lands)

palliate (to make an offense or crime seem less serious)

papal bull (an official document issued by the Roman pope and sealed with a *bulla)

parliamentarians (parliamentary forces—popularly known as Roundheads—in England around 1643)

peradventure (*Archaic*: perhaps; perchance)

percase (not in current dictionaries)

pernicious (causing great harm; destructive)

pestiferous (morally evil)

404

pestilence (a usually fatal epidemic disease, such as bubonic plague)
pike (a long spear formerly used by infantry, also the spike or sharp point, as on the tip of a halberd)
pillar (a person who holds a central or responsible position)
pink (*Nautical*: a sailing vessel with a narrow overhanging stern)
Plantagenets (Plantagenet: family name of a line of English kings from Henry II to Richard III {1154-1485}.)
ploughman (not in current dictionaries)
pontifical (a book of forms for ceremonies performed by a bishop)
popery (*Offensive*: doctrines, practices, and rituals of the Roman Catholic Church)
portuese (not in current dictionaries)
pravity (depravity)
prelacy (office or station of a prelate)
prelate (a high-ranking member of the clergy, especially a bishop)
prentice (*Archaic*: an apprentice)
Presbyterian (see Presbyterianism)
Presbyterianism (the form of church government in which elders, both lay people and ministers, govern)
priests . . . fared (no modern equivalent)
primate (a bishop of highest rank in a province or country)
prior (a monastic officer in charge of a priory or ranking next below the abbot of an abbey.)
procurator (a person authorized to manage the affairs of another; an agent—an employee of the Roman emperor in civil affairs, especially in finance and taxes, in management of imperial estates and properties, and in governing minor provinces)
profane (marked by contempt or irreverence for what is sacred: profane words; nonreligious in subject matter, form, or use; secular)
proffer (to offer for acceptance)
prolocutor (not in current dictionaries)
protest (*Archaic*: To proclaim or make known)
provinces (a territory governed as an administrative or political unit of a country or an empire—*Ecclesiastical*: A division of territory under the jurisdiction of an archbishop)

Q

quietism (a type of mysticism that regards the most perfect communion with God as coming only when the soul is in a state of quiet)

R

rabbins (not in current dictionaries)

rack (an instrument of torture on which the victim's body was stretched)
Ramadan (Ninth month of the Islamic year, the holy month of fasting ordained by the Koran for all adult Muslims. According to the Koran, the fast of Ramadan has been instituted so that believers "may cultivate piety." This particular month was designated because it is said it was the month during which *Muhammad {or Mohammed} received the first of the Koran's revelations.)
rector (an Anglican cleric who has charge of a parish and owns the tithes from it—a Roman Catholic priest appointed to be managerial as well as spiritual head of a church or other institution, such as a seminary or university)
redound (to have an effect or consequences; to contribute)
redressed (to set right; to make amends; to adjust)
Reformation (A 16th century movement in Western Europe that aimed at reforming many of the doctrines and practices of the Roman Catholic Church. When rebuffed and persecuted it developed into the Protestant churches.)
registers (formal or official recordings of items, names, or actions)
reguked (not in current dictionaries)
remand (send back; *Law*: send back into custody)
renegade (a person who rejects a religion, a cause, an allegiance, or a group for another)
reprehend (to reprove, censure)
resort (a customary or frequent going or gathering)
retinue (retainers or attendants accompanying a high-ranking person)
retire (withdraw)
roisting (not in current dictionaries)
ruddish (not in current dictionaries; probably now "ruddy")
runnagate (runagate: a renegade or deserter)
rustical (country people, or of a coarse, crude nature)

S

saloon (a large room or hall for entertainment or exhibitions)
scrivener (a professional copyist, a scribe)
sedition (conduct or language inciting rebellion against the authority of a state or country)
see (the official seat, center of authority, jurisdiction, or office of a bishop)
shaven crown (About the 8th century in Europe, a form of hairdressing in which the crown of the head is shaved was adopted by Christan monastic orders to indicate dedication to the service of God. The hairdressing was called *tonsure.)
sledge (a vehicle mounted on low runners drawn by work animals, such as horses or dogs, and used for transporting loads across ice, snow, and rough ground)

Smithfield (district of London north of St. Paul's Cathedral—in medieval times fairs, markets, and executions were held here)
sophistry (a likely but misleading or argument)
sore (causing misery, sorrow, or distress)
spirituality (the clergy)
stave (a stick or cane carried as an aid in walking or climbing—a stout stick used as a weapon)
stile (a set or series of steps for crossing a fence or wall)
stipend (a fixed and regular payment, such as a salary for services rendered or an allowance)
stocks (a device made up of a heavy wood frame with holes to hold the ankles and sometimes the wrists, used for punishment)
succour (*Chiefly British*: {succor} assistance in time of distress; relief)
suffragan (a bishop elected or appointed as an assistant to the bishop or ordinary of a diocese, having administrative and episcopal responsibilities but no jurisdictional functions)
supererogate (to do more than is required, ordered, or expected)
sustentation (something that sustains, a support, sustenance)

T

tempest (furious agitation, commotion, or tumult; an uproar)
thitherward (in that direction)
tinker (a traveling mender of metal household utensils)
tipcat (not in current dictionaries)
tipstaff (a staff with a metal tip, carried as a sign of office)
tonsure (the act of shaving the head or part of the head)
townsman (a man who is a resident of a town)
traitorly (treacherous)
transubstantiation (*Theology*: the doctrine stating that the bread and wine of the Eucharist are transformed into the body and blood of Jesus Christ, although their appearances remain the same.)
trouth (not found in current dictionaries)
trow (to think)
tush (used to express mild reproof, disapproval, or admonition)

V

vain (foolish)
verity (the quality or condition of being true, factual, or real; something, such as a statement, principle, or belief, that is true, especially an enduring truth)
vexed (irritated, distressed, or annoyed)
vicar (the priest of a parish in the Church of England who receives a stipend

or salary but does not receive the tithes of a parish)
visage (the face or facial expression of a person)
Voice of the Martyrs, Inc., The, P.O. Box 443, Bartlesville, OK 74005-0443 Phone: 918/337-8015 Fax: 918/337-9287
vouchsafe (to condescend to grant or bestow)
vulgar speech (language spoken by the common people)

W

want (*Middle English*: lacked)
wanting (*Middle English*: lacking)
wherefore (for what purpose or reason; why)
whit (the least bit)
Workum (city not found in current dictionaries and encyclopedias)
World Christian Encyclopedia, © 1997 by Global Evangelization Movement (published by Oxford University Press, NY, NY, 10016)
worried (to seize with the teeth and shake or tug at repeatedly: a dog worrying a bone—to attack roughly and repeatedly; harass.)
writ (*Law*: a written order issued by a court, commanding the party to whom it is addressed to perform or cease performing a specified act)

Appendix B

Disputation of Dr. Martin Luther
Concerning Penitence and Indulgences

In the desire and with the purpose of elucidating the truth, a disputation will be held on the underwritten propositions at Wittenberg, under the presidency of the Reverend Father Martin Luther, Monk of the Order of St. Augustine, Master of Arts and of Sacred Theology, and ordinary Reader of the same in that place. He therefore asks those who cannot be present and discuss the subject with us orally, to do so by letter in their absence. In the name of our Lord Jesus Christ. Amen.

1. Our Lord and Master Jesus Christ, in saying "Repent ye," etc., intended that the whole life of believers should be penitence.

2. This word cannot be understood of sacramental penance, that is, of the confession and satisfaction which are performed under the ministry of priests.

3. It does not, however, refer solely to inward penitence; nay such inward penitence is naught, unless it outwardly produces various mortifications of the flesh.

4. The penalty thus continues as long as the hatred of self—that is, true inward penitence—continues: namely, till our entrance into the kingdom of heaven.

5. The Pope has neither the will nor the power to remit any penalties, except those which he has imposed by his own authority, or by that of the canons.

6. The Pope has no power to remit any guilt, except by declaring and warranting it to have been remitted by God; or at most by remitting cases reserved for himself; in which cases, if his power were despised, guilt would certainly remain.

7. God never remits any man's guilt, without at the same time subjecting him, humbled in all things, to the authority of his representative the priest.

8. The penitential canons are imposed only on the living, and no burden ought to be imposed on the dying, according to them.

9. Hence the Holy Spirit acting in the Pope does well for us, in that, in his decrees, he always makes exception of the article of death and of necessity.

10. Those priests act wrongly and unlearnedly, who, in the case of the dying, reserve the canonical penances for purgatory.

11. Those tares about changing of the canonical penalty into the penalty of purgatory seem surely to have been sown while the bishops were asleep.

12. Formerly the canonical penalties were imposed not after, but before absolution, as tests of true contrition.

13. The dying pay all penalties by death, and are already dead to the canon laws, and are by right relieved from them.

14. The imperfect soundness or charity of a dying person necessarily brings with it great fear; and the less it is, the greater the fear it brings.

15. This fear and horror is sufficient by itself, to say nothing of other things, to constitute the pains of purgatory, since it is very near to the horror of despair.

16. Hell, purgatory, and heaven appear to differ as despair, almost despair, and peace of mind differ.

17. With souls in purgatory it seems that it must needs be that, as horror diminishes, so charity increases.

18. Nor does it seem to be proved by any reasoning or any scriptures, that they are outside of the state of merit or of the increase of charity.

19. Nor does this appear to be proved, that they are sure and confident of their own blessedness, at least all of them, though we may be very sure of it.

20. Therefore the Pope, when he speaks of the plenary remission of all penalties, does not mean simply of all, but only of those imposed by himself.

21. Thus those preachers of indulgences are in error who say that, by the indulgences of the Pope, a man is loosed and saved from all punishment.

22. For in fact he remits to souls in purgatory no penalty which they would have had to pay in this life according to the canons.

23. If any entire remission of all penalties can be granted to any one, it is certain that it is granted to none but the most perfect—that is, to very few.

24. Hence the greater part of the people must needs be deceived by this indiscriminate and high-sounding promise of release from penalties.

25. Such power as the Pope has over purgatory in general, such has every bishop in his own diocese, and every curate in his own parish, in particular.

26. The Pope acts most rightly in granting remission to souls, not by the power of the keys (which is of no avail in this case), but by the way of suffrage.

27. They preach mad, who say that the soul flies out of purgatory as soon as the money thrown into the chest rattles.

28. It is certain that, when the money rattles in the chest, avarice and gain may be increased, but the suffrage of the Church depends on the will of God alone.

29. Who knows whether all the souls in purgatory desire to be redeemed from it, according to the story told of Saints Severinus and Paschal?

30. No man is sure of the reality of his own contrition, much less of the attainment of plenary remission.

31. Rare as is a true penitent, so rare is one who truly buys indulgences— that is to say, most rare.

32. Those who believe that, through letters of pardon, they are made sure of their own salvation, will be eternally damned along with their teachers.

33. We must especially beware of those who say that these pardons from the Pope are that inestimable gift of God by which man is reconciled to God.

34. For the grace conveyed by these pardons has respect only to the penalties of sacramental satisfaction, which are of human appointment.

35. They preach no Christian doctrine, who teach that contrition is not necessary for those who buy souls out of purgatory or buy confessional licences.

36. Every Christian who feels true compunction has of right plenary remission of pain and guilt, even without letters of pardon.

37. Every true Christian, whether living or dead, has a share in all the benefits of Christ and of the Church given him by God, even without letters of pardon.

38. The remission, however, imparted by the Pope is by no means to be despised, since it is, as I have said, a declaration of the Divine remission.

39. It is a most difficult thing, even for the most learned theologians, to exalt at the same time in the eyes of the people the ample effect of pardons and the necessity of true contrition.

40. True contrition seeks and loves punishment; while the ampleness of pardons relaxes it, and causes men to hate it, or at least gives occasion for them to do so.

41. Apostolical pardons ought to be proclaimed with caution, lest the people should falsely suppose that they are placed before other good works of charity.

42. Christians should be taught that it is not the mind of the Pope that the buying of pardons is to be in any way compared to works of mercy.

43. Christians should be taught that he who gives to a poor man, or lends to a needy man, does better than if he bought pardons.

44. Because, by a work of charity, charity increases and the man becomes better; while, by means of pardons, he does not become better, but only freer from punishment.

45. Christians should be taught that he who sees any one in need, and passing him by, gives money for pardons, is not purchasing for himself the indulgences of the Pope, but the anger of God.

46. Christians should be taught that, unless they have superfluous wealth, they are bound to keep what is necessary for the use of their own households, and by no means to lavish it on pardons.

47. Christians should be taught that, while they are free to buy pardons, they are not commanded to do so.

48. Christians should be taught that the Pope, in granting pardons, has both more need and more desire that devout prayer should be made for him, than that money should be readily paid.

49. Christians should be taught that the Pope's pardons are useful, if they do not put their trust in them; but most hurtful, if through them they lose the fear of God.

50. Christians should be taught that, if the Pope were acquainted with the exactions of the preachers of pardons, he would prefer that the Basilica of St. Peter should be burnt to ashes, than that it should be built up with the skin, flesh and bones of his sheep.

51. Christians should be taught that, as it would be the duty, so it would be the wish of the Pope, even to sell, if necessary, the Basilica of St. Peter, and to give of his own money to very many of those from whom the preachers of pardons extract money.

52. Vain is the hope of salvation through letters of pardon, even if a commissary—nay, the Pope himself—were to pledge his own soul for them.

53. They are enemies of Christ and of the Pope who, in order that pardons may be preached, condemn the word of God to utter silence in other churches.

54. Wrong is done to the word of God when, in the same sermon, an equal or longer time is spent on pardons than on it.

55. The mind of the Pope necessarily is, that if pardons, which are a very small matter, are celebrated with single bells, single processions, and single ceremonies, the Gospel, which is a very great matter, should be preached with a hundred bells, a hundred processions, and a hundred ceremonies.

56. The treasures of the Church, whence the Pope grants indulgences, are neither sufficiently named nor known among the people of Christ.

57. It is clear that they are at least not temporal treasures, for these are not so readily lavished, but only accumulated, by many of the preachers.

58. Nor are they the merits of Christ and of the saints, for these, independently of the Pope, are always working grace to the inner man, and the cross, death, and hell to the outer man.

59. St. Lawrence said that the treasures of the Church are the poor of the Church, but he spoke according to the use of the word in his time.

60. We are not speaking rashly when we say that the keys of the Church, bestowed through the merits of Christ, are that treasure.

61. For it is clear that the power of the Pope is alone sufficient for the remission of penalties and of reserved cases.

62. The true treasure of the Church is the Holy Gospel of the glory and grace of God.

63. This treasure, however, is deservedly most hateful, because it makes the first to be last.

64. While the treasure of indulgences is deservedly most acceptable, because it makes the last to be first.

65. Hence the treasures of the Gospel are nets, wherewith of old they fished for the men of riches.

66. The treasures of indulgences are nets, wherewith they now fish for the riches of men.

67. Those indulgences, which the preachers loudly proclaim to be the greatest graces, are seen to be truly such as regards the promotion of gain.

68. Yet they are in reality in no degree to be compared to the grace of God and the piety of the cross.

69. Bishops and curates are bound to receive the commissaries of apostolical pardons with all reverence.

70. But they are still more bound to see to it with all their eyes, and take heed with all their ears, that these men do not preach their own dreams in place of the Pope's commission.

71. He who speaks against the truth of apostolical pardons, let him be anathema and accursed.

72. But he, on the other hand, who exerts himself against the wantonness and licence of speech of the preachers of pardons, let him be blessed.

73. As the Pope justly thunders against those who use any kind of contrivance to the injury of the traffic in pardons.

74. Much more is it his intention to thunder against those who, under the pretext of pardons, use contrivances to the injury of holy charity and of truth.

75. To think that Papal pardons have such power that they could absolve a man even if—by an impossibility—he had violated the Mother of God, is madness.

76. We affirm, on the contrary, that Papal pardons cannot take away even the least of venal sins, as regards its guilt.

77. The saying that, even if St. Peter were now Pope, he could grant no greater graces, is blasphemy against St. Peter and the Pope.

78. We affirm, on the contrary: that both he and any other Pope have greater graces to grant—namely, the Gospel, powers, gifts of healing, etc. (I Cor. xii. 9.)

79. To say that the cross set up among the insignia of the Papal arms is of equal power with the cross of Christ, is blasphemy.

80. Those bishops, curates, and theologians who allow such discourses to have currency among the people, will have to render an account.

81. This licence in the preaching of pardons makes it no easy thing, even for learned men, to protect the reverence due to the Pope against the calumnies, or, at all events, the keen questionings of the laity.

82. As for instance:—Why does not the Pope empty purgatory for the sake of most holy charity and of the supreme necessity of souls—this being the most just of all reasons—if he redeems an infinite number of souls for the sake of that most fatal thing, money, to be spent on building a basilica—this being a very slight reason?

83. Again: why do funeral masses and anniversary masses for the deceased continue, and why does not the Pope return, or permit the withdrawal of the funds bequeathed for this purpose, since it is a wrong to pray for those who are already redeemed?

84. Again: what is this new kindness of God and the Pope, in that, for money's sake, they permit an impious man and an enemy of God to redeem a pious soul which loves God, and yet do not redeem that same pious and beloved soul, out of free charity, on account of its own need?

85. Again: why is it that the penitential canons, long since abrogated and dead in themselves in very fact and not only by usage, are yet still redeemed with money, through the granting of indulgences, as if they were full of life?

86. Again: why does not the Pope, whose riches are at this day more ample than those of the wealthiest of the wealthy, build the one Basilica of St. Peter with his own money, rather than with that of poor believers?

87. Again: what does the Pope remit or impart to those who, through perfect contrition, have a right to plenary remission and participation?

88. Again: what greater good would the Church receive if the Pope, instead of once, as he does now, were to bestow these remissions and participations a hundred times a day on any one of the faithful ?

89. Since it is the salvation of souls, rather than money, that the Pope seeks by his pardons, why does he suspend the letters and pardons granted long ago, since they are equally efficacious?

90. To repress these scruples and arguments of the laity by force alone, and not to solve them by giving reasons, is to expose the Church and the Pope to the ridicule of their enemies, and to make Christian men unhappy.

91. If, then, pardons were preached according to the spirit and mind of the Pope, all these questions would be resolved with ease—nay, would not exist.

92. Away, then, with all those prophets who say to the people of Christ, "Peace, peace," and there is no peace!

93. Blessed be all those prophets who say to the people of Christ, "The cross, the cross," and there is no cross!

94. Christians should be exhorted to strive to follow Christ their Head through pains, deaths, and hells.

95. And thus trust to enter heaven through many tribulations, rather than in the security of peace.

PROTESTATION

I, Martin Luther, Doctor, of the Order of Monks at Wittenberg, desire to testify publicly that certain propositions against pontifical indulgences, as they call them, have been put forth by me. Now although, up to the present time, neither this most celebrated and renowned school of ours, nor any civil or ecclesiastical power has condemned me, yet there are, as I hear, some men of headlong and audacious spirit, who dare to pronounce me a heretic, as though the matter had been thoroughly looked into and studied. But on my part, as I have often done before, so now too, I implore all men, by the faith of Christ, either to point out to me a better way, if such a way has been divinely revealed to any, or at least to submit their opinion to the judgment of God and of the Church. For I am neither so rash as to wish that my sole opinion should be preferred to that of all other men, nor so senseless as to be willing, that the word of God should be made to give place to fables, devised by human reason.

Appendix C

Kings and Queens of England from 1327 to 1603

*Plantagenets (*Angevins)

Edward III	1327-77
Richard II	1377-99

House of Lancaster

Henry IV	1399-1413
Henry V	1413-22
Henry VI	1422-61

House of York

Edward IV	1461-83
Edward V	1483
Richard III	1483-85

Tudors

Henry VII	1485-1509
Henry VIII	1509-47
Edward VI	1547-53
Mary I	1553-58
Elizabeth I	1558-1603

Appendix D

Colleges of Cambridge University Founded from 1284 to 1596

College	Year Founded
Christ's College	1448 *(Founded as God's House, enlarged and renamed in 1505)*
Clare College	1326 *(Founded as University Hall, refounded in 1339)*
Corpus Christi College	1352
Emmanuel College	1584
Gonville and Caius College	1348 *(Founded as Gonville Hall in 1353, moved and renamed in 1558)*
Jesus College	1496
King's College	1441
King's Hall	1337
Magdalene College	542
Michaelhouse	1324
Peterhouse	1284
Queen's College	1448 *(Earlier known as College of St. Bernard {1446}, refounded in 1465)*
St. Catharine's College	1473
St. John's College	1511
Sidney Sussex College	1596 *(Consolidated and extended Michaelhouse and King's Hall)*
Trinity College	1546
Trinity Hall	1350

Colleges of Oxford University Founded from 1249 to 1571

College	Year Founded
All Souls College	1438
Brasenose College	1509
Christ College	1546
Corpus Christi College	1517
Exeter College	1314
Gloucester College	1283
Jesus College	1571
Lincoln College	1427
Magdalen College	1458
Merton College	1264
New College	1379
Oriel College	1326
The Queen's College	1340
St. Edmund Hall	c.1278
St. John's College	1555
Trinity College	1554-55
University College	1249

Appendix E

Roman Catholic Popes from 1000 to 1600

(Names of doubtful popes and *antipopes are
in parenthesis—note that out of the several
popes during the Great Papal Schism, only
those of the Roman line are listed by the
Pontifical Yearbook as being true popes.)

Name	Reign
Sylvester II	999-1003
John XVII	1003
John XVIII	1003-09
Sergius IV	1009-12
Benedict VIII	1012-24
(Gregory VI)	1012
John XIX	1024-33
Benedict IX	1033-45
Sylvester III	1045
Gregory VI	1045-46
Clement II	1046-47
Damasus II	1048
Leo IX	1049-54
Victor II	1055-57
Stephen IX	1057-58
(Benedict X)	1058-59
Nicholas II	1058-61
Alexander II	1061-73

(Honorius II)	10661-72
Gregory VII	1073-85
(Clement III)	1080; 1084-1100
Victor III	1086-87
Urban II	1088-99
Paschal II	1099-1118
(Theodoric or Theoderius)	1100-02
(Albert or Albertus)	1102
(Sylvester IV)	1105-11
Gelasius II	1118-19
(Gregory VIII)	1118-21
Callistus II	1119-24
Honorius II	1124-30
(Celestine II)	1124
Innocent II	1130-43
(Anacletus II)	1130-38
(Victor IV)	1138
Celestine II	1143-44
Lucius II	1144-45
Eugene or Eugenius III	1145-53
Anastasius IV	1153-54
Adrian IV	1154-59
Alexander III	1159-81
(Victor IV)	1159-64
(Paschal III)	1164-68
(Callistus or Calixtus III)	1168-78
(Innocent III)	1179-80
Lucius III	1181-85
Urban III	1185-87
Gregory VIII	1187
Clement III	1187-91
Celestine III	1191-98
Innocent III	1198-1216
Honorius III	1216-27
Gregory IX	1227-41

Celestine IV	1241
Innocent IV	1243-54
Alexander IV	1254-61
Urban IV	1261-64
Clement IV	1265-68
Gregory X	1271-76
Innocent V	1276
Adrian V	1276
John XXI	1276-77
Nicholas III	1277-80
Martin IV	1281-85
Honorius IV	1285-87
Nicholas IV	1288-92
Celestine V	1294
Boniface VIII	1294-1303
Benedict XI	1303-04
Clement V	1305-14
John XXII	1316-34
(Nicholas V)	1328-30
Benedict XII	1334-42
Clement VI	1342-52
Innocent VI	1352-62
Urban V	1362-70
Gregory XI	1370-78

Great Papal Schism

Urban VI - Roman line	1378-89
(Clement VII - Avignon line)	1378-94
Boniface IX - Roman line	1389-1404
(Benedict XIII - Avignon line)	1394-1423
Innocent VII -Roman line	1406-06
Gregory XII - Roman line	1406-15
(Alexander V - Pisan line)	1409-10
(John XXIII - Pisan line)	1410-15

End of Papal Schism

Martin V	1417-31
Eugene IV	1431-47
(Felix V)	1439-49
Nicholas V	1447-55
Callistus III	1445-58
Pius II	1458-64
Paul II	1464-71
Sixtus IV	1471-84
Innocent VIII	1484-92
Alexander VI	1492-1503
Pius III	1503
Julius II	1503-13
Leo X	1513-21
Adrian VI	1522-23
Clement VII	1523-34
Paul III	1534-49
Julius III	1550-55
Marcellus II	1555
Paul IV	1555-59
Pius IV	1559-65
Pius V	1566-72
Gregory XIII	1572-85
Sixtus V	1585-90
Urban VII	1590
Gregory XIV	1590-91
Innocent IX	1591
Clement VIII	1592-1605

Appendix F

Many Christians around the world are living under similar circumstances to those whose stories are told in this book. It's impossible to read these accounts without sensing their suffering and being challenged by their faith. By rewriting slightly Paul's commendation in 1 Thessalonians 1:6-8, it can truly be said of them: "In spite of severe suffering, the Lord's message rang out from you, and so you became a model to all believers—your faith in God has become known everywhere."

By reading the stories of these heroes of the faith, we are given greater insight into what it means to sacrifice ourselves for the sake of the Gospel. Martyrdom is more than being killed for Christ. It's living for Christ every moment of every day in the midst of persecution and life-threatening opposition. It's enduring great loss and suffering, yet praising God for all things. It's forgiving your persecutors and praying for their salvation. It's working to fulfill the Great Commission regardless of the inconveniences and dangers it imposes.

Even though more Christians have been martyred in this century than in all previous centuries, most of the Church is unaware of the large number of persecutions happening everyday around the world. Thankfully, there are organizations that have been raised by God to help them. We have listed several of them below. Dick Eastman of *Every Home for Christ* once wrote in his monthly newsletter that Christians can get involved with suffering Christians around the world in three ways: we can pray, we can give, or we can go.

The Voice of the Martyrs

P.O. Box 443

Bartlesville, OK 74005-0443

Telephone: 918-337-8015

Fax: 918-337-9287

Founded by Richard and Sabrina Wurmbrand, *Voice of the Martyrs* directly ministers to those living under persecution by giving hope, encouragement, literature, and whatever financial and material supplies are desperately needed. Pastor Wurmbrand is the author of *Tortured for Christ*, the story of fourteen years of persecutions he endured in communist prisons. His life and teachings exude a sweetness, compassion, and love that can only come from a vessel that has truly been broken and filled with the spirit of Christ. Tom White, who spent several months in a Cuban prison, is USA director for VOM.

Literature

Voice of the Martyrs offers a free monthly newsletter. Each month features a teaching from Brother Wurmbrand, along with recent information on Christians suffering persecution or martyrdom. A variety of books and videos are offered as resources for understanding the plight of those under persecution, understanding Christian suffering, and developing a more intimate relationship with the Lord.

Praying and Giving Opportunities

Specific prayer needs are related throughout the newsletter. On occasions, certain material items will be mentioned that are specifically needed by Christians in dire circumstances. See the map provided by VOM at the beginning of this book for countries where persecuted Christians need prayers.

Open Doors

with Brother Andrew

PO Box 27001, Santa Ana, CA 92799

Tel: 714-752-6600

e-mail: usa@opendoors.org

Web site: http://www.opendoors.org

Founded by Brother Andrew, author of *God's Smuggler*, Open Doors is a ministry that directly supports persecuted Christians through Bible and literature distribution and leadership training.

Literature

Free six-month's subscription to *Newsbrief* and *Prayer Force Alert*, gives information and events affecting Christians living under persecution.

Prayer Opportunities

Monthly *Prayer Alert* highlights certain individuals and situations needing urgent prayer. For some of those in prison, names and addresses are given so that believers can write letters of support or letters of appeal for their release.

Mission Opportunities

Open Doors accepts applications for short term (1-4 weeks) courier trips. Couriers take Bibles into lands not open to Christianity. Recent trips have been to China, Cuba,

Central America, and Vietnam. Open Doors goes where the need is the greatest.

Christian Solidarity International (CSI)

Zelglistrasse 64

P.O. Box 70

CH-8122 Binz (Zurich)

Switzerland

Tel: 41-1-980-4700 / Fax: 41-1-980-4715

CSI is an Interdenominational Human Rights Organization for Persecuted Christian and Other Victims of Oppression. Their particular focus is on forgotten peoples in forgotten lands— places that don't appear on TV screens or front pages of newspapers.

CSI states, "As mandated by the word of God (Matthew 25:39-40 and Hebrews 13:3), we believe in taking effective, appropriate action when Christians are persecuted—beaten, tortured, imprisoned, and even martyred—for their faith in Christ." Through their deeds of love, prayer, and active support they bring encouragement and strength to persecuted believers.

Literature and Opportunities

Publications on the accounts of the persecuted are available, some are translations from those written in other countries but not readily available through conventional means. Quarterly Newsletter, *Mission to the Persecuted,* gives related information and kinds of action to take in response.

Global Harvest Ministries

A.D. 2000 United Prayer Track

P.O. Box 63060 Colorado Springs, CO 80962-3060

Tel: 719-262-9922

Fax: 719-262-9920

e-mail: 74114.570@compuserve.com

C. Peter Wagner is president of Global Harvest Ministries, which networks with praying people in more than 120 nations. They specifically concentrate prayer in lands that are the least evangelized—and often those most hostile to the Gospel. Some of their organized prayer activities have been "Praying through the 10-40 Window," the annual "Ramadan Effort" (praying during Ramadan), and "30 Days of Prayer for the Hindu World."

Prayer and Go Opportunities

Literature is available to facilitate daily prayer for Christians in other lands. Each year Global Harvest Ministries, in conjunction with the Christian Information Network, sponsors prayer journeys through nations of the 10-40 window. Remarkable miracles and breakthroughs for the Gospel in other lands have been reported as a result of these concerted prayer efforts. For more information about participating in "Praying Through the Window III," contact: Christian Information Network, 11025 State Highway 83, Colorado Springs, CO 80921. Telephone: 719-5221040, Fax: 719-548-9000. Web site: http://www.horizonint.com/cin/html/prayerjourney.html

Literature

Bimonthly newsletter *Prayer Track News,* full of information on various global harvest prayer opportunities. Resource catalog, *The Arsenal*, contains a variety of related materials, including Peter Wagner's *Warfare Prayer Series.*

Giving Opportunities

Funds are specifically needed to establish National Prayer Centers in 120 nations of the world. These centers will be operated and run by committed Christian nationals who will coordinate and facilitate "the chief instrument that God has given us to open the way for lost people . . . to accept Jesus Christ and be saved . . . prayer."

Berry Publishing Services, Inc.

701 Main St., Evanston IL 60202

Tel: 847-869-1573 / Fax: 847-869-6921

Berry Publishing Services publishes *Missions Today —Short Term Missions Special Report.* In it they list a variety of ministries that offer short term programs for adults and youth that provide opportunities to serve the Lord in other lands, including some third world countries where Christians live under persecution.

International Christian Concern
2020 Pennslyvania Avenue, #941
Washington, DC 20006
Tel: 800-ICC-5441 or 301-989-1708
Web address: http://www.persecution.org

Index

A

G

H

CLASSICS IN MODERN ENGLISH

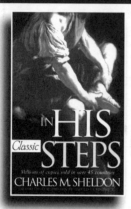

Classic

IN HIS STEPS

Millions of copies sold in over 45 countries

CHARLES M. SHELDON

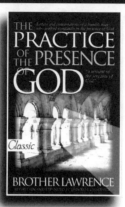

Entries and contemplations of a humble friar who walked constantly in the presence of God

THE PRACTICE OF THE PRESENCE OF GOD

"a servant in the presence of God."

Classic

BROTHER LAWRENCE

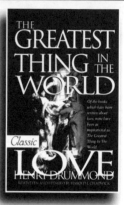

THE GREATEST THING IN THE WORLD

Of the books which have been written about love, none have been as inspirational as The Greatest Thing In The World

Classic

LOVE

HENRY DRUMMOND

REWRITTEN AND EDITED BY HAROLD J. CHADWICK

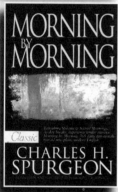

MORNING BY MORNING

Refreshing Morning & Sacred Mornings, to day breaks, experience tender mercies Morning by Morning, 365 daily devotionals topical into plain, modern English

Classic

CHARLES H. SPURGEON

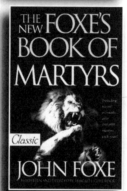

THE NEW FOXE'S BOOK OF MARTYRS

Including recent accounts of Christian martyrs each year.

Classic

JOHN FOXE

REWRITTEN AND EDITED BY HAROLD J. CHADWICK

THE CHRISTIAN'S Secret OF A HAPPY LIFE

Sensitively updated edition enhanced with thoughts for personal reflection

Classic

HANNAH WHITALL SMITH

REWRITTEN AND UPDATED BY HAROLD J. CHADWICK

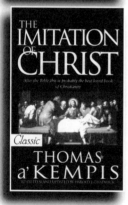

THE IMITATION OF CHRIST

After the Bible this is probably the best loved book of Christianity

Classic

THOMAS a' KEMPIS

REWRITTEN AND UPDATED BY HAROLD J. CHADWICK

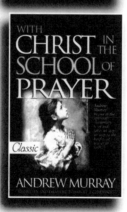

WITH CHRIST IN THE SCHOOL OF PRAYER

Andrew Murray became in the prayer and takes us up to the heights of Jesus' teachings on God's...

Classic

ANDREW MURRAY

REWRITTEN AND UPDATED BY HAROLD J. CHADWICK

THE PILGRIM'S PROGRESS IN MODERN ENGLISH

John Bunyan's Immortal Classic distinctively revised for the 21st Century reader

Classic

JOHN BUNYAN

REVISED AND EDITED BY L. EDWARD HAZELBAKER

THE CLASSICS COLLECTION